THE COMPLETE WORKS OF ROBERT BROWNING, VOLUME IV

Portrait of Robert Browning by Thomas Buchanan Read, 1853

The Complete Works of Robert Browning

With Variant Readings & Annotations

VOLUME IV

OHIO UNIVERSITY PRESS

ATHENS, OHIO 1973

Library of Congress Catalog Card Number: 68-18389
ISBN 8214-0115-7

Printed in the United States of America

CONTENTS

Preface

I contents

This edition of the works of Robert Browning is intended to be complete. It is expected to run to thirteen volumes and will contain:

1. The full contents of the first editions of Browning's work, arranged in chronological order. The poems included in *Dramatic Lyrics*, *Dramatic Romances and Lyrics*, and *Men and Women* appear in the order of their first publication rather than the order in which Browning rearranged them for later publication.

2. All prefaces, dedications, and advertisements which Browning wrote for his own works or for those of Elizabeth Barrett Browning and others.

3. The two known prose essays which Browning published: the review of a book on Tasso, generally referred to as "The Essay on Chatterton," and the preface for a collection of letters supposed to have been written by Percy Bysshe Shelley, generally referred to as "The Essay on Shelley."

4. The front matter and the table of contents of each of the collected editions (1849, 1863, 1868, 1888–89a, and 1889) which Browning himself saw through the press. The table of contents will include both the pagination of the first edition and of this edition.

5. Poems by Browning published during his lifetime but not collected by him.

6. Unpublished poems by Browning which have come to light since his death.

7. John Forster's *Thomas Wentworth, Earl of Strafford* to which Browning contributed significantly, though to what precise extent so far cannot be determined.

8. Variants from secondary materials (see section six of this preface).

II general textual principles: copy-text and variants

It is increasingly recognized that methods of editing nineteenth-century texts need to be reexamined and probably revised. The old fashioned notion that a nineteenth- or twentieth-century text could be simply reprinted from either the first or last edition is no longer tenable. Recent examination of the works of Hawthorne, Melville, Twain, Cooper, Mill and others, for example, reveal problems different from those arising from texts of earlier centuries, and also differing problems among recent writers which distinguish any one from the others.

Before we published Volume One of this edition, and after three years of intensive study of both the specific problems connected with Browning's texts and the adequacy of prevailing theory to solve them, we arrived at certain basic principles which we felt would produce an authoritative, useful edition of Browning's work. We recognized at that time, however, that after further practical experience with the text and with new information that would undoubtedly become available, we might want to elaborate upon and further document our initial statement of textual principles. We now feel that the time has come for a restatement. We are convinced that the principles and methods outlined in Volume One are basically sound. We will attempt here, however, to clarify any vagueness which might have existed in our original effort and to provide additional evidence which, we believe, will further increase the reasonableness of our choices and procedures.

Our first problem was to select an authoritative text, and to determine what was and what was not a legitimate variant to it. We have manuscripts for nineteen of Browning's thirty-four book publications. Others may become available during the time we are working on this edition. None, however, with the possible exception of *Asolando*, published on the day of Browning's death, can be said to represent the author's final intentions. Each of Browning's works went through a series of editions during his lifetime and each was revised by Browning himself. If, indeed, the manuscript and each successive edition were under Browning's control and if it can be established that in all probability the changes made in each were his own, then each represents Browning's final decision at the time, and must be considered as a possible copy-text. Thus the establishment of authorial control becomes the central concern of the editors. That Browning did exercise control over the publication of his works we shall demonstrate in due course.

Clearly in the case of a poet who was revising his work over a period of more than fifty years neither the original manuscript nor the first edition published from it can meet the accepted requirements for the copy-text. Nor would any one text, produced by a process of emendation and conflation, result in a single text more representative than any one we now have of what might be called the "real" Browning. To attempt to construct such a text would indicate not editorial responsibility, but flagrant violation of the editorial principle that the author's own decisions are, to the extent they are discernible, to be respected. Indeed, the position we found ourselves in—that of producing *a* text carrying the authority of *an* author—forced us to reconsider the commonly accepted understanding of the terms *text* and *author*.

Too often both text and author are considered as static entities, Platonic archetypes. We do not have space here to consider fully the philosophical implications of such an assumption and must of necessity restrict ourselves to a brief statement of a more practical nature. For those interested, we suggest that they read Morse Peckham's article "Reflections on the Foundations of Textual Criticism: Human Behavior and Better Editions," *Proof* 1 (1971). For a work that varies in a series of documents and editions, each having authorial authority, clearly there is no such empirical entity as *the* text. Indeed, grasp of this simple fact raises questions about the author himself. Which author—or the author at which stage in the process—is meant? Upon what basis can we ascribe greater authenticity to one than to the others? The young Browning who wrote *Pauline* in 1832, the maturing poet who revised it in 1863 and 1868, and the old man who put it in final form in 1888 and 1889 differ greatly. Each of these editions represented Browning's final decisions as he understood himself at the time. Each has its own authority, representing the author as he existed at that particular time. Clearly, to reduce the Browning of those diverse stages to a static entity renders him no less an artificial construction than to reduce a number of versions of a work to a similar artificially constructed single text. Neither of such constructions can be regarded as an empirical entity.

Our focus shifts, necessarily, from the *text* and the *author* considered as static metaphysical entities to the process of creating and editing involved in the compilation of a series of documents; and concern about the transmission of the text is redirected to the problem of understanding the character of the decisions by which the successive and varying versions of the work came to be.

It follows, therefore, that we are concerned more about authorial *function* and editorial *function* than about *author* and *editor*. Any writer's work consists of two processes: he generates a work, and he corrects or edits it by balancing his current conceptions of the coherence of what he has written, and his grasp of the conventions applicable to the kind of discourse he is composing as they then obtain and as he understands them. The two functions are not necessarily isolated and sequential. That is, he does not generate a statement once and then forever after merely edit it. The text itself remains fluid, subject to continuous recreation. The manuscript that goes to the printer for the first edition, no doubt, already represents a series of generations and revisions; likewise, the marked copy for each subsequent edition may and probably does represent both editing and recreation. The second and subsequent editions of *Pauline*, for example, containing as they do, material which not only clarifies and corrects but elaborates upon and, in some cases, changes the meaning of the original, represent more than editing. Following are characteristic examples of genuinely substantive changes that Browning made in the first edition:

525| *1833*: As would encircle me with praise and love;
1888: As straight encircle men with praise and love,
543–544| *1833*: First in the struggle, and again would make
All bow to it; and I would sink again.
1888: First in the struggle, fail again to make
All bow enslaved, and I again should sink.
564| *1833*: I was most happy, sweet, for all delights
1888: I seemed defiant, sweet, for old delights
875–876| *1833*: No less I feel that thou hast brought me bliss,
And that I still hope to win it back.
1888: No less song proves one word has brought me bliss,
Another still may win bliss surely back.

The cumulative impact of numerous such small changes have a profound effect upon the meaning of the revised poem.

This process of revision Browning continued throughout his life. One of the most curious alterations occurred in his revision of *Paracelsus*. In 1835, lines 649–650 of Part Two read:

Who in his own person acts his own creations.
Had you but told me this at first! . . . Hush! hush!

In 1849, Browning expanded this passage to include a statement of belief in the Christian doctrine of Incarnation which radically altered the meaning of the original:

Who in creation acts his own conceptions.
Shall man refuse to be aught less than God?
Man's weakness is his glory—for the strength
Which raises him near to heaven and near God's self,
Came spite of it: God's strength his glory is,
For thence came with our weakness sympathy
Which brought God down to earth, a man like us.
Had you but told me this at first! . . . Hush! hush!

In 1863, Browning restored the original reading, changing only capitalization and punctuation.

The inspiration to place Pompilia's rescue on St. George's Day came after the first draft of *The Ring and the Book* was written and is recorded as a revision on the manuscript that went to the printer. Other significant changes in the text of this work suggest that the process of creation continued long after the first edition was published. For the second edition of 1872 he added seventeen new lines and made hundreds of changes in both wording and punctuation, many of which went far beyond the scope of mere editing. For the final editions in 1888 and again in 1889 he made still other changes.

It appears to us, therefore, that in exercising his authorial-editorial functions the author's basis for his activity is continually changing, and may continue to change throughout his life. His grasp of both the coherence of his work and of the conventions may improve or deteriorate; he may come to feel that the conventions are either more or less binding on him. Author, then, as we use the term, refers not to a stable entity but to an unstable and continuously innovating continuum.

We recognize, of course, that individuals other than the author exercise, directly or indirectly, an editorial function. Sometimes, more common in the past than now, their intervention was direct and decisive. In the history of printing, the compositor, the printer, and the copyreader have been responsible for variants, and insofar as such variants reflect a grasp of the coherence of the work and of current conventions, they cannot be classified as errors. Nevertheless, they do not have authorial authority and in practice must be distinguished from those known to derive from the author himself. An error, in contrast, is a variant which self-evidently damages the coherence of the text and departs from the conventions, as the textual critic himself understands both factors as they were at work in the historical situation from which the work emerged. The history of printing has moved in the direction of trying to limit printers' errors, to train compositors to set only what is before them, and to restrict the copyreader to the detection of errors by requiring him to refer questionable variants to the editor or author. Both errors and arbitrary changes, originating other than with the author, cannot be regarded as legitimate parts of the text.

There is also the matter of house styling which may induce changes for which the author is not responsible, or only nominally so. The extent to which house styling is reflected in Browning's poetry will be discussed later. Still another kind of editorial assistance is that of the professional copyreader or the friend who reads the manuscript and suggests changes in it. To what extent do changes so made have authority? The question is a delicate one, almost incapable of irrefutable answer. If the author has no opportunity to reject or if he accepts the changes perfunctorily their status is dubious. If, however, the evidence indicates clearly that he was free to accept or reject them and does one or the other after careful deliberation, the decision must be regarded as his own.

At this point we may summarize. All changes in the text which are not obvious errors and for which the author himself is responsible are to be considered authoritative and accepted as legitimate parts of an authoritative text. This eliminates arbitrary changes by anyone other than the author, but includes those which might have originated with someone other than the author but deliberately accepted by him. This principle provides the basis both for the selection of the copy-text and for the recording of variants.

We question the theory that automatically regards all spelling and punctuation as accidentals, that is, as matters affecting the formal presentation of a text but not its meaning. To be genuinely accidental a variant must be one that in *no way* alters the meaning of the text. On the other hand, anything—word, syntax, punctuation, typography, for example—that might affect the meaning must be considered substantive. Likewise anything which affects the phonic character of the line must be regarded as substantive.

Spelling can delay the recognition of a semantic function, but if the current standards of spelling can be unequivocably substituted, then it is truly accidental, and so with word divisions and the like. Spelling may, however, alter the meaning of a poem by distorting the intended rhythm or sound pattern of a line, and in such a case, modernization would be a violation of the author's intention. No simple application of a theory which regards spelling automatically as an accidental is acceptable to a sensitive editor of poetic texts.

Punctuation is still a different matter, however. Whatever its meaning may be—and this is a matter very little understood—everyone feels that it is meaningful. Punctuation, under which we include paragraphing, does not merely affect the meaning but is part of the meaning. One reason is that punctuation is at least in part an attempt to record the character of junctures in the spoken language. Since Browning's mature poetic style is far closer to the spoken language than is normal expository prose and much other poetry, punctuation and all variants in punctuation in his works are of particular interest. It would seem to us irresponsible to ignore them.

Thus the study of a series of editorial decisions in a passage involving only punctuational variants can, and surely must, have both an interesting and important effect upon the interpretation of the passage. It seems to us, therefore, that particularly in the works of a nineteenth- or twentieth-century poet, punctuation variants must be considered a part of meaning and so recorded. Browning was especially sensitive to the rhetorical function of punctuation; and, many of the changes in punctuation which he made in his various editions reflect his concern to heighten or clarify meaning. A dramatic example is the way in which he replaced the indeterminate dash—so frequently used in the earlier drafts and early editions of his work—by other more precise marks of punctuation. Whatever else may be said about the signification of the dash, it is clear that its use suggests between the elements thus marked off and the rest of the sentence a looser relationship than that achieved by other marks of punctuation. It also signals a more radical break in the rhythmic pattern of the line than that suggested by commas, for example. In the 1833 edition of *Pauline,* there are 292 dashes. In the heavily revised edition of 1868 these have been reduced to 77. In the manuscript of *The Ring and the Book* there are considerably more dashes than there are in the first and subsequent editions. The number in Book I are reduced from 146 to 127 in the final edition; those in Book VIII, from 447 to 218. In almost every case the dash is replaced by some other mark of punctuation. The following examples, all taken from *Pauline,* but characteristic of Browning's practice elsewhere, illustrate how this revision in punctuation substantially alters the relation between the involved elements and certainly results in a very different rhythmic pattern and, most likely, in a different meaning.

700| *1833*: I am prepared—I have made life my own—
1868: I am prepared: I have made life my own.
703| *1833*: Thro' all conjuncture—I have lived all life
When it is most alive—when strangest fate
1868: Thro' all conjuncture, I have lived all life
When it is most alive, where strangest fate
740| *1833*: No—we will pass to morning—
Morning—the rocks and valleys and old woods.
1868: No, we will pass to morning—
Morning, the rocks and valleys and old woods.
788| *1833*: Air, air—fresh life-blood—thin and searching air—
1868: Air, air, fresh life-blood, thin and searching air,

The only serious question that remains, as we see it, is whether or not Browning was indeed responsible for the changes in punctuation that occur in the various stages of his work. Once that fact is established, we have no choice but to include them as substantive readings.

III THE BASIC MATERIALS

Aside from a handful of uncollected poems, all short, everything but *Asolando* went through two or more editions during Browning's lifetime. Except for *Pauline, Strafford,* and *Sordello,* everything published before 1849 was republished in newly edited form in the 1849 collection. *Strafford* and *Sordello* were newly edited for the collection of

1863, as were all other works in that edition. The 1868 collection added a newly revised *Pauline* and *Dramatis Personae* to the other works, which were themselves revised. The 1888–89a collection in sixteen volumes included everything so far published in volumes (certain poems published only in periodicals were not included; *Asolando* was added as Volume XVII after Browning's death). The printing of this edition was completed in July, 1889, and the exhaustion of some of the early volumes led Browning to correct the first ten volumes before he left for Italy in late August. The second edition of this sixteen volume collection is dated 1889 on the title pages; the first eight volumes of the first edition are dated 1888, the rest, 1889. We have designated Volumes IX to XVI of the first edition 1889a.

We have designated the existing manuscripts and editions either as primary or secondary materials. The primary materials include:

1. The manuscript of each volume (when such exists; see table at the end of preface);

2. The proof sheets (when such exist);

3. The original edition of each volume (and subsequent separate editions when such exist);

4. The collected editions over which Browning exercised editorial control:

1849—*Poems by Robert Browning*. Two Volumes. London: Chapman and Hall.

1863—*The Poetical Works.* Three Volumes. London: Chapman and Hall.

1868—*The Poetical Works.* Six Volumes. London: Smith, Elder and Company.

1888—*The Poetical Works.* Volumes 1–8. London: Smith, Elder and Company.

1889a—*The Poetical Works.* Volumes 9–16. London: Smith, Elder and Company.

1889—*The Poetical Works.* Volumes 1–16. London: Smith, Elder and Company.

(Vols. 1–10, a revision of 1888–1889a; Vols. 11–16, a reprint of 1889a.)

All other relevant materials now known to exist or which may be discovered while this edition is being prepared will be called secondary. Examples of such materials are: the copy of the first edition of *Pauline* which contains annotations by Browning and John Stuart Mill; the copies of the first edition of *Paracelsus* which contain corrections in Browning's hand; Elizabeth Barrett's suggestions for the revision of *A Soul's Tragedy* and certain poems in *Dramatic Romances and Lyrics* (1845); and the edition of *Strafford* by Miss Emily Hickey for which Browning made suggestions.

IV AUTHORIAL CONTROL

Given these diverse materials, we must first determine the nature of the decisions for the variants in order to establish the extent to which each may be given authorial authority. Any variant clearly an error we have corrected. This includes all obvious misprints, particularly dropped end line punctuation, and also inadvertent errors in paragraphing which are revealed when the printed versions of a text are compared with the manuscript. When, for example, a paragraph, indicated in the manuscript, comes between two lines the first of which falls in the first edition at the bottom of the page but in subsequent editions within the page of text, the paragraph may very well not be indicated in the latter. In such cases, we have restored what was unquestionably the author's intention, even though he himself failed to detect the error in proof.

Matters of spelling and typography present no real problems. Discrepancies between Browning's spelling and modern practices are few indeed and require no emendation. There are some discrepancies in the use of two possible spellings for the same word. For example, in the manuscript of *The Ring and the Book* Browning uses both *honour* and *honor*. In the first and subsequent editions, however, the form *honour* is used consistently. Whether Browning himself decided in proof to regularize his spelling or whether consistency was imposed upon him by the publisher we cannot say. In either case, however, the matter is immaterial since it in no way alters the meaning of Browning's statement. Similarly, the plural of *folk* in the manuscript and in the first and second edition of *The Ring and the Book* is *folks*. In the 1888 edition it has been changed to *folk*. That Browning himself was responsible for this change is suggested by the fact that one such example not corrected (*In a Balcony*, l. 184) in the 1888 edition is changed in Browning's hand for the 1889 reprinting. With such words we have accepted the form used in the 1888–1889 edition and recorded all variants therefrom because, in such instances, the phonic character of the line is changed. Materials of this sort are valuable not only to readers of Browning's poetry but also to students of language, particularly of orthography.

Typography is less a problem than it might be with poets whose meaning depends partly on the appearance of their poetry on the page. The issue, however, is not entirely irrelevant. The manner of printing the long lines of *La Saisiaz*, whether on one- or two-line spaces, for example, might control to some degree the reader's response to them. Nowhere, however, does Browning indicate that he wished to use typography to control meaning, and the inference is that whatever changes occur from edition to edition are the responsibility of the printer. We have made no effort to record them.

Changes in typography along with a number of others may reasonably be considered matters of house styling. A number of variants occur in the plays in the presentation of characters, place location, stage directions, and character designations all of which we record except: (1) accidentals for stage directions which involve only change in manner of statement such as *Enter Hampden* instead of *Hampden enters* (such accidentals are standardized to the 1889 text when they are used as drop words); (2) accidentals for stage directions such as *Aside* instead of *aside*, [*Aside*.] instead of [*Aside*], [STRAFFORD.] instead of [STRAFFORD]; (3) accidentals for character designations such as *Lady Carlisle* instead of *Car* or *Carlisle*.

During most of Browning's career, a space was left in the contraction of two words; thus "it's" was printed "it 's." These we have closed up in accordance with modern practices. Another matter almost certainly the result of house styling is the manner of indicating quotations. In the first edition of *Christmas Eve and Easter Day*, for example, and in the collected edition of 1863, each line of a quotation is preceded by a quotation mark. In contrast, in *Sordello* in both the first edition and in the collected edition of 1863, quotation marks are placed only at the beginning and end of a quotation. The first edition of *Sordello*, published by Edward Moxon, and that of *Christmas Eve and Easter Day*, published by Chapman and Hall, were both printed by Bradbury and Evans. It would seem in this case at least that the compositors printed the material they were given without attempting to make it conform to house styling. One might assume that the different publishers imposed their own practices upon the manuscript before submitting it to the printer. The 1863 collected edition, where these differences are maintained, serves only to confuse the issue, however. This edition also was published by Chapman and Hall, but printed by John Edward Taylor. Clearly here neither publisher nor printer bothered to follow a consistent practice. Browning too, presumably having read the proof, was content to let the inconsistencies stand. It was not until 1868 when Smith, Elder and Company both printed and published the new collected edition that a fairly consistent policy of indicating quotations was adopted for Browning's work. In general after the appearance of this edition, quotations are indicated by a quotation mark both at the beginning and end of the quotation and at the beginning of each new line within the quotation. Smith, Elder and Company printed the four titles following the 1868 collected edition. After those, the remaining were printed by Spottiswoode and Company. It would seem, therefore, that Browning's new and last publisher imposed house styling upon the poet in the manner of indicating quotations. The matter is not entirely clear, however, since some inconsistencies remain even in the last collected edition. The weight of the evidence, nevertheless, is that Browning deferred to his publisher on this matter. We regard the quotation marks, therefore, as genuine accidentals and in our text follow the modern practice—also that of Browning in many cases—of indicating a quotation with marks only at the beginning and the end.

The manuscript of *The Ring and the Book* throws considerable light upon not only this subject but related ones, all of which can best be discussed together. *The Ring and the Book* was printed and published by Smith, Elder and Company. The manuscript, in two bound volumes, is now in the British Museum. The first volume contains the material published in 1868; the second, that published in 1869. The first volume contains relatively few corrections, although those which do appear are undoubtedly in Browning's hand. Between the manuscript and the first edition, however, there are extensive differences, both in wording and punctuation. Clearly Browning or someone made extensive corrections, perhaps in the proofs. Unfortunately those proofs, as far as can now be determined, no longer exist. The second volume, in contrast, is very heavily corrected in Browning's hand, and the differences between the corrected manuscript and the first edition are considerably fewer. The second volume presumably received the revision that was made in the first volume only after the proofs had been printed. The corrected manuscript of the second volume is consistent with the printed first edition of volume one. The changes in both the first edition of books one through six and of volume two of the manuscript suggest that Browning himself made them in order to be more precise and expressive in his choice of words, to reflect more sensitively the nature of the juncture between rhetorical units, or better to utilize phonic and rhythmic patterns as part of his meaning. It appears that Browning wrote hurriedly, giving primary attention to wording and less to punctuation, being satisfied, as I have already suggested, to use a dash to indicate almost any break in thought or rhythm. Later, either in proof (the first six books) or on the manuscript itself (the last six books) he changed the dashes to other, more expressive marks of punctuation. The punctuation of the printed first six books and that of the manuscript of the last six books is consistent; both are consistent with Browning's practices elsewhere. The punctuational changes in *The Ring and the Book* we must conclude are those of Browning's own choice and not of house-styling.

In the matter of indicating quotations, however, the evidence, as we have already suggested, is that Browning accepted house styling. In the manuscript for the first six books, quotations begin and end with a quotation mark. In the first edition, however, quotation marks also precede each line of a quotation. In the last six books the latter practice is followed both in the manuscript and in the first edition. The inference is that Browning prepared his manuscript following one procedure and then changed it, perhaps in response to his new publisher's policies established in the 1868 edition of his collected poetry, in proof for the first six books and in the manuscript for the last six books.

Having eliminated obvious errors and having decided not to record variants clearly arising from house styling, we arrive finally at those variants, both word and punctuation, which are substantive, and which if they are Browning's, should be recognized as authoritative and recorded. Let us begin where the evidence is clear and irrefutable. Browning had complete control over the text for the 1888–1889 edition of his works. Professor Michael Hancher, editor of the correspondence between Browning and his publisher George Smith, has published an enlightening article in which he summarizes the relevant information contained in these letters. He concludes: "The evidence is clear that Browning undertook the 1888–1889 edition of his *Poetical Works* intent on controlling even the smallest minutiae of the text. Though he at one time considered supplying biographical and explanatory notes to the poems, he finally decided against such a scheme, concluding in his letter to Smith of 12 November 1887, 'I am correcting them carefully, and *that* must suffice.' " On January 13, 1888, he wrote, regarding the six-volume edition of his collected works published in 1868 which was to serve as the printer's copy for the final edition: "I have thoroughly corrected the six volumes of the Works, and can let you have them at once." Hancher continues: "Browning evidently kept a sharp eye on the production of all sixteen of the volumes, including those later volumes. . . . Browning returned proof for Volume 3 on 6 May 1888, commenting, 'I have had, as usual, to congratulate myself on the scrupulous accuracy of the Printers'; on 31 December he returned proofs of Volume II, 'corrected carefully'; and he returned 'the corrected Proofs of Vol. XV' on 1 May 1889." (All quotations are from Michael Hancher's "Browning and the Poetical Works of 1888–1889," *Browning Newsletter*, (Spring 1971): 25–27.

These letters certainly establish Browning's intent to control the text of the final edition of his work. There is concrete evidence that what he intended he achieved. By spring of 1889, it was evident that a new printing would be required. Browning informed James Dykes Campbell that he was making corrections which the publisher would incorporate in the new printing. Browning offered to transcribe the corrections into Campbell's own set. The copies of the volumes corrected in Browning's hand are now in the British Museum and contain on the fly leaf of volume one a note by Campbell which explains precisely what happened. Browning proposed to correct the entire edition before reprinting. Before he left for Italy on August 29, 1889, he had completed his corrections for the first ten volumes. His death in Venice a few months later prevented him from finishing the task as far as we presently know. When the new printing appeared in 1889 the first ten volumes incorporated Browning's emendations. Campbell says that the corrections numbered "upwards of 250" (there are 247). It should be recognized, of course, that this marked copy was not the one used by the printer and that even Browning in transferring the changes from one text to another might have erred. Nevertheless, these changes are indisputably Browning's and are those which, according to his own statement, he proposed to make in the new edition. They are, therefore, unquestionably authoritative. The matter is further complicated, however, by the fact that a second list of corrections for Volumes IV-X, in Browning's hand and in his possession at the time of his death, exists. It was included in lot 179 of the Sotheby, Wilkinson, and Hodge's auction of Browning materials in 1913. It was purchased at that time and eventually found its way to Brown University where it is now located. This list does not correspond exactly to the Dykes Campbell list, and neither corresponds in all points to the 1889 printing. It is clear, however, that in general changes were made in the 1889 printing as Browning directed. Those which were not made are largely end of line punctuation marks and appear, since they were obvious corrections in the 1888 edition required by the meaning of the text, to be printers' errors. The one genuine exception is the failure to change *Utopia* to *Eutopia*. There are also four examples in which the printers made changes other than those Browning designated on either of the extant lists of corrections:

Pauline, l. 332:
1888: caves
B's correction: caves,
1889: caves:
King Victor and King Charles, Second Year, Part I, l. 31:
1888: give pretext
B's correction: give a pretext
1889: give the pretext
"Up at a Villa—Down in the City," l. 61:
1888: handle.
B's correction: handle,
1889: handle
The Ring and the Book, IX, l. 1492:
1888: afterward
B's correction: afterward.
1889: afterward!

There is no certain way of accounting for these discrepancies. Browning himself may have erred in transcribing the changes from his original list or he might, at a later date, have dictated the changes that appear in the 1889 text. The printers might have unconsciously made the substitutions. There is no evidence, however, to suggest that the changes were made deliberately by anyone who wished to alter the text. They remain isolated changes more logically accounted for as errors than as anything else. It seems conclusive, both from Browning's stated intention and his practice that for this final edition Browning and Browning alone was responsible.

The strong probability exists that by at least 1863 Browning had principal control over the editorial function. Writing to Chapman in the 1850s he shows concern for punctuation ("I attach importance to the mere stops . . ."). Hancher cites evidence of Browning's close supervision of the 1868 edition of his collected works. Mrs. Orr reports his resentment of those who garbled his text by misplacing his stops (*Life*, 357–358). She continues that his punctuation "was always made with the fullest sense of its significance to any but the baldest style, and of its special importance to his own (*Life*, 360)." We note also that she says he sent proof sheets to his French friend Joseph Milsand for correction (*Life*, 265). There is no evidence, however, that in seeking such help, Browning relinquished his own final editorial function.

That he was solely responsible from the beginning for all changes of words and lines seems obvious. In 1847 Elizabeth Barrett made suggestions for numerous changes in *A Soul's Tragedy* and some of the poems which compose *Dramatic Romances and Lyrics* (for a full list see *New Poems by Robert Browning and Elizabeth Barrett Browning*, ed. Sir Frederick G. Kenyon [New York, 1915], pp. 140–76). Some of these Browning accepted and others he rejected. Obviously he did not defer automatically even to her, although he professes great confidence in her literary judgment. Those which he accepted after deliberation, we regard as his own. Careful examination of the manuscripts and the first editions reveal no information to suggest that anyone other than Browning tampered with his wording between submission of the manuscript and the appearance of the first edition. Such changes as do occur are consistent with what we know of Browning's practices and suggest that in every case he himself made the change. In the case of *Paracelsus* and *The Ring and the Book*, if these two sizable manuscripts may be regarded as representative, there is every reason to indicate that such changes as appear in the first edition were those which Browning himself made.

The history of the *Paracelsus* text is of the highest interest and importance. The manuscript of that poem exhibits either an ignorance of punctuation conventions or a refusal to consider them very seriously. For whatever reason, Browning exhibits in this manuscript a wide latitude of innovation even from a variety of conflicting current punctuational conventions. The manuscript shows, however, house styling, or the exercise of the editorial function by someone other than Browning for one leaf in Act I and all but the first and last pages of Act III. Several other pages show editorial changes in punctuation which may be Browning's. What precisely happened to the styling of some of the manuscript before it was finally printed is uncertain. Either a new manuscript was prepared, or proof was set up from the manuscript as it stood after partial editing and was then thoroughly revised. The manuscript shows signs of heavy use, indications for the signatures (corrected for one signature), and what are compositors' names. The second possibility, then, seems the more likely. The results are significant. First, although the printed punctuation of the edited portions of the manuscript does not correspond with that editing, it is in the same style as that editing. Second, the printed punctuation of the unedited portions is in the same style as the printed versions of the edited portions, and thus of the editing in the manuscript. Third, subsequent published works for which no manuscript exists are in the same style as the printed 1835 *Paracelsus*.

The next available manuscript of major significance, that for *Christmas Eve and Easter Day*, prepared for the printer by Elizabeth and Robert, shows virtually no variation from the first edition of 1850. All evidence indicates that from 1835 onward Browning was responsible for variants to be found in the several editions of his work over which he had nominal supervision except those listed above as excluded.

V CHOICE OF TEXT

One cannot reasonably say that the 1889 text or any single one of the others best represent the "real" Robert Browning. There is no way of establishing objectively the greater accuracy or the greater artistic merit of any one of these texts. It could be argued that the 1888–1889a text, emended to conform to the corrections listed in the Dykes Campbell and the Brown University lists of corrections, would provide the most authoritative text since obviously there are differences between the lists and the 1889 printing. This would assume, however, that Browning made those and only those corrections included on these two lists, and that all others were non-authorial, an assumption for which there is no evidence. Indeed, it was Browning's practice to continue to make changes in his texts even after printing had begun. Moreover, it is not a choice between certainty and uncertainty. The important discrepancies between the lists themselves introduce doubts about Browning's final intentions, quite apart both the 1888–1889a and the 1889 texts, which can be resolved only by editorial decision. It would seem, therefore, best in absence of certainty to assume that Browning might have made changes up until the time of his death, and to base the copy text on all available possible evidence: the 1889 edition of the first ten volumes and the 1888 edition of the last six volumes, collated with all previous editions and emended according to the Dykes Campbell and the Brown

University list of corrections. In cases where conflicting readings result it becomes the responsibility of the editors to make a choice based upon the apparent demands of the text and to supply the reader with all the information which influenced their decision.

Indeed, our experience so far has shown that Browning was a careful but imperfect proofreader. This fact requires us to make editorial decisions based upon all the evidence available to us rather than upon a single text. It would seem even that in rare cases he failed during his latter years to grasp fully the syntax of his earlier works. Our problem, as far as punctuation goes, is made easier by Browning's obvious tendency to remove from a rhetorical to a syntactical use of punctuation as he grew older.

We propose, therefore, to print the 1889 text (emended as suggested above) for the first ten volumes; the 1889a text for the last six volumes (similarly emended) the 1889 edition of *Asolando;* all corrected to eliminate both errors and the consequence of house styling. In case of the 1889a, the Large Paper Edition limited to 250 copies rather than the trade edition will be used to insure that our basic copy text is that of an early impression. Errors include printers' mistakes and apparent Browning errors. These emendations are based on the historical collation as far as possible. The only alteration which we have made in the arrangement of the copy-text is to rearrange the materials so that they appear in the order of their first publication. This involves restoring to their original order the poems included in *Dramatic Lyrics, Dramatic Romances and Lyrics,* and *Men and Women.*

By presenting this text accompanied by the variant readings from manuscripts and subsequent editions, we provide the reader not only an acceptable text but the materials necessary to reconstruct any portion of Browning's work as it developed over the years. This enables him both to study the work in its variant forms and the poetic process by which it came into existence.

VI LISTING OF EMENDATIONS

All emendations to the text (based on principles established above) are listed at the beginning of the annotations for each work. This practice is initiated with Volume IV. Volume V will contain an appendix giving the emendations and their justification for the first three volumes.

VII NUMBERING OF LINES

Poetic lines are numbered in the traditional manner by considering the unit to be the complete poetic line. In prose passages the line unit is the type line of this edition.

VIII PRESENTATION OF VARIANTS

The presentation of variants is not entirely conventional. Indeed, there is no one way to offer variants. We feel justified, therefore, in having developed a method consistent with the principles of good textual practice and appropriate to the particular requirements of our present task. We believe that it has the advantage of presenting the history of the variants in the order in which they appeared, from the first form through the final one, and in a way in which the full text of each line of each edition is most accurately and readily reconstructed.

In presenting the variants from the 1889 text we print at the bottom of the page variants found in the manuscripts, when available, and in the first and subsequent editions—that is, variants found in the primary materials. It seems to us that we can give a clearer, more concise notion of Browning's editorial function if we separate primary materials from secondary materials as these are defined in item III. Moreover, we must assume that additional manuscripts may become available between now and the time the last volume of this edition is published, making a supplemental volume of variants necessary. We have decided, therefore, that it would be logical to place all variants derived from secondary materials together in a final volume. This final volume will also include *Thomas Wentworth, Earl of Strafford* by John Forster, to which Browning's contribution was apparently considerable but is so far indeterminable.

TABLE OF SIGNS

All signs used by Browning himself have been avoided. The symbols essential to an understanding of the variant notes are set out in the following table of signs:

§ . . . §	Editor's note
<>	Words omitted
/	Line break
//,///, . . .	Line break plus one or more lines without internal variants

All variants are placed at the bottom of the page of text to which they refer. A variant is generally preceded and followed by a pickup and a drop word (example *a*). No note terminates with a punctuation mark unless the punctuation mark comes at the end of a line. If a variant drops or adds a punctuation mark, the next word is added (example *b*). If the normal pickup word has appeared previously in the same line, the note begins with the word preceding it. If the normal drop word appears subsequently in the line, the next word is added (example *c*). If a single capitalized pickup word occurs within the line, it is accompanied by the preceding word. No pickup word, however, is used for any variant consisting of an internal change, for example, a hyphen in a compounded word, an apostrophe, a tense change, or a spelling change. Nor is a drop word used when the variant comes at the end of a line (example *e*). Illustrations from *Sordello*:

a 611| *1840:* but that appeared *1863:* but this appeared

b 1) at end of line:

109| *1840:* it, "taken <> intrigue:" *1863:* it, taken <> intrigue.

2) 82| *1840:* forests like *1863:* forests, like

c 183| *1840:* after clue and *1863:* after clue, and

77| *1840:* Who managed <> that night by

1863: She managed <> that, night by night, *1888:* by night

d 1) a single capitalized pickup word:

61| *1840:* Now—nor, this *1863:* Now—not this

2) a single capitalized pickup word within line:

295| *1840:* at Padua to repulse the

1863: at Padua who repulsed the

e 1) 285| *1840:* shall *1863:* should

2) at end of line:

86| *1840:* sky: *1863:* sky.

Each recorded variant will be assumed to be incorporated in the next edition if there is no indication otherwise.

All character designations which appear in variant entries will conform to the 1889 text as it appears in this edition. In typing variants in the plays, we ignore character designations unless the designation comes within a numbered line, in which case we treat it as any other word. In such cases, therefore, it is used as pickup or drop word. When it is used as a pickup word, however, the general rule regarding pickup words which begin with a capital letter does not apply.

IX ANNOTATIONS

Browning scholarship is not yet fully mature. The notes we have presented, therefore, are not intended to be exhaustive or final. The format of the edition has been planned to allow for revision of the notes without disturbing the text. If the text proves satisfactory, it can be reprinted indefinitely with new sets of notes.

As a general principle, we have annotated proper names, phrases that function as proper names, and words or groups of words the full meaning of which requires factual, historical, or literary background. Thus, we have attempted to hold interpretation to a minimum, although we realize that the act of selection itself is to some extent interpretative.

Specifically, we have annotated the following: (1) proper names; (2) geographical locations; (3) allusions to Biblical and other literature; (4) words not included in *Webster's Collegiate Dictionary*, Seventh Edition (since some limits must be imposed upon our work and because this dictionary is generally accepted and readily available. We annotate words used by Browning in a sense other than that given in this dictionary. For a more accurate understanding we have relied heavily upon Samuel Johnson's dictionary); and (5) other items requiring factual information which is not of current common knowledge or easily available. All passages in a language other than English are translated into English. Occasional quotations from Browning's sources are included when such source quotations seem especially pertinent and are of difficult access.

For notes, particularly on historical figures and events, we have tended to prefer fullness and even to risk the tangential and unessential. As a result, some of the information provided may be perhaps unnecessary for the mature scholar. On the other hand, it is impossible to assume that all who use this edition—the ordinary reader and the undergraduate and graduate student, for example—will be fully equipped to assimilate unaided all of Browning's copious literary, historical, and mythological allusions. Thus we have directed our efforts toward an audience conceived as a continuum from the relatively uninformed to the trained.

TABLE OF ABBREVIATIONS AND SHORT TITLES USED IN ANNOTATIONS

B	Browning
B.U.	Ms. corrections located at Brown University
D.C.	Corrections in Dykes Campbell copy
DeVane, *Hdk.*	William C. DeVane. *A Browning Handbook.* New York: Appleton-Century-Croft, 1955.
Griffin and Minchin	W. H. Griffin and H. C. Minchin. *The Life of Robert Browning.* New York: Macmillan, 1910.
Hood, *Ltrs.*	Thurman L. Hood, ed. *Letters of Robert Browning Collected by T. J. Wise.* New Haven: Yale University Press, 1933.
Orr, *Hkb.*	Mrs. Sutherland Orr. *Handbook to the Works of Robert Browning.* New Edition. Revised and in part Part Rewritten by Fredric G. Kenyon. Boston and New York: Houghton Mifflin Company, 1891.
P-C	Charlotte Porter and Helen A. Clarke, eds. *The Complete Works of Robert Browning.* 12 vols. Issued first in 1898 and reissued frequently. It appeared in 1910 as the De Luxe Edition and in 1912 as the Pocket Edition. New York: Crowell and Company.

The following manuscripts are known to exist in the locations indicated:

Paracelsus
Forster and Dyce Collection,
Victoria and Albert Museum, Kensington

Christmas-Eve and Easter-Day
Forster and Dyce Collection,
Victoria and Albert Museum, Kensington

Dramatis Personae
Pierpont Morgan Library, New York

The Ring and the Book
British Museum

Balaustion's Adventure
Balliol College Library, Oxford

Prince Hohenstiel-Schwangau
Balliol College Library, Oxford

Fifine at the Fair
Balliol College Library, Oxford

Red Cotton Night-Cap Country
Balliol College Library, Oxford

Aristophanes' Apology
Balliol College Library, Oxford

The Inn Album
Balliol College Library, Oxford

Of Pacchiarotto and How He Worked in Distemper
Balliol College Library, Oxford

The Agamemnon of Aeschylus
Balliol College Library, Oxford

La Saisaiz and The Two Poets of Croisic
Balliol College Library, Oxford

Dramatic Idyls First Series
Balliol College Library, Oxford

Dramatic Idyls Second Series
Balliol College Library, Oxford

Jocoseria
Balliol College Library, Oxford

Ferishtah's Fancies
Balliol College Library, Oxford

Parleyings With Certain People of Importance in Their Day
Balliol College Library, Oxford
Asolando
Pierpont Morgan Library, New York

Each manuscript is fully described in this edition in the section given to annotations on the corresponding text.

The following manuscripts are not known to be extant:

Pauline
Strafford
Sordello
Pippa Passes
King Victor and King Charles
"The Essay on Chatterton"
Dramatic Lyrics
The Return of the Druses
A Blot in the 'Scutcheon
Colombe's Birthday
Dramatic Romances and Lyrics
Luria
A Soul's Tragedy
"The Essay on Shelley"
Men and Women

We should like to request that anyone with information about any of the manuscripts which are presently unknown to the scholarly world communicate with the Director of the Ohio University Press, Athens, Ohio.

XI REQUEST FOR CORRECTIONS

We have tried to make this edition free from error, but we know that the history of printing proves that such an ambition is impossible of fulfillment. We urgently request that whoever discovers errors will report them to the Ohio University Press, Athens, Ohio, where a file of such errors will be kept so that any future printings can take advantage of such reports. A cumulative list of such errors will be printed as an appendix beginning with Volume V.

XII ACKNOWLEDGMENTS

We express our appreciation especially to the following: the Ohio University Press, the Ohio University Library, and the Ohio University English Department for providing money and services which have made it possible for us to assemble the vast materials required for preparation of this edition; The Armstrong Browning Library, Baylor University, Waco, Texas, and its director Professor Jack Herring for various favors;

The Beinecke Rare Book and Manuscript Library, Yale University, and its director, Mr. H. W. Liebert, for materials used in this volume. We have also received valuable assistance in securing and preparing materials to appear in later volumes from the British Museum; Balliol College Library, Oxford, and its librarian Mr. E. V. Quinn; Mr. Philip Kelley, New York; and Mr. John Murray, London. For permission to use the ms. copy of Browning's corrections of volumes 4–10 of the 1888–1889a edition, we are indebted to the owner of the MS., The John Hay Library, Brown University.

We are indebted to the Historical Society of Pennsylvania, Philadelphia, for permission to reproduce the oil portrait of Robert Browning painted in Italy in 1853 by the American painter Thomas Buchanan Read (1822–1872).

The Editors
Athens, Ohio

TABLE OF EDITIONS REFERRED TO IN VOLUME IV

1843	*Bells and Pomegranates,* No. V. *A Blot in the 'Scutcheon.* London: Edward Moxon.
1843a	*Bells and Pomegranates,* No. V. *A Blot in the 'Scutcheon.* Second Edition. London: Edward Moxon.
1844	*Bells and Pomegranates,* No. VI. *Colombe's Birthday.* London: Edward Moxon.
1845	*Bells and Pomegranates,* No. VII. *Dramatic Romances and Lyrics.* London: Edward Moxon.
1846	*Bells and Pomegranates,* No. VIII and Last. *Luria.* London: Edward Moxon.
1849	*Poems* Two Volumes. London: Chapman and Hall.
1863	*The Poetical Works.* Three Volumes. London: Chapman and Hall.
1868	*The Poetical Works.* Six Volumes. London: Smith, Elder, and Company.
1888	*The Poetical Works.* Volumes 1–8. London: Smith, Elder, and Company.
1889a	*The Poetical Works.* Volumes 9–16. London: Smith, Elder, and Company.
1889	*The Poetical Works.* Sixteen Volumes. London: Smith, Elder, and Company.

A BLOT IN THE 'SCUTCHEON

Edited by Thomas F. Wilson

COLOMBE'S BIRTHDAY

Edited by Park Honan

DRAMATIC ROMANCES AND LYRICS

Edited by Raymond Fitch

LURIA

Edited by Morse Peckham

BELLS AND POMEGRANATES, NUMBER V.

A BLOT IN THE 'SCUTCHEON

A TRAGEDY

Edited by Thomas F. Wilson

A BLOT IN THE 'SCUTCHEON

A TRAGEDY

1843: Bells and Pomegranates. / No. V.—A Blot in the 'Scutcheon. / A Tragedy, / in Three Acts. / By Robert Browning, / author of "Paracelsus." / London: Edward Moxon, Dover Street. / MDCCCXLIII. *1843a:* of "Paracelsus." / Second Edition. *1849:* A Blot <> Tragedy. *1863:* § with first page of text § Tragedy. / 1843. *1869:* § on page with title § *1888:* § on separate page § A / Blot <> Tragedy.

PERSONS.

MILDRED TRESHAM

GUENDOLEN TRESHAM

THOROLD, EARL TRESHAM

AUSTIN TRESHAM

HENRY, EARL MERTOUN

GERALD, *and other retainers of* LORD TRESHAM

TIME, 17—

1843, 1843a: Theatre Royal, Drury Lane, / February 11, 1843. § top of page § Miss Helen Faucit / Mrs. Sterling / Mr. Phelps / Mr. Hudson / Mr. Anderson / M. G. Bennett § minor characters listed in separate columns § Thorold, Lord Tresham *1863:* Thorold, Earl Tresham *1843:* Gerard / Other Retainers *1863:* Gerald, and other

A BLOT IN THE 'SCUTCHEON

1843

ACT I

SCENE I—*The interior of a lodge in* LORD TRESHAM'S *park. Many* Retainers *crowded at the window, supposed to command a view of the entrance to his mansion.* GERARD, *the warrener, his back to a table on which are flagons, etc.*

1ST RETAINER Ay, do! push, friends, and then you'll push down me!
—What for? Does any hear a runner's foot
Or a steed's trample or a coach-wheel's cry?
Is the Earl come or his least poursuivant?
But there's no breeding in a man of you
Save Gerard yonder: here's a half-place yet,
Old Gerard!
GERARD Save your courtesies, my friend.
Here is my place.
2ND RETAINER Now, Gerard, out with it!
What makes you sullen, this of all the days
I' the year? Today that young rich bountiful
Handsome Earl Mertoun, whom alone they match
With our Lord Tresham through the country-side,
Is coming here in utmost bravery
To ask our master's sister's hand?
GERARD What then?
2ND RETAINER What then? Why, you, she speaks to, if she meets
Your worship, smiles on as you hold apart

---

§ Ed. 1843, 1843a, 1849, 1863, 1868, 1888, 1889: No MS in an ancestral line extant. §
1| *1843:* Ay—do—push friends <> me. *1843a:* push, friends *1863:* Ay, do! push *1868:* me! 2| *1843:* foot, *1868:* foot 3| *1843:* trample, or *1868:* trample or
9| *1843:* sullen this *1849:* sullen, this 10| *1843:* that young, rich, bountiful, *1849:* that, young *1863:* that young *1868:* young rich bountiful 12| *1843:* thro' *1863:* through 14| *1843:* our Master's Sister's *1868:* master's sister's 15| *1843:* you

The boughs to let her through her forest walks,
You, always favourite for your no-deserts,
You've heard, these three days, how Earl Mertoun sues
To lay his heart and house and broad lands too
At Lady Mildred's feet: and while we squeeze
Ourselves into a mousehole lest we miss
One congee of the least page in his train,
You sit o' one side—"there's the Earl," say I—
"What then?" say you!

3RD RETAINER I'll wager he has let
Both swans he tamed for Lady Mildred swim
Over the falls and gain the river!

GERARD Ralph,
Is not tomorrow my inspecting-day
For you and for your hawks?

4TH RETAINER Let Gerard be!
He's coarse-grained, like his carved black cross-bow stock.
Ha, look now, while we squabble with him, look!
Well done, now—is not this beginning, now,
To purpose?

1ST RETAINER Our retainers look as fine—
That's comfort. Lord, how Richard holds himself
With his white staff! Will not a knave behind
Prick him upright?

4TH RETAINER He's only bowing, fool!
The Earl's man bent us lower by this much.

1ST RETAINER That's comfort. Here's a very cavalcade!

3RD RETAINER I don't see wherefore Richard, and his troop
Of silk and silver varlets there, should find
Their perfumed selves so indispensable
On high days, holidays! Would it so disgrace
Our family, if I, for instance, stood—
In my right hand a cast of Swedish hawks,
A leash of greyhounds in my left?—

---

she *1863:* you, she 17| *1843:* thro' *1863:* through 19| *1843:* heard these <> days how *1849:* heard, these <> days, how 20| *1843:* heart, and house, and <> too, *1868:* heart and house and <> too 21| *1843:* feet—and *1863:* feet: and 24| *1843:* the Earl" say *1843a:* the Earl," say 25| *1843:* then," say *1888:* then?" say 26| *1843:* for Lady Mildred, swim *1888:* for Lady Mildred swim 34| *1843:* comfort! Lord *1863:* comfort. Lord 42| *1843:* days—holy days!—Would *1843a:* days, holy days! Would *1849:* holy-days *1863:* holidays 43| *1843:* Our Family *1868:* family 45| *1843:* left? *GERARD* With *1849:*

GERARD —With Hugh
The logman for supporter, in his right
The bill-hook, in his left the brushwood-shears!
3RD RETAINER Out on you, crab! What next, what next? The Earl!
1ST RETAINER Oh Walter, groom, our horses, do they match
The Earl's? Alas, that first pair of the six—
They paw the ground—Ah Walter! and that brute
Just on his haunches by the wheel!
6TH RETAINER Ay—ay!
You, Philip, are a special hand, I hear,
At soups and sauces: what's a horse to you?
D'ye mark that beast they've slid into the midst
So cunningly?—then, Philip, mark this further;
No leg has he to stand on!
1ST RETAINER No? That's comfort.
2ND RETAINER Peace, Cook! The Earl descends. Well, Gerard, see
The Earl at least! Come, there's a proper man,
I hope! Why, Ralph, no falcon, Pole or Swede,
Has got a starrier eye.
3RD RETAINER His eyes are blue:
But leave my hawks alone!
4TH RETAINER So young, and yet
So tall and shapely!
5TH RETAINER Here's Lord Tresham's self!
There now—there's what a nobleman should be!
He's older, graver, loftier, he's more like
A House's head.
2ND RETAINER But you'd not have a boy
—And what's the Earl beside?—possess too soon
That stateliness?
1ST RETAINER Our master takes his hand—
Richard and his white staff are on the move—

---

left?—*GERARD*—With 46| *1843:* supporter—in *1868:* supporter, in 47| *1843:* bill-hook—in <> brushwood shears. *1849:* brushwood-shears! *1868:* bill-hook, in 49| *1843:* Oh, Walter *1868:* Oh Walter 51| *1843:* ground—Ah, Walter *1868:* ground—Ah Walter 52| *1843: 6th RETAINER* Ay—Ay! *1888: 6th RETAINER* Ay—ay! 54| *1843:* sauces—what's *1863:* sauces: what's 58| *1843:* Peace, Cook. The Earl descends.—Well *1849:* Peace, Cook! The *1888:* descends. Well 60| *1843:* hope! Why Ralph *1843a:* hope! Why, Ralph 61| *1843:* eye—*3rd RETAINER* <> blue— *1863:* eye. *3rd RETAINER* *1888:* blue: 66| *1843:* A House's Head! *2nd RETAINER* *1868:* head *1888:* head. *2nd RETAINER* 68| *1843: 1st RETAINER* Our Master *1868:* master 71| *1843:*

Back fall our people—(tsh!—there's Timothy
Sure to get tangled in his ribbon-ties,
And Peter's cursed rosette's a-coming off!)
—At last I see our lord's back and his friend's;
And the whole beautiful bright company
Close round them—in they go!
[*Jumping down from the window-bench, and making for the table and its jugs.*]
Good health, long life,
Great joy to our Lord Tresham and his House!

6TH RETAINER My father drove his father first to court,
After his marriage-day—ay, did he!

2ND RETAINER God bless
Lord Tresham, Lady Mildred, and the Earl!
Here, Gerard, reach your beaker!

GERARD Drink, my boys!
Don't mind me—all's not right about me—drink!

2ND RETAINER [*aside.*] He's vexed, now, that he let the show escape!
[*To* GERARD.] Remember that the Earl returns this way.

GERARD That way?

2ND RETAINER Just so.

GERARD Then my way's here.
[*Goes.*]

2ND RETAINER Old Gerard
Will die soon—mind, I said it! He was used
To care about the pitifullest thing
That touched the House's honour, not an eye
But his could see wherein: and on a cause
Of scarce a quarter this importance, Gerard
Fairly had fretted flesh and bone away
In cares that this was right, nor that was wrong,
Such point decorous, and such square by rule—
He knew such niceties, no herald more:

---

ribbon-ties— *1863:* ribbon ties— *1868:* ribbon-ties— *1888:* ribbon-ties, 72| *1843:* a coming *1849:* a-coming 73| *1843:* our Lord's <> friend's— *1868:* lord's *1888:* friend's; 77| *1843:* court *1849:* court, *1863:* to Court, *1868:* court, 78| *1843:* ay did *1843a:* ay, did 80| *1843:* Here Gerard <> boys: *1843a:* Here, Gerard *1868:* boys! 81| *1843:* drink. *1849:* drink! 83| *1843:* way— *1868:* way. 85| *1843:* mind I said it: he *1849:* mind, I said it! He 87| *1843:* honor—not *1849:* honor, not *1863:* honour 88| *1843:* wherein—and *1863:* wherein: and 91| *1843:* wrong; *1843a:* wrong, 92| *1843:* Such a point <> such by *1863:* such square by *1888:* Such point 93| *1843:* (He <> more) *1863:*

And now—you see his humour: die he will!
2ND RETAINER God help him! Who's for the great servants'-hall
To hear what's going on inside? They'd follow
Lord Tresham into the saloon.
3RD RETAINER I!—
4TH RETAINER I!—
Leave Frank alone for catching, at the door,
Some hint of how the parley goes inside!
Prosperity to the great House once more!
Here's the last drop!
1ST RETAINER Have at you! Boys, hurrah!

SCENE II—*A Saloon in the Mansion.*

Enter LORD TRESHAM, LORD MERTOUN, AUSTIN, *and* GUENDOLEN.

TRESHAM I welcome you, Lord Mertoun, yet once more,
To this ancestral roof of mine. Your name
—Noble among the noblest in itself,
Yet taking in your person, fame avers,
New price and lustre,—(as that gem you wear,
Transmitted from a hundred knightly breasts,
Fresh chased and set and fixed by its last lord,
Seems to re-kindle at the core)—your name
Would win you welcome!—
MERTOUN Thanks!
TRESHAM —But add to that,
The worthiness and grace and dignity
Of your proposal for uniting both
Our Houses even closer than respect
Unites them now—add these, and you must grant
One favour more, nor that the least,—to think
The welcome I should give;—'tis given! My lord,
My only brother, Austin: he's the king's.

He <> more: 94| *1843:* humour—die *1863:* humour: die 95| *1843:* servants' hall *1849:* servants'-hall 100| *1843:* more— *1868:* more!

6| *1843:* a thousand knightly *1849:* a hundred knightly 7| *1843:* Fresh-chased *1849:* Fresh chased 9| *1843:* welcome! *MERTOUN* <> *TRESHAM* But *1849:* welcome!—*MERTOUN* <> *TRESHAM*—But 14| *1843:* favor *1863:* favour 16| *1843:* brother, Austin—he's the King's. *1868:* king's. *1888:* brother, Austin: he's

Our cousin, Lady Guendolen—betrothed
To Austin: all are yours.

MERTOUN I thank you—less
For the expressed commendings which your seal,
And only that, authenticates—forbids
My putting from me . . . to my heart I take
Your praise . . . but praise less claims my gratitude,
Than the indulgent insight it implies
Of what must needs be uppermost with one
Who comes, like me, with the bare leave to ask,
In weighed and measured unimpassioned words,
A gift, which, if as calmly 'tis denied,
He must withdraw, content upon his cheek,
Despair within his soul. That I dare ask
Firmly, near boldly, near with confidence
That gift, I have to thank you. Yes, Lord Tresham,
I love your sister—as you'd have one love
That lady . . . oh more, more I love her! Wealth,
Rank, all the world thinks me, they're yours, you know,
To hold or part with, at your choice—but grant
My true self, me without a rood of land,
A piece of gold, a name of yesterday,
Grant me that lady, and you . . . Death or life?

GUENDOLEN [*apart to* AUSTIN.] Why, this is loving, Austin!

AUSTIN He's so young!

GUENDOLEN Young? Old enough, I think, to half surmise
He never had obtained an entrance here,
Were all this fear and trembling needed.

AUSTIN Hush!
He reddens.

GUENDOLEN Mark him, Austin; that's true love!
Ours must begin again.

TRESHAM We'll sit, my lord.

21| *1843:* me . . to *1888:* me . . . to 22| *1843:* praise . . but <> gratitude *1849:* gratitude, *1888:* praise . . . but 25| *1843:* ask *1849:* ask, 26| *1843:* words *1849:* words, 27| *1843:* which if as quietly denied, *1849:* which, if as calmly 'tis denied, 29| *1843:* soul:—that *1863:* soul. That 31| *1843:* you for. Lord *1849:* you.—Yes, Lord *1863:* you. Yes 33| *1843:* lady . . oh <> her. Wealth, *1849:* her! Wealth, *1888:* lady . . . oh 34| *1843: me* *1868:* me 36| *1843: me* *1868:* me 38| *1843:* lady and *1849:* lady, and 39| *1843: is* *1868:* is 41| *1843:* here *1849:* here, 43| *1843:* him, Austin, that's *1849:* him, Austin; that's

Ever with best desert goes diffidence.
I may speak plainly nor be misconceived.
That I am wholly satisfied with you
On this occasion, when a falcon's eye
Were dull compared with mine to search out faults,
Is somewhat. Mildred's hand is hers to give
Or to refuse.
MERTOUN But you, you grant my suit?
I have your word if hers?
TRESHAM My best of words
If hers encourage you. I trust it will.
Have you seen Lady Mildred, by the way?
MERTOUN I . . . I . . . our two demesnes, remember, touch;
I have been used to wander carelessly
After my stricken game: the heron roused
Deep in my woods, has trailed its broken wing
Thro' thicks and glades a mile in yours,—or else
Some eyass ill-reclaimed has taken flight
And lured me after her from tree to tree,
I marked not whither. I have come upon
The lady's wondrous beauty unaware,
And—and then . . . I have seen her.
GUENDOLEN [*aside to* AUSTIN.] Note that mode
Of faltering out that, when a lady passed,
He, having eyes, did see her! You had said—
"On such a day I scanned her, head to foot;
Observed a red, where red should not have been,
Outside her elbow; but was pleased enough
Upon the whole." Let such irreverent talk
Be lessoned for the future!
TRESHAM What's to say
May be said briefly. She has never known
A mother's care; I stand for father too.
Her beauty is not strange to you, it seems—

55| *1843:* I . . I . . our <> touch— *1863:* touch; *1888:* I . . . I . . . our 57| *1843:* game—the *1863:* game: the 58| *1843:* woods has *1849:* woods, has 62| *1843:* whither . . I *1863:* whither. I 63| *1843:* The Lady's *1863:* lady's 64| *1843:* then . . I *1888:* then . . . I 65| *1843:* that when <> passed *1863:* that, when <> passed, 67| *1843:* her head *1849:* her, head 69| *1843:* elbow, but *1849:* elbow; but 73| *1843:* too— *1849:* too. 74| *1843:* you it *1849:* you, it

You cannot know the good and tender heart,
Its girl's trust and its woman's constancy,
How pure yet passionate, how calm yet kind,
How grave yet joyous, how reserved yet free
As light where friends are—how imbued with lore
The world most prizes, yet the simplest, yet
The . . . one might know I talked of Mildred—thus
We brothers talk!

MERTOUN I thank you.

TRESHAM In a word,
Control's not for this lady; but her wish
To please me outstrips in its subtlety
My power of being pleased: herself creates
The want she means to satisfy. My heart
Prefers your suit to her as 'twere its own.
Can I say more?

MERTOUN No more—thanks, thanks—no more!

TRESHAM This matter then discussed . . .

MERTOUN —We'll waste no breath
On aught less precious. I'm beneath the roof
Which holds her: while I thought of that, my speech
To you would wander—as it must not do,
Since as you favour me I stand or fall.
I pray you suffer that I take my leave!

TRESHAM With less regret 'tis suffered, that again
We meet, I hope, so shortly.

MERTOUN We? again?—
Ah yes, forgive me—when shall . . . you will crown
Your goodness by forthwith apprising me
When . . . if . . . the lady will appoint a day

76| *1843:* trust, and *1868:* trust and 79| *1843:* embued *1863:* imbued 81| *1843:* The . . one *1888:* The . . . one 85| *1843:* pleased—herself *1863:* pleased: herself 89| *1843: MERTOUN* . . We'll *1863: MERTOUN*—We'll 90| *1843:* precious—I'm *1863:* precious. I'm 91| *1843:* That holds <> think *1843a:* thought *1868:* Which holds 93| *1843:* favor *1863:* favour 97| *1843:* shall . . you *1888:* shall . . . you 99| *1843:* When . . if . . the Lady *1863:* lady *1888:* When

For me to wait on you—and her.
TRESHAM So soon
As I am made acquainted with her thoughts
On your proposal—howsoe'er they lean—
A messenger shall bring you the result.
MERTOUN You cannot bind me more to you, my lord.
Farewell till we renew . . . I trust, renew
A converse ne'er to disunite again.
TRESHAM So may it prove!
MERTOUN You, lady, you, sir, take
My humble salutation!
GUENDOLEN AND AUSTIN Thanks!
TRESHAM Within there!

[SERVANTS *enter.* TRESHAM *conducts* MERTOUN *to the door. Meantime* AUSTIN *remarks,*

Well,
Here I have an advantage of the Earl,
Confess now! I'd not think that all was safe
Because my lady's brother stood my friend!
Why, he makes sure of her—"do you say, yes—
She'll not say, no,"—what comes it to beside?
I should have prayed the brother, "speak this speech,
For Heaven's sake urge this on her—put in this—
Forget not, as you'd save me, t'other thing,—
Then set down what she says, and how she looks,
And if she smiles, and" (in an under breath)
"Only let her accept me, and do you
And all the world refuse me, if you dare!"
GUENDOLEN That way you'd take, friend Austin? What a shame
I was your cousin, tamely from the first
Your bride, and all this fervour's run to waste!
Do you know you speak sensibly today?
The Earl's a fool.
AUSTIN Here's Thorold. Tell him so!
TRESHAM [*returning.*] Now, voices, voices! 'St! the lady's first!

. . . if . . . the 105| *1843:* renew . . I *1888:* renew . . . I 107| *1843: MERTOUN* You, Lady, you, Sir *1868:* lady <> sir 110| *1843:* now; *I'd* *1849:* now! *I'd* *1868:* now! I'd 111| *1843:* friend. *1868:* friend! 113| *1843:* no"—what *1868:* no,"—what 114| *1843: I* *1868:* I 118| *1843:* smiles," and, in <> breath, *1849:* and (in <> breath) *1868:* smiles, and" (in 120| *1843:* me if *1849:* me, if 122| *1843:* cousin,—tamely *1843a:* cousin, tamely 127| *1843:* not . . come

How seems he?—seems he not . . . come, faith give fraud
The mercy-stroke whenever they engage!
Down with fraud, up with faith! How seems the Earl?
A name! a blazon! if you knew their worth,
As you will never! come—the Earl?

GUENDOLEN He's young.

TRESHAM What's she? an infant save in heart and brain.
Young! Mildred is fourteen, remark! And you . . .
Austin, how old is she?

GUENDOLEN There's tact for you!
I meant that being young was good excuse
If one should tax him . . .

TRESHAM Well?

GUENDOLEN —With lacking wit.

TRESHAM He lacked wit? Where might he lack wit, so please you?

GUENDOLEN In standing straighter than the steward's rod
And making you the tiresomest harangue,
Instead of slipping over to my side
And softly whispering in my ear, "Sweet lady,
Your cousin there will do me detriment
He little dreams of: he's absorbed, I see,
In my old name and fame—be sure he'll leave
My Mildred, when his best account of me
Is ended, in full confidence I wear
My grandsire's periwig down either cheek.
I'm lost unless your gentleness vouchsafes" . . .

TRESHAM . . . "To give a best of best accounts, yourself,
Of me and my demerits." You are right!
He should have said what now I say for him.
Yon golden creature, will you help us all?
Here's Austin means to vouch for much, but you
—You are . . . what Austin only knows! Come up,
All three of us: she's in the library
No doubt, for the day's wearing fast. Precede!

1888: not . . . come 129| *1843:* fraud—up *1863:* fraud, up 133| *1843:* you . . *1888:* you . . . 136| *1843:* him . . *TRESHAM* *1888:* him . . . *TRESHAM* 138| *1843:* straiter *1863:* straighter 139| *1843:* harangues, *1868:* harangue, 143| *1843:* of—he's *1863:* of: he's 148| *1843:* vouchsafes" . . *1888:* vouchsafes" . . . 149| *1843:* . . "To *1888:* . . . "To 152| *1843:* You golden *1868:* Yon golden 154| *1843:* are . . what *1888:* are . . . what 155| *1843:* us—she's <> the

GUENDOLEN Austin, how we must—!

TRESHAM Must what? Must speak truth,
Malignant tongue! Detect one fault in him!
I challenge you!

GUENDOLEN Witchcraft's a fault in him,
For you're bewitched.

TRESHAM What's urgent we obtain
Is, that she soon receive him—say, to-morrow—
Next day at furthest.

GUENDOLEN Ne'er instruct me!

TRESHAM Come!
—He's out of your good graces, since forsooth,
He stood not as he'd carry us by storm
With his perfections! You're for the composed
Manly assured becoming confidence!
—Get her to say, "to-morrow," and I'll give you . . .
I'll give you black Urganda, to be spoiled
With petting and snail-paces. Will you? Come!

SCENE III—MILDRED's *chamber. A painted window overlooks the park.*
MILDRED *and* GUENDOLEN.

GUENDOLEN Now, Mildred, spare those pains. I have not left
Our talkers in the library, and climbed
The wearisome ascent to this your bower
In company with you,—I have not dared . . .
Nay, worked such prodigies as sparing you
Lord Mertoun's pedigree before the flood,

Library *1863:* us: she's *1868:* library 162| *1843:* farthest *1863:* furthest 163| *1843:* graces since, forsooth, *1868:* graces, since forsooth, 165| *1843:* composed, *1868:* composed 166| *1843:* Manly, assured, becoming *1868:* Manly assured becoming 167| *1843:* you . . *1888:* you . . .

2| *1843:* the Library *1868:* library 4| *1843:* dared . . *1888:* dared . . .

Which Thorold seemed in very act to tell
—Or bringing Austin to pluck up that most
Firm-rooted heresy—your suitor's eyes,
He would maintain, were grey instead of blue—
I think I brought him to contrition!—Well,
I have not done such things, (all to deserve
A minute's quiet cousin's talk with you,)
To be dismissed so coolly.

MILDRED Guendolen!
What have I done? what could suggest . . .

GUENDOLEN There, there!
Do I not comprehend you'd be alone
To throw those testimonies in a heap,
Thorold's enlargings, Austin's brevities,
With that poor silly heartless Guendolen's
Ill-timed misplaced attempted smartnesses—
And sift their sense out? now, I come to spare you
Nearly a whole night's labour. Ask and have!
Demand, be answered! Lack I ears and eyes?
Am I perplexed which side of the rock-table
The Conqueror dined on when he landed first,
Lord Mertoun's ancestor was bidden take—
The bow-hand or the arrow-hand's great meed?
Mildred, the Earl has soft blue eyes!

MILDRED My brother—
Did he . . . you said that he received him well?

7| *1843:* tell— *1868:* tell 10| *1843:* gray *1863:* grey 13| *1843:* cousin's-talk *1863:* cousin's talk 14| *1843:* coolly! *MILDRED* Guendolen, *1868: MILDRED* Guendolen! *1888:* coolly. *MILDRED* 15| *1843:* done . . what <> suggest . . *GUENDOLEN* *1868:* done? what *1888:* suggest . . . *GUENDOLEN* 19| *1843:* poor, silly, heartless *1868:* poor silly heartless 20| *1843:* Ill-timed, misplaced, attempted *1868:* Ill-timed misplaced attempted 24| *1863:* rock-table, *1868:* side, of <> rock-table *1888:* side of 29| *1843:* he . . you *1888:* he . . .

GUENDOLEN If I said only "well" I said not much.
Oh, stay—which brother?
MILDRED Thorold! who—who else?
GUENDOLEN Thorold (a secret) is too proud by half,—
Nay, hear me out—with us he's even gentler
Than we are with our birds. Of this great House
The least retainer that e'er caught his glance
Would die for him, real dying—no mere talk:
And in the world, the court, if men would cite
The perfect spirit of honour, Thorold's name
Rises of its clear nature to their lips.
But he should take men's homage, trust in it,
And care no more about what drew it down.
He has desert, and that, acknowledgment;
Is he content?
MILDRED You wrong him, Guendolen.
GUENDOLEN He's proud, confess; so proud with brooding o'er
The light of his interminable line,
An ancestry with men all paladins,
And women all . . .
MILDRED Dear Guendolen, 'tis late!
When yonder purple pane the climbing moon
Pierces, I know 'tis midnight.
GUENDOLEN Well, that Thorold
Should rise up from such musings, and receive
One come audaciously to graft himself
Into this peerless stock, yet find no flaw,
No slightest spot in such an one . . .
MILDRED Who finds
A spot in Mertoun?
GUENDOLEN Not your brother; therefore,
Not the whole world.
MILDRED I am weary, Guendolen.
Bear with me!
GUENDOLEN I am foolish.
MILDRED Oh no, kind!

---

you 30| *1843:* much— *1888:* much. 38| *1843:* honor *1849:* honour 39| *1843:* lips: *1863:* lips. 47| *1843:* all . . *MILDRED* *1888:* all . . . *MILDRED* 55| *1843: MILDRED* I'm weary, Guendolen.— *1868:* I am *1888:* weary, Guendolen. 56| *1843: MILDRED* Oh, no; kind— *1868: MILDRED* Oh no *1888:*

But I would rest.

GUENDOLEN Good night and rest to you!
I said how gracefully his mantle lay
Beneath the rings of his light hair?

MILDRED Brown hair.

GUENDOLEN Brown? why, it *is* brown: how could you know that?

MILDRED How? did not you—Oh, Austin 'twas, declared
His hair was light, not brown—my head!—and look,
The moon-beam purpling the dark chamber! Sweet,
Good night!

GUENDOLEN Forgive me—sleep the soundlier for me!

[*Going, she turns suddenly.*]

Mildred!
Perdition! all's discovered! Thorold finds
—That the Earl's greatest of all grandmothers
Was grander daughter still—to that fair dame
Whose garter slipped down at the famous dance! [*Goes.*]

MILDRED Is she—can she be really gone at last?
My heart! I shall not reach the window. Needs
Must I have sinned much, so to suffer.

[*She lifts the small lamp which is suspended before the Virgin's image in the window, and places it by the purple pane.*] There!

[*She returns to the seat in front.*]

Mildred and Mertoun! Mildred, with consent
Of all the world and Thorold, Mertoun's bride!
Too late! 'Tis sweet to think of, sweeter still
To hope for, that this blessed end soothes up
The curse of the beginning; but I know
It comes too late: 'twill sweetest be of all
To dream my soul away and die upon. [*A noise without.*]
The voice! Oh why, why glided sin the snake
Into the paradise Heaven meant us both?

[*The window opens softly. A low voice sings.*]

---

kind! 57| *1843:* you. *1863:* you! 59| *1843: MILDRED* Brown hair! *1868: MILDRED* Brown hair. 60| *1843: is* brown—how *1888: is* brown: how 61| *1843:* you—Oh Austin *1868:* you—Oh, Austin 62| *1843:* and, look, *1868:* and look, 65| *1843:* discovered.—Thorold *1863:* discovered! Thorold 70| *1843:* heart —I <> window! Needs *1863:* heart! I <> window. Needs 71| *1843:* suffer! *1888:* suffer. 73| *1843:* and Thorold,—Mertoun's *1863:* and Thorold, Mertoun's 77| *1843:* late—'twill *1868:* late: 'twill 78| *1843:* upon! *1868:* upon. 79| *1843:* voice! Oh, why *1868:* voice! Oh why 80| *1843:* the Paradise *1868:*

There's a woman like a dew-drop, she's so purer than the purest;
And her noble heart's the noblest, yes, and her sure faith's the surest:
And her eyes are dark and humid, like the depth on depth of lustre
Hid i' the harebell, while her tresses, sunnier than the wild-grape cluster,
Gush in golden-tinted plenty down her neck's rose-misted marble:
Then her voice's music . . . call it the well's bubbling, the bird's warble!

[*A figure wrapped in a mantle appears at the window.*]

And this woman says, "My days were sunless and my nights were moonless,
"Parched the pleasant April herbage, and the lark's heart's outbreak tuneless,
"If you loved me not!" And I who—(ah, for words of flame!) adore her,
Who am mad to lay my spirit prostrate palpably before her—

[*He enters, approaches her seat, and bends over her.*]

I may enter at her portal soon, as now her lattice takes me,
And by noontide as by midnight make her mine, as hers she makes me!

[*The* Earl *throws off his slouched hat and long cloak.*]

My very heart sings, so I sing, Beloved!
MILDRED Sit, Henry—do not take my hand!
MERTOUN 'Tis mine.
The meeting that appalled us both so much
Is ended.
MILDRED What begins now?
MERTOUN Happiness
Such as the world contains not.
MILDRED That is it.
Our happiness would, as you say, exceed
The whole world's best of blisses: we—do we
Deserve that? Utter to your soul, what mine
Long since, Beloved, has grown used to hear,

paradise 81| *1843:* *purest,* *1849:* *purest;* 86| *1843:* music . . call *1888:* music . . . call 89| *1843:* her! *1868:* her, 91| *1843:* me. *1849:* me, 93| *1843:* beloved! *1863:* sing, Beloved! *1868:* beloved! *1888:* sing, Beloved! 94| *1843:* hand. *MERTOUN* <> mine! *1868:* hand! *MERTOUN* <> mine. 101| *1843:* beloved *1863:* since, Beloved *1868:* beloved *1888:* since, Beloved 102| *1843:*

Like a death-knell, so much regarded once,
And so familiar now; this will not be!
MERTOUN Oh, Mildred, have I met your brother's face
Compelled myself—if not to speak untruth,
Yet to disguise, to shun, to put aside
The truth, as—what had e'er prevailed on me
Save you, to venture? Have I gained at last
Your brother, the one scarer of your dreams,
And waking thoughts' sole apprehension too?
Does a new life, like a young sunrise, break
On the strange unrest of our night, confused
With rain and stormy flaw—and will you see
No dripping blossoms, no fire-tinted drops
On each live spray, no vapour steaming up,
And no expressless glory in the East?
When I am by you, to be ever by you,
When I have won you and may worship you,
Oh, Mildred, can you say "this will not be"?
MILDRED Sin has surprised us, so will punishment.
MERTOUN No—me alone, who sinned alone!
MILDRED The night
You likened our past life to—was it storm
Throughout to you then, Henry?
MERTOUN Of your life
I spoke—what am I, what my life, to waste
A thought about when you are by me?—you
It was, I said my folly called the storm
And pulled the night upon. 'Twas day with me—
Perpetual dawn with me.
MILDRED Come what, come will,
You have been happy: take my hand!
MERTOUN [*after a pause.*] How good
Your brother is! I figured him a cold—
Shall I say, haughty man?
MILDRED They told me all.

---

death-knell so *1849:* death-knell, so [104]| *1843:* face, *1888:* face [107]| *1843:* as what *1868:* as—what [116]| *1843:* east? *1863:* the East? [119]| *1843:* be?" *1863:* be"? *1868:* be?" *1888:* be"? [120]| *1843:* us; so *1888:* us, so [124]| *1843:* life to *1849:* life, to [127]| *1843:* upon.—'Twas *1868:* upon. 'Twas [129]| *1843:* happy—take <> *MERTOUN* How *1849: MERTOUN* [*after a pause*] How *1863:*

I know all.

MERTOUN It will soon be over.

MILDRED Over?

Oh, what is over? what must I live through
And say, "'tis over"? Is our meeting over?
Have I received in presence of them all
The partner of my guilty love—with brow
Trying to seem a maiden's brow—with lips
Which make believe that when they strive to form
Replies to you and tremble as they strive,
It is the nearest ever they approached
A stranger's . . . Henry, yours that stranger's . . . lip—
With cheek that looks a virgin's, and that is . . .
Ah God, some prodigy of thine will stop
This planned piece of deliberate wickedness
In its birth even! some fierce leprous spot
Will mar the brow's dissimulating! I
Shall murmur no smooth speeches got by heart,
But, frenzied, pour forth all our woeful story,
The love, the shame, and the despair—with them
Round me aghast as round some cursed fount
That should spirt water, and spouts blood. I'll not
. . . Henry, you do not wish that I should draw
This vengeance down? I'll not affect a grace
That's gone from me—gone once, and gone for ever!

MERTOUN Mildred, my honour is your own. I'll share
Disgrace I cannot suffer by myself.
A word informs your brother I retract
This morning's offer; time will yet bring forth
Some better way of saving both of us.

MILDRED I'll meet their faces, Henry!

MERTOUN [*after a pause.*] How good

MERTOUN When? to-morrow!

MILDRED Oh, Henry, not to-morrow!

---

happy: take 133| *1843:* thro' *1863:* through 134| *1843:* over?" Is *1863:* over"? Is *1868:* over?" Is *1888:* over"? Is 136| *1843:* love,—with *1888:* love—with 141| *1843:* stranger's . . Henry *1888:* stranger's . . . Henry
142| *1843:* a Virgin's <> *is . . .* *1843a:* virgin's *1868:* is . . . 143| *1843:* Ah, God! some *1863:* of Thine *1868:* Ah God, some <> of thine 145| *1843:* even—some *1868:* even! some 146| *1843:* dissimulating—I *1868:* dissimulating! I
150| *1843:* as men round *1888:* as round 155| *1843:* honor *1863:* honour
158| *1843:* offer . . time *1843a:* offer; time 160| *1843:* faces, Mertoun! *MERTOUN*

Next day! I never shall prepare my words
And looks and gestures sooner.—How you must
Despise me!
MERTOUN Mildred, break it if you choose,
A heart the love of you uplifted—still
Uplifts, thro' this protracted agony,
To heaven! but Mildred, answer me,—first pace
The chamber with me—once again—now, say
Calmly the part, the . . . what it is of me
You see contempt (for you did say contempt)
—Contempt for you in! I would pluck it off
And cast it from me!—but no—no, you'll not
Repeat that?—will you, Mildred, repeat that?
MILDRED Dear Henry!
MERTOUN I was scarce a boy—e'en now
What am I more? And you were infantine
When first I met you; why, your hair fell loose
On either side! My fool's-cheek reddens now
Only in the recalling how it burned
That morn to see the shape of many a dream
—You know we boys are prodigal of charms
To her we dream of—I had heard of one,
Had dreamed of her, and I was close to her,
Might speak to her, might live and die her own,
Who knew? I spoke. Oh, Mildred, feel you not
That now, while I remember every glance
Of yours, each word of yours, with power to test
And weigh them in the diamond scales of pride,
Resolved the treasure of a first and last
Heart's love shall have been bartered at its worth,
—That now I think upon your purity
And utter ignorance of guilt—your own
Or other's guilt—the girlish undisguised
Delight at a strange novel prize—(I talk

<> to-morrow? *1863:* faces, Henry! *MERTOUN* *1868:* to-morrow! 163| *1843:* sooner!—How *1863:* sooner.—How 167| *1843:* To Heaven! but, Mildred *1868:* heaven! but Mildred 169| *1843:* the . . what *1888:* the . . . what 171| *1843:* in? I *1849:* in! I 174| *1843:* Dear Henry—*MERTOUN* *1863:* Dear Henry! *MERTOUN* 176| *1843:* you—why *1868:* you; why 177| *1843:* side!—my fool's cheek *1863:* fool's-cheek *1868:* side! My 179| *1843:* dream! *1849:* dream 184| *1843:* knew?—I spoke— Oh *1863:* spoke. Oh *1868:* knew? I <> Oh Mildred *1888:* spoke. Oh, Mildred 187| *1843:* of Pride, *1863:* pride, 189| *1843:* worth;

A silly language, but interpret, you!)
If I, with fancy at its full, and reason
Scarce in its germ, enjoined you secrecy,
If you had pity on my passion, pity
On my protested sickness of the soul
To sit beside you, hear you breathe, and watch
Your eyelids and the eyes beneath—if you
Accorded gifts and knew not they were gifts—
If I grew mad at last with enterprise
And must behold my beauty in her bower
Or perish—(I was ignorant of even
My own desires—what then were you?) if sorrow—
Sin—if the end came—must I now renounce
My reason, blind myself to light, say truth
Is false and lie to God and my own soul?
Contempt were all of this!

MILDRED Do you believe . . .
Or, Henry, I'll not wrong you—you believe
That I was ignorant. I scarce grieve o'er
The past. We'll love on; you will love me still.

MERTOUN Oh, to love less what one has injured! Dove,
Whose pinion I have rashly hurt, my breast—
Shall my heart's warmth not nurse thee into strength?
Flower I have crushed, shall I not care for thee?
Bloom o'er my crest, my fight-mark and device!
Mildred, I love you and you love me.

MILDRED Go!
Be that your last word. I shall sleep to-night.

MERTOUN This is not our last meeting?

MILDRED One night more.

MERTOUN And then—think, then!

MILDRED Then, no sweet courtship-days,
No dawning consciousness of love for us,
No strange and palpitating births of sense
From words and looks, no innocent fears and hopes,
Reserves and confidences: morning's over!

MERTOUN How else should love's perfected noontide follow?

1843a: worth, 212| *1843:* past! We'll <> on—you <> still! *1863:* The Past *1868:* past <> on; you *1888:* past. We'll <> still. 216| *1843:* crush'd *1849:* crushed 217| *1843:* crest my *1863:* crest, my 218| *1843:* me! *MILDRED*

All the dawn promised shall the day perform.
MILDRED So may it be! but——
You are cautious, Love?
Are sure that unobserved you scaled the walls?
MERTOUN Oh, trust me! Then our final meeting's fixed
To-morrow night?
MILDRED Farewell! Stay, Henry . . . wherefore?
His foot is on the yew-tree bough; the turf
Receives him: now the moonlight as he runs
Embraces him—but he must go—is gone.
Ah, once again he turns—thanks, thanks, my Love!
He's gone. Oh, I'll believe him every word!
I was so young, I loved him so, I had
No mother, God forgot me, and I fell.
There may be pardon yet: all's doubt beyond.
Surely the bitterness of death is past.

1888: me. *MILDRED* 228| *1849:* love? *1888:* cautious, Love? 230| *1843:* fixed? *1888:* fixed 231| *1843: MILDRED* Farewell! Stay, Henry . . wherefore? *1888: MILDRED* Farewell! Stay, Henry . . . wherefore? 232| *1843:* bough—the *1863:* bough; the 233| *1843:* him—now *1863:* him: now 234| *1843:* gone— *1863:* gone. 235| *1843:* love! *1888:* my Love! 236| *1843:* gone—Oh I'll *1863:* gone. Oh *1888:* gone. Oh, I'll 237 *1843:* young—I <> so—I *1868:* young, I <> so, I 238| *1843:* mother—God <> me—and *1868:* mother, God <> me, and 239| *1843:* yet—all's *1863:* yet: all's 240| *1843:* past! *1888:* past.

ACT II

SCENE—*The Library.*

Enter LORD TRESHAM, *hastily.*

TRESHAM This way! In, Gerard, quick!
[*As* GERARD *enters,* TRESHAM *secures the door.*]
Now speak! or, wait—
I'll bid you speak directly. [*Seats himself.*]
Now repeat
Firmly and circumstantially the tale
You just now told me; it eludes me; either
I did not listen, or the half is gone
Away from me. How long have you lived here?
Here in my house, your father kept our woods
Before you?

GERARD —As his father did, my lord.
I have been eating, sixty years almost,
Your bread.

TRESHAM Yes, yes. You ever were of all
The servants in my father's house, I know,
The trusted one. You'll speak the truth.

GERARD I'll speak
God's truth. Night after night . . .

TRESHAM Since when?

GERARD At least
A month—each midnight has some man access
To Lady Mildred's chamber.

TRESHAM Tush, "access"—
No wide words like "access" to me!

GERARD He runs

1| *1843:* way—In *1863:* way! In 6| *1843:* me—How *1863:* me. How 7| *1843:* house your *1849:* house, your 9| *1843:* eating sixty years, almost, *1868:* eating, sixty years almost, 10| *1843: TRESHAM* Yes, yes—You *1863: TRESHAM* Yes, yes. You 13| *1843:* truth: night after *1863:* truth. Night after 16| *1843:*

Along the woodside, crosses to the South,
Takes the left tree that ends the avenue . . .
TRESHAM The last great yew-tree?
GERARD You might stand upon
The main boughs like a platform. Then he . . .
TRESHAM Quick!
GERARD Climbs up, and, where they lessen at the top,
—I cannot see distinctly, but he throws,
I think—for this I do not vouch—a line
That reaches to the lady's casement—
TRESHAM —Which
He enters not! Gerard, some wretched fool
Dares pry into my sister's privacy!
When such are young, it seems a precious thing
To have approached,—to merely have approached,
Got sight of, the abode of her they set
Their frantic thoughts upon. He does not enter?
Gerard?
GERARD There is a lamp that's full i' the midst,
Under a red square in the painted glass
Of Lady Mildred's . . .
TRESHAM Leave that name out! Well?
That lamp?
GERARD —Is moved at midnight higher up
To one pane—a small dark-blue pane; he waits
For that among the boughs: at sight of that,
I see him, plain as I see you, my lord,
Open the lady's casement, enter there . . .
TRESHAM —And stay?
GERARD An hour, two hours.
TRESHAM And this you saw

---

me!" *GERARD* *1849:* me! *GERARD* 17| *1843:* south *1863:* the South, 20| *1843:* platform . . Then he . . *TRESHAM* *1863:* platform. Then *1888:* he . . . *TRESHAM* 21| *1843:* . . Climbs *1863:* Climbs 24| *1843:* the Lady's casement. *TRESHAM* Which *1849:* casement—*TRESHAM*—Which *1888:* lady's 25| *1843:* not! Gerard—some *1868:* not! Gerard, some 27| *1843:* young it *1849:* young, it 28| *1843:* merely have approached— *1849:* merely have approached, 29| *1843:* of the *1849:* of, the 30| *1843:* upon! He *1888:* upon. He 31| *1843:* in *1888:* i' 33| *1843:* Of Lady Mildred's . . *TRESHAM* *1868:* Of Lady Mildred's . . . *TRESHAM* 35| *1843:* dark-blue pane—he *1863:* dark-blue pane; he 36| *1843:* boughs; at *1863:* boughs: at 38| *1843:* the Lady's *1868:* lady's

Once?—twice?—quick!

GERARD Twenty times.

TRESHAM And what brings you
Under the yew-trees?

GERARD The first night I left
My range so far, to track the stranger stag
That broke the pale, I saw the man.

TRESHAM Yet sent
No cross-bow shaft through the marauder?

GERARD But
He came, my lord, the first time he was seen,
In a great moonlight, light as any day,
From Lady Mildred's chamber.

TRESHAM [*after a pause.*] You have no cause
—Who could have cause to do my sister wrong?

GERARD Oh, my lord, only once—let me this once
Speak what is on my mind! Since first I noted
All this, I've groaned as if a fiery net
Plucked me this way and that—fire if I turned
To her, fire if I turned to you, and fire
If down I flung myself and strove to die.
The lady could not have been seven years old
When I was trusted to conduct her safe
Through the deer-herd to stroke the snow-white fawn
I brought to eat bread from her tiny hand
Within a month. She ever had a smile
To greet me with—she . . . if it could undo
What's done, to lop each limb from off this trunk . . .
All that is foolish talk, not fit for you—
I mean, I could not speak and bring her hurt
For Heaven's compelling. But when I was fixed
To hold my peace, each morsel of your food
Eaten beneath your roof, my birth-place too,
Choked me. I wish I had grown mad in doubts

42| *1843:* far to *1849:* far, to 44| *1843:* thro' *1863:* through 47| *1843:* cause— *1863:* cause 49| *1868:* Oh my *1888:* Oh, my 52| *1843:* fire, if *1888:* fire if 53| *1843:* and fire, *1888:* and fire 57| *1843:* Thro' *1863:* Through 60| *1843:* she . . if *1888:* she . . . if 61| *1843:* done to <> trunk . . *1863:* done, to *1888:* trunk . . . 64| *1843:* compelling: but *1863:* compelling.

What it behoved me do. This morn it seemed
Either I must confess to you, or die:
Now it is done, I seem the vilest worm
That crawls, to have betrayed my lady.
TRESHAM   No—
No, Gerard!
GERARD   Let me go!
TRESHAM   A man, you say:
What man? Young? Not a vulgar hind? What dress?
GERARD A slouched hat and a large dark foreign cloak
Wraps his whole form; even his face is hid;
But I should judge him young: no hind, be sure!
TRESHAM Why?
GERARD   He is ever armed: his sword projects
Beneath the cloak.
TRESHAM   Gerard,—I will not say
No word, no breath of this!
GERARD   Thanks, thanks, my lord! [*Goes.*]
TRESHAM [*paces the room. After a pause.*]
Oh, thought's absurd!—as with some monstrous fact
Which, when ill thoughts beset us, seems to give
Merciful God that made the sun and stars,
The waters and the green delights of earth,
The lie! I apprehend the monstrous fact—
Yet know the maker of all worlds is good,
And yield my reason up, inadequate
To reconcile what yet I do behold—
Blasting my sense! There's cheerful day outside:
This is my library, and this the chair
My father used to sit in carelessly
After his soldier-fashion, while I stood
Between his knees to question him: and here
Gerard our grey retainer,—as he says,

But   68| *1843:* me to do   *1849:* me do   *1868:* me to do   *1888:* me do   71| *1843:* my Lady! *TRESHAM*   *1868:* lady   *1888:* lady. *TRESHAM*   72| *1843:* No—Gerard <> say—   *1868:* No, Gerard <> say: 75| *1843:* form: even   *1863:* form; even   76| *1843:* young; no   *1863:* young: no   77–78| *1843:* sword / Projects beneath   *1849:* sword projects / Beneath   80| *1843:* absurd here! like some   *1849:* absurd!—as with some   81| *1843:* That, when ill-thoughts   *1849:* ill thoughts   *1868:* Which, when   82| *1843:* Merciful Heaven that <> stars   *1849:* Merciful God that   *1868:* stars,   85| *1843:* the Maker   *1868:* maker   88| *1843:* outside—   *1868:* outside: 89| *1843:* library—and   *1868:* library, and   90| *1843:* carelessly,   *1868:* carelessly   92| *1843:* him—and   *1849:* here,   *1863:* him: and   *1888:* here   93| *1843:*

Fed with our food, from sire to son, an age,—
Has told a story—I am to believe!
That Mildred . . . oh, no, no! both tales are true,
Her pure cheek's story and the forester's!
Would she, or could she, err—much less, confound
All guilts of treachery, of craft, of . . . Heaven
Keep me within its hand!—I will sit here
Until thought settle and I see my course.
Avert, oh God, only this woe from me!

[*As he sinks his head between his arms on the table,* GUENDOLEN'S *voice is heard at the door.*]

Lord Tresham! [*She knocks.*] Is Lord Tresham there?

[TRESHAM, *hastily turning, pulls down the first book above him and opens it.*]

TRESHAM Come in! [*She enters.*]
Ha, Guendolen!—good morning.

GUENDOLEN Nothing more?

TRESHAM What should I say more?

GUENDOLEN Pleasant question! more?
This more. Did I besiege poor Mildred's brain
Last night till close on morning with "the Earl,"
"The Earl"—whose worth did I asseverate
Till I am very fain to hope that . . . Thorold,
What is all this? You are not well!

TRESHAM Who, I?
You laugh at me.

GUENDOLEN Has what I'm fain to hope,
Arrived then? Does that huge tome show some blot
In the Earl's 'scutcheon come no longer back
Than Arthur's time?

TRESHAM When left you Mildred's chamber?

GUENDOLEN Oh, late enough, I told you! The main thing
To ask is, how I left her chamber,—sure,

gray *1863:* grey 94| *1843:* food from <> son an *1863:* food, from <> son, an 96| *1843:* oh no, no *1888:* oh, no, no 100| *1863:* within Its *1868:* its 101| *1843:* settles *1868:* settle 104| *1843:* Ah Guendolen—good *1849:* Ah, Guendolen *1868:* Ha Guendolen *1888:* Ha, Guendolen!—good 106| *1843:* more! Did *1868:* more. Did 107| *1843:* the Earl"— *1868:* the Earl," 111| *1843:* hope *1868:* hope, 112| *1843:* Arrived, then *1868:* Arrived then 115| *1843:* Oh late *1888:* Oh, late 116| *1843:* chamber. Sure, *1849:* chamber,—sure,

Content yourself, she'll grant this paragon
Of Earls no such ungracious . . .

TRESHAM Send her here!

GUENDOLEN Thorold?

TRESHAM I mean—acquaint her, Guendolen,
—But mildly!

GUENDOLEN Mildly?

TRESHAM Ah, you guessed aright!
I am not well: there is no hiding it.
But tell her I would see her at her leisure—
That is, at once! here in the library!
The passage in that old Italian book
We hunted for so long is found, say, found—
And if I let it slip again . . . you see,
That she must come—and instantly!

GUENDOLEN I'll die
Piecemeal, record that, if there have not gloomed
Some blot i' the 'scutcheon!

TRESHAM Go! or, Guendolen,
Be you at call,—with Austin, if you choose,—
In the adjoining gallery! There, go! [GUENDOLEN *goes.*]
Another lesson to me! You might bid
A child disguise his heart's sore, and conduct
Some sly investigation point by point
With a smooth brow, as well as bid me catch
The inquisitorial cleverness some praise.
If you had told me yesterday, "There's one
You needs must circumvent and practise with,
Entrap by policies, if you would worm
The truth out: and that one is—Mildred!" There,
There—reasoning is thrown away on it!
Prove she's unchaste . . . why, you may after prove
That she's a poisoner, traitress, what you will!
Where I can comprehend nought, nought's to say.

119| *1843:* her, Guendolen,— *1868:* her, Guendolen, 120| *1843:* guess'd *1863:* guessed 121| *1843:* well—there *1863:* well: there 123| *1843:* the Library! *1868:* library! 125| *1843:* say,—found— *1888:* say, found— 126| *1843:* again . . you *1888:* again . . . you 129| *1843:* the 'Scutcheon *1849:* 'scutcheon 131| *1843:* gallery—There *1863:* gallery! There 132| *1843:* you *1868:* me! You 136| *1843:* praise! *1888:* praise. 140| *1843:* out—and <> is Mildred!" There— *1863:* out: and *1868:* is Mildred!" There, 142| *1843:* unchaste . . why you *1863:* why, you *1888:* unchaste . . . why 144| *1843:* say, *1888:* say.

Or do, or think. Force on me but the first
Abomination,—then outpour all plagues,
And I shall ne'er make count of them.

Enter MILDRED.

MILDRED What book
Is it I wanted, Thorold? Guendolen
Thought you were pale; you are not pale. That book?
That's Latin surely.
TRESHAM Mildred, here's a line,
(Don't lean on me: I'll English it for you)
"Love conquers all things." What love conquers them?
What love should you esteem—best love?
MILDRED True love.
TRESHAM I mean, and should have said, whose love is best
Of all that love or that profess to love?
MILDRED The list's so long: there's father's, mother's, husband's . . .
TRESHAM Mildred, I do believe a brother's love
For a sole sister must exceed them all.
For see now, only see! there's no alloy
Of earth that creeps into the perfect'st gold
Of other loves—no gratitude to claim;
You never gave her life, not even aught
That keeps life—never tended her, instructed,
Enriched her—so, your love can claim no right
O'er her save pure love's claim: that's what I call
Freedom from earthliness. You'll never hope
To be such friends, for instance, she and you,
As when you hunted cowslips in the woods
Or played together in the meadow hay.
Oh yes—with age, respect comes, and your worth
Is felt, there's growing sympathy of tastes,
There's ripened friendship, there's confirmed esteem:

145| *1843:* think! Force *1888:* think. Force 147| *1843:* them! *1888:* them. 149| *1843:* pale—you <> not pale! That *1868:* pale: you <> not pale. That *1888:* were pale; you 150| *1843:* surely! *TRESHAM* Mildred—here's a line— *1863: TRESHAM* Mildred, here's *1868:* surely. *TRESHAM* <> line, 151| *1843:* me—I'll *1868:* me: I'll 156| *1843:* long—there's *1868:* long: there's 158| *1843:* all! *1868:* all. 162| *1843:* life—not even the dross *1849:* not even aught *1868:* life, not 164| *1843:* so your *1888:* so, your 165| *1843:* hers <> claim—that's *1863:* claim: that's *1868:* her 168| *1843:* woods, *1868:* woods 172| *1843:* esteem, *1868:*

—Much head these make against the new-comer!
The startling apparition, the strange youth—
Whom one half-hour's conversing with, or, say,
Mere gazing at, shall change (beyond all change
This Ovid ever sang about) your soul
. . . Her soul, that is,—the sister's soul! With her
'Twas winter yesterday; now, all is warmth,
The green leaf's springing and the turtle's voice,
"Arise and come away!" Come whither?—far
Enough from the esteem, respect, and all
The brother's somewhat insignificant
Array of rights! All which he knows before,
Has calculated on so long ago!
I think such love, (apart from yours and mine,)
Contented with its little term of life,
Intending to retire betimes, aware
How soon the background must be place for it,
—I think, am sure, a brother's love exceeds
All the world's love in its unworldliness.
MILDRED What is this for?
TRESHAM This, Mildred, is it for!
Or, no, I cannot go to it so soon!
That's one of many points my haste left out—
Each day, each hour throws forth its silk-slight film
Between the being tied to you by birth,
And you, until those slender threads compose
A web that shrouds her daily life of hopes
And fears and fancies, all her life, from yours:
So close you live and yet so far apart!
And must I rend this web, tear up, break down
The sweet and palpitating mystery
That makes her sacred? You—for you I mean,
Shall I speak, shall I not speak?
MILDRED Speak!
TRESHAM I will.

---

esteem: 174| *1843:* apparition—the *1868:* apparition, the 177| *1843:* about!) your *1868:* about) your 178| *1843:* . . . *Her* soul that *1849:* soul, that *1868:* . . . Her 184| *1843:* all <> before— *1868:* rights! All <> before, 189| *1843:* back-ground *1863:* background 190| *1843:* I *1863:*—I 193| *1843:* Oh, no *1868:* Or, no 199| *1843:* yours— *1868:* yours: 204| *1843:* speak—shall *1868:*

Is there a story men could—any man
Could tell of you, you would conceal from me?
I'll never think there's falsehood on that lip.
Say "There is no such story men could tell,"
And I'll believe you, though I disbelieve
The world—the world of better men than I,
And women such as I suppose you. Speak!
[*After a pause.*] Not speak? Explain then! Clear it up then! Move
Some of the miserable weight away
That presses lower than the grave! Not speak?
Some of the dead weight, Mildred! Ah, if I
Could bring myself to plainly make their charge
Against you! Must I, Mildred? Silent still?
[*After a pause.*] Is there a gallant that has night by night
                    Admittance to your chamber?
[*After a pause.*]   Then, his name!
Till now, I only had a thought for you:
But now,—his name!
MILDRED   Thorold, do you devise
Fit expiation for my guilt, if fit
There be! 'Tis nought to say that I'll endure
And bless you,—that my spirit yearns to purge
Her stains off in the fierce renewing fire:
But do not plunge me into other guilt!
Oh, guilt enough! I cannot tell his name.
TRESHAM Then judge yourself! How should I act? Pronounce!
MILDRED Oh, Thorold, you must never tempt me thus!
To die here in this chamber by that sword
Would seem like punishment: so should I glide,
Like an arch-cheat, into extremest bliss!

---

speak, shall   207| *1843:* lip! *1868:* lip.   209| *1843:* tho' *1863:* though   210| *1843:* world . . the *1863:* world—the   211| *1843:* you—Speak! *1863:* you. Speak!   212| *1843:* clear up all, then *1849:* clear it up, then *1868:* then! Clear it up then   220| *1843:* you— *1863:* you: 223| *1843:* 'tis *1868:* be! 'Tis   225| *1843:* fire— *1863:* fire: 231| *1843:* punishment—so <> glide *1849:* glide, *1868:* punishment: so   232| *1843:* arch-cheat into *1849:* arch-cheat, into

'Twere easily arranged for me: but you—
What would become of you?

TRESHAM — And what will now
Become of me? I'll hide your shame and mine
From every eye; the dead must heave their hearts
Under the marble of our chapel-floor;
They cannot rise and blast you. You may wed
Your paramour above our mother's tomb;
Our mother cannot move from 'neath your foot.
We too will somehow wear this one day out:
But with to-morrow hastens here—the Earl!
The youth without suspicion face can come
From Heaven, and heart from . . . whence proceed such hearts?
I have despatched last night at your command
A missive bidding him present himself
To-morrow—here—thus much is said; the rest
Is understood as if 'twere written down—
"His suit finds favour in your eyes." Now dictate
This morning's letter that shall countermand
Last night's—do dictate that!

MILDRED — But, Thorold—if
I will receive him as I said?

TRESHAM — The Earl?

MILDRED — I will receive him.

TRESHAM [*starting up.*] — Ho there! Guendolen!

GUENDOLEN *and* AUSTIN *enter.*

233| *1843:* me! but *1868:* me: but 238| *1843:* you! You *1868:* you. You 239| *1843:* our Mother's tomb: *1849:* mother's tomb; 243| *1843:* suspicion faces come *1849:* suspicion that faces come *1888:* suspicion face can come 244| *1843:* and hearts from *1868:* heaven: *1888:* From Heaven, and heart from 247| *1843:* Tomorrow here <> said—the *1863:* said; the *1868:* Tomorrow—here 249| *1843:* favor <> eyes, "—now *1863:* favour <> eyes:"—now *1888:* eyes." Now 252| *1843:* *TRESHAM The Earl?* *1868:* *TRESHAM* The Earl? 253| *1843:* him! *TRESHAM*

And, Austin, you are welcome, too! Look there!
The woman there!

AUSTIN AND GUENDOLEN How? Mildred?

TRESHAM Mildred once!
Now the receiver night by night, when sleep
Blesses the inmates of her father's house,
—I say, the soft sly wanton that receives
Her guilt's accomplice 'neath this roof which holds
You, Guendolen, you, Austin, and has held
A thousand Treshams—never one like her!
No lighter of the signal-lamp her quick
Foul breath near quenches in hot eagerness
To mix with breath as foul! no loosener
O' the lattice, practised in the stealthy tread,
The low voice and the noiseless come-and-go!
Not one composer of the bacchant's mien
Into—what you thought Mildred's, in a word!
Know her!

GUENDOLEN Oh, Mildred, look to me, at least!
Thorold—she's dead, I'd say, but that she stands
Rigid as stone and whiter!

TRESHAM You have heard . . .

GUENDOLEN Too much! You must proceed no further.

MILDRED Yes—
Proceed! All's truth. Go from me!

TRESHAM All is truth,
She tells you! Well, you know, or ought to know,
All this I would forgive in her. I'd con
Each precept the harsh world enjoins, I'd take
Our ancestors' stern verdicts one by one,
I'd bind myself before them to exact
The prescribed vengeance—and one word of hers,
The sight of her, the bare least memory
Of Mildred, my one sister, my heart's pride

1868: him. *TRESHAM* 254| *1843:* welcome too *1868:* welcome, too 260| *1843:* You Guendolen, you Austin *1849:* You, Guendolen, you, Austin 262| *1843:* signal lamp *1863:* signal-lamp 265| *1843:* Of *1888:* O' 267| *1843:* the Bacchant's *1868:* bacchant's 269| *1843: GUENDOLEN* Oh, Mildred look *1868: GUENDOLEN* Oh Mildred, look *1888: GUENDOLEN* Oh, Mildred 272| *1843:* you <> further! *MILDRED* *1868:* much! You <> further. *Mildred* 273| *1843:* Proceed—All's truth! Go *1863:* Proceed! All's *1868:* truth. Go 275| *1843:* her—I'd *1849:* her. I'd

Above all prides, my all in all so long,
Would scatter every trace of my resolve.
What were it silently to waste away
And see her waste away from this day forth,
Two scathed things with leisure to repent,
And grow acquainted with the grave, and die
Tired out if not at peace, and be forgotten?
It were not so impossible to bear.
But this—that, fresh from last night's pledge renewed
Of love with the successful gallant there,
She calmly bids me help her to entice,
Inveigle an unconscious trusting youth
Who thinks her all that's chaste and good and pure,
—Invites me to betray him . . . who so fit
As honour's self to cover shame's arch-deed?
—That she'll receive Lord Mertoun—(her own phrase)—
This, who could bear? Why, you have heard of thieves,
Stabbers, the earth's disgrace, who yet have laughed,
"Talk not to me of torture—I'll betray
No comrade I've pledged faith to!"—you have heard
Of wretched women—all but Mildreds—tied
By wild illicit ties to losels vile
You'd tempt them to forsake; and they'll reply
"Gold, friends, repute, I left for him, I find
In him, why should I leave him then for gold,
Repute or friends?"—and you have felt your heart
Respond to such poor outcasts of the world
As to so many friends; bad as you please,
You've felt they were God's men and women still,
So, not to be disowned by you. But she

283| *1843:* Had scattered <> resolve! *1863:* Would scatter *1868:* resolve.
287| *1843:* die, *1868:* die
289| *1843:* This were <> bear! *1849:* It were *1868:* bear.
292| *1843:* She'll calmly bid *1863:* She calmly bids
294| *1843:* chaste, and good, and *1868:* chaste and good and
295| *1843:* —Invite <> him . . who *1863:* —Invites *1868:* him . . . who
296| *1843:* honor's *1863:* honour's
297| *1843:* receive Lord Mertoun—(that's her phrase)— *1849:* receive Lord Mertoun—(her own phrase)—
298| *1843:* This who <> thieves *1849:* This, who <> thieves,
299| *1843:* Stabbers—the <> disgrace—who *1849:* Stabbers, the *1868:* disgrace, who
300| *1843:* not of tortures to me—I'll *1868:* not to me of torture—I'll
301| *1843:* to"—you *1849:* to!"—you
303| *1843:* In wild *1849:* By wild
304| *1843:* forsake, and *1849:* forsake; and
305| *1843:* him, I have *1868:* him, I find
307| *1843:* Repute, or friends?" and *1849:* friends?"—and *1868:* Repute or
311| *1843:* So not <> you! but she, *1863:* So, not <> you! But *1868:* you. But she

That stands there, calmly gives her lover up
As means to wed the Earl that she may hide
Their intercourse the surelier: and, for this,
I curse her to her face before you all.
Shame hunt her from the earth! Then Heaven do right
To both! It hears me now—shall judge her then!
[*As* MILDRED *faints and falls,* TRESHAM *rushes out.*]
AUSTIN Stay, Tresham, we'll accompany you!
GUENDOLEN We?
What, and leave Mildred? We? Why, where's my place
But by her side, and where yours but by mine?
Mildred—one word! Only look at me, then!
AUSTIN No, Guendolen! I echo Thorold's voice.
She is unworthy to behold . . .
GUENDOLEN Us two?
If you spoke on reflection, and if I
Approved your speech—if you (to put the thing
At lowest) you the soldier, bound to make
The king's cause yours and fight for it, and throw
Regard to others of its right or wrong,
—If with a death-white woman you can help,
Let alone sister, let alone a Mildred,
You left her—or if I, her cousin, friend
This morning, playfellow but yesterday,
Who said, or thought at least a thousand times,
"I'd serve you if I could," should now face round
And say, "Ah, that's to only signify
I'd serve you while you're fit to serve yourself:
So long as fifty eyes await the turn

314| *1843:* the safelier! and, for that, *1849:* the surelier! and, for this, *1868:* surelier: and
315| *1843:* all! *1863:* all. 318| *1843:* Stay Tresham *1843a:* Stay, Tresham
319| *1843:* why where's *1843a:* why, where's *1868:* Why 321| *1843:* word—only <> me then! *1849:* me, then! *1868:* word! Only 322| *1843:* No Guendolen <> voice! *1849:* No, Guendolen *1868:* voice. 323| *1843:* behold . . *GUENDOLEN* *1868:* behold . . . *GUENDOLEN* 324| *1843:* reflection and *1849:* reflection, and 326| *1843:* you, the *1868:* you the 327| *1843:* The King's <> yours, and fight *1868:* king's <> yours and fight 333| *1843:* Who've said or <> times *1843a:* said, or <> times, *1863:* Who said 335| *1843:* say "Ah *1863:* say, "Ah *1868:* say, "Ah that's *1888:* say, "Ah, that's 336| *1843:* yourself— *1888:* yourself:

Of yours to forestall its yet half-formed wish,
I'll proffer my assistance you'll not need—
When every tongue is praising you, I'll join
The praisers' chorus—when you're hemmed about
With lives between you and detraction—lives
To be laid down if a rude voice, rash eye,
Rough hand should violate the sacred ring
Their worship throws about you,—then indeed,
Who'll stand up for you stout as I?" If so
We said, and so we did,—not Mildred there
Would be unworthy to behold us both,
But we should be unworthy, both of us,
To be beheld by—by—your meanest dog,
Which, if that sword were broken in your face
Before a crowd, that badge torn off your breast,
And you cast out with hooting and contempt,
—Would push his way thro' all the hooters, gain
Your side, go off with you and all your shame
To the next ditch you choose to die in! Austin,
Do you love me? Here's Austin, Mildred,—here's
Your brother says he does not believe half—
No, nor half that—of all he heard! He says,
Look up and take his hand!

AUSTIN Look up and take
My hand, dear Mildred!

MILDRED I—I was so young!
Beside, I loved him, Thorold—and I had
No mother; God forgot me: so, I fell.

GUENDOLEN Mildred!

MILDRED Require no further! Did I dream
That I could palliate what is done? All's true.
Now, punish me! A woman takes my hand?

338| *1863:* forestal *1868:* forestall 347| *1843:* said and <> did, not *1849:* did,—not *1868:* said, and 350| *1843:* dog *1849:* dog, 351| *1843:* your sight *1849:* your face 353| *1843:* hootings *1868:* hooting 356| *1843:* chose *1868:* choose 358| *1843:* believe one half— *1849:* believe half— 359| *1843:* all he's heard *1843a:* all he heard 362| *1843:* him Thorold *1843a:* him, Thorold 363| *1843:* mother—God <> me—so I fell! *1868:* mother; God <> me: so I fell. *1888:* so, I 365| *1843:* all's *1843a:* done? All's 366| *1843:* hand! *1868:* hand?

Let go my hand! You do not know, I see.
I thought that Thorold told you.

GUENDOLEN What is this?
Where start you to?

MILDRED Oh, Austin, loosen me!
You heard the whole of it—your eyes were worse,
In their surprise, than Thorold's! Oh, unless
You stay to execute his sentence, loose
My hand! Has Thorold gone, and are you here?

GUENDOLEN Here, Mildred, we two friends of yours will wait
Your bidding; be you silent, sleep or muse!
Only, when you shall want your bidding done,
How can we do it if we are not by?
Here's Austin waiting patiently your will!
One spirit to command, and one to love
And to believe in it and do its best,
Poor as that is, to help it—why, the world
Has been won many a time, its length and breadth,
By just such a beginning!

MILDRED I believe
If once I threw my arms about your neck
And sunk my head upon your breast, that I
Should weep again.

GUENDOLEN Let go her hand now, Austin!
Wait for me. Pace the gallery and think
On the world's seemings and realities,

---

[367]| *1843:* see— *1868:* see. [369]| *1843: MILDRED* Oh Austin *1888: MILDRED* Oh, Austin [370]| *1843:* worse *1849:* worse, [371]| *1843:* surprise than *1849:* surprise, than [373]| *1843:* hand! Has Thorold left and *1849:* hand! Has Thorold gone, and [386]| *1843:* again! *GUENDOLEN* <> Austin. *1868:* again. *GUENDOLEN* <> Austin! [387]| *1843:* me.—Pace *1863:* me. Pace [388]| *1843:*

Until I call you. [AUSTIN *goes.*]
MILDRED No—I cannot weep.
No more tears from this brain—no sleep—no tears!
O Guendolen, I love you!
GUENDOLEN Yes: and "love"
Is a short word that says so very much!
It says that you confide in me.
MILDRED Confide!
GUENDOLEN Your lover's name, then! I've so much to learn,
Ere I can work in your behalf!
MILDRED My friend,
You know I cannot tell his name.
GUENDOLEN At least
He is your lover? and you love him too?
MILDRED Ah, do you ask me that?—but I am fallen
So low!
GUENDOLEN You love him still, then?
MILDRED My sole prop
Against the guilt that crushes me! I say,
Each night ere I lie down, "I was so young—
I had no mother, and I loved him so!"
And then God seems indulgent, and I dare
Trust him my soul in sleep.
GUENDOLEN How could you let us
E'en talk to you about Lord Mertoun then?
MILDRED There is a cloud around me.
GUENDOLEN But you said
You would receive his suit in spite of this?
MILDRED I say there is a cloud . . .
GUENDOLEN No cloud to me!
Lord Mertoun and your lover are the same!
MILDRED What maddest fancy . . .
GUENDOLEN [*calling aloud.*] Austin! (spare your pains—
When I have got a truth, that truth I keep)—
MILDRED By all you love, sweet Guendolen, forbear!

---

realities *1863:* realities, 389| *1843:* weep! *1868:* weep. 397| *1843: is* *1868:* is 400| *1843:* say *1849:* say, 401| *1843:* down, I <> young *1849:* down, "I <> young— 402| *1843:* mother—and <> so! *1849:* so!" *1868:* mother, and 404| *1863:* Trust Him *1868:* him 408| *1843:* cloud . . *GUENDOLEN* *1868:* cloud . . . *GUENDOLEN* 410| *1843:* Austin! (Spare *1888:* spare 411| *1843:* truth that *1849:* truth, that 413| *1843:* you . . *GUENDOLEN* . . Just *1849:*

Have I confided in you . . .

GUENDOLEN Just for this!

Austin!—Oh, not to guess it at the first!
But I did guess it—that is, I divined,
Felt by an instinct how it was: why else
Should I pronounce you free from all that heap
Of sins which had been irredeemable?
I felt they were not yours—what other way
Than this, not yours? The secret's wholly mine!

MILDRED If you would see me die before his face . . .

GUENDOLEN I'd hold my peace! And if the Earl returns
To-night?

MILDRED Ah Heaven, he's lost!

GUENDOLEN I thought so. Austin!

Enter AUSTIN.

Oh, where have you been hiding?

AUSTIN Thorold's gone,
I know not how, across the meadow-land.
I watched him till I lost him in the skirts
O' the beech-wood.

GUENDOLEN Gone? All thwarts us.

MILDRED Thorold too?

GUENDOLEN I have thought. First lead this Mildred to her room.
Go on the other side; and then we'll seek
Your brother: and I'll tell you, by the way,
The greatest comfort in the world. You said
There was a clue to all. Remember, Sweet,
He said there was a clue! I hold it. Come!

GUENDOLEN Just *1868:* you . . . *GUENDOLEN* 415| *1843: did* <> divined— *1868:* did <> divined, 416| *1843:* was—why *1868:* was: why 421| *1843:* face . . *1868:* face . . . 423| *1843: MILDRED* Ah, Heaven <> so! Austin! *1868: MILDRED* Ah Heaven <> so. Austin! 424| *1843:* Oh where *1863:* Oh, where 427| *1843:* Of <> us! *MILDRED* *1868:* us. *MILDRED* *1888:* O' 429| *1843:* side: and *1868:* side; and 430| *1843:* brother; and *1868:* brother: and 432| *1843:* clew <> sweet, *1863:* clue <>Sweet, *1868:* sweet, *1888:* all. Remember, Sweet, 433| *1843:* clew *1863:* clue

ACT III

SCENE I—*The end of the Yew-tree Avenue under* MILDRED'S *window. A light seen through a central red pane.*

Enter TRESHAM *through the trees.*

Again here! But I cannot lose myself.
The heath—the orchard—I have traversed glades
And dells and bosky paths which used to lead
Into green wild-wood depths, bewildering
My boy's adventurous step. And now they tend
Hither or soon or late; the blackest shade
Breaks up, the thronged trunks of the trees ope wide,
And the dim turret I have fled from, fronts
Again my step; the very river put
Its arm about me and conducted me
To this detested spot. Why then, I'll shun
Their will no longer: do your will with me!
Oh, bitter! To have reared a towering scheme
Of happiness, and to behold it razed,
Were nothing: all men hope, and see their hopes
Frustrate, and grieve awhile, and hope anew.
But I . . . to hope that from a line like ours
No horrid prodigy like this would spring,
Were just as though I hoped that from these old
Confederates against the sovereign day,
Children of older and yet older sires,
Whose living coral berries dropped, as now
On me, on many a baron's surcoat once,
On many a beauty's whimple—would proceed

5| *1843:* step; and *1863:* step. And 8| *1843:* from fronts *1863:* from, fronts
12| *1843:* longer—do *1868:* longer: do 16| *1843:* anew: *1863:* anew.
17| *1843:* But I . . to *1888:* But I . . . to 21| *1843:* sires *1863:* sires, 22| *1843:* (Whose *1863:* Whose 24| *1843:* whimple) would *1863:* whimple—would

No poison-tree, to thrust, from hell its root,
Hither and thither its strange snaky arms.
Why came I here? What must I do? [*A bell strikes.*] A bell?
Midnight! and 'tis at midnight . . . Ah, I catch
—Woods, river, plains, I catch your meaning now,
And I obey you! Hist! This tree will serve.

[*He retires behind one of the trees. After a pause, enter* MERTOUN *cloaked as before.*]

MERTOUN Not time! Beat out thy last voluptuous beat
Of hope and fear, my heart! I thought the clock
I' the chapel struck as I was pushing through
The ferns. And so I shall no more see rise
My love-star! Oh, no matter for the past!
So much the more delicious task to watch
Mildred revive: to pluck out, thorn by thorn,
All traces of the rough forbidden path
My rash love lured her to! Each day must see
Some fear of hers effaced, some hope renewed:
Then there will be surprises, unforeseen
Delights in store. I'll not regret the past.

[*The light is placed above in the purple pane.*]

And see, my signal rises, Mildred's star!
I never saw it lovelier than now
It rises for the last time. If it sets,
'Tis that the re-assuring sun may dawn.

[*As he prepares to ascend the last tree of the avenue,* TRESHAM *arrests his arm.*

Unhand me—peasant, by your grasp! Here's gold.
'Twas a mad freak of mine. I said I'd pluck
A branch from the white-blossomed shrub beneath
The casement there. Take this, and hold your peace.

TRESHAM Into the moonlight yonder, come with me!

25| *1843:* thrust from Hell *1849:* thrust, from *1888:* hell 27| *1843:* here? what <> do!— <> —a Bell? *1843a:* bell? *1849:* here? What <> do?— <> —A *1863:* do? <> A 30| *1843:* serve! *1868:* serve. 33| *1843:* In <> thro' *1863:* through *1888:* I' 35| *1843:* the Past! *1849:* past! *1863:* the Past! *1868:* past! 36| *1843:* to see *1888:* to watch 37| *1843:* revive—to *1849:* revive: to 40| *1843:* renewed! *1868:* renewed: 42| *1843:* the Past! *1849:* the past! *1863:* the Past! *1868:* the past! *1888:* past. 43| *1843:* rises! Mildred's *1868:* rises, Mildred's 45| *1843:* time! If it sets *1849:* sets, *1863:* time. If 46| *1843:* may rise! *1849:* may dawn! *1863:* dawn. 50| *1843:* there! Take *1868:* there.

Out of the shadow!
MERTOUN I am armed, fool!
TRESHAM Yes,
Or no? You'll come into the light, or no?
My hand is on your throat—refuse!—
MERTOUN That voice!
Where have I heard . . . no—that was mild and slow.
I'll come with you. [*They advance.*]
TRESHAM You're armed: that's well. Declare
Your name: who are you?
MERTOUN (Tresham!—she is lost!)
TRESHAM Oh, silent? Do you know, you bear yourself
Exactly as, in curious dreams I've had
How felons, this wild earth is full of, look
When they're detected, still your kind has looked!
The bravo holds an assured countenance,
The thief is voluble and plausible,
But silently the slave of lust has crouched
When I have fancied it before a man.
Your name!
MERTOUN I do conjure Lord Tresham—ay,
Kissing his foot, if so I might prevail—
That he for his own sake forbear to ask
My name! As heaven's above, his future weal
Or woe depends upon my silence! Vain!
I read your white inexorable face.
Know me, Lord Tresham! [*He throws off his disguises.*]
TRESHAM Mertoun!
[*After a pause.*] Draw now!
MERTOUN Hear me
But speak first!
TRESHAM Not one least word on your life!
Be sure that I will strangle in your throat

Take 52| *1843:*—Out *1888:* Out 53| *1843:* no?—You'll *1863:* no? You'll 55| *1843:* heard . . no—*that* *1849:* that *1888:* heard . . . no 56–57| *1843:* you! *TRESHAM* <> armed—that's well. / Your *1863:* armed: that's *1868:* you. *TRESHAM* *1888:* well. Declare / Your 57| *1843:* name—who <> *MERTOUN* Tresham <> lost! *1863: MERTOUN* (Tresham <> lost!) *1888:* name: who 59| *1843:* as in *1849:* as, in 61| *1843:* look'd! *1849:* looked! 62| *1843:* countenance— *1849:* countenance, 63| *1843:* plausible— *1849:* plausible, 65| *1843:* man! *1868:* man. 66| *1843:* name? *MERTOUN* *1888:* name! *MERTOUN* 69| *1843:* name! As Heaven's *1868:* heaven's 71| *1843:* face!

The least word that informs me how you live
And yet seem what you seem! No doubt 'twas you
Taught Mildred still to keep that face and sin.
We should join hands in frantic sympathy
If you once taught me the unteachable,
Explained how you can live so, and so lie.
With God's help I retain, despite my sense,
The old belief—a life like yours is still
Impossible. Now draw!

MERTOUN Not for my sake,
Do I entreat a hearing—for your sake,
And most, for her sake!

TRESHAM Ha ha, what should I
Know of your ways? A miscreant like yourself,
How must one rouse his ire? A blow?—that's pride
No doubt, to him! One spurns him, does one not?
Or sets the foot upon his mouth, or spits
Into his face! Come! Which, or all of these?

MERTOUN 'Twixt him and me and Mildred, Heaven be judge!
Can I avoid this? Have your will, my lord!

[*He draws and, after a few passes, falls.*]

TRESHAM You are not hurt?

MERTOUN You'll hear me now!

TRESHAM But rise!

MERTOUN Ah, Tresham, say I not "you'll hear me now!"
And what procures a man the right to speak
In his defence before his fellow man,
But—I suppose—the thought that presently
He may have leave to speak before his God
His whole defence?

TRESHAM Not hurt? It cannot be!
You made no effort to resist me. Where
Did my sword reach you? Why not have returned

1868: face. 76| *1843:* yet are what you are! No *1849:* yet seem what you seem! No 77| *1843:* sin! *1868:* sin. 80| *1843:* lie! *1868:* lie. 81| *1843:* help I will keep despite my sense *1849:* help I retain, despite my sense, 83| *1843:* Impossible! Now *1868:* Impossible. Now 85| *1843: TRESHAM* Ha, ha *1868: TRESHAM* Ha ha 87| *1843:* ire?—A <> that's great *1849:* that's pride *1868:* ire? A 88| *1843:* him! one *1868:* him! One 89| *1843:* mouth—or *1868:* mouth, or 90| *1843:* face—come—which *1849:* face! Come *1868:* face! Come! Which 91| *1843:* him, and me, and *1868:* him and me and 92| *1843:* my Lord! *1863:* lord! 94| *1868:* Ah Tresham *1888:* Ah, Tresham 96| *1843:* fellow-man, *1888:*

My thrusts? Hurt where?
MERTOUN My lord—
TRESHAM How young he is!
MERTOUN Lord Tresham, I am very young, and yet
I have entangled other lives with mine.
Do let me speak, and do believe my speech!
That when I die before you presently,—
TRESHAM Can you stay here till I return with help?
MERTOUN Oh, stay by me! When I was less than boy
I did you grievous wrong and knew it not—
Upon my honour, knew it not! Once known,
I could not find what seemed a better way
To right you than I took: my life—you feel
How less than nothing were the giving you
The life you've taken! But I thought my way
The better—only for your sake and hers:
And as you have decided otherwise,
Would I had an infinity of lives
To offer you! Now say—instruct me—think!
Can you, from the brief minutes I have left,
Eke out my reparation? Oh think—think!
For I must wring a partial—dare I say,
Forgiveness from you, ere I die?
TRESHAM I do
Forgive you.
MERTOUN Wait and ponder that great word!
Because, if you forgive me, I shall hope
To speak to you of—Mildred!
TRESHAM Mertoun, haste
And anger have undone us. 'Tis not you
Should tell me for a novelty you're young,
Thoughtless, unable to recall the past.

---

fellow man, 105| *1843:* speak—and <> speech, *1863:* speak! and *1868:* speak, and <> speech! 109| *1843:* wrong, and *1868:* wrong and 110| *1843:* honor *1863:* honour 113| *1843:* nothing had been giving *1868:* nothing were the giving 115| *1843:* hers. *1868:* hers: 116| *1843:* But as *1849:* And as 118| *1843:* you!—now *1863:* you! Now *1868:* think *1888:* think! 119| *1843:* you from out the minutes <> left *1868:* you from the brief minutes *1888:* you, from <> left, 120| *1843:* reparation? Oh—think—think— *1868:* reparation? Oh think—think! 122| *1843:* you ere *1849:* you, ere 125| *1843: TRESHAM* Mertoun—haste *1868: TRESHAM* Mertoun, haste 127| *1843:* young— *1868:* young, 128| *1843:* Thoughtless—unable <> the Past! *1849:* past! *1863:* the

Be but your pardon ample as my own!
MERTOUN Ah, Tresham, that a sword-stroke and a drop
Of blood or two, should bring all this about!
Why, 'twas my very fear of you, my love
Of you—(what passion like a boy's for one
Like you?)—that ruined me! I dreamed of you—
You, all accomplished, courted everywhere,
The scholar and the gentleman. I burned
To knit myself to you: but I was young,
And your surpassing reputation kept me
So far aloof! Oh, wherefore all that love?
With less of love, my glorious yesterday
Of praise and gentlest words and kindest looks,
Had taken place perchance six months ago.
Even now, how happy we had been! And yet
I know the thought of this escaped you, Tresham!
Let me look up into your face; I feel
'Tis changed above me: yet my eyes are glazed.
Where? where?
[*As he endeavours to raise himself, his eye catches the lamp.*]
Ah, Mildred! What will Mildred do?
Tresham, her life is bound up in the life
That's bleeding fast away! I'll live—must live,
There, if you'll only turn me I shall live
And save her! Tresham—oh, had you but heard!
Had you but heard! What right was yours to set
The thoughtless foot upon her life and mine,
And then say, as we perish, "Had I thought,
All had gone otherwise"? We've sinned and die:
Never you sin, Lord Tresham! for you'll die,

Past! *1868:* Thoughtless, unable <> past. 130| *1843:* Ah Tresham *1849:* Ah, Tresham *1868:* Ah Tresham *1888:* Ah, Tresham 132| *1843:* you—my *1868:* you, my 133| *1843:* passion's *1868:* passion 135| *1843:* You—all accomplished—courted every where— *1849:* You, all accomplished, courted every where, *1863:* everywhere, 137| *1843:* you—but *1863:* you: but 139| *1843:* aloof—oh *1863:* aloof! Oh 140| *1843:* love my *1849:* love, my 141| *1843:* gentle <> looks *1849:* looks, *1868:* gentlest 142| *1843:* ago! *1868:* ago. 143| *1843:* now—how *1868:* now, how 145| *1843:* face—I *1868:* face; I 146| *1843:* me—yet <> glazed— *1849:* glazed. *1868:* me: yet 149| *1843:* away!—I'll *1868:* away! I'll 150| *1843:* There! if *1868:* There, if 151| *1863:* her! Tresham—Oh *1868:* oh 152| *1843:* right have you to *1863:* right was yours to 155| *1843:* otherwise." We've *1888:* otherwise"? We've 156| *1843: you* sin

And God will judge you.
TRESHAM Yes, be satisfied!
That process is begun.
MERTOUN And she sits there
Waiting for me! Now, say you this to her—
You, not another—say, I saw him die
As he breathed this, "I love her"—you don't know
What those three small words mean! Say, loving her
Lowers me down the bloody slope to death
With memories . . . I speak to her, not you,
Who had no pity, will have no remorse,
Perchance intend her . . . Die along with me,
Dear Mildred! 'tis so easy, and you'll 'scape
So much unkindness! Can I lie at rest,
With rude speech spoken to you, ruder deeds
Done to you?—heartless men shall have my heart,
And I tied down with grave-clothes and the worm,
Aware, perhaps, of every blow—oh God!—
Upon those lips—yet of no power to tear
The felon stripe by stripe! Die, Mildred! Leave
Their honourable world to them! For God
We're good enough, though the world casts us out.
[*A whistle is heard.*]
TRESHAM Ho, Gerard!

Enter GERARD, AUSTIN *and* GUENDOLEN, *with lights.*

No one speak! You see what's done.
I cannot bear another voice.
MERTOUN There's light—

Lord Tresham!—for *1849:* you sin, Lord *1868:* sin, Lord Tresham! for 157| *1843:* satisfied— *1868:* satisfied! 159| *1843:* me.—Now say *1849:* me. Now *1863:* me! Now, say 160| *1843:* You—not *1868:* You, not 161| *1843:* this—"I <> her"—(you *1863:* her"—you *1868:* this, "I 162| *1843:* mean) say *1863:* mean! Say 164| *1843:* her—not you *1849:* you, *1868:* her, not 165| *1843:* pity—will *1868:* pity, will 166| *1843:* her—Die *1843a:* her . . . Die 167| *1843:* Dear Mildred!—'tis so easy—and *1868:* Dear Mildred! 'tis so easy, and 170| *1843:* you—heartless men to have *1868:* you?—heartless men shall have 172| *1843:* blow—Oh *1868:* oh 174| *1843:* by stripe? Die <> leave *1849:* by stripe? Die, Mildred! Leave *1868:* by stripe! Die 175| *1843:* honorable <> them—for *1849:* honourable *1868:* them! For 176| *1843:* tho' <> out! *1863:* though *1868:* out. 177| *1843:* you <>done! *1868:* speak! You <> done. 178| *1843:* voice!

Light all about me, and I move to it.
Tresham, did I not tell you—did you not
Just promise to deliver words of mine
To Mildred?

TRESHAM I will bear those words to her.

MERTOUN Now?

TRESHAM Now. Lift you the body, and leave me
The head.

[*As they have half raised* MERTOUN, *he turns suddenly.*]

MERTOUN I knew they turned me: turn me not from her!
There! stay you! there! [*Dies.*]

GUENDOLEN [*after a pause.*] Austin, remain you here
With Thorold until Gerard comes with help:
Then lead him to his chamber. I must go
To Mildred.

TRESHAM Guendolen, I hear each word
You utter. Did you hear him bid me give
His message? Did you hear my promise? I,
And only I, see Mildred.

GUENDOLEN She will die.

TRESHAM Oh no, she will not die! I dare not hope
She'll die. What ground have you to think she'll die?
Why, Austin's with you!

AUSTIN Had we but arrived
Before you fought!

TRESHAM There was no fight at all.
He let me slaughter him—the boy! I'll trust
The body there to you and Gerard—thus!
Now bear him on before me.

AUSTIN Whither bear him?

TRESHAM Oh, to my chamber! When we meet there next,

MERTOUN *1868:* voice. *MERTOUN* 179| *1843:* me and *1863:* me, and 183| *1843:* TRESHAM Now! Lift <> body, Gerard, and *1863:* TRESHAM Now. Lift *1868:* body, and 184| *1843:* me—turn *1868:* me: turn 186| *1843:* help— *1868:* help: 189| *1843:* utter—did *1868:* utter. Did 191| *1843:* see Mildred! *GUENDOLEN* *1868:* see Mildred. *GUENDOLEN* 195| *1843:* all! *1868:* all. 196| *1843:* him—these boys!—I'll *1849:* him—the boy *1863:* boy! I'll 199| *1843:* chamber.

We shall be friends. [*They bear out the body of* MERTOUN.]
Will she die, Guendolen?

GUENDOLEN Where are you taking me?

TRESHAM He fell just here.
Now answer me. Shall you in your whole life
—You who have nought to do with Mertoun's fate,
Now you have seen his breast upon the turf,
Shall you e'er walk this way if you can help?
When you and Austin wander arm-in-arm
Through our ancestral grounds, will not a shade
Be ever on the meadow and the waste—
Another kind of shade than when the night
Shuts the woodside with all its whispers up?
But will you ever so forget his breast
As carelessly to cross this bloody turf
Under the black yew avenue? That's well!
You turn your head: and I then?—

GUENDOLEN What is done
Is done. My care is for the living. Thorold,
Bear up against this burden: more remains
To set the neck to!

TRESHAM Dear and ancient trees
My fathers planted, and I loved so well!
What have I done that, like some fabled crime
Of yore, lets loose a Fury leading thus
Her miserable dance amidst you all?
Oh, never more for me shall winds intone
With all your tops a vast antiphony,
Demanding and responding in God's praise!
Hers ye are now, not mine! Farewell—farewell!

When *1863:* chamber! When 201| *1843:* here! *1868:* here. 206| *1843:* arm in arm *1863:* arm-in-arm 207| *1843:* Thro' *1863:* Through 210| *1843:* up! *1863:* up? 211| *1843:* forget this night *1849:* forget his breast 212| *1843:* As willingly to *1868:* As carelessly to 214| *1843:* head! and *I* *1868:* head: and I 215| *1843:* done! My *1868:* done. My 216| *1843:* burthen—more *1863:* burden *1868:* burden: more 220| *1843:* fury—free to lead *1849:* fury leading thus *1888:* a Fury 222| *1843:* Oh never *1849:* Oh, never 225| *1843:* now—not <> Farewell—Farewell! *1868:* now, not <> Farewell—farewell!

SCENE II—MILDRED'S *chamber.* MILDRED *alone.*

He comes not! I have heard of those who seemed
Resourceless in prosperity,—you thought
Sorrow might slay them when she listed; yet
Did they so gather up their diffused strength
At her first menace, that they bade her strike,
And stood and laughed her subtlest skill to scorn.
Oh, 'tis not so with me! The first woe fell,
And the rest fall upon it, not on me:
Else should I bear that Henry comes not?—fails
Just this first night out of so many nights?
Loving is done with. Were he sitting now,
As so few hours since, on that seat, we'd love
No more—contrive no thousand happy ways
To hide love from the loveless, any more.
I think I might have urged some little point
In my defence, to Thorold; he was breathless
For the least hint of a defence: but no,
The first shame over, all that would might fall.
No Henry! Yet I merely sit and think
The morn's deed o'er and o'er. I must have crept
Out of myself. A Mildred that has lost
Her lover—oh, I dare not look upon
Such woe! I crouch away from it! 'Tis she,
Mildred, will break her heart, not I! The world
Forsakes me: only Henry's left me—left?
When I have lost him, for he does not come,
And I sit stupidly . . . Oh Heaven, break up
This worse than anguish, this mad apathy,
By any means or any messenger!

TRESHAM [*without.*] Mildred!

MILDRED Come in! Heaven hears me!

[*Enter* TRESHAM.] You? alone?

Oh, no more cursing!

TRESHAM Mildred, I must sit.

3| *1843:* listed—yet *1868:* listed; yet 7| *1843:* me; the *1868:* me! The
11| *1843:* with! were <> now *1849:* with! Were <> now, *1868:* with. Were
14| *1843:* more! *1868:* more. 16| *1843:* defence to *1849:* defence, to
17| *1843:* defence; but no! *1868:* defence: but no, 25| *1843:* me—only *1868:* me:

There—you sit!
MILDRED Say it, Thorold—do not look
The curse! deliver all you come to say!
What must become of me? Oh, speak that thought
Which makes your brow and cheeks so pale!
TRESHAM My thought?
MILDRED All of it!
TRESHAM How we waded—years ago—
After those water-lilies, till the plash,
I know not how, surprised us; and you dared
Neither advance nor turn back: so, we stood
Laughing and crying until Gerard came—
Once safe upon the turf, the loudest too,
For once more reaching the relinquished prize!
How idle thoughts are, some men's, dying men's!
Mildred,—
MILDRED You call me kindlier by my name
Than even yesterday: what is in that?
TRESHAM It weighs so much upon my mind that I
This morning took an office not my own!
I might . . . of course, I must be glad or grieved,
Content or not, at every little thing
That touches you. I may with a wrung heart
Even reprove you, Mildred; I did more:
Will you forgive me?
MILDRED Thorold? do you mock?
Or no . . . and yet you bid me . . . say that word!
TRESHAM Forgive me, Mildred!—are you silent, Sweet?
MILDRED [*starting up.*] Why does not Henry Mertoun come to-night?

---

only 33| *1843:* curse—deliver *1868:* curse! deliver 34| *1843:* me? Oh speak *1888:* me? Oh, speak 37| *1843:* water-lilies till *1849:* water-lilies, till 38| *1843:* us and *1849:* us; and 39| *1843:* back, so we *1863:* back: so *1868:* so, we 41| *1843:* loudest, too *1868:* loudest too, 43| *1843:* are—some men's—dying *1868:* are, some men's, dying 45| *1843:* yesterday—what *1868:* yesterday: what 48| *1843:* might . . of *1888:* might . . . of 50| *1843:* you—I *1868:* you. I 51| *1843:* more— *1863:* more: 52| *1843:* me! *MILDRED* <> mock? . . *1849:* me? *MILDRED* *1863:* mock? 53| *1843:* no . . and <> me . . say <> word! . . *1849:* word! *1888:* no . . . and <> me . . . say 54| *1843:* sweet? *1863:* silent, Sweet? *1868:*

Are you, too, silent?

[*Dashing his mantle aside, and pointing to his scabbard, which is empty.*]

Ah, this speaks for you!
You've murdered Henry Mertoun! Now proceed!
What is it I must pardon? This and all?
Well, I do pardon you—I think I do.
Thorold, how very wretched you must be!

TRESHAM He bade me tell you . . .

MILDRED What I do forbid
Your utterance of! So much that you may tell
And will not—how you murdered him . . . but, no!
You'll tell me that he loved me, never more
Than bleeding out his life there: must I say
"Indeed," to that? Enough! I pardon you.

TRESHAM You cannot, Mildred! for the harsh words, yes:
Of this last deed Another's judge: whose doom
I wait in doubt, despondency and fear.

MILDRED Oh, true! There's nought for me to pardon! True!
You loose my soul of all its cares at once.
Death makes me sure of him for ever! You
Tell me his last words? He shall tell me them,
And take my answer—not in words, but reading
Himself the heart I had to read him late,
Which death . . .

TRESHAM Death? You are dying too? Well said
Of Guendolen! I dared not hope you'd die:
But she was sure of it.

MILDRED Tell Guendolen
I loved her, and tell Austin . . .

TRESHAM Him you loved:

---

silent, sweet? *1888:* silent, Sweet? 56| *1843: you,* too *1868:* you, too 57| *1843:* now *1868:* murdered Henry Mertoun! Now 61| *1843:* you . . *MILDRED* *1888:* you . . . *MILDRED* 62| *1843:* so <> *may* *1849:* may *1868:* of! So 63| *1843:* him . . but *1888:* him . . . but 65| *1843:* there—must *1868:* there: must 66| *1843:* you! *1868:* you. 68| *1843:* deed Another's Judge—whose *1868:* judge: whose 69| *1843:* despondency, and *1868:* despondency and 70| *1843:* Oh true *1868:* Oh, true 71| *1843:* loosed <>once— *1868:* loose <> once. 72| *1843:* ever! *You* *1868:* ever! You 73| *1843:* words? *He* *1868:* words? He 76| *1843:* you *1868:* *TRESHAM* Death? You 77| *1843:* die— *1863:* die: 79| *1843: TRESHAM* . . Him

And me?

MILDRED Ah, Thorold! Was't not rashly done
To quench that blood, on fire with youth and hope
And love of me—whom you loved too, and yet
Suffered to sit here waiting his approach
While you were slaying him? Oh, doubtlessly
You let him speak his poor confused boy's-speech
—Do his poor utmost to disarm your wrath
And respite me!—you let him try to give
The story of our love and ignorance,
And the brief madness and the long despair—
You let him plead all this, because your code
Of honour bids you hear before you strike:
But at the end, as he looked up for life
Into your eyes—you struck him down!

TRESHAM No! No!
Had I but heard him—had I let him speak
Half the truth—less—had I looked long on him
I had desisted! Why, as he lay there,
The moon on his flushed cheek, I gathered all
The story ere he told it: I saw through
The troubled surface of his crime and yours
A depth of purity immovable,
Had I but glanced, where all seemed turbidest
Had gleamed some inlet to the calm beneath;
I would not glance: my punishment's at hand.
There, Mildred, is the truth! and you—say on—
You curse me?

MILDRED As I dare approach that Heaven
Which has not bade a living thing despair,
Which needs no code to keep its grace from stain,

---

you loved— *1863: TRESHAM* Him you loved: 80| *1843: MILDRED* Ah Thorold! was't *1849: MILDRED* Ah, Thorold *1868: MILDRED* Ah Thorold! Was't *1888: MILDRED* Ah, Thorold 82| *1843:* me, *you* loved I think, and *1849:* me, whom you loved too, and *1863:* me—whom 84| *1868:* him? Oh doubtlessly *1888:* him? Oh, doubtlessly 88| *1843:* loves, and *1868:* love and 89| *1843:* madness, and *1868:* madness and 91| *1843:* honor <> strike— *1849:* strike: *1863:* honour 93| *1843: TRESHAM* No! no! *1888: TRESHAM* No! No! 95| *1843:* him, *1868:* him 98| *1843:* it! I saw thro' *1863:* through *1868:* it: I 100| *1843:* immovable! *1868:* immovable. *1888:* immovable, 102| *1843:* beneath! *1868:* beneath; 103| *1843:* glance—my *1868:* glance: my 107| *1863:* keep Its *1868:*

But bids the vilest worm that turns on it
Desist and be forgiven,—I—forgive not,
But bless you, Thorold, from my soul of souls! [*Falls on his neck.*]
There! Do not think too much upon the past!
The cloud that's broke was all the same a cloud
While it stood up between my friend and you;
You hurt him 'neath its shadow: but is that
So past retrieve? I have his heart, you know;
I may dispose of it: I give it you!
It loves you as mine loves! Confirm me, Henry! [*Dies.*]

TRESHAM I wish thee joy, Beloved! I am glad
In thy full gladness!

GUENDOLEN [*without.*] Mildred! Tresham!
[*Entering with* AUSTIN.] Thorold,
I could desist no longer. Ah, she swoons!
That's well.

TRESHAM Oh, better far than that!

GUENDOLEN She's dead!
Let me unlock her arms!

TRESHAM She threw them thus
About my neck, and blessed me, and then died:
You'll let them stay now, Guendolen!

AUSTIN Leave her
And look to him! What ails you, Thorold?

GUENDOLEN White
As she, and whiter! Austin! quick—this side!

AUSTIN A froth is oozing through his clenched teeth,
Both lips, where they're not bitten through, are black:
Speak, dearest Thorold!

TRESHAM Something does weigh down

---

keep its 108| *1863:* on It *1868:* it 111| *1843:* There! do <> the Past! *1849:* past! *1863:* the Past! *1868:* past! *1888:* There! Do 113| *1843:* you! *1868:* you; 114| *1843:* shadow—but *1863:* shadow: but 115| *1843:* know— *1863:* know; 116| *1843:* it—I *1863:* it: I 118| *1843:* beloved *1863:* joy, Beloved *1868:* beloved *1888:* joy, Beloved 121| *1843:* well—*TRESHAM* Oh! better *1863:* well. *TRESHAM* *1868:* *TRESHAM* Oh, better 123| *1843:* died. *1863:* died: 124| *1843:*—You'll *1868:* You'll 126| *1843:* she—and <> Austin—quick *1863:* whiter! Austin! quick *1868:* she, and 127| *1843:* thro' <> teeth— *1863:* through *1868:* teeth; 128| *1843:* thro' <> black! *1863:* through *1868:* black:

My neck beside her weight: thanks: I should fall
But for you, Austin, I believe!— there, there,
'Twill pass away soon!—ah,—I had forgotten:
I am dying.
GUENDOLEN Thorold—Thorold—why was this?
TRESHAM I said, just as I drank the poison off,
The earth would be no longer earth to me,
The life out of all life was gone from me.
There are blind ways provided, the foredone
Heart-weary player in this pageant-world
Drops out by, letting the main masque defile
By the conspicuous portal: I am through—
Just through!
GUENDOLEN Don't leave him, Austin! Death is close.
TRESHAM Already Mildred's face is peacefuller.
I see you, Austin—feel you: here's my hand,
Put yours in it—you, Guendolen, yours too!
You're lord and lady now—you're Treshams; name
And fame are yours: you hold our 'scutcheon up.
Austin, no blot on it! You see how blood
Must wash one blot away: the first blot came
And the first blood came. To the vain world's eye
All's gules again: no care to the vain world,
From whence the red was drawn!
AUSTIN No blot shall come!
TRESHAM I said that: yet it did come. Should it come,
Vengeance is God's, not man's. Remember me! [*Dies.*]
GUENDOLEN [*letting fall the pulseless arm.*] Ah, Thorold, we can but—
remember you!

130| *1843:* weight—thanks—I *1849:* weight: thanks: I 131| *1843:* there—there— *1849:* there, there— *1868:* there, there, 132| *1843:* forgotten— *1868:* forgotten: 136| *1843:* me! *1868:* me. 139| *1843:* main Masque *1849:* masque 140| *1843:* conspicuous Portal:—I am thro'— *1843a:* portal:—I *1849:* through— *1868:* portal: I 141| *1843:* through!—*GUENDOLEN* <> death *1863:* through! *GUENDOLEN* *1868:* him, Austin! Death 142| *1843:* peacefuller! *1868:* peacefuller. 143| *1843:* feel you—here's *1868:* feel you: here's 144| *1843:* it—You *1863:* you 145| *1843:* You're Lord and Lady now—You're Tresham's—— name *1843a:* now—You're Treshams—Name *1863:* you're Treshams; name *1868:* lord and lady 146| *1843:* yours—You hold our 'Scutcheon *1863:* yours: you *1868:* 'scutcheon 147| *1843:* no Blot *1868:* blot 150| *1843:* again—no <> world *1849:* world, *1863:* again: no 152| *1843:* that—yet *1863:* that: yet <> come! Should *1868:* come. Should 153| *1843:* is God's not man's—Remember *1843a:* man's. Remember *1863:* is God's, not 154| *1868:* Ah Thorold *1888:* Ah, Thorold

BY THE SAME AUTHOR.

I.

PARACELSUS. A POEM.

Price 6s. boards.

II.

SORDELLO. A POEM.

Price 6s. 6d. boards.

III.

BELLS AND POMEGRANATES.

No. I.—PIPPA PASSES. *Price 6d.*

No. II.—KING VICTOR AND KING CHARLES. *Price 1s.*

No. III.—DRAMATIC LYRICS. *Price 1s.*

No. IV.—THE RETURN OF THE DRUSES. *Price 1s.*

BELLS AND POMEGRANATES, NO. VI.

COLOMBE'S BIRTHDAY

Edited by Park Honan

COLOMBE'S BIRTHDAY:

A PLAY.

Ivy and violet, what do ye here
With blossom and shoot in the warm spring-weather,
Hiding the arms of Monchenci and Vere?—Hanmer.

1844: Bells and Pomegranates / No. VI.—Colombe's <> Play, / in five acts / By Robert Browning, / Author of "Paracelsus." / "Ivy <> Vere?" Hanmer. / London: / Edward Moxon, Dover Street. / MDCCCXLIV. *1849:* Colombe's <> Play. / "Ivy *1863:* § on page with dedication and persons § *1868:* § on page with dedication § *1888:* § on separate page § Play / Ivy <> Vere?—Hanmer.

NO ONE LOVES AND HONOURS BARRY CORNWALL MORE THAN DOES ROBERT BROWNING; WHO, HAVING NOTHING BETTER THAN THIS PLAY TO GIVE HIM IN PROOF OF IT, MUST SAY SO.

LONDON: 1844.

1844: § on page with persons § Dedication. No <> than Robert <> so. March, 1844. *1849:* than Robert Browning does; who <> so. § Date omitted § *1863:* § on page with title and persons § than does Robert Browning; who <> so. London, 1844. *1868:* § on page with title § *1888:* § on separate page § London: 1844.

PERSONS.

COLOMBE OF RAVESTEIN, *Duchess of Juliers and Cleves.*

SABYNE, ADOLF, *her attendants.*

GUIBERT, GAUCELME, MAUFROY, CLUGNET, *courtiers.*

VALENCE, *advocate of Cleves.*

PRINCE BERTHOLD, *claimant of the Duchy.*

MELCHIOR, *his confidant.*

PLACE.—*The Palace at Juliers.*

TIME, 16—.

COLOMBE'S BIRTHDAY

1844

ACT I

MORNING

SCENE—*A corridor leading to the Audience-chamber.*

GAUCELME, CLUGNET, MAUFROY *and other* COURTIERS, *round* GUIBERT, *who is silently reading a paper: as he drops it at the end—*

GUIBERT That this should be her birthday; and the day
We all invested her, twelve months ago,
As the late Duke's true heiress and our liege;
And that this also must become the day . . .
Oh, miserable lady!
1ST COURTIER Ay, indeed?
2ND COURTIER Well, Guibert?
3RD COURTIER But your news, my friend, your news!
The sooner, friend, one learns Prince Berthold's pleasure,
The better for us all: how writes the Prince?
Give me! I'll read it for the common good.
GUIBERT In time, sir,—but till time comes, pardon me!
Our old Duke just disclosed his child's retreat,
Declared her true succession to his rule,
And died: this birthday was the day, last year,
We convoyed her from Castle Ravestein—
That sleeps out trustfully its extreme age
On the Meuse' quiet bank, where she lived queen
Over the water-buds,—to Juliers' court

---

§ Ed. 1844, 1849, 1863, 1868, 1888, 1889; see Notes for information about MS. §
9| *1844:* me—I'll <> good— *1863:* good. *1868:* me! I'll 10| *1844:* sir—but, till *1868:* sir,—but till 13| *1844:* day last year *1849:* day, last year, 16| *1844:* where queen she lived *1849:* where she lived queen 17| *1844:* to Juliers' Court *1863:*

With joy and bustle. Here again we stand;
Sir Gaucelme's buckle's constant to his cap:
To-day's much such another sunny day!
GAUCELME Come, Guibert, this outgrows a jest, I think!
You're hardly such a novice as to need
The lesson, you pretend.
GUIBERT   What lesson, sir?
That everybody, if he'd thrive at court,
Should, first and last of all, look to himself?
Why, no: and therefore with your good example,
(—Ho, Master Adolf!)—to myself I'll look.

Enter ADOLF.

GUIBERT The Prince's letter; why, of all men else,
Comes it to me?
ADOLF   By virtue of your place,
Sir Guibert! 'Twas the Prince's express charge,
His envoy told us, that the missive there
Should only reach our lady by the hand
Of whosoever held your place.
GUIBERT   Enough!   [ADOLF *retires.*]
Then, gentles, who'll accept a certain poor
Indifferently honourable place,
My friends, I make no doubt, have gnashed their teeth
At leisure minutes these half-dozen years,
To find me never in the mood to quit?
Who asks may have it, with my blessing, and—
This to present our lady. Who'll accept?
You,—you,—you? There it lies, and may, for me!
MAUFROY   [*a youth, picking up the paper, reads aloud.*]
"Prince Berthold, proved by titles following
Undoubted Lord of Juliers, comes this day
To claim his own, with licence from the Pope,
The Emperor, the Kings of Spain and France" . . .

---

court 18| *1844:* bustle: here <> stand— *1849:* stand; *1863:* bustle. Here 19| *1844:* cap *1863:* cap: 21| *1844:* Come, Guibert—this outgoes a *1849:* this outgrows a *1863:* Come, Guibert, this 23| *1844:* lesson you *1849:* lesson, you 26| *1844:* therefore, with *1868:* therefore with 39| *1844:*—Who *1888:* Who 40| *1844: This* *1868:* This 41| *1844:* lies and *1849:* lies, and 45| *1844:*

GAUCELME Sufficient "titles following," I judge!
Don't read another! Well,—"to claim his own?"
MAUFROY "—And take possession of the Duchy held
Since twelve months, to the true heir's prejudice,
By" . . . Colombe, Juliers' mistress, so she thinks,
And Ravestein's mere lady, as we find.
Who wants the place and paper? Guibert's right.
I hope to climb a little in the world,—
I'd push my fortunes,—but, no more than he,
Could tell her on this happy day of days,
That, save the nosegay in her hand, perhaps,
There's nothing left to call her own. Sir Clugnet,
You famish for promotion; what say you?
CLUGNET [*an old man.*] To give this letter were a sort, I take it,
Of service: services ask recompense:
What kind of corner may be Ravestein?
GUIBERT The castle? Oh, you'd share her fortunes? Good!
Three walls stand upright, full as good as four,
With no such bad remainder of a roof.
CLUGNET Oh,—but the town?
GUIBERT Five houses, fifteen huts;
A church whereto was once a spire, 'tis judged;
And half a dyke, except in time of thaw.
CLUGNET Still, there's some revenue?
GUIBERT Else Heaven forfend!
You hang a beacon out, should fogs increase;
So, when the Autumn floats of pine-wood steer
Safe 'mid the white confusion, thanks to you,
Their grateful raftsman flings a guilder in;
—That's if he mean to pass your way next time.
CLUGNET If not?
GUIBERT Hang guilders, then! He blesses you.

France" . . *1888:* France" . . . 48| *1844:* "And *1863:* "—And 50| *1844:* By" . . . Colombe, Juliers' Mistress *1863:* mistress 51| *1844:* find! *1888:* find. 52| *1844:* right! *1868:* right. 57| *1844:* own! Sir *1868:* own. Sir 60| *1844:* recompence *1863:* recompense 62| *1844:* castle?—Oh *1888:* castle? Oh 65| *1844:* the Town <> huts, *1849:* huts; *1863:* town 66| *1844:* judged, *1849:* judged; 68| *1844:* forefend! *1868:* forfend! 70| *1844:* So when *1863:* So, when 72| *1844:* The grateful *1849:* Their grateful 73| *1844:* means *1868:* mean 74| *1844:* then—he <> you! *1863:* you § Missing punctuation probably a

CLUGNET What man do you suppose me? Keep your paper!
And, let me say, it shows no handsome spirit
To dally with misfortune: keep your place!
GAUCELME Some one must tell her.
GUIBERT Some one may: you may!
GAUCELME Sir Guibert, 'tis no trifle turns me sick
Of court-hypocrisy at years like mine,
But this goes near it. Where's there news at all?
Who'll have the face, for instance, to affirm
He never heard, e'en while we crowned the girl,
That Juliers' tenure was by Salic law;
That one, confessed her father's cousin's child,
And, she away, indisputable heir,
Against our choice protesting and the Duke's,
Claimed Juliers?—nor, as he preferred his claim,
That first this, then another potentate,
Inclined to its allowance?—I or you,
Or any one except the lady's self?
Oh, it had been the direst cruelty
To break the business to her! Things might change:
At all events, we'd see next masque at end,
Next mummery over first: and so the edge
Was taken off sharp tidings as they came,
Till here's the Prince upon us, and there's she
—Wreathing her hair, a song between her lips,
With just the faintest notion possible
That some such claimant earns a livelihood
About the world, by feigning grievances—
Few pay the story of, but grudge its price,
And fewer listen to, a second time.

---

printer's error. § *1868:* you! *1888:* then! He <> you. [76]| *1844:* And let me say it shows *1863:* And, let <> it, shows *1868:* say, it shows [78]| *1863:* you may § Missing punctuation probably a printer's error. § *1868:* you may! [85]| *1844:* And one *1849:* That one [89]| *1844:* another, potentate, *1849:* another potentate, [90]| *1844:* allowance?—I, or *1868:* allowance?—I or [93]| *1844:* change— *1863:* change: [101]| *1844:* world by <> grievances *1849:* world, by *1863:* grievances— [102]| *1844:* of but *1849:* of, but [103]| *1844:* to a *1849:* to, a

Your method proves a failure; now try mine!
And, since this must be carried . . .

GUIBERT [*snatching the paper from him.*] By your leave!
Your zeal transports you! 'Twill not serve the Prince
So much as you expect, this course you'd take.
If she leaves quietly her palace,—well;
But if she died upon its threshold,—no:
He'd have the trouble of removing her.
Come, gentles, we're all—what the devil knows!
You, Gaucelme, won't lose character, beside:
You broke your father's heart superiorly
To gather his succession—never blush!
You're from my province, and, be comforted,
They tell of it with wonder to this day.
You can afford to let your talent sleep.
We'll take the very worst supposed, as true:
There, the old Duke knew, when he hid his child
Among the river-flowers at Ravestein,
With whom the right lay! Call the Prince our Duke!
There, she's no Duchess, she's no anything
More than a young maid with the bluest eyes:
And now, sirs, we'll not break this young maid's heart
Coolly as Gaucelme could and would! No haste!
His talent's full-blown, ours but in the bud:
We'll not advance to his perfection yet—
Will we, Sir Maufroy? See, I've ruined Maufroy
For ever as a courtier!

GAUCELME Here's a coil!
And, count us, will you? Count its residue,
This boasted convoy, this day last year's crowd!
A birthday, too, a gratulation day!
I'm dumb: bid that keep silence!

MAUFROY AND OTHERS Eh, Sir Guibert?

104| *1844:* mine— *1863:* mine! 105| *1849:* leave *1863:* leave! 107| *1844:* take; *1863:* take. 108| *1844:* well: *1863:* well; 110| *1844:* her! *1863:* her. 111| *1844:* knows: *1849:* knows! 112| *1844:* beside— *1888:* beside: 116| *1844:* day— *1868:* day. 117–121| *1844:* sleep! / There <> child, / With <> lay! Let the Prince be Duke! *1849:* sleep! / We'll take the very worst supposed, as true— / There <> child / Among the river-flowers at Ravestein, / With <> lay! Call the Prince our Duke! *1863:* true: / There *1868:* sleep. / We'll 123| *1844:* eyes— *1868:* eyes: 125| *1844:* So coolly as he could *1849:* Coolly as Gaucelme could 126| *1844:* bud— *1868:* bud: 129| *1844:* coil— *1863:* coil! 132| *1844:* too—a gratulation-day! *1868:* too, a *1888:* gratulation day! 133| *1844:* *that* *1868:*

He's right: that does say something: that's bare truth.
Ten—twelve, I make: a perilous dropping off!
GUIBERT Pooh—is it audience hour? The vestibule
Swarms too, I wager, with the common sort
That want our privilege of entry here.
GAUCELME Adolf! [*Re-enter* ADOLF.] Who's outside?
GUIBERT Oh, your looks suffice!
Nobody waiting?
MAUFROY [*looking through the door-folds.*] Scarce our number!
GUIBERT 'Sdeath!
Nothing to beg for, to complain about?
It can't be! Ill news spreads, but not so fast
As thus to frighten all the world!
GAUCELME The world
Lives out of doors, sir—not with you and me
By presence-chamber porches, state-room stairs,
Wherever warmth's perpetual: outside's free
To every wind from every compass-point,
And who may get nipped needs be weather-wise.
The Prince comes and the lady's People go;
The snow-goose settles down, the swallows flee—
Why should they wait for winter-time? 'Tis instinct.
Don't you feel somewhat chilly?
GUIBERT That's their craft?
And last year's crowders-round and criers-forth
That strewed the garlands, overarched the roads,
Lighted the bonfires, sang the loyal songs!
Well 'tis my comfort, you could never call me
The People's Friend! The People keep their word—
I keep my place: don't doubt I'll entertain
The People when the Prince comes, and the People
Are talked of! Then, their speeches—no one tongue

---

that 135| *1844:* dropping-off! *1868:* dropping off! 136| *1844:* audience-hour *1863:* audience hour 146| *1844:* perpetual. Outside's *1849:* perpetual: outside's 147| *1868:* compass-point *1888:* compass-point. 149| *1844:* and the People go; 'tis instinct: *1849:* and the lady's People go; 150–152| *1844:* flee—/ Don't *1849:* flee—/ Why should they wait for winter-time? 'Tis instinct; / Don't *1888:* instinct. 153| *1844:* criers-forth, *1868:* criers-forth 155| *1844:* Lit up the bonfires <> songs— *1849:* songs! *1868:* Lighted the bonfires 156| *1844:* Well, 'tis my comfort you *1849:* comfort, you *1868:* Well 'tis 160| *1844:* of!—Then *1863:* of!

Found respite, not a pen had holiday
—For they wrote, too, as well as spoke, these knaves!
Now see: we tax and tithe them, pill and poll,
They wince and fret enough, but pay they must
—We manage that,—so, pay with a good grace
They might as well, it costs so little more.
But when we've done with taxes, meet folk next
Outside the toll-booth and the rating-place,
In public—there they have us if they will,
We're at their mercy after that, you see!
For one tax not ten devils could extort—
Over and above necessity, a grace;
This prompt disbosoming of love, to wit—
Their vine-leaf wrappage of our tribute penny,
And crowning attestation, all works well.
Yet this precisely do they thrust on us!
These cappings quick, these crook-and-cringings low,
Hand to the heart, and forehead to the knee,
With grin that shuts the eyes and opes the mouth—
So tender they their love; and, tender made,
Go home to curse us, the first doit we ask.
As if their souls were any longer theirs!
As if they had not given ample warrant
To who should clap a collar on their neck,
Rings in their nose, a goad to either flank,
And take them for the brute they boast themselves!

Then 165| *1844:* so pay *1863:* so, pay 170| *1844:* see— *1863:* see! 171| *1844:* extort, *1849:* extort; *1863:* extort— 172| *1844:* grace, *1849:* grace; 174| *1844:* vine-leaf-wrappage <> tribute-penny, *1863:* vine-leaf wrappage *1888:* tribute penny, 175| *1844:* And crowning attestation *1849:* well— *1863:* well. *1868:* And crowding attestation § see Ed. notes § 176| *1844:* us,— *1849:* us! 177| *1844:* quick, and crook-and-cringings *1868:* quick, these crook-and-cringings 180| *1844:* and tender *1863:* and, tender 181–183| *1844:* curse you, the first doit you ask; / As if they had *1849:* ask; / As if their souls were any longer theirs! / As *1863:* ask. / As if their souls *1868:* curse us, the first doit we ask.

Stay—there's a bustle at the outer door—
And somebody entreating . . . that's my name!
Adolf,—I heard my name!
ADOLF 'Twas probably
The suitor.
GUIBERT Oh, there is one?
ADOLF With a suit
He'd fain enforce in person.
GUIBERT The good heart
—And the great fool! Just ope the mid-door's fold!
Is that a lappet of his cloak, I see?
ADOLF If it bear plenteous sign of travel . . . ay,
The very cloak my comrades tore!
GUIBERT Why tore?
ADOLF He seeks the Duchess' presence in that trim:
Since daybreak, was he posted hereabouts
Lest he should miss the moment.
GUIBERT Where's he now?
ADOLF Gone for a minute possibly, not more:
They have ado enough to thrust him back.
GUIBERT Ay—but my name, I caught?
ADOLF Oh, sir—he said
—What was it?—You had known him formerly,
And, he believed, would help him did you guess
He waited now; you promised him as much:
The old plea! 'Faith, he's back,—renews the charge!
[*Speaking at the door.*] So long as the man parleys, peace outside—
Nor be too ready with your halberts, there!
GAUCELME My horse bespattered, as he blocked the path,

187| *1844:*—Stay *1863:* Stay 190| *1844:* The Suitor *1868:* suitor
192| *1844:* fold— *1863:* fold! *1888:* fold 194| *1844:* signs *1868:* sign
195| *1844:* comrade *1849:* comrades 197| *1844:* daybreak was *1849:* daybreak, was 199| *1844:* more. *1868:* more: 201| *1844:* name I *1849:* name, I
202| *1844:*—What said he?—You *1849:*—What was it?—You 204| *1844:* now—you <> much— *1868:* now; you <> much: 205| *1844:* plea!—'Faith *1863:* plea! Faith 206| *1844:* outside! *1868:* outside— 208| *1844:* path, *1888:*

A thin sour man, not unlike somebody.
ADOLF He holds a paper in his breast, whereon
He glances when his cheeks flush and his brow
At each repulse—
GAUCELME I noticed he'd a brow.
ADOLF So glancing, he grows calmer, leans awhile
Over the balustrade, adjusts his dress,
And presently turns round, quiet again,
With some new pretext for admittance.—Back!
[*To* GUIBERT.]—Sir, he has seen you! Now cross halberts! Ha—
Pascal is prostrate—there lies Fabian too!
No passage! Whither would the madman press?
Close the doors quick on me!
GUIBERT Too late! He's here.

Enter, hastily and with discomposed dress, VALENCE.

VALENCE Sir Guibert, will you help me?—me, that come
Charged by your townsmen, all who starve at Cleves,
To represent their heights and depths of woe
Before our Duchess and obtain relief!
Such errands barricade such doors, it seems:
But not a common hindrance drives me back
On all the sad yet hopeful faces, lit
With hope for the first time, which sent me forth.
Cleves, speak for me! Cleves' men and women, speak!
Who followed me—your strongest—many a mile
That I might go the fresher from their ranks,
—Who sit—your weakest—by the city gates,
To take me fuller of what news I bring
As I return—for I must needs return!
—Can I? 'Twere hard, no listener for their wrongs,
To turn them back upon the old despair—
Harder, Sir Guibert, than imploring thus—
So, I do—any way you please—implore!
If you . . . but how should you remember Cleves?

---

path 209| *1844:* man not *1863:* man, not 218| *1844:* too— *1868:* too! 220| *1844:* late—he's *1868:* late! He's 221| *1844:* me?—Me *1888:* me?—me 228| *1844:* forth! *1868:* forth. 229| *1844:* women, speak— *1868:* women, speak! 232| *1844:* city-gates, *1863:* city gates, 238| *1844:* So I *1863:* So,

Yet they of Cleves remember you so well!
Ay, comment on each trait of you they keep,
Your words and deeds caught up at second hand,—
Proud, I believe, at bottom of their hearts,
O' the very levity and recklessness
Which only prove that you forget their wrongs.
Cleves, the grand town, whose men and women starve,
Is Cleves forgotten? Then, remember me!
You promised me that you would help me once,
For other purpose: will you keep your word?
GUIBERT And who may you be, friend?
VALENCE Valence of Cleves.
GUIBERT Valence of . . . not the advocate of Cleves,
I owed my whole estate to, three years back?
Ay, well may you keep silence! Why, my lords,
You've heard, I'm sure, how, Pentecost three years,
I was so nearly ousted of my land
By some knave's pretext—(eh? when you refused me
Your ugly daughter, Clugnet!)—and you've heard
How I recovered it by miracle
—(When I refused her!) Here's the very friend,
—Valence of Cleves, all parties have to thank!
Nay, Valence, this procedure's vile in you!
I'm no more grateful than a courtier should,
But politic am I—I bear a brain,
Can cast about a little, might require
Your services a second time. I tried
To tempt you with advancement here to court
—"No!"—well, for curiosity at least
To view our life here—"No!"—our Duchess, then,—

I 241| *1844:*—Ay *1888:* Ay 244| *1844:* Of *1888:* O' 245| *1844:* prove yourself forget *1849:* prove that you forget 246| *1844:* Cleves the <> town whose *1849:* Cleves, the <> town, whose 247| *1844:* forgotten?—Then remember *1863:* forgotten?—Then, remember *1888:* forgotten? Then 248| *1844:* once *1888:* once, 251| *1844:* the Advocate of Cleves *1863:* the Advocate of Cleves, *1868:* advocate 256| *1844:* pretext,—(eh *1863:* knaves'-pretext *1888:* knave's pretext—(eh 257| *1844:* daughter, Clugnet,)—and *1868:* daughter, Clugnet!)—and 259| *1844:* her)! Here's *1863:* her!) Here's 261| *1844:* you— *1868:* you! 265| *1844:* time! I *1868:* time. I 267| *1844:*—"No"—well *1849:*—"No!"—well 268| *1844:* here—"no"—our *1849:* here—"No!"—our

A pretty woman's worth some pains to see,
Nor is she spoiled, I take it, if a crown
Complete the forehead pale and tresses pure . . .
VALENCE Our city trusted me its miseries,
And I am come.
GUIBERT So much for taste! But "come,"—
So may you be, for anything I know,
To beg the Pope's cross, or Sir Clugnet's daughter,
And with an equal chance you get all three.
If it was ever worth your while to come,
Was not the proper way worth finding too?
VALENCE Straight to the palace-portal, sir, I came—
GUIBERT —And said?—
VALENCE —That I had brought the miseries
Of a whole city to relieve.
GUIBERT —Which saying
Won your admittance? You saw me, indeed,
And here, no doubt, you stand: as certainly,
My intervention, I shall not dispute,
Procures you audience; which, if I procure,—
That paper's closely written—by Saint Paul,
Here flock the Wrongs, follow the Remedies,
Chapter and verse, One, Two, A, B and C!
Perhaps you'd enter, make a reverence,
And launch these "miseries" from first to last?
VALENCE How should they let me pause or turn aside?
GAUCELME [*to* VALENCE.] My worthy sir, one question! You've come straight
From Cleves, you tell us: heard you any talk
At Cleves about our lady?
VALENCE Much.
GAUCELME And what?
VALENCE Her wish was to redress all wrongs she knew.

269| *1844:*—A *1863:* A 271| *1844:* Completes *1868:* Complete 275| *1844:* cross or *1849:* cross, or 276| *1844:* three! *1888:* three. 279| *1844:* palace-portal, Sir *1849:* sir 285| *1844:* audience; but, if so I do— *1849:* audience; which, if I procure, *1863:* procure,— 288| *1844:* C— *1868:* C! 292| *1844:* worthy Sir, one question: you've *1849:* sir *1868:* question! You've 293| *1844:*

GAUCELME That, you believed?
VALENCE You see me, sir!
GAUCELME —Nor stopped
Upon the road from Cleves to Juliers here,
For any—rumours you might find afloat?
VALENCE I had my townsmen's wrongs to busy me.
GAUCELME This is the lady's birthday, do you know?
—Her day of pleasure?
VALENCE —That the great, I know,
For pleasure born, should still be on the watch
To exclude pleasure when a duty offers:
Even as, for duty born, the lowly too
May ever snatch a pleasure if in reach:
Both will have plenty of their birthright, sir!
GAUCELME [*aside to* GUIBERT.] Sir Guibert, here's your man! No scruples now—
You'll never find his like! Time presses hard.
I've seen your drift and Adolf's too, this while,
But you can't keep the hour of audience back
Much longer, and at noon the Prince arrives.
[*Pointing to* VALENCE.] Entrust him with it—fool no chance away!
GUIBERT Him?
GAUCELME —With the missive! What's the man to her?
GUIBERT No bad thought! Yet, 'tis yours, who ever played
The Tempting serpent: else 'twere no bad thought!
I should—and do—mistrust it for your sake,
Or else . . .

Enter an OFFICIAL *who communicates with* ADOLF.

ADOLF The Duchess will receive the court.
GUIBERT Give us a moment, Adolf! Valence, friend,

---

us—heard *1849:* us: heard 296| *1844:* That you *1849:* That, you 300| *1844:* the Lady's birthday do *1849:* birthday, do *1863:* lady's 301| *1844:* the Great *1849:* VALENCE—I know that the *1863:* great *1868:* VALENCE—That the great, I know, 302| *1844:* For Pleasure *1863:* pleasure 303| *1844:* exclude Pleasure <> a Duty *1863:* pleasure <> duty 304| *1844:* for Duty <> the Lowly *1849:* as, the Lowly too, for Duty born, *1863:* lowly <> duty *1868:* as, for duty born, the lowly too 305| *1844:* a Pleasure *1863:* pleasure 312| *1844: him* *1868:* him 313| *1844:*—Him *1888:* Him 314| *1844:* thought!—Yet, 'tis yours—who *1868:* yours, who *1888:* thought! Yet 315| *1844:* serpent—else, 'twere *1863:* serpent: else *1868:* else 'twere 317| *1844:* receive the Court! *1868:* court! *1888:*

I'll help you. We of the service, you're to mark,
Have special entry, while the herd . . . the folk
Outside, get access through our help alone;
—Well, it is so, was so, and I suppose
So ever will be: your natural lot is, therefore,
To wait your turn and opportunity,
And probably miss both. Now, I engage
To set you, here and in a minute's space,
Before the lady, with full leave to plead
Chapter and verse, and A, and B, and C,
To heart's content.
VALENCE I grieve that I must ask,—
This being, yourself admit, the custom here,—
To what the price of such a favour mounts?
GUIBERT Just so! You're not without a courtier's tact.
Little at court, as your quick instinct prompts,
Do such as we without a recompense.
VALENCE Yours is?—
GUIBERT A trifle: here's a document
'Tis some one's duty to present her Grace—
I say, not mine—these say, not theirs—such points
Have weight at court. Will you relieve us all
And take it? Just say, "I am bidden lay
This paper at the Duchess' feet!"
VALENCE No more?
I thank you, sir!
ADOLF Her Grace receives the court.
GUIBERT [*aside.*] Now, *sursum corda*, quoth the mass-priest! Do—
Whoever's my kind saint, do let alone
These pushings to and fro, and pullings back;
Peaceably let me hang o' the devil's arm
The downward path, if you can't pluck me off

---

court. 319| *1844:* you: we *1868:* you! We *1888:* you. We 320| *1844:* folks *1888:* folk 321| *1844:* alone *1863:* alone. *1868:* alone; 323| *1844:* be—your *1863:* be: your 327| *1844:* lady with *1863:* lady, with 328| *1844:* verse, and A., and B., and C., *1849:* verse, and A, and B, and C, 329| *1844:* ask, *1863:* ask,— 330| *1844:* From this yourself admit the <> here, *1849:* This being, yourself admit, the *1863:* here,— 331| *1844:* What will the <> favour be? *1849:* To what the <> favour mounts? 332| *1844:* tact! *1868:* tact. 334| *1844:* recompence. *1863:* recompense. 339| *1844:* it?—Just *1863:* it? Just 340| *1844:* feet." VALENCE *1868:* feet!" VALENCE 341| *1844:* the Court! *1868:* court! *1888:* court.

Completely! Let me live quite his, or yours!
[*The* COURTIERS *begin to range themselves, and move toward the door.*]
After me, Valence! So, our famous Cleves
Lacks bread? Yet don't we gallants buy their lace?
And dear enough—it beggars me, I know,
To keep my very gloves fringed properly.
This, Valence, is our Great State Hall you cross;
Yon grey urn's veritable marcasite,
The Pope's gift: and those salvers testify
The Emperor. Presently you'll set your foot
. . . But you don't speak, friend Valence!

VALENCE I shall speak.

GAUCELME [*aside to* GUIBERT.] Guibert—it were no such ungraceful thing
If you and I, at first, seemed horror-struck
With the bad news. Look here, what you shall do.
Suppose you, first, clap hand to sword and cry
"Yield strangers our allegiance? First I'll perish
Beside your Grace!"—and so give me the cue
To . . .

GUIBERT —Clap your hand to note-book and jot down
That to regale the Prince with? I conceive.
[*To* VALENCE.] Do, Valence, speak, or I shall half suspect
You're plotting to supplant us, me the first,
I' the lady's favour! Is't the grand harangue
You mean to make, that thus engrosses you?
—Which of her virtues you'll apostrophize?
Or is't the fashion you aspire to start,
Of that close-curled, not unbecoming hair?
Or what else ponder you?

VALENCE My townsmen's wrongs.

347| *1844:* his or *1849:* his, or 348| *1844:* me, Valence! So our *1863:* me, Valence! So, our 351| *1844:* properly! *1868:* properly. 352| *1844:* cross: *1863:* cross; 354| *1844:* gift; and *1863:* gift: and 358| *1844:* horrorstruck *1863:* horror-struck 359| *1844:* news? Look <> do! *1849:* news. Look *1888:* do. 360| *1844:* you first clap *1849:* you, first, clap 362| *1844:* your Grace"!—And *1849:* and *1863:* your Grace!"—and 363| *1844:* GUIBERT Clap *1868:* GUIBERT—Clap 364| *1844:* conceive! *1868:* conceive. 367| *1844:* the Lady's favour: is't *1863:* lady's *1868:* favour! Is't 368| *1844:* make that *1849:* make, that 369| *1844:* apostrophise? *1863:* apostrophize? 370| *1844:* start *1849:* start, 372| *1844:*—Or <> wrongs! [*Exeunt omnes.* *1849:* wrongs! *1868:* Or <> wrongs.

ACT II

NOON

SCENE—*The Prescence-chamber.*

The DUCHESS *and* SABYNE.

THE DUCHESS Announce that I am ready for the court!
SABYNE 'Tis scarcely audience-hour, I think; your Grace
May best consult your own relief, no doubt,
And shun the crowd: but few can have arrived.
THE DUCHESS Let those not yet arrived, then, keep away!
'Twas me, this day last year at Ravestein,
You hurried. It has been full time, beside,
This half-hour. Do you hesitate?
SABYNE Forgive me!
THE DUCHESS Stay, Sabyne; let me hasten to make sure
Of one true thanker: here with you begins
My audience, claim you first its privilege!
It is my birth's event they celebrate:
You need not wish me more such happy days,
But—ask some favour! Have you none to ask?
Has Adolf none, then? this was far from least
Of much I waited for impatiently,
Assure yourself! It seemed so natural
Your gift, beside this bunch of river-bells,
Should be the power and leave of doing good
To you, and greater pleasure to myself.
You ask my leave to-day to marry Adolf?

1| *1844:* the Court! *1868:* court! 2| *1844:* think—your *1868:* think; your 4| *1844:* crowd; but if there's few arrived . . . *1849:* but few can have arrived . . . *1868:* crowd: but <> arrived. 6| *1844:* me this day, last *1849:* me, this *1868:* me <> day last 12| *1844:* celebrate— *1863:* celebrate: 17| *1844:* yourself! So natural it seemed, *1849:* yourself! It seemed so natural 19–21| *1844:* leave to do you good; / You *1849:* leave of doing good / To you, and greater pleasure to myself: / You 21| *1863:*

The rest is my concern.
SABYNE Your Grace is ever
Our lady of dear Ravestein,—but, for Adolf . . .
THE DUCHESS "But"? You have not, sure, changed in your regard
And purpose towards him?
SABYNE We change?
THE DUCHESS Well then? Well?
SABYNE How could we two be happy, and, most like,
Leave Juliers, when—when . . . but 'tis audience-time!
THE DUCHESS "When, if you left me, I were left indeed!"
Would you subjoin that?—Bid the court approach!
—Why should we play thus with each other, Sabyne?
Do I not know, if courtiers prove remiss,
If friends detain me, and get blame for it,
There is a cause? Of last year's fervid throng
Scarce one half comes now.
SABYNE [*aside.*] One half? No, alas!
THE DUCHESS So can the mere suspicion of a cloud
Over my fortunes, strike each loyal heart.
They've heard of this Prince Berthold; and, forsooth,
Some foolish arrogant pretence he makes,
May grow more foolish and more arrogant,
They please to apprehend! I thank their love.
Admit them!
SABYNE [*aside.*] How much has she really learned?
THE DUCHESS Surely, whoever's absent, Tristan waits?
—Or at least Romuald, whom my father raised
From nothing—come, he's faithful to me, come!
(Sabyne, I should but be the prouder—yes,
The fitter to comport myself aright)
Not Romuald? Xavier—what said he to that?
For Xavier hates a parasite, I know! [SABYNE *goes out.*]
THE DUCHESS Well, sunshine's everywhere, and summer too.

---

myself. 23| *1844:* My Lady <> Ravenstein *1849:* Our Lady <> Ravestein *1868:* lady 25| *1844.* SABYNE *We* change! THE *1868:* SABYNE We change? THE 27| *1844:* when . . . when *1863:* when—when 28| *1844:* indeed"— *1863:* indeed!" 29| *1844:* the Court *1868:* court 34| *1844:* now! SABYNE *1868:* now. SABYNE 36| *1844:* fortunes strike *1863:* fortunes, strike 38| *1844:* Each foolish <> makes *1849:* makes, *1868:* Some foolish 39| *1844:* More foolish <> arrogant may grow, *1849:* May grow more <> arrogant, 40| *1844:* love! *1868:* love. 46| *1844:* And fitter *1868:* The fitter 49| *1844:* too; *1863:* too.

Next year 'tis the old place again, perhaps—
The water-breeze again, the birds again.
—It cannot be! It is too late to be!
What part had I, or choice in all of it?
Hither they brought me; I had not to think
Nor care, concern myself with doing good
Or ill, my task was just—to live,—to live,
And, answering ends there was no need explain,
To render Juliers happy—so they said.
All could not have been falsehood: some was love,
And wonder and obedience. I did all
They looked for: why then cease to do it now?
Yet this is to be calmly set aside,
And—ere next birthday's dawn, for aught I know,
Things change, a claimant may arrive, and I . . .
It cannot nor it shall not be! His right?
Well then, he has the right, and I have not,
—But who bade all of you surround my life
And close its growth up with your ducal crown
Which, plucked off rudely, leaves me perishing?
I could have been like one of you,—loved, hoped,
Feared, lived and died like one of you—but you
Would take that life away and give me this,
And I will keep this! I will face you! Come!

Enter the COURTIERS *and* VALENCE.

THE COURTIERS Many such happy mornings to your Grace!
THE DUCHESS [*aside, as they pay their devoir.*] The same words, the same faces,—the same love!
I have been overfearful. These are few;
But these, at least, stand firmly: these are mine.
As many come as may; and if no more,
'Tis that these few suffice—they do suffice!

51| *1844:* birds again *1863:* birds again. 52| *1844:* . . . It cannot *1863:*—It cannot 59| *1844:* falsehood! Some *1868:* falsehood: some 60| *1844:* obedience—I *1863:* obedience. I 61| *1844:* look'd for! Why *1849:* looked *1863:* for: why 66| *1844:* right, I have it not, *1849:* right, and I have not, 68| *1844:* your Ducal *1868:* ducal 69| *1844:* pluck'd *1849:* plucked 73| *1844:* you—Come! *1863:* you! Come! 75| *1844:* words—the same faces *1868:* words, the same faces 76| *1844:* over-fearful <> few— *1863:* few; *1868:* overfearful 77| *1844:* firmly—these are mine! *1863:* firmly: these *1868:* mine. 78| *1844:* may,

What succour may not next year bring me? Plainly,
I feared too soon. [*To the* COURTIERS.] I thank you, sirs: all thanks!

VALENCE [*aside, as the* DUCHESS *passes from one group to another, conversing.*]
'Tis she—the vision this day last year brought,
When, for a golden moment at our Cleves,
She tarried in her progress hither. Cleves
Chose me to speak its welcome, and I spoke
—Not that she could have noted the recluse
—Ungainly, old before his time—who gazed.
Well, Heaven's gifts are not wasted, and that gaze
Kept, and shall keep me to the end, her own!
She was above it—but so would not sink
My gaze to earth! The People caught it, hers—
Thenceforward, mine; but thus entirely mine,
Who shall affirm, had she not raised my soul
Ere she retired and left me—them? She turns—
There's all her wondrous face at once! The ground
Reels and . . . [*suddenly occupying himself with his paper.*]
These wrongs of theirs I have to plead!

THE DUCHESS [*to the* COURTIERS.] Nay, compliment enough! and kindness' self
Should pause before it wish me more such years.
'Twas fortunate that thus, ere youth escaped,
I tasted life's pure pleasure—one such, pure,
Is worth a thousand, mixed—and youth's for pleasure:
Mine is received; let my age pay for it.

GAUCELME So, pay, and pleasure paid for, thinks your Grace,
Should never go together?

GUIBERT How, Sir Gaucelme?
Hurry one's feast down unenjoyingly
At the snatched breathing-intervals of work?
As good you saved it till the dull day's-end

and *1863:* may; and 80| *1844:* me! Plainly *1863:* me? Plainly, 81| *1844:* soon! [*To* *1863:* soon. [*To* 83| *1844:* When for <> Cleves *1863:* When, for <> Cleves, 87| *1844:* gazed— *1863:* gazed. 88| *1844:* . . . Well *1863:* Well 94| *1844:* them?—She *1863:* them? She 97| *1844:* enough! And *1863:* enough! and 99| *1844:* thus ere <> escaped *1849:* thus, ere <> escaped, 103| *1844:* pay and *1849:* pay, and 106| *1844:* § First point may be broken comma, broken hyphen, or unintended: § snatched-breathing-intervals *1849:* snatched

When, stiff and sleepy, appetite is gone.
Eat first, then work upon the strength of food!
THE DUCHESS True: you enable me to risk my future,
By giving me a past beyond recall.
I lived, a girl, one happy leisure year:
Let me endeavour to be the Duchess now!
And so,—what news, Sir Guibert, spoke you of?
[*As they advance a little, and* GUIBERT *speaks*—]
—That gentleman?
VALENCE [*aside.*] I feel her eyes on me.
GUIBERT [*to* VALENCE.] The Duchess, sir, inclines to hear your suit.
Advance! He is from Cleves.
VALENCE [*coming forward. Aside.*] Their wrongs—their wrongs!
THE DUCHESS And you, sir, are from Cleves? How fresh in mind,
The hour or two I passed at queenly Cleves!
She entertained me bravely, but the best
Of her good pageant seemed its standers-by
With insuppressive joy on every face!
What says my ancient famous happy Cleves?
VALENCE Take the truth, lady—you are made for truth!
So think my friends: nor do they less deserve
The having you to take it, you shall think,
When you know all—nay, when you only know
How, on that day you recollect at Cleves,
When the poor acquiescing multitude
Who thrust themselves with all their woes apart
Into unnoticed corners, that the few,
Their means sufficed to muster trappings for,
Might fill the foreground, occupy your sight
With joyous faces fit to bear away
And boast of as a sample of all Cleves
—How, when to daylight these crept out once more,
Clutching, unconscious, each his empty rags

---

breathing-intervals 108–110| *1844:* gone! / THE <> Future, *1849:* gone! / Eat first, then work upon the strength of it! / THE *1868:* gone. / Eat <> of food! / THE <> future, 111| *1844:* a Past *1868:* past 112| *1844:* A girl <> year I lived: *1849:* I lived, a <> year: 113| *1844:* be Duchess *1849:* be the Duchess 115| *1844:* me! *1868:* me. 116| *1844:* suit! *1868:* suit. 118| *1844:* mind *1849:* mind, 120| *1844:* entertained us bravely *1849:* entertained me bravely 121| *1849:* standers-by, *1868:* standers-by 123| *1844:* ancient, famous, happy *1868:* ancient famous happy 125| *1844:* nor less do they deserve *1849:* nor do they less deserve 131| *1844:* few *1863:* few, 137| *1844:* inconscious *1849:*

Whence the scant coin, which had not half bought bread,
That morn he shook forth, counted piece by piece,
And, well-advisedly, on perfumes spent them
To burn, or flowers to strew, before your path
—How, when the golden flood of music and bliss
Ebbed, as their moon retreated, and again
Left the sharp black-point rocks of misery bare
—Then I, their friend, had only to suggest
"Saw she the horror as she saw the pomp!"
And as one man they cried "He speaks the truth:
Show her the horror! Take from our own mouths
Our wrongs and show them, she will see them too!"
This they cried, lady! I have brought the wrongs.

THE DUCHESS Wrongs? Cleves has wrongs—apparent now and thus?
I thank you! In that paper? Give it me!

VALENCE (There, Cleves!) In this! (What did I promise, Cleves?)
Our weavers, clothiers, spinners are reduced
Since . . . Oh, I crave your pardon! I forget
I buy the privilege of this approach,
And promptly would discharge my debt. I lay
This paper humbly at the Duchess' feet. [*Presenting* GUIBERT'S *paper.*]

GUIBERT Stay! for the present . . .

THE DUCHESS Stay, sir? I take aught
That teaches me their wrongs with greater pride
Than this your ducal circlet. Thank you, sir!

[*The* DUCHESS *reads hastily; then, turning to the* COURTIERS—]

What have I done to you? Your deed or mine
Was it, this crowning me? I gave myself
No more a title to your homage, no,
Than church-flowers, born this season, wrote the words
In the saint's-book that sanctified them first.
For such a flower, you plucked me; well, you erred—

---

unconscious 140| *1844:* spent *1849:* spent them 146| *1844:* pomp"— *1849:* pomp!"— *1868:* pomp!" 147| *1844:* truth— *1868:* truth: 148| *1844:* horror—take *1849:* horror! Take 150| *1844:*—This *1868:* This 151| *1844:* has wrongs—which now and thus I know? *1849:* has wrongs—apparent now and thus? 152| *1844:* you—in that paper?—Give *1863:* paper? Give *1868:* you! In 155| *1844:* pardon—I *1863:* pardon! I 158| *1844: This* <> feet! *1868:* This <> feet. 159| *1844:* Stay—for *1863:* Stay! for 161| *1844:* your Ducal *1868:* ducal 165| *1844:* church-flowers born this season gave the *1849:* church-flowers, born this season, wrote the 167| *1844:* flower you plucked me—well *1849:* flower, you

Well, 'twas a weed; remove the eye-sore quick!
But should you not remember it has lain
Steeped in the candles' glory, palely shrined,
Nearer God's Mother than most earthly things?
—That if't be faded 'tis with prayer's sole breath—
That the one day it boasted was God's day?
Still, I do thank you! Had you used respect,
Here might I dwindle to my last white leaf,
Here lose life's latest freshness, which even yet
May yield some wandering insect rest and food:
So, fling me forth, and—all is best for all!
[*After a pause.*] Prince Berthold, who art Juliers' Duke it seems—
The King's choice, and the Emperor's, and the Pope's—
Be mine, too! Take this People! Tell not me
Of rescripts, precedents, authorities,
—But take them, from a heart that yearns to give!
Find out their love,—I could not; find their fear,—
I would not; find their like,—I never shall,
Among the flowers! [*Taking off her coronet.*]

Colombe of Ravestein
Thanks God she is no longer Duchess here!

VALENCE [*advancing to* GUIBERT.] Sir Guibert, knight, they call you—this of mine
Is the first step I ever set at court.
You dared make me your instrument, I find;
For that, so sure as you and I are men,
We reckon to the utmost presently:
But as you are a courtier and I none,
Your knowledge may instruct me. I, already,
Have too far outraged, by my ignorance

1863: me! well *1868:* me; well 168| *1844:* weed—remove *1868:* weed: remove *1888:* weed; remove 174| *1844:* But I <> you—had <> respect *1849:* Still, I *1863:* you! Had *1868:* respect, 175| *1844:* to the last <> leaf *1849:* to my last <> leaf, 176| *1844:* Till losing the poor relic which *1849:* Here lose life's latest freshness, which 177| *1844:* insect life and *1863:* insect rest and 178| *1844:* forth and *1849:* forth, and 179| *1844:* art Juliers' Duke, it *1888:* art Juliers' Duke it 180| *1844:* The Pope's choice and the Emperor's, and the Kings'— *1849:* The King's choice, and the Emperor's, and the Pope's— 181| *1844:* people *1863:* this People 185| *1844:* never will *1849:* never shall, 186| *1844:* flowers. [*Taking* *1849:* flowers! [*Taking* 188| *1844:* Sir Guibert,—knight *1868:* Sir Guibert, knight

Of courtier-ways, this lady, to proceed
A second step and risk addressing her:
—I am degraded—you, let me address!
Out of her presence, all is plain enough
What I shall do—but in her presence, too,
Surely there's something proper to be done.
[*To the others.*] You, gentles, tell me if I guess aright—
May I not strike this man to earth?

THE COURTIERS [*as* GUIBERT *springs forward, withholding him.*]
Let go!
—The clothiers' spokesman, Guibert? Grace a churl?

THE DUCHESS [*to* VALENCE.] Oh, be acquainted with your party, sir!
He's of the oldest lineage Juliers boasts;
A lion crests him for a cognizance;
"Scorning to waver"—that's his 'scutcheon's word;
His office with the new Duke—probably
The same in honour as with me; or more,
By so much as this gallant turn deserves.
He's now, I dare say, of a thousand times
The rank and influence that remain with her
Whose part you take! So, lest for taking it
You suffer . . .

VALENCE I may strike him then to earth?

GUIBERT [*falling on his knee.*] Great and dear lady, pardon me! Hear once!
Believe me and be merciful—be just!
I could not bring myself to give that paper
Without a keener pang than I dared meet
—And so felt Clugnet here, and Maufroy here
—No one dared meet it. Protestation's cheap,—
But, if to die for you did any good,
[*To* GAUCELME.] Would not I die, sir? Say your worst of me!
But it does no good, that's the mournful truth.
And since the hint of a resistance, even,
Would just precipitate, on you the first,
A speedier ruin—I shall not deny,

196| *1844:* lady to *1849:* lady, to 197| *1844:* her *1868:* her:
198| *1844:* you let *1849:* you, let *1888:* you let § see Ed. notes §
199| *1844:* presence all *1849:* presence, all 201| *1844:* done! *1868:* done.
204| *1844:*—The Clothiers' *1868:* clothiers' 207| *1844:* cognisance; *1888:* cognizance; 211| *1844:* deserves; *1863:* deserves: *1868:* deserves. 224| *1844:*

Saving myself indubitable pain,
I thought to give you pleasure (who might say?)
By showing that your only subject found
To carry the sad notice, was the man
Precisely ignorant of its contents;
A nameless, mere provincial advocate;
One whom 'twas like you never saw before,
Never would see again. All has gone wrong;
But I meant right, God knows, and you, I trust!
THE DUCHESS A nameless advocate, this gentleman?
—(I pardon you, Sir Guibert!)
GUIBERT [*rising, to* VALENCE.] Sir, and you?
VALENCE —Rejoice that you are lightened of a load.
Now, you have only me to reckon with.
THE DUCHESS One I have never seen, much less obliged?
VALENCE Dare I speak, lady?
THE DUCHESS Dare you! Heard you not
I rule no longer?
VALENCE Lady, if your rule
Were based alone on such a ground as these
[*Pointing to the* COURTIERS.]
Could furnish you,—abjure it! They have hidden
A source of true dominion from your sight.
THE DUCHESS You hear them—no such source is left . . .
VALENCE Hear Cleves!
Whose haggard craftsmen rose to starve this day,
Starve now, and will lie down at night to starve,
Sure of a like tomorrow—but as sure
Of a most unlike morrow-after-that,
Since end things must, end howsoe'er things may.
What curbs the brute-force instinct in its hour?
What makes—instead of rising, all as one,
And teaching fingers, so expert to wield

---

truth: *1849:* truth. 229| *1844:* to get you pleasure, who <> say? *1849:* to give you pleasure (who <> say?) 230| *1844:* In that <> subject we could find *1849:* By showing that <> subject found 237| *1844:* gentleman?— *1888:* gentleman? 238| *1844: to* VALENCE] .—Sir, and you?— *1888: to* VALENCE] . Sir, and you? 239| *1844:* Rejoice *1849:*—Rejoice 240| *1844:* with! *1868:* with. 241| *1844:* obliged?— *1888:* obliged? 248| *1844:* rose this day to starve, *1849:* rose to starve this day, 249| *1844:* Are starving now <> night *1849:* Starve now <> night to starve, 252–254| *1844:* may. / What makes, instead *1849:* may. / What curbs the brute-force instinct in its hour? / What *1863:* makes—instead 255| *1844:* fingers

Their tool, the broadsword's play or carbine's trick,
—What makes that there's an easier help, they think,
For you, whose name so few of them can spell,
Whose face scarce one in every hundred saw,—
You simply have to understand their wrongs,
And wrongs will vanish—so, still trades are plied,
And swords lie rusting, and myself stand here?
There is a vision in the heart of each
Of justice, mercy, wisdom, tenderness
To wrong and pain, and knowledge of its cure:
And these embodied in a woman's form
That best transmits them, pure as first received,
From God above her, to mankind below.
Will you derive your rule from such a ground,
Or rather hold it by the suffrage, say,
Of this man—this—and this?

THE DUCHESS [*after a pause.*] You come from Cleves:
How many are at Cleves of such a mind?

VALENCE [*from his paper.*] "We, all the manufacturers of Cleves—"

THE DUCHESS Or stay, sir—lest I seem too covetous—
Are you my subject? such as you describe,
Am I to you, though to no other man?

VALENCE [*from his paper.*]—"Valence, ordained your Advocate at Cleves"—

THE DUCHESS [*replacing the coronet.*] Then I remain Cleves' Duchess! Take you note,
While Cleves but yields one subject of this stamp,
I stand her lady till she waves me off!
For her sake, all the Prince claims I withhold;
Return his missive with its due contempt!

[*Casting it away.*]

[so *1849:* fingers, so 256| *1844:* tool] the *1849:* tool, the 258| *1844:* And you *1849:* For you 259| *1844:* one for every <> saw, *1849:* one in every *1863:* saw,— 260| *1844:* That you have simply to receive their *1849:* You simply have to understand their 262–269| *1844:* here? / Will *1849:* § adds 263–268 § 264| *1849:* wisdom; tenderness *1868:* wisdom, tenderness 265| *1849:* cure— *1863:* cure: 266| *1849:* these, embodied *1868:* these embodied 271| *1844:* this—and this—and this? THE <> Cleves— *1849:* this man—this—and *1863:* from Cleves. *1888:* from Cleves: 273| *1844:* of Cleves"— *1868:* of Cleves—" 275| *1844:* describe *1868:* describe, 276| *1844:* you—though *1863:* you, though 280| *1844:* her

GUIBERT [*picking it up.*]—Which to the Prince I will deliver, lady,
(Note it down, Gaucelme)—with your message too!
THE DUCHESS I think the office is a subject's, sir!
—Either . . . . how style you him?—my special guarder
The Marshal's—for who knows but violence
May follow the delivery?—Or, perhaps,
My Chancellor's—for law may be to urge
On its receipt!—Or, even my Chamberlain's—
For I may violate established form!
[*To* VALENCE.] Sir,—for the half-hour till this service ends,
Will you become all these to me?
VALENCE [*falling on his knee.*] My liege!
THE DUCHESS Give me! [*The* COURTIERS *present their badges of office.*]
[*Putting them by.*] Whatever was their virtue once,
They need new consecration. [*Raising* VALENCE.] Are you mine?
I will be Duchess yet! [*She retires.*]
THE COURTIERS Our Duchess yet!
A glorious lady! Worthy love and dread!
I'll stand by her,—And I, whate'er betide!
GUIBERT [*to* VALENCE.] Well done, well done, sir! I care not who knows,
You have done nobly and I envy you—
Tho' I am but unfairly used, I think:
For when one gets a place like this I hold,
One gets too the remark that its mere wages,
The pay and the preferment, make our prize.
Talk about zeal and faith apart from these,
We're laughed at—much would zeal and faith subsist
Without these also! Yet, let these be stopped,
Our wages discontinue,—then, indeed,
Our zeal and faith, (we hear on every side,)
Are not released—having been pledged away

Lady *1849:* lady 284| *1844:* deliver, Lady, *1868:* lady, 285| *1844:* [Note <> Gaucelme]—with *1888:* (Note <> Gaucelme)—with 287| *1844:*—Either . . . how *1888:*—Either . . . . how 289| *1844:* delivery!—Or *1868:* delivery?—Or 294| *1844:* My Liege! *1868:* liege! 295| *1844: by.*]—Whatever *1888: by.*] Whatever 296| *1844:* There needs new consecration! [*Raising* *1849:* They need *1868:* consecration. [*Raising* 297| *1844:*—I *1888:* I 299| *1844:* and *1888:* her,—And 300| *1844:* knows *1849:* knows, 301| *1849:* nobly, and *1868:* nobly and 305| *1844:* prize— *1863:* prize. 308–310| *1844:* stopped, / Our <> faith, we <> side, *1849:* stopped, / Our wages discontinue,—then, indeed, / Our *1863:*

I wonder, for what zeal and faith in turn?
Hard money purchased me my place! No, no—
I'm right, sir—but your wrong is better still,
If I had time and skill to argue it.
Therefore, I say, I'll serve you, how you please—
If you like,—fight you, as you seem to wish—
(The kinder of me that, in sober truth,
I never dreamed I did you any harm) . . .
GAUCELME —Or, kinder still, you'll introduce, no doubt,
His merits to the Prince who's just at hand,
And let no hint drop he's made Chancellor
And Chamberlain and Heaven knows what beside!
CLUGNET [*to* VALENCE.] You stare, young sir, and threaten! Let me say,
That at your age, when first I came to court,
I was not much above a gentleman;
While now . . .
VALENCE —You are Head-Lackey? With your office
I have not yet been graced, sir!
OTHER COURTIERS [*to* CLUGNET.] Let him talk!
Fidelity, disinterestedness,
Excuse so much! Men claim my worship ever
Who staunchly and steadfastly . . .

Enter ADOLF.

ADOLF The Prince arrives.
COURTIERS Ha? How?
ADOLF He leaves his guard a stage behind
At Aix, and enters almost by himself.
1ST COURTIER The Prince! This foolish business puts all out.
2ND COURTIER Let Gaucelme speak first!
3RD COURTIER Better I began
About the state of Juliers: should one say

---

faith, (we <> side,) 312| *1844:* wonder with what *1863:* wonder, with *1868:* wonder, for what 313| *1844:* 'Twas money *1849:* Hard money 319| *1844:* harm)— *1863:* harm) . . . 322| *1844:* made Chancellor, *1868:* made Chancellor 323| *1844:* And Chamberlain, and *1868:* And Chamberlain and 328| *1844:* graced, Sir *1849:* sir *1868:* talk *1888:* talk! 329| *1844:* Fidelity—disinterestedness— *1863:* Fidelity, disinterestedness, 330| *1844:* claimed *1868:* claim 331| *1844:* Who, staunch and <> arrives! *1863:* Who, staunchly and *1868:* Who staunchly <> arrives. 334| *1844:* out! *1868:* out. 336| *1844:* of

All's prosperous and inviting him?

4TH COURTIER —Or rather,

All's prostrate and imploring him?

5TH COURTIER That's best.

Where's the Cleves' paper, by the way?

4TH COURTIER [*to* VALENCE.] Sir—sir—

If you but lend that paper—trust it me,

I'll warrant . . .

5TH COURTIER Softly, sir—the Marshal's duty!

CLUGNET Has not the Chamberlain a hearing first

By virtue of his patent?

GAUCELME Patents?—Duties?

All that, my masters, must begin again!

One word composes the whole controversy:

We're simply now—the Prince's!

THE OTHERS Ay—the Prince's!

Enter SABYNE.

SABYNE Adolf! Bid . . . Oh, no time for ceremony!

Where's whom our lady calls her only subject?

She needs him. Who is here the Duchess's?

VALENCE [*starting from his reverie.*] Most gratefully I follow to her feet.

Juliers—should *1863:* of Juliers: should [337]| *1844:* rather *1868:* rather, [338]| *1844:* him! 5 <> best! *1868:* him?,5 <> best. [340]| *1844:* but give that *1868:* but lend that [345]| *1844:* controversy— *1863:* controversy: [349]| *1844:* him! Who *1868:* him. Who [350]| *1844:* feet! [*Exit.* *1849:* feet! *1868:* feet.

ACT III

AFTERNOON

SCENE—*The Vestibule.*

Enter PRINCE BERTHOLD *and* MELCHIOR.

BERTHOLD A thriving little burgh this Juliers looks.
[*Half-apart.*] Keep Juliers, and as good you kept Cologne:
Better try Aix, though!—
MELCHIOR Please't your Highness speak?
BERTHOLD [*as before.*] Aix, Cologne, Frankfort,—Milan;—Rome!—
MELCHIOR The Grave.
More weary seems your Highness, I remark,
Than sundry conquerors whose path I've watched
Through fire and blood to any prize they gain.
I could well wish you, for your proper sake,
Had met some shade of opposition here
—Found a blunt seneschal refuse unlock,
Or a scared usher lead your steps astray.
You must not look for next achievement's palm
So easily: this will hurt your conquering.
BERTHOLD My next? Ay, as you say, my next and next!
Well, I am tired, that's truth, and moody too,
This quiet entrance-morning: listen why!
Our little burgh, now, Juliers—'tis indeed
One link, however insignificant,
Of the great chain by which I reach my hope,
—A link I must secure; but otherwise,
You'd wonder I esteem it worth my grasp.
Just see what life is, with its shifts and turns!

4| *1844:* MELCHIOR—The *1888:* MELCHIOR The 5| *1844:*—More *1888:* More
13| *1844:* So easy: this <> conquering! *1863:* So easily: this *1868:* conquering.
14| *1844:* next? Ay—as *1888:* next? Ay, as 16| *1844:* entrance-morning; listen *1868:* entrance-morning: listen 19| *1844:* hope— *1863:* hope, 21| *1844:* esteemed *1849:* esteem'd *1863:* esteemed *1868:* esteem 22| *1844:* is with *1849:* is,

It happens now—this very nook—to be
A place that once . . . not a long while since, neither—
When I lived an ambiguous hanger-on
Of foreign courts, and bore my claims about,
Discarded by one kinsman, and the other
A poor priest merely,—then, I say, this place
Shone my ambition's object; to be Duke—
Seemed then, what to be Emperor seems now.
My rights were far from judged as plain and sure
In those days as of late, I promise you:
And 'twas my day-dream, Lady Colombe here
Might e'en compound the matter, pity me,
Be struck, say, with my chivalry and grace
(I was a boy!)—bestow her hand at length,
And make me Duke, in her right if not mine.
Here am I, Duke confessed, at Juliers now.
Hearken: if ever I be Emperor,
Remind me what I felt and said today!
MELCHIOR All this consoles a bookish man like me.
—And so will weariness cling to you. Wrong,
Wrong! Had you sought the lady's court yourself,—
Faced the redoubtables composing it,
Flattered this, threatened that man, bribed the other,—
Pleaded by writ and word and deed, your cause,—
Conquered a footing inch by painful inch,—
And, after long years' struggle, pounced at last
On her for prize,—the right life had been lived,
And justice done to divers faculties
Shut in that brow. Yourself were visible
As you stood victor, then; whom now—(your pardon!)

---

with 24| *1844:* once . . . but a short while *1868:* once . . . not a long while *1888:* once . . not 30| *1844:* then what *1863:* then, what 31| *1844:* from being judged apparent, *1849:* judged as plain *1888:* from judged as plain and sure 32| *1844:* you— *1863:* you: 37| *1844:* me Duke in *1849:* me Duke, in 38| *1844:* now! *1868:* now. 40| *1844:* Will you remind me this, I feel and say? *1849:* Remind me what I felt and said to-day! 41| *1844:* me! *1868:* me. 42| *1844:* you! Wrong— *1863:* you! Wrong, *1868:* you. Wrong, 43–45| *1844:* the Lady's <> yourself,—/ Flattered <> that, and bribed *1849:* yourself,—/ Faced the redoubtables composing it,/ Flattered <> that man, bribed *1868:* lady's 46| *1844:* Pleaded, by *1868:* Pleaded by 47| *1844:* Conquered yourself a <> by inch,— *1849:* Conquered a <> by painful inch,— 51| *1844:* Safe in that brow: yourself *1849:* Shut in *1863:* brow. Yourself 52| *1844:* victor,—you, whom *1849:* victor, then! whom *1868:* then:

I am forced narrowly to search and see,
So are you hid by helps—this Pope, your uncle—
Your cousin, the other King! You are a mind,—
They, body: too much of mere legs-and-arms
Obstructs the mind so! Match these with their like:
Match mind with mind!

BERTHOLD And where's your mind to match?
They show me legs-and-arms to cope withal!
I'd subjugate this city—where's its mind? [*The* COURTIERS *enter slowly.*]

MELCHIOR Got out of sight when you came troops and all!
And in its stead, here greets you flesh-and-blood:
A smug œconomy of both, this first! [*As* CLUGNET *bows obsequiously.*]
Well done, gout, all considered!—I may go?

BERTHOLD Help me receive them!

MELCHIOR Oh, they just will say
What yesterday at Aix their fellows said—
At Treves, the day before! Sir Prince, my friend,
Why do you let your life slip thus?—Meantime,
I have my little Juliers to achieve—
The understanding this tough Platonist,
Your holy uncle disinterred, Amelius:
Lend me a company of horse and foot,
To help me through his tractate—gain my Duchy!

BERTHOLD And Empire, after that is gained, will be—?

MELCHIOR To help me through your uncle's comment, Prince! [*Goes.*]

BERTHOLD Ah? Well: he o'er-refines—the scholar's fault!
How do I let my life slip? Say, this life,
I lead now, differs from the common life
Of other men in mere degree, not kind,

---

whom *1888:* then; whom 53| *1844:* Narrowly am I forced to <> see— *1849:* I am forced narrowly to *1888:* see, 54| *1844:* So by your uncle are you hid, this Pope, *1849:* So are you hid by helps—this Pope, your uncle— 55| *1844:* a Mind,— *1863:* mind,— 56| *1844:* They, Body *1863:* body 57| *1844:* like— *1863:* like: 58| *1844:* But, mind with *1849:* Match mind with 62| *1844:* flesh-and-blood— *1888:* flesh-and-blood: 66| *1844:* said, *1849:* said,— *1888:* said 67| *1844:* before!—Sir *1888:* before! Sir 68| *1844:* thus?—Mean time, *1863:* thus?—Meantime, 70| *1844:* tough Platonist *1849:* tough Platonist, 71| *1844:* disinterred, Amelius— *1849:* disinters *1863:* disinterred *1888:* disinterred, Amelius: 72| *1844:* foot *1849:* foot, 76| *1844:* Ah? Well! He *1849:* he *1868:* Ah? Well: he 77| *1844:* this life *1849:* this life,

Of joys and griefs,—still there is such degree—
Mere largeness in a life is something, sure,—
Enough to care about and struggle for,
In this world: for this world, the size of things;
The sort of things, for that to come, no doubt.
A great is better than a little aim:
And when I wooed Priscilla's rosy mouth
And failed so, under that grey convent-wall,
Was I more happy than I should be now
[*By this time, the* COURTIERS *are ranged before him.*]
If failing of my Empire? Not a whit.
—Here comes the mind, it once had tasked me sore
To baffle, but for my advantages!
All's best as 'tis: these scholars talk and talk. [*Seats himself.*]

THE COURTIERS Welcome our Prince to Juliers!—to his heritage!
Our dutifullest service proffer we!

CLUGNET I, please your Highness, having exercised
The function of Grand Chamberlain at court,
With much acceptance, as men testify . . .

BERTHOLD I cannot greatly thank you, gentlemen!
The Pope declares my claim to the Duchy founded
On strictest justice—you concede it, therefore,
I do not wonder: and the kings my friends
Protest they mean to see such claim enforced,—

80–82| *1844:* and sorrows,—such degree there is— / Enough <> for *1849:* and griefs,—still there is such degree— / Mere largeness in a life is something, sure,— / Enough <> for, *1888:* degree / Mere 83| *1844:* the Size *1863:* size 84| *1844:* The Sort <> doubt! *1863:* sort *1868:* doubt. 85| *1844:* aim— *1863:* aim: 87| *1844:* convent wall, *1849:* convent-wall, 89| *1844:* whit! *1868:* whit. 90| *1844:* the Mind it *1849:* the Mind, it *1863:* mind 91| *1844:* baffle, let advantages alone! *1849:* baffle, but for my advantages! 92| *1844:* 'tis—these <> and talk! *1868:* 'tis: these <> and talk. 93| *1844:* his Heritage! *1868:* heritage! 95| *1844:* please't *1849:* please 96| *1844:* at Court, *1863:* court, 100| *1844:* justice; if you *1888:* justice—you 101| *1844:* wonder—and the Kings *1849:* kings *1863:* wonder: and 102| *1844:* Protesting they will see <> enforced, *1888:* Protest they mean to see

You easily may offer to assist.
But there's a slight discretionary power
To serve me in the matter, you've had long,
Though late you use it. This is well to say—
But could you not have said it months ago?
I'm not denied my own Duke's truncheon, true—
'Tis flung me—I stoop down, and from the ground
Pick it, with all you placid standers-by:
And now I have it, gems and mire at once,
Grace go with it to my soiled hands, you say!
GUIBERT (By Paul, the advocate our doughty friend
Cuts the best figure!)
GAUCELME If our ignorance
May have offended, sure our loyalty . . .
BERTHOLD Loyalty? Yours? Oh—of yourselves you speak!
I mean the Duchess all this time, I hope!
And since I have been forced repeat my claims
As if they never had been urged before,
As I began, so must I end, it seems.
The formal answer to the grave demand!
What says the lady?
COURTIERS [*one to another.*] 1ST COURTIER Marshall! 2ND COURTIER Orator!
GUIBERT A variation of our mistress' way!
Wipe off his boots' dust, Clugnet!—that, he waits!
1ST COURTIER Your place!
2ND COURTIER Just now it was your own!
GUIBERT The devil's!
BERTHOLD [*to* GUIBERT.] Come forward, friend—you with the paper, there!
Is Juliers the first city I've obtained?
By this time, I may boast proficiency
In each decorum of the circumstance.
Give it me as she gave it—the petition,
Demand, you style it! What's required, in brief?

<> enforced,— 103| *1844:* assist us. *1888:* assist. 110| *1844:* standers-by— *1888:* standers-by: 113| *1844:* the Advocate *1868:* advocate 116| *1844:* Loyalty? Yours?—Oh *1888:* Loyalty? Yours? Oh 117| *1844:* —I mean *1888:* I mean 119| *1844:* been made before, *1888:* been urged before, 120| *1844:* so probably I end. *1849:* so must I end, it seems. 121| *1844:* demand— *1863:* demand! 124| *1844:* that he *1849:* that, he 126| *1844:* paper there! *1849:* paper, there! 128| *1844:* time I *1849:* time, I 129| *1844:* circumstance! *1868:* circumstance. 130| *1844:* petition *1888:* petition, 131| *1844:* (Demand <>

What title's reservation, appanage's
Allowance? I heard all at Treves, last week.
GAUCELME [*to* GUIBERT.] "Give it him as she gave it!"
GUIBERT And why not?
[*To* BERTHOLD.] The lady crushed your summons thus together,
And bade me, with the very greatest scorn
So fair a frame could hold, inform you . . .
COURTIERS Stop—
Idiot!
GUIBERT —Inform you she denied your claim,
Defied yourself! (I tread upon his heel,
The blustering advocate!)
BERTHOLD By heaven and earth!
Dare you jest, sir?
GUIBERT Did they at Treves, last week?
BERTHOLD [*starting up.*] Why then, I look much bolder than I knew,
And you prove better actors than I thought:
Since, as I live, I took you as you entered
For just so many dearest friends of mine,
Fled from the sinking to the rising power
—The sneaking'st crew, in short, I e'er despised!
Whereas, I am alone here for the moment,
With every soldier left behind at Aix!
Silence? That means the worst? I thought as much!
What follows next then?
COURTIERS Gracious Prince, he raves!
GUIBERT He asked the truth and why not get the truth?
BERTHOLD Am I a prisoner? Speak, will somebody?
—But why stand paltering with imbeciles?
Let me see her, or . . .
GUIBERT Her, without her leave,
Shall no one see: she's Duchess yet!
COURTIERS [*footsteps without, as they are disputing.*] Good chance!

---

it)—what's *1868:* Demand <> it—What's *1888:* it! What's 133| *1844:* Allowance?—I <> week! *1868:* week. *1888:* Allowance? I 138| *1844:* Idiot!—GUIBERT *1863:* Idiot! GUIBERT 140| *1844:* blustering Advocate <> By Heaven *1849:* heaven *1868:* advocate 141| *1844:* GUIBERT Did he at Treves last *1849:* GUIBERT Did they at Treves, last 143| *1844:* thought— *1863:* thought, *1868:* thought— *1888:* thought: 148| *1844:* moment! *1849:* moment— *1863:* moment, 150| *1844:* worst—I *1868:* worst? I 151| *1844:* COURTIERS Gracious Prince—he *1888:* COURTIERS Gracious Prince, he 152| *1844:* not have the *1849:* not get the 155| *1844:* GUIBERT Her without *1849:* GUIBERT Her, without 156| *1844:* see—she's

She's here—the Lady Colombe's self!

BERTHOLD 'Tis well!

[*Aside.*] Array a handful thus against my world?
Not ill done, truly! Were not this a mind
To match one's mind with? Colombe! Let us wait!
I failed so, under that grey convent wall!
She comes.

GUIBERT The Duchess! Strangers, range yourselves!

[*As the* DUCHESS *enters in conversation with* VALENCE, BERTHOLD *and the* COURTIERS *fall back a little.*]

THE DUCHESS Presagefully it beats, presagefully,
My heart: the right is Berthold's and not mine.

VALENCE Grant that he has the right, dare I mistrust
Your power to acquiesce so patiently
As you believe, in such a dream-like change
Of fortune—change abrupt, profound, complete?

THE DUCHESS Ah, the first bitterness is over now!
Bitter I may have felt it to confront
The truth, and ascertain those natures' value
I had so counted on; that was a pang:
But I did bear it, and the worst is over.
Let the Prince take them!

VALENCE And take Juliers too?
—Your people without crosses, wands and chains—
Only with hearts?

THE DUCHESS There I feel guilty, sir!
I cannot give up what I never had:
For I ruled these, not them—these stood between.
Shall I confess, sir? I have heard by stealth
Of Berthold from the first; more news and more:
Closer and closer swam the thundercloud,
But I was safely housed with these, I knew.
At times when to the casement I would turn,

1868: see: she's 160| *1844:* with? Colombe!—Let *1888:* with? Colombe! Let
161| *1844:* gray convent-wall, *1849:* grey convent-wall! *1868:* convent wall!
162| *1844:* comes! GUIBERT *1868:* comes. GUIBERT 164| *1844:* heart—the <> mine! *1863:* heart: the *1868:* mine. 172| *1844:* on—that <> pang— *1868:* on; that <> pang: 173| *1844:* over: *1868:* over. 174| *1844:* VALENCE —And *1888:* VALENCE And 175| *1844:* —Your People <> wands, and *1868:* people <> wands and 178| *1844:* For these I ruled, not *1868:* For I ruled these, not
180| *1844:* first—more news and more— *1849:* first: more news and more; *1863:* first; more news and more: 181| *1844:* thunder-cloud, *1868:* thunder cloud, *1888:* thundercloud, 182| *1844:* knew! *1888:* knew. 183| *1844:*

At a bird's passage or a flower-trail's play,
I caught the storm's red glimpses on its edge—
Yet I was sure some one of all these friends
Would interpose: I followed the bird's flight
Or plucked the flower: some one would interpose!
VALENCE Not one thought on the People—and Cleves there!
THE DUCHESS Now, sadly conscious my real sway was missed,
Its shadow goes without so much regret:
Else could I not again thus calmly bid you,
Answer Prince Berthold!
VALENCE   Then you acquiesce?
THE DUCHESS Remember over whom it was I ruled!
GUIBERT [*stepping forward.*] Prince Berthold, yonder, craves an audience, lady!
THE DUCHESS [*to* VALENCE.] I only have to turn, and I shall face
Prince Berthold! Oh, my very heart is sick!
It is the daughter of a line of Dukes
This scornful insolent adventurer
Will bid depart from my dead father's halls!
I shall not answer him—dispute with him—
But, as he bids, depart! Prevent it, sir!
Sir—but a mere day's respite! Urge for me
—What I shall call to mind I should have urged
When time's gone by: 'twill all be mine, you urge!
A day—an hour—that I myself may lay
My rule down! 'Tis too sudden—must not be!
The world's to hear of it! Once done—for ever!
How will it read, sir? How be sung about?
Prevent it!
BERTHOLD [*approaching.*] Your frank indignation, lady,

---

turn *1849:* times, when <> turn, *1888:* times when 186| *1844:* of those about me *1849:* of all these friends 187| *1844:* interpose—I <> flight, *1863:* interpose: I *1868:* flight 188| *1844:* flower—some *1888:* flower: some 189| *1863:* § omitted punctuation probably printer's error § there *1868:* there! 190| *1844:* So, sadly *1868:* Now, sadly 195| *1844:* audience, Lady! *1868:* lady! 198| *1844:* line of Dukes, *1888:* Dukes 203| *1844:* a day's sole respite *1849:* a mere day's respite 205| *1844:* by—'twill <> mine you *1849:* mine, you *1888:* by: 'twill 210| *1844:* indignation, Lady, *1868:* lady, 211| *1844:* me! Overbold I seem— *1868:* me.

Cannot escape me. Overbold I seem;
But somewhat should be pardoned my surprise
At this reception,—this defiance, rather.
And if, for their and your sake, I rejoice
Your virtues could inspire a trusty few
To make such gallant stand in your behalf,
I cannot but be sorry, for my own,
Your friends should force me to retrace my steps:
Since I no longer am permitted speak
After the pleasant peaceful course prescribed
No less by courtesy than relationship—
Which I remember, if you once forgot.
But never must attack pass unrepelled.
Suffer that, through you, I demand of these,
Who controverts my claim to Juliers?

THE DUCHESS —Me
You say, you do not speak to—

BERTHOLD Of your subjects
I ask, then: whom do you accredit? Where
Stand those should answer?

VALENCE [*advancing*.] The lady is alone.

BERTHOLD Alone, and thus? So weak and yet so bold?

VALENCE I said she was alone—

BERTHOLD And weak, I said.

VALENCE When is man strong until he feels alone?
It was some lonely strength at first, be sure,
Created organs, such as those you seek,
By which to give its varied purpose shape:
And, naming the selected ministrants,
Took sword, and shield, and sceptre,—each, a man!

Overbold I seem; 212–214| *1844:* surprise. / And <> sakes *1849:* surprise, / At this reception,—this defiance, rather. / And *1888:* surprise / At </> sake 217–221| *1844:* own, / Since <> speak / No <> relationship *1849:* own, / Your friends should force me to retrace my steps, / Since <> speak / After the pleasant peaceful course prescribed / No *1868:* steps. / Since *1888:* steps: / Since <//> relationship— 222| *1844:* —If you forgot once, I remember now! *1849:* Which, if you once forgot, I still remember: *1863:* remember. *1868:* Which I remember, if you once forgot. 223| *1844:* But, unrepelled, attack must never pass. *1849:* But never must attack pass unrepelled. 224| *1844:* Suffer, through you, your subjects I demand, *1849:* Suffer, that through you, I demand of these, *1888:* Suffer that, through 225| *1844:* THE DUCHESS—Me, *1888:* THE DUCHESS—Me
226| *1844:* say you *1849:* say, you 227| *1844:* ask then *1849:* ask, then
228| *1844:* [*advancing*.] The Lady is alone! *1868:* lady *1888:* alone. 230| *1844:* BERTHOLD—And *1888:* BERTHOLD And 234| *1844:* shape— *1888:* shape:

That strength performed its work and passed its way:
You see our lady: there, the old shapes stand!
—A Marshal, Chamberlain, and Chancellor—
"Be helped their way, into their death put life
And find advantage!"—so you counsel us.
But let strength feel alone, seek help itself,—
And, as the inland-hatched sea-creature hunts
The sea's breast out,—as, littered 'mid the waves
The desert-brute makes for the desert's joy,
So turns our lady to her true resource,
Passing o'er hollow fictions, worn-out types,
—And I am first her instinct fastens on.
And prompt I say, as clear as heart can speak,
The People will not have you; nor shall have!
It is not merely I shall go bring Cleves
And fight you to the last,—though that does much,
And men and children,—ay, and women too,
Fighting for home, are rather to be feared
Than mercenaries fighting for their pay—
But, say you beat us, since such things have been,
And, where this Juliers laughed, you set your foot
Upon a steaming bloody plash—what then?
Stand you the more our lord that there you stand?
Lord it o'er troops whose force you concentrate,
A pillared flame whereto all ardours tend—
Lord it 'mid priests whose schemes you amplify,
A cloud of smoke 'neath which all shadows brood—
But never, in this gentle spot of earth,
Can you become our Colombe, our play-queen,
For whom, to furnish lilies for her hair,
We'd pour our veins forth to enrich the soil.
—Our conqueror? Yes!—Our despot? Yes!—Our Duke?

238| *1844:* our Lady *1868:* lady 240| *1844:* Be *1849:* "Be 241| *1844:* advantage,—so <> us! *1849:* advantage!"—so <> us: *1863:* us. 244| *1844:* waves, *1868:* waves 245–248| *1844:* joy, / —So, I <> on; *1849:* joy, / So turns our lady to her true resource, / Passing o'er hollow fictions, worn-out types, / —So <> on! *1868:* types, / —And I <> on. 249| *1844:* say so clear *1849:* say, so *1863:* say, as clear 252| *1844:* last, though <> much,— *1849:* last,—though <> much, 259| *1844:* our Lord as there *1849:* our Lord that there *1868:* lord 262| *1844:* it 'mongst priests *1849:* it 'mid priests 266| *1844:* Whom we, to *1849:* For whom, to 267| *1844:* Would pour <> soil!

Know yourself, know us!
BERTHOLD [*who has been in thought.*] Know your lady, also!
[*Very deferentially.*]—To whom I needs must exculpate myself
For having made a rash demand, at least.
Wherefore to you, sir, who appear to be
Her chief adviser, I submit my claims, [*Giving papers.*]
But, this step taken, take no further step,
Until the Duchess shall pronounce their worth.
Here be our meeting-place; at night, its time:
Till when I humbly take the lady's leave!
[*He withdraws. As the* DUCHESS *turns to* VALENCE, *the* COURTIERS *interchange glances and come forward a little.*]
1ST COURTIER So, this was their device!
2ND COURTIER No bad device!
3RD COURTIER You'd say they love each other, Guibert's friend
From Cleves, and she, the Duchess!
4TH COURTIER —And moreover,
That all Prince Berthold comes for, is to help
Their loves!
5TH COURTIER Pray, Guibert, what is next to do?
GUIBERT [*advancing.*] I laid my office at the Duchess' foot—
OTHERS And I—and I—and I!
THE DUCHESS I took them, sirs.
GUIBERT [*apart to* VALENCE.] And now, sir, I am simple knight again—
Guibert, of the great ancient house, as yet
That never bore affront; whate'er your birth,—
As things stand now, I recognize yourself
(If you'll accept experience of some date)
As like to be the leading man o' the time,
Therefore as much above me now, as I
Seemed above you this morning. Then, I offered
To fight you: will you be as generous

1849: We'd pour *1888:* soil. 271| *1844:* demand at *1849:* demand, at 273| *1844:* The chief *1849:* Her chief 276| *1844:* meeting-place, at night its time— *1849:* meeting-place; at night, its time: 277| *1844:* the Lady's *1863:* lady's 279–282| *1844:* 3 COURTIER They <> friend and she! / 4 COURTIER Plainly! 5 COURTIER *1849:* 3 COURTIER You'd say they <> friend / From Cleves, and she, the Duchess! 4 COURTIER—And moreover, / That all Prince Berthold comes for, is to help / Their loves! 5 COURTIER 283| *1844:* lay <> foot! *1849:* laid <> foot— 284| *1844:* sirs! *1868:* sirs. 285| *1844:* GUIBERT [*to* <> sir, simple knight again am I— *1849:* GUIBERT [*apart to* <> sir, I am simple knight again— 286| *1844:* Guibert of *1849:* Guibert, of 287| *1844:* affront: whate'er *1863:* affront; whate'er 291| *1844:* And so as

And now fight me?
VALENCE Ask when my life is mine!
GUIBERT ('Tis hers now!)
CLUGNET [*apart to* VALENCE, *as* GUIBERT *turns from him.*]
You, sir, have insulted me
Grossly,—will grant me, too, the selfsame favour
You've granted him, just now, I make no question?
VALENCE I promise you, as him, sir.
CLUGNET Do you so?
Handsomely said! I hold you to it, sir.
You'll get me reinstated in my office
As you will Guibert!
THE DUCHESS I would be alone!
[*They begin to retire slowly; as* VALENCE *is about to follow*—]
Alone, sir—only with my heart: you stay!
GAUCELME You hear that? Ah, light breaks upon me! Cleves—
It was at Cleves some man harangued us all—
With great effect,—so those who listened said,
My thoughts being busy elsewhere: was this he?
Guibert,—your strange, disinterested man!
Your uncorrupted, if uncourtly friend!
The modest worth you mean to patronize!
He cares about no Duchesses, not he—
His sole concern is with the wrongs of Cleves!
What, Guibert? What, it breaks on you at last?
GUIBERT Would this hall's floor were a mine's roof! I'd back
And in her very face . . .
GAUCELME Apply the match
That fired the train,—and where would you be, pray?
GUIBERT With him!
GAUCELME Stand, rather, safe outside with me!
The mine's charged: shall I furnish you the match
And place you properly? To the antechamber!

1849: Therefore as 295| *1844:* ('Tis Hers <> CLUGNET [*advancing to* VALENCE]. You *1849:* hers <> CLUGNET [*apart to* VALENCE, *as* GUIBERT *turns from him*]. You 298| *1844:* you as him, sir! CLUGNET *1849:* you, as *1868:* sir. CLUGNET 299| *1844:* sir! *1868:* sir. 302–313| *1844:* heart,—you stay! / GUIBERT Would *1849:* § adds 303–312 § 302| *1863:* § omission of punctuation probably printer's error: § stay *1868:* heart: you stay! 309| *1849:* patronise! *1863:* patronize! 311| *1849:* sole contest is *1868:* sole concern is 313| *1844:* roof!—I'll back *1849:* roof—I'd back *1888:* roof! I'd 315| *1844:* fires <> where will you *1849:* fired <> where would you 317| *1844:* charged—shall *1888:* charged: shall 318| *1844:* properly?—To the

GUIBERT Can you?

GAUCELME Try me! Your friend's in fortune!

GUIBERT Quick—
To the antechamber! He is pale with bliss!

GAUCELME No wonder! Mark her eyes!

GUIBERT To the antechamber!

[*The* COURTIERS *retire.*]

THE DUCHESS Sir, could you know all you have done for me
You were content! You spoke, and I am saved.

VALENCE Be not too sanguine, lady! Ere you dream,
That transient flush of generosity
Fades off, perchance. The man, beside, is gone,—
Him we might bend; but see, the papers here—
Inalterably his requirement stays,
And cold hard words have we to deal with now.
In that large eye there seemed a latent pride,
To self-denial not incompetent,
But very like to hold itself dispensed
From such a grace: however, let us hope!
He is a noble spirit in noble form.
I wish he less had bent that brow to smile
As with the fancy how he could subject
Himself upon occasion to—himself!
From rudeness, violence, you rest secure;
But do not think your Duchy rescued yet!

---

ante-chamber! *1863:* antechamber! *1888:* properly? To 319| *1844:* me!—Your *1888:* me! Your 320| *1844:* ante-chamber!—He *1863:* antechamber *1888:* antechamber! He 321| *1844:* ante-chamber! *1863:* antechamber! 323| *1844:* spoke and <> saved! *1849:* spoke, and *1888:* saved. 324| *1844:* sanguine, Lady! Ere now, even, *1849:* sanguine, Lady! Ere you dream, *1868:* lady 326–328| *1844:* perchance! The man and mood are gone— / Inalterably *1849:* man, beside, is gone,— / Whom we might bend; but see the papers here— / Inalterably *1863:* see, the *1868:* gone,— / Him we *1888:* perchance. The man 330| *1844:* there was a <> pride *1849:* there seemed a <> pride, 333| *1844:* grace—however *1863:* grace: however 334| *1844:* form! *1863:* form.

THE DUCHESS You,—who have opened a new world to me,
Will never take the faded language up
Of that I leave? My Duchy—keeping it,
Or losing it—is that my sole world now?
VALENCE Ill have I spoken if you thence despise
Juliers; although the lowest, on true grounds,
Be worth more than the highest rule, on false:
Aspire to rule, on the true grounds!
THE DUCHESS Nay, hear—
False, I will never—rash, I would not be!
This is indeed my birthday—soul and body,
Its hours have done on me the work of years.
You hold the requisition: ponder it!
If I have right, my duty's plain: if he—
Say so, nor ever change a tone of voice!
At night you meet the Prince; meet me at eve!
Till when, farewell! This discomposes you?
Believe in your own nature, and its force
Of renovating mine! I take my stand
Only as under me the earth is firm:
So, prove the first step stable, all will prove.
That first, I choose: [*Laying her hand on his.*]—the next to take, choose you! [*She withdraws.*]
VALENCE [*after a pause.*] What drew down this on me?—on me, dead once,
She thus bids live,—since all I hitherto

342| *1844:* it *1849:* it, 349| *1844:* my Birthday *1868:* birthday 351| *1844:* the Requisition *1863:* requisition 352| *1844:* right—my <> if He— *1863:* right, my <> he— 353| *1844:* so—nor *1863:* so, nor 354| *1844:* night the Prince you meet—meet <> eve, *1849:* night you meet the Prince—meet <> eve; *1863:* the Prince; meet <> eve: *1868:* eve!
357| *1844:* mine. I *1868:* mine! I 358| *1844:* firm— *1863:* firm: 359| *1844:* will be! *1863:* will prove! *1868:* will prove. 360| *1844:* choose— [*Laying* *1888:* choose: [*Laying* 361| *1844:* me! On me—dead once— *1863:* me? On me, dead once,

Thought dead in me, youth's ardours and emprise,
Burst into life before her, as she bids
Who needs them. Whither will this reach, where end?
Her hand's print burns on mine . . . Yet she's above—
So very far above me! All's too plain:
I served her when the others sank away,
And she rewards me as such souls reward—
The changed voice, the suffusion of the cheek,
The eye's acceptance, the expressive hand,
—Reward, that's little, in her generous thought,
Though all to me . . .
                                        I cannot so disclaim
Heaven's gift, nor call it other than it is!
She loves me!
[*Looking at the* PRINCE's *papers.*]—Which love, these, perchance, forbid.
Can I decide against myself—pronounce
She is the Duchess and no mate for me?
—Cleves, help me! Teach me,—every haggard face,—
To sorrow and endure! I will do right
Whatever be the issue. Help me, Cleves!

1868: me?—on 363| *1844:* emprize, *1863:* emprise, 365| *1844:* them!—Whither *1863:* them! Whither *1868:* them. Whither 366| *1844:* mine . . Yet *1849:* mine . . . Yet 367| *1844:* plain— *1863:* plain: 369–372| *1844:* souls reward— / —Reward <> little, that is nought to her, *1849:* souls reward— / The changed voice, the suffusion of the cheek, / The eye's acceptance, the expressive hand— / —Reward <> little, in her generous thought, *1863:* hand, / —Reward 373| *1844:* me . . . I *1849:* me . . . ¶ I 374| *1844:* gift nor *1849:* gift, nor 375| *1844:* these forbid, perchance! *1849:* these, perchance, forbid! *1863:* forbid. *1868:* these perchance *1888:* these, perchance 380| *1844:* issue—help me, Cleves! [*Exit.* *1849:* me, Cleves! *1863:* issue. Help

ACT IV

EVENING

S C E N E—*An Antechamber.*

Enter the COURTIERS.

MAUFROY Now, then, that we may speak—how spring this mine?
GAUCELME Is Guibert ready for its match? He cools!
Not so friend Valence with the Duchess there!
"Stay, Valence! Are not you my better self?"
And her cheek mantled—
GUIBERT Well, she loves him, sir:
And more,—since you will have it I grow cool,—
She's right: he's worth it.
GAUCELME For his deeds today?
Say so!
GUIBERT What should I say beside?
GAUCELME Not this—
For friendship's sake leave this for me to say—
That we're the dupes of an egregious cheat!
This plain unpractised suitor, who found way
To the Duchess through the merest die's turn-up
A year ago, had seen her and been seen,
Loved and been loved.
GUIBERT Impossible!
GAUCELME —Nor say,
How sly and exquisite a trick, moreover,
Was this which—taking not their stand on facts

1| *1844:* Now then *1888:* Now, then 4| *1844:* "Stay, Valence—are *1863:* "Stay, Valence! are *1868:* "Stay, Valence! Are 5| *1844:* sir— *1863:* sir: 11| *1844:* plain, unpractised *1868:* plain unpractised 12| *1844:* thro' <> turn-up— *1863:* through *1868:* turn-up 13| *1844:* ago had *1849:* ago, had 14| *1844:* been loved—GUIBERT *1863:* been loved. GUIBERT 16| *1844:* not his stand *1849:* not

Boldly, for that had been endurable,
But worming on their way by craft, they choose
Resort to, rather,—and which you and we,
Sheep-like, assist them in the playing-off!
The Duchess thus parades him as preferred,
Not on the honest ground of preference,
Seeing first, liking more, and there an end—
But as we all had started equally,
And at the close of a fair race he proved
The only valiant, sage and loyal man.
Herself, too, with the pretty fits and starts,—
The careless, winning, candid ignorance
Of what the Prince might challenge or forego—
She had a hero in reserve! What risk
Ran she? This deferential easy Prince
Who brings his claims for her to ratify
—He's just her puppet for the nonce! You'll see,—
Valence pronounces, as is equitable,
Against him: off goes the confederate:
As equitably, Valence takes her hand!
THE CHANCELLOR You run too fast: her hand, no subject takes.
Do not our archives hold her father's will?
That will provides against such accident,
And gives next heir, Prince Berthold, the reversion

---

their stand 18| *1844:* But, worming in his way by craft, he chose *1849:* in their way by craft, they choose *1863:* worming on their *1868:* But worming 20| *1844:* assist him in the playing off! *1849:* assist them in *1888:* playing-off! 21| *1844:* The fruit is, she prefers him to ourselves, *1849:* The Duchess thus parades him as preferred, 22| *1844:* the simple ground *1849:* the honest ground 23| *1844:* First seeing, liking more, and so an *1849:* Seeing first, liking more, and there an 26| *1844:* sage, and *1868:* sage and 27| *1844:* And she, too *1863:* Herself, too 28| *1844:* And careless *1849:* The careless 32| *1844:* That brings *1849:* Who brings 37| *1844:* fast—her hand no <> takes! *1849:* hand, no *1863:* fast: her <> takes. 38| *1844:* our Archives <> father's Will? *1863:* archives <> will? 39| *1844:* Against such accident that will provides, *1849:* That will provides against such accident,

Of Juliers, which she forfeits, wedding so.
GAUCELME I know that, well as you,—but does the Prince?
Knows Berthold, think you, that this plan, he helps,
For Valence's ennoblement,—would end,
If crowned with the success which seems its due,
In making him the very thing he plays,
The actual Duke of Juliers? All agree
That Colombe's title waived or set aside,
He is next heir.
THE CHANCELLOR Incontrovertibly.
GAUCELME Guibert, your match, now, to the train!
GUIBERT Enough!
I'm with you: selfishness is best again.
I thought of turning honest—what a dream!
Let's wake now!
GAUCELME Selfish, friend, you never were:
'Twas but a series of revenges taken
On your unselfishness for prospering ill.
But now that you're grown wiser, what's our course?
GUIBERT —Wait, I suppose, till Valence weds our lady,
And then, if we must needs revenge ourselves,
Apprise the Prince.
GAUCELME —The Prince, ere then dismissed
With thanks for playing his mock part so well?
Tell the Prince now, sir! Ay, this very night,
Ere he accepts his dole and goes his way,
Explain how such a marriage makes him Duke,
Then trust his gratitude for the surprise!
GUIBERT —Our lady wedding Valence all the same
As if the penalty were undisclosed?
Good! If she loves, she'll not disown her love,

41–49| *1844:* so. / he <> heir? THE <> Incontrovertibly! *1849:* § adds 42–48 § 49| *1849:* heir. ¶ THE *1863:* THE CHANCELLOR Incontrovertibly. 51| *1844:* you—selfishness <> again! *1863:* you: selfishness *1868:* again. 53| *1844:* were— *1863:* were: 55| *1844:* Upon unselfishness that prospered ill. *1849:* On your unselfishness for prospering ill. 57| *1844:* our Lady, *1863:* lady, 58–61| *1844:* And then apprise the Prince—GAUCELME—Ere then, retired? / Tell <> night— *1849:* And then, if we must needs revenge ourselves, / Apprise the Prince—GAUCELME—The Prince, ere then dismissed / With thanks for playing his mock part so well? / Tell *1863:* the Prince. GAUCELME *1888:* night, 62–67| *1844:* way, / Tell what has been, declare what's like to be, / And really makes him all he feigned himself; / Then <> surprise! / GUIBERT Good! I am sure she'll not *1849:* way, / Explain how such a marriage makes him Duke, / Then

Throw Valence up. I wonder you see that.

GAUCELME The shame of it—the suddenness and shame!
Within her, the inclining heart—without,
A terrible array of witnesses—
And Valence by, to keep her to her word,
With Berthold's indignation or disgust!
We'll try it!—Not that we can venture much.
Her confidence we've lost for ever: Berthold's
Is all to gain.

GUIBERT Tonight, then, venture we!
Yet—if lost confidence might be renewed?

GAUCELME Never in noble natures! With the base ones,—
Twist off the crab's claw, wait a smarting-while,
And something grows and grows and gets to be
A mimic of the lost joint, just so like
As keeps in mind it never, never will
Replace its predecessor! Crabs do that:
But lop the lion's foot—and . . .

GUIBERT To the Prince!

GAUCELME [*aside.*] And come what will to the lion's foot, I pay you,
My cat's-paw, as I long have yearned to pay.
[*Aloud.*] Footsteps! Himself! 'Tis Valence breaks on us,
Exulting that their scheme succeeds. We'll hence—
And perfect ours ! Consult the archives, first—
Then, fortified with knowledge, seek the Hall!

CLUGNET [*to* GAUCELME *as they retire.*] You have not smiled so since your father died!

<> surprise! / GUIBERT—Our Lady wedding Valence all the same / As if the penalty were undisclosed! / Good! If she loves, she'll *1863:* lady *1868:* undisclosed? / Good
68| *1844:* up—I <> that! *1863:* up. I <> that. 69–72| *1844:* and shame! / With Valence there, to keep *1849:* and shame! / Within her, the inclining heart—without, / A terrible array of witnesses— / With Valence by, to *1863:* witnesses— / And Valence 73| *1844:* And Berthold's own reproaches or disgust— *1849:* And Berthold's indignation or *1863:* With Berthold's <> disgust! 74| *1844:* much! *1849:* much: *1863:* much. 75| *1844:* ever—his *1849:* ever—Berthold's *1863:* ever.—Berthold's *1868:* ever: Berthold's 76| *1844:* Must be to gain! GUIBERT *1849:* Is all to *1868:* gain. GUIBERT 77| *1844:* Yet—may a lost love never be *1849:* Yet—if lost confidence might be 78| *1844:* natures: with *1849:* natures! With
81| *1844:* the joint, and just *1849:* the lost joint, just 84| *1844:* the Lion's foot and—GUIBERT *1849:* foot—and GUIBERT *1863:* lion's <> and . . . GUIBERT 85| *1844:* you *1863:* you, 86| *1844:* pay! *1888:* pay. 87| *1844:* Footsteps . . Himself <> us! *1863:* Footsteps! Himself <> us, 88| *1844:* Waits her to boast their <> succeeds!—We'll *1849:* Exulting that their *1863:* succeeds. We'll 89–91| *1844:* ours!

As they retire, enter VALENCE *with papers.*

VALENCE So must it be! I have examined these
With scarce a palpitating heart—so calm,
Keeping her image almost wholly off,
Setting upon myself determined watch,
Repelling to the uttermost his claims:
And the result is—all men would pronounce
And not I, only, the result to be—
Berthold is heir; she has no shade of right
To the distinction which divided us,
But, suffered to rule first, I know not why,
Her rule connived at by those Kings and Popes,
To serve some devil's-purpose,—now 'tis gained,
Whate'er it was, the rule expires as well.
—Valence, this rapture . . . selfish can it be?
Eject it from your heart, her home!—It stays!
Ah, the brave world that opens on us both!
—Do my poor townsmen so esteem it? Cleves,—
I need not your pale faces! This, reward
For service done to you? Too horrible!
I never served you: 'twas myself I served—
Nay, served not—rather saved from punishment
Which, had I failed you then, would plague me now.
My life continues yours, and your life, mine.
But if, to take God's gift, I swerve no step—
Cleves! If I breathe no prayer for it—if she, [*Footsteps without.*]
Colombe, that comes now, freely gives herself—
Will Cleves require, that, turning thus to her,

To the Archives, and the Hall! / CLUGNET *1849:* ours! Consult the Archives, first— / Then, fortified with knowledge, seek the Hall! / CLUGNET *1863:* archives 96| *1844:* claims, *1888:* claims: 97| *1844:* is . . . all *1868:* is—all 99| *1844:* is Heir *1863:* heir 101–105| *1844:* suffered rule first by these Kings and Popes / To serve some devil's-purpose,—now 'tis gain'd, / To serve some devil's-purpose must withdraw! / —Valence <> rapture . . selfish *1849:* suffered to rule first I know not why, / Her rule connived at by those Kings and Popes, / To serve some devil's-purpose,—now 'tis gained, / Whate'er it was, the rule expires as well. / —Valence *1863:* first, I *1888:* rapture . . . selfish 107| *1844:* opens to us *1849:* opens on us 108| *1844:* . . . Do *1863:*—Do 110| *1844:* to them? Too *1849:* to you? Too 111| *1844:* served them—'twas <> served! *1849:* served you—'twas *1863:* you: 'twas *1868:* myself I served— 112| *1844:* Nay—served *1863:* Nay, served 113| *1844:* now! *1888:* now. 114| *1844:* mine— *1863:* mine. 116| *1844:* Cleves,—if no prayer I breathe for *1849:* Cleves!—if I

I . . .

Enter PRINCE BERTHOLD.

Pardon, sir! I did not look for you
Till night, i' the Hall; nor have as yet declared
My judgment to the lady.
BERTHOLD So I hoped.
VALENCE And yet I scarcely know why that should check
The frank disclosure of it first to you—
What her right seems, and what, in consequence,
She will decide on.
BERTHOLD That I need not ask.
VALENCE You need not: I have proved the lady's mind:
And, justice being to do, dare act for her.
BERTHOLD Doubtless she has a very noble mind.
VALANCE Oh, never fear but she'll in each conjuncture
Bear herself bravely! She no whit depends
On circumstance; as she adorns a throne,
She had adorned . . .
BERTHOLD A cottage—in what book
Have I read that, of every queen that lived?
A throne! You have not been instructed, sure,
To forestall my request?
VALENCE 'Tis granted, sir!
My heart instructs me. I have scrutinized
Your claims . . .
BERTHOLD Ah—claims, you mean, at first preferred?
I come, before the hour appointed me,

---

breathe no prayer for *1868:* Cleves!—If *1888:* Cleves! If I 119| *1844:* I . . . —Pardon, sir—I had not looked for *1849:* sir—I did not look for *1863:* I . . . Pardon *1868:* sir! I 120| *1849:* in *1888:* i' 121| *1844:* the Lady! BERTHOLD *1863:* lady. BERTHOLD 122–125| *1844:* yet I scarce know wherefore that prevents / Disclosing it to you—disclosing even / What she determines—BERTHOLD *1849:* yet I scarcely know why that should check / The frank disclosure of it first to you— / WHat her right seems, and what, in consequence, / She will decide on—BERTHOLD *1888:* on. BERTHOLD
126| *1844:* the Lady's mind— *1863:* lady's *1888:* mind: 128| *1844:* mind! *1863:* mind. 130| *1844:* bravely; she *1863:* bravely! she *1868:* bravely! She
131| *1844:* throne *1849:* throne, 132| *1844:* adorned . . BERTHOLD . . A hovel—in *1849:* BERTHOLD . . A cottage—in *1863:* BERTHOLD A *1888:* adorned . . . BERTHOLD
133| *1844:* that of *1849:* that, of 134| *1844:* throne? You *1868:* throne! You
135| *1844:* sir— *1868:* sir! 136| *1844:* me—I *1849:* me. I 137| *1844:* preferred! *1868:* preferred? 138| *1844:* Before our late appointment, sir, I come,

To pray you let those claims at present rest,
In favour of a new and stronger one.
VALENCE You shall not need a stronger: on the part
O' the lady, all you offer I accept,
Since one clear right suffices: yours is clear.
Propose!
BERTHOLD I offer her my hand.
VALENCE Your hand?
BERTHOLD A Duke's, yourself say; and, at no far time,
Something here whispers me—an Emperor's.
The lady's mind is noble: which induced
This seizure of occasion ere my claims
Were—settled, let us amicably say!
VALENCE Your hand!
BERTHOLD (He will fall down and kiss it next!)
Sir, this astonishment's too flattering,
Nor must you hold your mistress' worth so cheap.
Enhance it, rather,—urge that blood is blood—
The daughter of the Burgraves, Landgraves, Markgraves,
Remains their daughter! I shall scarce gainsay.
Elsewhere or here, the lady needs must rule:
Like the imperial crown's great chrysoprase,
They talk of—somewhat out of keeping there,
And yet no jewel for a meaner cap.
VALENCE You wed the Duchess?
BERTHOLD Cry you mercy, friend!
Will the match also influence fortunes here?
A natural solicitude enough.
Be certain, no bad chance it proves for you!
However high you take your present stand,

1849: I come, before the hour appointed me, 139| *1844:* rest— *1863:* rest, 142| *1844:* Of *1888:* O' 143| *1844:* is clear: *1849:* is clear. 145| *1844:* A Duke's yourself say, and at *1849:* A Duke's, yourself say; and, at 146| *1844:* me—the Emperor's. *1888:* me—an Emperor's. 147| *1844:* The Lady's <> noble; which *1863:* lady's *1888:* noble: which 151| *1844:* Sir—this <> flattering— *1849:* Sir, this *1863:* flattering, 152| *1844:* cheap! *1863:* cheap. 153| *1844:* it rather *1849:* it, rather 155| *1844:* daughter—I <> gainsay! *1849:* daughter; I *1868:* daughter! I <> gainsay. 156| *1844:* here the Lady <> rule— *1849:* here, the <> rule: *1863:* lady 157| *1844:* the Imperial *1863:* imperial 158| *1844:* They tell me—somewhat *1849:* They talk of—somewhat 159| *1844:* cap! *1863:* cap. 161| *1844:* The match will influence many fortunes *1849:* Will the match influence *1868:* match also influence fortunes 162| *1844:* natural enough solicitude! *1849:* natural solicitude enough! *1868:* enough. 163| *1844:* certain no

There's prospect of a higher still remove—
For Juliers will not be my resting-place,
And, when I have to choose a substitute
To rule the little burgh, I'll think of you
Who need not give your mates a character.
And yet I doubt your fitness to supplant
The grey smooth Chamberlain: he'd hesitate
A doubt his lady could demean herself
So low as to accept me. Courage, sir!
I like your method better: feeling's play
Is franker much, and flatters me beside.

VALENCE I am to say, you love her?

BERTHOLD Say that too!
Love has no great concernment, thinks the world,
With a Duke's marriage. How go precedents
In Juliers' story—how use Juliers' Dukes?
I see you have them here in goodly row;
Yon must be Luitpold—ay, a stalwart sire!
Say, I have been arrested suddenly
In my ambition's course, its rocky course,
By this sweet flower: I fain would gather it
And then proceed: so say and speedily
—(Nor stand there like Duke Luitpold's brazen self!)
Enough, sir: you possess my mind, I think.
This is my claim, the others being withdrawn,
And to this be it that, i' the Hall to-night,
Your lady's answer comes; till when, farewell! [*He retires.*]

VALENCE [*after a pause.*] The heavens and earth stay as they were; my heart

---

1849: certain, no 167–169| *1844:* And when <> substitute / You need <> character! *1849:* And, when <> substitute / To rule the little burgh, I'll think of you. / You *1868:* character. *1888:* of you / Who need 171| *1844:* The grew smooth Chamberlain—he'd *1849:* The grey smooth *1863:* smooth Chamberlain: he'd 174| *1844:* better—feeling's *1863:* better: feeling's 178| *1844:* marriage—How *1863:* marriage. How 179–181| *1844:* use Juliers' Dukes? / (Yon <> Luitpold,—ay <> sire!) *1849:* use Juliers' Dukes? / I see you have them here in goodly row; / Yon <> sire! *1888:* be Luitpold—ay 182| *1844:*—Say *1888:* Say 183| *1844:* course . . say, rocky *1849:* course, its rocky 184| *1844:* flower—I *1863:* flower: I 185| *1844:* proceed—so <> speedily— *1863:* speedily *1888:* proceed: so 188–190| *1844:* To this claim, be it in the Hall at night / Your Lady's *1849:* This is my claim, the others being withdrawn, / And to this, be it that, in the Hall to-night, / Your *1863:* this be < / > lady's *1888:* i' 191| *1844:* The Heavens <> were—my *1849:* heavens *1863:* were; my

Beats as it beat: the truth remains the truth.
What falls away, then, if not faith in her?
Was it my faith, that she could estimate
Love's value, and, such faith still guiding me,
Dare I now test her? Or grew faith so strong
Solely because no power of test was mine?

Enter the DUCHESS.

THE DUCHESS My fate, sir! Ah, you turn away. All's over.
But you are sorry for me? Be not so!
What I might have become, and never was,
Regret with me! What I have merely been,
Rejoice I am no longer! What I seem
Beginning now, in my new state, to be,
Hope that I am!—for, once my rights proved void,
This heavy roof seems easy to exchange
For the blue sky outside—my lot henceforth.
VALENCE And what a lot is Berthold's!
THE DUCHESS How of him?
VALENCE He gathers earth's whole good into his arms;
Standing, as man now, stately, strong and wise,
Marching to fortune, not surprised by her:
One great aim, like a guiding-star, above—
Which tasks strength, wisdom, stateliness, to lift
His manhood to the height that takes the prize;
A prize not near—lest overlooking earth
He rashly spring to seize it—nor remote,

192| *1844:* it beat—the truth remains the truth! *1863:* it beat: the truth remains *1868:* remains the truth. 193| *1844:* away, if not my faith *1849:* away, then, if not faith 195| *1844:* value,—and *1868:* value, and 196| *1844:* Dare I to test her now,—or had I faith *1849:* Dare I now test her?—or grew faith so strong *1868:* her? Or 198| *1844:* away—all's over! *1863:* away:all's *1868:* away. All's over. 199| *1844:* me—be *1863:* me? be *1868:* me? Be 201| *1844:* me; what *1868:* me! What 202| *1844:* longer; what I now *1849:* what I seem *1868:* longer! What 203| *1844:* Begin, a simple woman now, to *1849:* Beginning now, in my new state, to 204| *1844:* am,—for, now my rights are void, *1849:* for, once my rights proved void, *1868:* am!—for 206| *1844:* henceforth! *1868:* henceforth. 207–211| *1844:* him? / VALENCE He stands, a man, now; stately <> wise— / One <> guiding-star, before— *1849:* him? / VALENCE He gathers earth's whole good into his arms, / Standing, as man, now, stately <> wise— / Marching to fortune, not surprised by her: / One <> guiding-star, above— *1863:* man now < / > her. / One *1868:* arms; / Standing <> wise, / Marching 212–223| *1844:* stateliness to follow, / As, not its substance, but its shine he tracks, / Nor dreams of more than, just evolving these / To fulness, will suffice him to life's end. / After *1849:*

So that he rest upon his path content:
But day by day, while shimmering grows shine,
And the faint circlet prophesies the orb,
He sees so much as, just evolving these,
The stateliness, the wisdom and the strength,
To due completion, will suffice this life,
And lead him at his grandest to the grave.
After this star, out of a night he springs;
A beggar's cradle for the throne of thrones
He quits; so, mounting, feels each step he mounts,
Nor, as from each to each exultingly
He passes, overleaps one grade of joy.
This, for his own good:—with the world, each gift
Of God and man,—reality, tradition,
Fancy and fact—so well environ him,
That as a mystic panoply they serve—
Of force, untenanted, to awe mankind,
And work his purpose out with half the world,
While he, their master, dexterously slipt
From such encumbrance, is meantime employed
With his own prowess on the other half.
Thus shall he prosper, every day's success
Adding, to what is he, a solid strength—
An aëry might to what encircles him,
Till at the last, so life's routine lends help,
That as the Emperor only breathes and moves,
His shadow shall be watched, his step or stalk
Become a comfort or a portent, how
He trails his ermine take significance,—
Till even his power shall cease to be most power,
And men shall dread his weakness more, nor dare
Peril their earth its bravest, first and best,
Its typified invincibility.

---

stateliness, to lift / § adds 213–222 § / After 216| *1849:* rests *1863:* rest 225| *1844:* quits, so *1863:* quits; so 229| *1844:* man,—Reality, Tradition, *1863:* reality, tradition, 230| *1844:* and Fact *1863:* fact 236| *1844:* In his own prowess with the *1849:* With his own prowess on the 237| *1844:* So shall he go on, every *1849:* Thus shall he prosper, every 238| *1844:* is He *1863:* he 239| *1844:* airy *1849:* aëry 240| *1844:* routine shall grow, *1849:* routine lends help, 243| *1844:* portent; how *1863:* portent, how 245| *1844:* cease his power to be, *1849:* cease to be most power, 246–248| *1844:* And most his weakness men shall fear, nor vanquish / Their typified *1849:* And men shall dread his weakness more, nor dare /

Thus shall he go on, greatening, till he ends—
The man of men, the spirit of all flesh,
The fiery centre of an earthly world!
THE DUCHESS Some such a fortune I had dreamed should rise
Out of my own—that is, above my power
Seemed other, greater potencies to stretch—
VALENCE For you?
THE DUCHESS It was not I moved there, I think:
But one I could,—though constantly beside,
And aye approaching,—still keep distant from,
And so adore. 'Twas a man moved there.
VALENCE Who?
THE DUCHESS I felt the spirit, never saw the face.
VALENCE See it! 'Tis Berthold's! He enables you
To realize your vision.
THE DUCHESS Berthold?
VALENCE Duke—
Emperor to be: he proffers you his hand.
THE DUCHESS Generous and princely!
VALENCE He is all of this.
THE DUCHESS Thanks, Berthold, for my father's sake! No hand
Degrades me.
VALENCE You accept the proffered hand?
THE DUCHESS That he should love me!
VALENCE "Loved" I did not say.
Had that been—love might so incline the Prince
To the world's good, the world that's at his foot,—
I do not know, this moment, I should dare
Desire that you refused the world—and Cleves—
The sacrifice he asks.
THE DUCHESS Not love me, sir?

Peril their earth its bravest, first and best, / Its typified 249| *1844:* So shall he go on, so at last shall end, *1849:* on, greatening, till he ends *1863:* Thus shall <> ends— 251| *1844:* earthy *1868:* earthly 258| *1844:* adore. A man 'twas moved there! VALENCE *1849:* adore. 'Twas a man moved *1868:* there. VALENCE 259| *1844:* face! *1863:* face. 261| *1844:* realise <> vision! THE *1863:* realize <> vision. THE 264| *1844:* sake—no *1863:* sake! no *1868:* sake! No 265| *1844:* me! VALENCE *1888:* me. VALENCE 266| *1844:* say! *1888:* say. 267| *1844:* been—so might love incline *1849:* been—love might so incline 268| *1844:* foot, *1849:* foot,— 269| *1844:* know this moment I *1849:* know, this moment, I 270| *1844:* Give counsel you refuse the *1849:* Desire that you refused the 271| *1844:*

VALENCE He scarce affirmed it.
THE DUCHESS May not deeds affirm?
VALENCE What does he? . . . Yes, yes, very much he does!
All the shame saved, he thinks, and sorrow saved—
Immitigable sorrow, so he thinks,—
Sorrow that's deeper than we dream, perchance.
THE DUCHESS Is not this love?
VALENCE So very much he does!
For look, you can descend now gracefully:
All doubts are banished, that the world might have,
Or worst, the doubts yourself, in after-time,
May call up of your heart's sincereness now.
To such, reply, "I could have kept my rule—
Increased it to the utmost of my dreams—
Yet I abjured it." This, he does for you:
It is munificently much.
THE DUCHESS Still "much!"
But why is it not love, sir? Answer me!
VALENCE Because not one of Berthold's words and looks
Had gone with love's presentment of a flower
To the beloved: because bold confidence,
Open superiority, free pride—
Love owns not, yet were all that Berthold owned:
Because where reason, even, finds no flaw,
Unerringly a lover's instinct may.
THE DUCHESS You reason, then, and doubt?
VALENCE I love, and know.
THE DUCHESS You love? How strange! I never cast a thought
On that. Just see our selfishness! You seemed
So much my own . . . I had no ground—and yet,
I never dreamed another might divide

---

asks! THE *1863:* asks. THE 272| *1844:* deeds say more? *1849:* deeds affirm? 273| *1844:* he? . . . Yes—yes—very *1863:* he? . . . Yes, yes, very 274| *1844:* saved he *1849:* saved, he 276| *1844:* perchance! *1888:* perchance. 278| *1844:* gracefully— *1863:* gracefully: 279| *1844:* banished that *1849:* banished, that 281| *1844:* now: *1863:* now. 282| *1844:* reply, "My rule I could have kept— *1849:* reply, "I <> kept my rule— 284| *1844:* Yet abjured all!" This, Berthold does *1849:* Yet I abjured it!" This, he does *1868:* it." This 285| *1844:* much! THE DUCHESS Still "much"! *1849:* THE DUCHESS Still "much!" *1868:* much. THE 290| *1844:* pride *1849:* pride— 291| *1844:* not, and were *1849:* not, yet were 295| *1844:* love?—How *1888:* love? How 296| *1844:* that! Just <>

My power with you, much less exceed it.
VALENCE Lady,
I am yours wholly.
THE DUCHESS Oh, no, no, not mine!
'Tis not the same now, never more can be.
—Your first love, doubtless. Well, what's gone from me?
What have I lost in you?
VALENCE My heart replies—
No loss there! So, to Berthold back again:
This offer of his hand, he bids me make—
Its obvious magnitude is well to weigh.
THE DUCHESS She's . . . yes, she must be very fair for you!
VALENCE I am a simple advocate of Cleves.
THE DUCHESS You! With the heart and brain that so helped me,
I fancied them exclusively my own,
Yet find are subject to a stronger sway!
She must be . . . tell me, is she very fair?
VALENCE Most fair, beyond conception or belief.
THE DUCHESS Black eyes?—no matter! Colombe, the world leads
Its life without you, whom your friends professed
The only woman: see how true they spoke!
One lived this while, who never saw your face,
Nor heard your voice—unless . . . Is she from Cleves?
VALENCE Cleves knows her well.
THE DUCHESS Ah—just a fancy, now!
When you poured forth the wrongs of Cleves,—I said,
—Thought, that is, afterward . . .
VALENCE You thought of me?
THE DUCHESS Of whom else? Only such great cause, I thought,

---

selfishness—you *1863:* selfishness! you *1868:* selfishness! You *1888:* that. Just 299| *1844:* it! VALENCE *1863:* it. VALENCE 300| *1844:* wholly! THE *1863:* wholly. THE *1888:* wholly THE 301| *1844:* be! *1868:* be. 302| *1844:* doubtless! Well *1868:* doubtless. Well 304–306| *1844:* there! . . So of Berthold's proposition,—/ Its <> weigh! *1849:* there! . . . So to Berthold back again! / This offer of his hand, he bids me make—/ Its *1863:* there! So, to < // > weigh. *1868:* again: / This 308| *1844:* simple Advocate *1868:* advocate 309| *1844:* me *1849:* me, 310| *1844:* fancied both exclusively *1849:* fancied them exclusively 311| *1888:* sway 313| *1844:* belief! *1868:* belief. 314| *1844:* matter! Colombe—the *1849:* matter! Colombe, the 316| *1844:* The single woman —see <> they were! *1849:* The only woman <> they spoke! *1888:* woman: see 319| *1844:* well! THE *1868:* well. THE 322| *1844:* Of what else? Only

For such effect: see what true love can do!
Cleves is his love. I almost fear to ask
. . . And will not. This is idling: to our work!
Admit before the Prince, without reserve,
My claims misgrounded; then may follow better
. . . When you poured out Cleves' wrongs impetuously,
Was she in your mind?

VALENCE All done was done for her
—To humble me!

THE DUCHESS She will be proud at least.

VALENCE She?

THE DUCHESS When you tell her.

VALENCE That will never be.

THE DUCHESS How—are there sweeter things you hope to tell?
No, sir! You counselled me,—I counsel you
In the one point I—any woman—can.
Your worth, the first thing; let her own come next—
Say what you did through her, and she through you—
The praises of her beauty afterward!
Will you?

VALENCE I dare not.

THE DUCHESS Dare not?

VALENCE She I love
Suspects not such a love in me.

THE DUCHESS You jest.

VALENCE The lady is above me and away.
Not only the brave form, and the bright mind,
And the great heart, combine to press me low—
But all the world calls rank divides us.

THE DUCHESS Rank!
Now grant me patience! Here's a man declares
Oracularly in another's case—
Sees the true value and the false, for them—
Nay, bids them see it, and they straight do see.

---

such a cause *1849:* such great cause *1863:* Of whom else 323| *1844:* effect—see *1863:* effect: see 324| *1844:* love! I *1849:* love!—I *1868:* love. I 325| *1844:* . . . Nor will not! This is idling—to *1863:* . . . And will not. This is idling: to 329| *1844:* her— *1863:* her 330| *1844:* least! *1863:* To *1868:*—To <> least. 331| *1844:* her VALENCE <> be! *1863:* her. VALENCE <> be. 334| *1844:* woman can! *1849:* woman—can! *1868:* can. 338| *1844:* not! THE *1863:* not. THE 339| *1844:* jest! *1868:* jest. 340| *1844:* away! *1868:* away. 343| *1844:* THE DUCHESS Rank? *1888:* THE DUCHESS Rank! 347| *1844:* do

You called my court's love worthless—so it turned:
I threw away as dross my heap of wealth,
And here you stickle for a piece or two!
First—has she seen you?
VALENCE Yes.
THE DUCHESS She loves you, then.
VALENCE One flash of hope burst; then succeeded night:
And all's at darkest now. Impossible!
THE DUCHESS We'll try: you are—so to speak—my subject yet?
VALENCE As ever—to the death.
THE DUCHESS Obey me, then!
VALENCE I must.
THE DUCHESS Approach her, and . . . no! first of all
Get more assurance. "My instructress," say,
"Was great, descended from a line of kings,
And even fair"—(wait why I say this folly)—
"She said, of all men, none for eloquence,
Courage, and (what cast even these to shade)
The heart they sprung from,—none deserved like him
Who saved her at her need: if she said this,
What should not one I love, say?"
VALENCE Heaven—this hope—
Oh, lady, you are filling me with fire!
THE DUCHESS Say this!—nor think I bid you cast aside
One touch of all the awe and reverence;

---

see! *1868:* do see. 351| *1844:* VALENCE Yes! THE *1863:* VALENCE Yes. THE 352| *1844:* burst—then <> night— *1863:* burst; then <> night: 354| *1844:* are—somehow—my *1849:* are—so to speak—my 355| *1844:* death! THE *1868:* death. THE 356| *1844:* must! THE <> her and . . . No! First *1849:* her, and *1863:* must. THE *1868:* no! first 357| *1844:* assurance; my instructress, say, *1849:* assurance; "my instructress," say, *1863:* assurance. "My 358| *1844:* Was *1849:* "Was 359| *1844:* fair—(wait *1849:* fair"—(wait 360| *1844:* She *1849:* "She 361| *1844:* and, what <> shade, *1849:* and (what <> shade) 363| *1844:* need—if *1863:* need: if 364| *1844:* say? VALENCE *1849:* say?" VALENCE 367| *1844:* all that awe and reverence! *1863:* all the awe *1868:*

Nay, make her proud for once to heart's content
That all this wealth of heart and soul's her own!
Think you are all of this,—and, thinking it,
. . . (Obey!)
VALENCE I cannot choose.
THE DUCHESS Then, kneel to her!
[VALENCE *sinks on his knee.*]
I dream!
VALENCE Have mercy! Yours, unto the death,—
I have obeyed. Despise, and let me die!
THE DUCHESS Alas, sir, is it to be ever thus?
Even with you as with the world? I know
This morning's service was no vulgar deed
Whose motive, once it dares avow itself,
Explains all done and infinitely more,
So, takes the shelter of a nobler cause.
Your service named its true source,—loyalty!
The rest's unsaid again. The Duchess bids you,
Rise, sir! The Prince's words were in debate.
VALENCE [*rising.*] Rise? Truth, as ever, lady, comes from you!
I should rise—I who spoke for Cleves, can speak
For Man—yet tremble now, who stood firm then.
I laughed—for 'twas past tears—that Cleves should starve
With all hearts beating loud the infamy,
And no tongue daring trust as much to air:
Yet here, where all hearts speak, shall I be mute?
Oh, lady, for your own sake look on me!
On all I am, and have, and do—heart, brain,
Body and soul,—this Valence and his gifts!
I was proud once: I saw you, and they sank,
So that each, magnified a thousand times,

---

reverence; 368| *1844:* Nay—make *1888:* Nay, make 371| *1844:* choose! THE *1863:* choose. THE 373| *1844:* die. *1868:* die! 379–380| *1844:* So takes <> a meaner cause, / Whence rising, its effects may amply show. / Your *1849:* a nobler cause. / Your *1863:* So, takes 383| *1844:* Rise! Truth <> ever, Lady *1863:* Rise? Truth *1868:* lady 384| *1844:* rise—I that spoke *1863:* rise—I who spoke 385| *1844:* now, that stood firm then! *1863:* now, who stood *1888:* then. 386| *1844:* laughed . . . for <> tears . . . that *1849:* laughed—for <> tears—that 388| *1844:* air— *1849:* air! *1868:* air: 390| *1844:* Oh lady *1888:* Oh, lady 392| *1844:* gifts— *1849:* gifts! 393| *1844:* once—I saw you—and *1868:* once: I saw you, and 394| *1844:* each magnified <> times *1868:* each, magnified <> times,

Were nothing to you—but such nothingness,
Would a crown gild it, or a sceptre prop,
A treasure speed, a laurel-wreath enhance?
What is my own desert? But should your love
Have . . . there's no language helps here . . . singled me,—
Then—oh, that wild word "then!"—be just to love,
In generosity its attribute!
Love, since you pleased to love! All's cleared—a stage
For trial of the question kept so long:
Judge you—Is love or vanity the best?
You, solve it for the world's sake—you, speak first
What all will shout one day—you, vindicate
Our earth and be its angel! All is said.
Lady, I offer nothing—I am yours:
But, for the cause' sake, look on me and him,
And speak!
THE DUCHESS I have received the Prince's message:
Say, I prepare my answer!
VALENCE Take me, Cleves! [*He withdraws.*]
THE DUCHESS Mournful—that nothing's what it calls itself!
Devotion, zeal, faith, loyalty—mere love!
And, love in question, what may Berthold's be?
I did ill to mistrust the world so soon:
Already was this Berthold at my side.
The valley-level has its hawks no doubt:
May not the rock-top have its eagles, too?
Yet Valence . . . let me see his rival then!

395| *1844:* nothingness *1863:* nothingness. *1868:* nothingness, 396| *1844:* What would <> gild, or *1849:* Would <> gild it, or 399| *1844:* here . . singled *1888:* here . . . singled 400| *1844:* Then . . Oh <> then"! . . be *1849:* Then—Oh <> then!"—be *1868:* oh 402| *1844:* Love, as you pleased love! All is cleared *1849:* Love, since you pleased to love! All's cleared 403| *1844:* long *1863:* long; *1868:* long: 404| *1844:* For you—Is Love or Vanity *1863:* Judge you *1868:* love or vanity 405| *1844:* sake—you, say first *1849:* sake—you, speak first 408| *1844:* yours, *1868:* yours: 409| *1844:* But for <> him *1868:* But, for *1888:* him, 415| *1844:* soon— *1868:* soon: 416| *1844:* side! *1863:* side. 417| *1844:* hawks, no *1868:* hawks no 419| *1844:* his Rival then! [*Exit.* *1849:* then! *1863:* rival

ACT V

NIGHT

S C E N E—*The Hall.*

Enter BERTHOLD *and* MELCHIOR.

MELCHIOR And here you wait the matter's issue?
BERTHOLD Here.
MELCHIOR I don't regret I shut Amelius, then.
But tell me, on this grand disclosure,—how
Behaved our spokesman with the forehead?
BERTHOLD Oh,
Turned out no better than the foreheadless—
Was dazzled not so very soon, that's all!
For my part, this is scarce the hasty showy
Chivalrous measure you give me credit of.
Perhaps I had a fancy,—but 'tis gone.
—Let her commence the unfriended innocent
And carry wrongs about from court to court?
No, truly! The least shake of fortune's sand,
—My uncle-Pope chokes in a coughing fit,
King-cousin takes a fancy to blue eyes,—
And wondrously her claims would brighten up;
Forth comes a new gloss on the ancient law,
O'er-looked provisoes, o'er-past premises,

2| *1844:* then! *1863:* then. 4| *1844:* BERTHOLD Oh,—he *1849:* BERTHOLD Oh, 6| *1844:* soon—that's *1863:* soon, that's 7| *1844:* hasty, showy, *1868:* hasty showy 8–10| *1844:* of! / —Let her commence unfriended innocent, *1849:* of! / Perhaps I had the fancy,—but 'tis gone— / —Let her commence the unfriended *1863:* of. / Perhaps I had a fancy <> gone. / —Let *1888:* innocent 12| *1844:* No truly <> of Fortune's *1849:* No, truly *1863:* fortune's 13| *1844:*—My uncle chokes in his next coughing-fit, *1849:*—My uncle-Pope chokes in a coughing-fit, *1868:* coughing fit, 14| *1844:* King Philip takes *1868:* King-cousin takes 15| *1844:* up! *1868:* up; 17| *1844:* provisoes, past o'er premises, *1888:* provisoes, o'er-past premises,

Follow in plenty. No: 'tis the safe step.
The hour beneath the convent-wall is lost:
Juliers and she, once mine, are ever mine.

MELCHIOR Which is to say, you, losing heart already,
Elude the adventure.

BERTHOLD Not so—or, if so—
Why not confess at once that I advise
None of our kingly craft and guild just now
To lay, one moment, down their privilege
With the notion they can any time at pleasure
Retake it: that may turn out hazardous.
We seem, in Europe, pretty well at end
O' the night, with our great masque: those favoured few
Who keep the chamber's top, and honour's chance
Of the early evening, may retain their place
And figure as they list till out of breath.
But it is growing late: and I observe
A dim grim kind of tipstaves at the doorway
Not only bar new-comers entering now,
But caution those who left, for any cause,
And would return, that morning draws too near;
The ball must die off, shut itself up. We—
I think, may dance lights out and sunshine in,
And sleep off headache on our frippery:
But friend the other, who cunningly stole out,
And, after breathing the fresh air outside,
Means to re-enter with a new costume,
Will be advised go back to bed, I fear.
I stick to privilege, on second thoughts.

MELCHIOR Yes—you evade the adventure: and, beside,
Give yourself out for colder than you are.
King Philip, only, notes the lady's eyes?

18–20| *1844:* plenty—No—'tis the safer step. / Juliers *1849:* step. / The hour beneath the convent-wall is lost— / Juliers *1863:* plenty. No: 'tis </> lost: / Juliers *1868:* mine are *1888:* safe < // > mine, are 22| *1844:* adventure! BERTHOLD *1868:* adventure. BERTHOLD 23| *1849:* once, that *1888:* once that 27| *1844:* it—that <> hazardous! *1863:* it? that *1868:* it: that <> hazardous. 33| *1844:* late; and *1868:* late: and 40| *1844:* frippery— *1863:* frippery: 41–43| *1844:* out, / And thinks re-enter with a fresh costume, *1849:* out, / And, after breathing the fresh air outside, / Means to re-enter with a new costume, 45| *1844:* thoughts! *1868:* thoughts. 46| *1844:* adventure!—And *1868:* adventure: and 48| *1844:*—King 1868:

Don't they come in for somewhat of the motive
With you too?
BERTHOLD Yes—no: I am past that now.
Gone 'tis: I cannot shut my soul to fact.
Of course, I might by forethought and contrivance
Reason myself into a rapture. Gone:
And something better come instead, no doubt.
MELCHIOR So be it! Yet, all the same, proceed my way,
Though to your ends; so shall you prosper best!
The lady,—to be won for selfish ends,—
Will be won easier my unselfish . . . call it,
Romantic way.
BERTHOLD Won easier?
MELCHIOR Will not she?
BERTHOLD There I profess humility without bound:
Ill cannot speed—not I—the Emperor.
MELCHIOR And I should think the Emperor best waived,
From your description of her mood and way.
You could look, if it pleased you, into hearts;
But are too indolent and fond of watching
Your own—you know that, for you study it.
BERTHOLD Had you but seen the orator her friend,
So bold and voluble an hour before,
Abashed to earth at aspect of the change!
Make her an Empress? Ah, that changed the case!
Oh, I read hearts! 'Tis for my own behoof,
I court her with my true worth: wait the event!
I learned my final lesson on that head
When years ago,—my first and last essay—
Before the priest my uncle could by help

King 49| *1844:* in somewhat *1849:* in for somewhat 50| *1844:* now! *1868:* now. 51| *1844:* 'tis—I <> my eyes to *1863:* 'tis: I *1868:* my soul to 52| *1844:* course I *1849:* course, I 53| *1844:* rapture. Gone! *1868:* rapture. Gone: 54| *1844:* better's *1863:* better 55| *1844:* it! Yet, proceed my way, the same, *1849:* it! Yet, all the same, proceed my way, 56| *1844:* end <> best. *1868:* ends <> best! 58| *1844:* unselfish . . call *1868:* unselfish . . . call 60| *1844:* bound! *1868:* bound: 61| *1844:* the Emperor! *1868:* the Emperor. 63| *1844:* way! *1868:* way. 66| *1844:* it! *1863:* it. 67–71| *1844:* friend / Abashed <> change! / . . Oh <> hearts! And for *1849:* friend, / So bold and voluble an hour before, / Abashed <> change! / Make her an Empress? Ah, that changed the case! / . . Oh *1863:* case! / Oh *1868:* hearts! 'Tis for 72| *1844:* worth—see the *1863:* worth: see *1868:* worth: wait the 74| *1844:* essay! *1868:* essay— 75| *1844:* Before my uncle could obtain the

Of his superior, raise me from the dirt—
Priscilla left me for a Brabant lord
Whose cheek was like the topaz on his thumb.
I am past illusion on that score.

MELCHIOR Here comes
The lady—

BERTHOLD And there you go. But do not! Give me
Another chance to please you! Hear me plead!

MELCHIOR You'll keep, then, to the lover, to the man?

Enter the DUCHESS—*followed by* ADOLF *and* SABYNE *and, after an interval, by the* COURTIERS.

BERTHOLD Good auspice to our meeting!

THE DUCHESS May it prove!
—And you, sir, will be Emperor one day?

BERTHOLD (Ay, that's the point!) I may be Emperor.

THE DUCHESS 'Tis not for my sake only, I am proud
Of this you offer: I am prouder far
That from the highest state should duly spring
The highest, since most generous, of deeds.

BERTHOLD (Generous—still that!) You underrate yourself.
You are, what I, to be complete, must gain—
Find now, and may not find, another time.
While I career on all the world for stage,
There needs at home my representative.

THE DUCHESS —Such, rather, would some warrior-woman be—
One dowered with lands and gold, or rich in friends—
One like yourself.

BERTHOLD Lady, I am myself,
And have all these: I want what's not myself,
Nor has all these. Why give one hand two swords?
Here's one already: be a friend's next gift

---

ear *1868:* Before the priest my uncle could by help 76| *1844:* superior, help me *1868:* superior, raise me 77| *1844:* a Brabant Duke *1868:* a Brabant lord 78| *1844:* thumb— *1849:* thumb. 80| *1844:* go! But *1868:* go. But 81| *1844:* you. Hear *1868:* you! Hear 82| *1844:* the gallant, to *1849:* the lover, to 85| *1844:* (Ay—that's the point.) I *1849:* point!) I *1868:* (Ay, that's 86| *1844:* only I *1849:* only, I 91| *1844:* must have— *1888:* must gain— 94| *1844:* representative— *1863:* representative. 97| *1844:* yourself! BERTHOLD *1868:*

A silk glove, if you will—I have a sword.
THE DUCHESS You love me, then?
BERTHOLD Your lineage I revere,
Honour your virtue, in your truth believe,
Do homage to your intellect, and bow
Before your peerless beauty.
THE DUCHESS But, for love—
BERTHOLD A further love I do not understand.
Our best course is to say these hideous truths,
And see them, once said, grow endurable:
Like waters shuddering from their central bed,
Black with the midnight bowels of the earth,
That, once up-spouted by an earthquake's throe,
A portent and a terror—soon subside,
Freshen apace, take gold and rainbow hues
In sunshine, sleep in shadow, and at last
Grow common to the earth as hills or trees—
Accepted by all things they came to scare.
THE DUCHESS You cannot love, then?
BERTHOLD —Charlemagne, perhaps!
Are you not over-curious in love-lore?
THE DUCHESS I have become so, very recently.
It seems, then, I shall best deserve esteem,
Respect, and all your candour promises,
By putting on a calculating mood—
Asking the terms of my becoming yours?
BERTHOLD Let me not do myself injustice, neither.
Because I will not condescend to fictions
That promise what my soul can ne'er acquit,
It does not follow that my guarded phrase
May not include far more of what you seek,
Than wide profession of less scrupulous men.
You will be Empress, once for all: with me
The Pope disputes supremacy—you stand,

---

yourself. BERTHOLD 101| *1844:* sword! *1868:* sword. 102| *1844:* revere— *1863:* revere, 104| *1844:* to intelligence, and *1849:* to your intellect, and 105| *1844:* Before a peerless *1849:* Before your peerless 108| *1844:* endurable. *1863:* endurable: 113| *1844:* hues, *1849:* hues 114| *1844:* Under the sun and in the air,—at *1849:* In sunshine, sleep in shadow,—and, at last, *1863:* shadow, and *1868:* and at last 124| *1844:* neither! *1868:* neither *1888:* neither. 129| *1844:* professions *1868:* profession 130| *1844:* all—with *1863:* all: with 131| *1844:*

And none gainsays, the earth's first woman.
THE DUCHESS That—
Or simple Lady of Ravestein again?
BERTHOLD The matter's not in my arbitrament:
Now I have made my claims—which I regret—
Cede one, cede all.
THE DUCHESS This claim then, you enforce?
BERTHOLD The world looks on.
THE DUCHESS And when must I decide?
BERTHOLD When, lady? Have I said thus much so promptly
For nothing?—Poured out, with such pains, at once
What I might else have suffered to ooze forth
Droplet by droplet in a lifetime long—
For aught less than as prompt an answer, too?
All's fairly told now: who can teach you more?
THE DUCHESS I do not see him.
BERTHOLD I shall ne'er deceive.
This offer should be made befittingly
Did time allow the better setting forth
The good of it, with what is not so good,
Advantage, and disparagement as well:
But as it is, the sum of both must serve.
I am already weary of this place;
My thoughts are next stage on to Rome. Decide!
The Empire—or,—not even Juliers now!
Hail to the Empress—farewell to the Duchess!
[*The* COURTIERS, *who have been drawing nearer and nearer, interpose.*]
GAUCELME —"Farewell," Prince? when we break in at our risk—

---

stand *1868:* stand, 132| *1844:* the Earth's first woman! THE *1863:* earth's *1868:* woman. THE 134| *1844:* arbitrement! *1868:* arbitrament: 136| *1844:* all! THE *1868:* all. THE 138| *1844:* "When," Lady <> much at first *1849:* much so promptly *1863:* When, Lady *1868:* lady 139| *1844:* nothing? Poured *1868:* nothing?—Poured 141| *1844:* life-time long, *1863:* lifetime *1868:* long— 143| *1844:* now—who *1863:* now: who 144| *1844:* him! BERTHOLD <> deceive! *1863:* him. BERTHOLD <> deceive. 145| *1844:* offer had been made more leisurely *1849:* made befittingly *1863:* offer should be made 146–148| *1844:* Would time <> setting off / Advantage <> well— *1849:* setting forth / The good of it, with what is not so good, / Advantage *1868:* Did time < // > well: 150| *1844:* place— *1868:* place; 151–153| *1844:* to Rome. Now, either / Hail <> farewell to the Lady! *1849:* to Rome. Decide! / The Empire—or,—not even Juliers now! / Hail <> farewell to the Duchess! 154| *1844:* COURTIERS. . . "Farewell <> risk . . . *1849:* risk— *1863:*

CLUGNET Almost upon court-licence trespassing—
GAUCELME —To point out how your claims are valid yet!
You know not, by the Duke her father's will,
The lady, if she weds beneath her rank,
Forfeits her Duchy in the next heir's favour—
So 'tis expressly stipulate. And if
It can be shown 'tis her intent to wed
A subject, then yourself, next heir, by right
Succeed to Juliers.
BERTHOLD What insanity?—
GUIBERT Sir, there's one Valence, the pale fiery man
You saw and heard this morning—thought, no doubt,
Was of considerable standing here:
I put it to your penetration, Prince,
If aught save love, the truest love for her
Could make him serve the lady as he did!
He's simply a poor advocate of Cleves
—Creeps here with difficulty, finds a place
With danger, gets in by a miracle,
And for the first time meets the lady's face—
So runs the story: is that credible?
For, first—no sooner in, than he's apprised
Fortunes have changed; you are all-powerful here,
The lady as powerless: he stands fast by her!
THE DUCHESS [*aside.*] And do such deeds spring up from love alone?
GUIBERT But here occurs the question, does the lady
Love him again? I say, how else can she?
Can she forget how he stood singly forth
In her defence, dared outrage all of us,
Insult yourself—for what, save love's reward?

COURTIERS—"Farewell *1868:* GAUCELME—"Farewell 155| *1844:* (Almost upon Court-licence trespassing) . . *1849:* trespassing)— *1863:* Almost upon court-licence trespassing— 156| *1844:* COURTIERS To *1849:* COURTIERS—To *1868:* GAUCELME—To 157| *1844:* her Father's *1863:* father's 162–163| *1844:* yourself . . . BERTHOLD What insolence? . . . *1849:* yourself, next heir, by right / Succeed to Juliers. BERTHOLD What insanity? . . . 163| *1863:* insanity? *1868:* insanity?— 164| *1844:* one Valence—the *1868:* one Valence, the 165| *1849:* heard, this *1868:* heard this 166| *1844:* here— *1863:* here: 168| *1844:* her, *1868:* her 169| *1844:* Had made him *1863:* Could make him 173| *1844:* meets the Lady's *1863:* lady's 174| *1844:* story—is *1863:* story: is 177| *1844:* The Lady as powerless—he *1849:* powerless: he *1863:* lady 178| *1844:* (And <> from Love alone?) *1849:* love *1863:* And <> alone? 179| *1844:* does the Lady *1863:* lady 180| *1844:* say, How *1868:* how 183| *1844:* what save *1863:* what,

THE DUCHESS [*aside.*] And is love then the sole reward of love?
GUIBERT But, love him as she may and must—you ask,
Means she to wed him? "Yes," both natures answer!
Both, in their pride, point out the sole result;
Nought less would he accept nor she propose.
For each conjecture was she great enough
—Will be, for this.
CLUGNET Though, now that this is known,
Policy, doubtless, urges she deny . . .
THE DUCHESS —What, sir, and wherefore?—since I am not sure
That all is any other than you say!
You take this Valence, hold him close to me,
Him with his actions: can I choose but look?
I am not sure, love trulier shows itself
Than in this man, you hate and would degrade,
Yet, with your worst abatement, show me thus.
Nor am I—(thus made look within myself,
Ere I had dared)—now that the look is dared—
Sure that I do not love him!
GUIBERT Hear you, Prince?
BERTHOLD And what, sirs, please you, may this prattle mean
Unless to prove with what alacrity
You give your lady's secrets to the world?
How much indebted, for discovering
That quality, you make me, will be found
When there's a keeper for my own to seek.
COURTIERS "Our lady?"
BERTHOLD —She assuredly remains.
THE DUCHESS Ah, Prince—and you too can be generous?
You could renounce your power, if this were so,

---

save 184| *1844:* (And is Love <> of Love?) *1849:* love <> love?) *1863:* And <> of love? 185| *1844:* must . . you ask *1849:* must—you ask, 187| *1844:* result— *1868:* result; 188| *1844:* propose! *1868:* propose. 189| *1844:* each conjuncture was <> enough— *1863:* enough *1868:* each conjecture was 190| *1844:* this! CLUGNET *1868:* this. CLUGNET 193| *1844:* say? *1868:* say! 195| *1844:* action . . can *1849:* actions: can 198| *1844:* Yet with *1849:* Yet, with <> thus: *1863:* thus. 199| *1844:* myself *1849:* myself, 200| *1844:* dared,)—now *1868:* dared)—now 202| *1844:* mean? *1863:* mean 203| *1844:*—Unless *1868:* Unless 204| *1844:* your Lady's <> world— *1863:* lady's <> world? 205| *1844:*—But how indebted *1849:*—How much indebted *1868:* How 207| *1844:* When next a <> my own's to seek! *1868:* When there's a <> my own to seek. 208| *1844:* Our Lady? BERTHOLD . . . She <> remains! *1849:* "Our Lady?"

And let me, as these phrase it, wed my love
Yet keep my Duchy? You perhaps exceed
Him, even, in disinterestedness!
BERTHOLD How, lady, should all this affect my purpose?
Your will and choice are still as ever, free.
Say, you have known a worthier than myself
In mind and heart, of happier form and face—
Others must have their birthright: I have gifts,
To balance theirs, not blot them out of sight.
Against a hundred alien qualities,
I lay the prize I offer. I am nothing:
Wed you the Empire?
THE DUCHESS And my heart away?
BERTHOLD When have I made pretension to your heart?
I give none. I shall keep your honour safe;
With mine I trust you, as the sculptor trusts
Yon marble woman with the marble rose,
Loose on her hand, she never will let fall,
In graceful, slight, silent security.
You will be proud of my world-wide career,
And I content in you the fair and good.
What were the use of planting a few seeds
The thankless climate never would mature—
Affections all repelled by circumstance?
Enough: to these no credit I attach,—
To what you own, find nothing to object.
Write simply on my requisition's face
What shall content my friends—that you admit,
As Colombe of Ravestein, the claims therein,
Or never need admit them, as my wife—
And either way, all's ended!
THE DUCHESS Let all end!

BERTHOLD—She *1868:* lady <> remains. 211| *1844:* these argue, wed *1849:* these phrase it, wed 212| *1844:* And keep *1849:* Yet keep 214| *1844:* How Lady *1849:* How, Lady *1863:* lady 215| *1844:* free! *1868:* free. 216| *1844:* Say you *1849:* Say, you 217| *1844:* face; *1863:* face— 218| *1844:* birthright! I have gifts, *1863:* birthright: I *1888:* gifts. § see Ed. Notes § 219| *1844:* sight! *1863:* sight. 220| *1844:* hundred other qualities, *1868:* hundred alien qualities, 221| *1844:* nothing— *1868:* nothing: 224| *1844:* safe— *1863:* safe; 225| *1844:* you as *1849:* you, as 231| *1849:* seeds, *1888:* seeds 236| *1844:* my Requisition's *1863:* requisition's 240| *1844:* ended. THE *1868:*

BERTHOLD The requisition!
GUIBERT —Valence holds, of course!
BERTHOLD Desire his presence! [ADOLF *goes out.*]
COURTIERS [*to each other.*] Out it all comes yet;
He'll have his word against the bargain yet;
He's not the man to tamely acquiesce.
One passionate appeal—upbraiding even,
May turn the tide again. Despair not yet! [*They retire a little.*]
BERTHOLD [*to* MELCHIOR.] The Empire has its old success, my friend!
MELCHIOR You've had your way: before the spokesman speaks,
Let me, but this once, work a problem out,
And ever more be dumb! The Empire wins?
To better purpose have I read my books!

Enter VALENCE.

MELCHIOR [*to the* COURTIERS.] Apart, my masters! [*To* VALENCE.] Sir, one word with you!
I am a poor dependant of the Prince's—
Pitched on to speak, as of slight consequence.
You are no higher, I find: in other words,
We two, as probably the wisest here,
Need not hold diplomatic talk like fools.
Suppose I speak, divesting the plain fact
Of all their tortuous phrases, fit for them?
Do you reply so, and what trouble saved!
The Prince, then—an embroiled strange heap of news
This moment reaches him—if true or false,
All dignity forbids he should inquire

---

ended! THE 241| *1844:* The Requisition! COURTIERS—Valence *1863:* requisition *1868:* requisition! GUIBERT—Valence 242| *1844:* yet! *1868:* yet; 243| *1844:* bargain still! *1868:* bargain yet; 244| *1844:* acquiesce! *1868:* acquiesce. 246| *1844:* Might turn <> again! Despair *1868:* May turn <> again. Despair 248| *1844:* way . . before the spokesman comes, *1849:* way: before *1868:* spokesman speaks, 250| *1863:* dumb. The *1868:* dumb! The 251| *1844:* purpose I have read *1868:* purpose have I read 253| *1844:* dependent of the Princes'— *1849:* the Prince's— *1868:* dependant 254| *1844:* consequence: *1863:* consequence; *1868:* consequence. 255| *1844:* find—in *1863:* find: in 257| *1844:* fools: *1863:* fools. 258| *1844:* So, I shall speak *1849:* Suppose I speak 259| *1844:* them— *1863:* them? 260| *1844:* trouble's saved! *1863:* trouble saved! 263| *1844:*

In person, or by worthier deputy;
Yet somehow must inquire, lest slander come:
And so, 'tis I am pitched on. You have heard
His offer to your lady?
VALENCE Yes.
MELCHIOR —Conceive
Her joy thereat?
VALENCE I cannot.
MELCHIOR No one can.
All draws to a conclusion, therefore.
VALENCE [*aside.*] So!
No after-judgment—no first thought revised—
Her first and last decision!—me, she leaves,
Takes him; a simple heart is flung aside,
The ermine o'er a heartless breast embraced.
Oh Heaven, this mockery has been played too oft!
Once, to surprise the angels—twice, that fiends
Recording, might be proud they chose not so—
Thrice, many thousand times, to teach the world
All men should pause, misdoubt their strength, since men
Can have such chance yet fail so signally,
—But ever, ever this farewell to Heaven,
Welcome to earth—this taking death for life—
This spurning love and kneeling to the world—
Oh Heaven, it is too often and too old!
MELCHIOR Well, on this point, what but an absurd rumour
Arises—these, its source—its subject, you!
Your faith and loyalty misconstruing,
They say, your service claims the lady's hand!
Of course, nor Prince nor lady can respond:

---

enquire *1863:* inquire 265| *1844:* enquire *1863:* inquire 266| *1844:* so 'tis *1863:* so, 'tis 267| *1844:* your Lady? VALENCE Yes! MELCHIOR Conceive *1849:* VALENCE Yes. MELCHIOR—Conceive *1863:* lady 268| *1844:* thereat?—VALENCE I cannot! MELCHIOR <> can! *1849:* cannot. MELCHIOR <> can: *1863:* thereat? VALENCE *1888:* can. 271| *1844:* leaves— *1868:* leaves, 272| *1844:* him—a *1868:* him; a 273| *1844:* embraced! *1868:* embraced. 276| *1844:* Might record, hug themselves they *1849:* Recording, might be proud they 279| *1844:* Could have the chance *1849:* have such chance *1868:* Can have 280| *1844:* ever—ever—this <> heaven, *1863:* to Heaven, *1868:* ever, ever this 283| *1863:* heaven *1868:* Oh Heaven 284| *1844:* point—what *1868:* point, what 287| *1844:* The lady's hand your service claims, they say! *1849:* They say, your service claims the lady's hand! 288| *1844:* nor Prince nor Lady can respond— *1863:* respond: *1868:* lady

Yet something must be said: for, were it true
You made such claim, the Prince would . . .

VALENCE Well, sir,—would?

MELCHIOR —Not only probably withdraw his suit,
But, very like, the lady might be forced
Accept your own. Oh, there are reasons why!
But you'll excuse at present all save one,—
I think so. What we want is, your own witness,
For, or against—her good, or yours: decide!

VALENCE [*aside.*] Be it her good if she accounts it so!
[*After a contest.*] For what am I but hers, to choose as she?
Who knows how far, beside, the light from her
May reach, and dwell with, what she looks upon?

MELCHIOR [*to the* PRINCE.] Now to him, you!

BERTHOLD [*to* VALENCE.] My friend acquaints you, sir,
The noise runs . . .

VALENCE —Prince, how fortunate are you,
Wedding her as you will, in spite of noise,
To show belief in love! Let her but love you,
All else you disregard! What else can be?
You know how love is incompatible
With falsehood—purifies, assimilates
All other passions to itself.

MELCHIOR Ay, sir:
But softly! Where, in the object we select,
Such love is, perchance, wanting?

VALENCE Then indeed,
What is it you can take?

MELCHIOR Nay, ask the world!
Youth, beauty, virtue, an illustrious name,
And influence o'er mankind.

VALENCE When man perceives . . .
—Ah, I can only speak as for myself!

289| *1844:* said—for *1868:* said: for 290| *1844:* sir, would? *1863:* sir,—would? 291| *1844:* Not *1849:*—Not 293| *1844:* own.—Oh <> why, *1849:* why! *1868:* own. Oh 294| *1844·* save this,— *1868:* save one,— 295| *1844:* is your *1849:* is, your 302| *1844:* VALENCE . . Prince *1863:* VALENCE —Prince 303| *1844:* of it, *1868:* of noise, 309| *1844:* softly! Where in *1863:* softly! Where, in 310| *1844:* VALENCE Then, indeed, *1868:* VALENCE Then indeed, 311| *1844:* MELCHIOR Nay—ask *1868:* MELCHIOR Nay, ask 313| *1844:* o'er the world! VALENCE *1849:* o'er mankind! VALENCE *1863:* mankind.

THE DUCHESS Speak for yourself!
VALENCE May I!—no, I have spoken,
And time's gone by. Had I seen such an one,
As I loved her—weighing thoroughly that word—
So should my task be to evolve her love:
If for myself!—if for another—well.
BERTHOLD Heroic truly! And your sole reward,—
The secret pride in yielding up love's right?
VALENCE Who thought upon reward? And yet how much
Comes after—oh, what amplest recompense!
Is the knowledge of her, nought? the memory, nought?
——Lady, should such an one have looked on you,
Ne'er wrong yourself so far as quote the world
And say, love can go unrequited here!
You will have blessed him to his whole life's end—
Low passions hindered, baser cares kept back,
All goodness cherished where you dwelt—and dwell.
What would he have? He holds you—you, both form
And mind, in his,—where self-love makes such room
For love of you, he would not serve you now
The vulgar way,—repluse your enemies,
Win you new realms, or best, to save the old
Die blissfully—that's past so long ago!
He wishes you no need, thought, care of him—
Your good, by any means, himself unseen,
Away, forgotten!—He gives that life's task up,
As it were . . . but this charge which I return—
[*Offers the requisition, which she takes.*]

VALENCE 315| *1863:* yourself. VALENCE *1868:* yourself! VALENCE
316| *1844:* by!—Had <> one— *1863:* one, *1868:* by. Had 318| *1844:* love— *1863:* love: 319| *1844:* myself—! if <> well! *1849:* myself!—if *1863:* well.
321| *1844:* up your own? *1868:* up love's right? 323| *1844:* after—Oh what <> recompence! *1863:* recompense! *1868:* oh *1888:* oh, what 326| *1844:* world, *1868:* world 331| *1844:* have? He has you—you, the form, *1849:* have? He holds you—you, both form, *1868:* form 332| *1844:* And you, the mind, where self-love made such *1849:* And mind, in his,—where self-love makes such 335| *1844:* best, in saving you *1868:* saving old *1888:* best, to save the old 339| *1844:* forgotten,—he *1849:*

Wishing your good.
THE DUCHESS [*having subscribed it.*] And opportunely, sir—
Since at a birthday's close, like this of mine,
Good wishes gentle deeds reciprocate.
Most on a wedding-day, as mine is too,
Should gifts be thought of: yours comes first by right.
Ask of me!
BERTHOLD He shall have whate'er he asks,
For your sake and his own.
VALENCE [*aside.*] If I should ask—
The withered bunch of flowers she wears—perhaps,
One last touch of her hand, I never more
Shall see! [*After a pause, presenting his paper to the* PRINCE.]
Cleves' Prince, redress the wrongs of Cleves!
BERTHOLD I will, sir!
THE DUCHESS [*as* VALENCE *prepares to retire.*]—Nay, do out your duty, first!
You bore this paper; I have registered
My answer to it: read it and have done! [VALENCE *reads it.*]
I take him—give up Juliers and the world.
This is my Birthday.
MELCHIOR Berthold, my one hero
Of the world she gives up, one friend worth my books,
Sole man I think it pays the pains to watch,—
Speak, for I know you through your Popes and Kings!
BERTHOLD [*after a pause.*] Lady, well rewarded! Sir, as well deserved!
I could not imitate—I hardly envy—
I do admire you. All is for the best.
Too costly a flower were this, I see it now,
To pluck and set upon my barren helm

---

forgotten!—He 341| *1844:* good! THE *1868:* good. THE 344| *1844:* wedding day *1888:* wedding-day 345| *1844:* gifts go forward: yours *1849:* gifts be thought of: yours 347| *1844:* For his sake and for yours! VALENCE *1849:* For your sake and his own! VALENCE *1868:* own. VALENCE 349–350| *1844:* of . . . [*After* <> PRINCE.] Redress *1849:* of her hand. I never more / Shall see <> [*After* PRINCE.] Cleves' Prince, redress 351| *1863:* sir. THE *1888:* sir! THE 352| *1844:* paper: I *1863:* paper; I 354| *1844:*—I <> world! *1868:* I <> world. 355| *1844:* my Birth-day *1863:* my Birthday 361| *1844:* you! All <> best! *1868:* you. All <> best. 362| *1844:* were you, I *1868:* were this, I 363| *1844:* and put upon *1849:* and set

To wither—any garish plume will do.
I'll not insult you and refuse your Duchy—
You can so well afford to yield it me,
And I were left, without it, sadly lorn.
As it is—for me—if that will flatter you,
A somewhat wearier life seems to remain
Than I thought possible where . . . 'faith, their life
Begins already! They're too occupied
To listen: and few words content me best.
[*Abruptly to the* COURTIERS.] I am your Duke, though! Who obey me here?

THE DUCHESS Adolf and Sabyne follow us—

GUIBERT [*starting from the* COURTIERS.]—And I?
Do I not follow them, if I mayn't you?
Shall not I get some little duties up
At Ravestein and emulate the rest?
God save you, Gaucelme! 'Tis my Birthday, too!

BERTHOLD You happy handful that remain with me
. . . That is, with Dietrich the black Barnabite
I shall leave over you—will earn your wages
Or Dietrich has forgot to ply his trade!
Meantime,—go copy me the precedents
Of every installation, proper styles
And pedigrees of all your Juliers' Dukes—
While I prepare to plod on my old way,
And somewhat wearily, I must confess!

THE DUCHESS [*with a light joyous laugh as she turns from them.*] Come, Valence, to our friends, God's earth . . .

VALENCE [*as she falls into his arms.*]—And thee!

---

upon 364| *1844:* do! *1868:* do. 365| *1844:* your rule— *1849:* your Duchy— 367| *1844:* sadly off! *1868:* off. *1888:* sadly lorn. 371| *1844:* already—they're *1868:* already! They're 372| *1844:* listen—and <> best! *1868:* listen: and <> best. 375| *1844:* may'nt *1849:* mayn't 378| *1844:* Birth-day *1863:* Birthday 381| *1844:* wages, *1888:* wages 384| *1844:* styles, *1868:* styles 386| *1844:* to go on *1868:* to plod on 388| *1844:* friends—God's earth—VALENCE <> thee!/*Curtain falls* THE END. *1849:* thee! *1863:* earth . . . VALENCE *1868:* friends, God's

BY THE SAME AUTHOR.

I.

PARACELSUS. A POEM.

Price 6*s*. *boards*.

II.

SORDELLO. A POEM.

Price 6*s*. 6*d*. *boards*.

III.

BELLS AND POMEGRANATES.

No. I.—PIPPA PASSES. *Price* 1*s*.

No. II.—KING VICTOR AND KING CHARLES. *Price* 1*s*.

No. III.—DRAMATIC LYRICS. *Price* 1*s*.

No. IV.—THE RETURN OF THE DRUSES. *Price* 1*s*.

No. V.—A BLOT IN THE 'SCUTCHEON. *Price* 1*s*.

Nearly Ready.

No. VII.—DRAMATIC ROMANCES AND LYRICS.

No. VIII.—A SOUL'S TRAGEDY.

BELLS AND POMEGRANATES, NUMBER VII.

DRAMATIC ROMANCES AND LYRICS

Edited by Raymond Fitch

DRAMATIC ROMANCES

1845: Bells and Pomegranates. / No. VII. / Dramatic Romances & Lyrics. / By Robert Browning, / Author of "Paracelsus." *1849:* Dramatic <> Lyrics. *1863:* Lyrics, Romances, Men, and Women. § See Ed. Notes and Table of Contents for the redistribution in 1863 of the original contents of Bells and Pomegranates, No. VIII. This arrangement was retained in 1868, 1888 and 1889. §

INSCRIBED TO JOHN KENYON, ESQ., IN THE HOPE THAT A RECOLLECTION OF HIS OWN SUCCESSFUL "RHYMED PLEA FOR TOLERANCE" MAY INDUCE HIM TO ADMIT GOOD-NATUREDLY THIS HUMBLER PROSE ONE OF HIS VERY SINCERE FRIEND, R. B.

NOV. 1845.

§ appears only in 1845 on contents page §

In this volume are collected and redistributed the pieces first published in 1842, 1845 and 1855, respectively, under the titles of "Dramatic Lyrics," "Dramatic Romances," and "Men and Women."

Part of these were inscribed to my dear friend John Kenyon: I hope the whole may obtain the honour of an association with his memory.

R. B.

1863: § appeared facing first page of text § *1868:* § appeared in section preceding *Dramatic Lyrics* § In a late edition were collected <> Women." It is not worth while to disturb this arrangement. ¶ Part of the Poems were *1888:* § omitted §

Page

1845:

1849:

1855:

MEN AND WOMEN.

VOLUME I.

Volume II.

1863:

LYRICS.

Romances.

Men, and Women.

DRAMATIC ROMANCES AND LYRICS

1845

"HOW THEY BROUGHT THE GOOD NEWS FROM GHENT TO AIX"

[16—]

I

I sprang to the stirrup, and Joris, and he;
I galloped, Dirck galloped, we galloped all three;
"Good speed!" cried the watch, as the gate-bolts undrew;
"Speed!" echoed the wall to us galloping through;
Behind shut the postern, the lights sank to rest,
And into the midnight we galloped abreast.

II

Not a word to each other; we kept the great pace
Neck by neck, stride by stride, never changing our place;
I turned in my saddle and made its girths tight,
Then shortened each stirrup, and set the pique right,
Rebuckled the cheek-strap, chained slacker the bit,
Nor galloped less steadily Roland a whit.

III

'Twas moonset at starting; but while we drew near
Lokeren, the cocks crew and twilight dawned clear;
At Boom, a great yellow star came out to see;
At Düffeld, 'twas morning as plain as could be;
And from Mecheln church-steeple we heard the half-chime,
So, Joris broke silence with, "Yet there is time!"

---

§ Ed. 1845, 1849, 1863, 1868, 1888, 1889. For earlier single publications see note to specific poem. No MS known to be extant. §

"HOW THEY BROUGHT THE GOOD NEWS FROM GHENT TO AIX"
§ Subsequent placement: *1863:* DL § [1]| *1845:* and He; *1849:* he; [2]| *1845:* all Three; *1849:* three; [8]| *1845:* stride for stride *1849:* stride by stride

IV

At Aershot, up leaped of a sudden the sun,
And against him the cattle stood black every one,
To stare thro' the mist at us galloping past,
And I saw my stout galloper Roland at last,
With resolute shoulders, each butting away
The haze, as some bluff river headland its spray:

V

And his low head and crest, just one sharp ear bent back
For my voice, and the other pricked out on his track;
And one eye's black intelligence,—ever that glance
O'er its white edge at me, his own master, askance!
And the thick heavy spume-flakes which aye and anon
His fierce lips shook upwards in galloping on.

VI

By Hasselt, Dirck groaned; and cried Joris, "Stay spur!
Your Roos galloped bravely, the fault's not in her,
We'll remember at Aix"—for one heard the quick wheeze
Of her chest, saw the stretched neck and staggering knees,
And sunk tail, and horrible heave of the flank,
As down on her haunches she shuddered and sank.

VII

So, we were left galloping, Joris and I,
Past Looz and past Tongres, no cloud in the sky;
The broad sun above laughed a pitiless laugh,
'Neath our feet broke the brittle bright stubble like chaff;
Till over by Dalhem a dome-spire sprang white,
And "Gallop," gasped Joris, "for Aix is in sight!"

18| *1845:* So Joris *1868:* So, Joris 24| *1845:* haze as <> spray. *1849:* haze, as *1868:* spray: 37| *1845:* So left were we galloping *1849:* So we were left galloping

VIII

"How they'll greet us!"—and all in a moment his roan
Rolled neck and croup over, lay dead as a stone;
And there was my Roland to bear the whole weight
Of the news which alone could save Aix from her fate,
With his nostrils like pits full of blood to the brim,
And with circles of red for his eye-sockets' rim.

IX

Then I cast loose my buffcoat, each holster let fall,
Shook off both my jack-boots, let go belt and all,
Stood up in the stirrup, leaned, patted his ear,
Called my Roland his pet-name, my horse without peer;
Clapped my hands, laughed and sang, any noise, bad or good,
Till at length into Aix Roland galloped and stood.

X

And all I remember is—friends flocking round
As I sat with his head 'twixt my knees on the ground;
And no voice but was praising this Roland of mine,
As I poured down his throat our last measure of wine,
Which (the burgesses voted by common consent)
Was no more than his due who brought good news from Ghent.

1868: So, we 43| *1845:* us "—and *1849:* us! "—and 55| *1845:* is, friends *1888:* is—friends 56| *1845:* sate <> ground, *1863:* sat <> ground;

PICTOR IGNOTUS

FLORENCE, 15—

I could have painted pictures like that youth's
Ye praise so. How my soul springs up! No bar
Stayed me—ah, thought which saddens while it soothes!
—Never did fate forbid me, star by star,
To outburst on your night with all my gift
Of fires from God: nor would my flesh have shrunk
From seconding my soul, with eyes uplift
And wide to heaven, or, straight like thunder, sunk
To the centre, of an instant; or around
Turned calmly and inquisitive, to scan
The licence and the limit, space and bound,
Allowed to truth made visible in man.
And, like that youth ye praise so, all I saw,
Over the canvas could my hand have flung,
Each face obedient to its passion's law,
Each passion clear proclaimed without a tongue;
Whether Hope rose at once in all the blood,
A-tiptoe for the blessing of embrace,
Or Rapture drooped the eyes, as when her brood
Pull down the nesting dove's heart to its place;
Or Confidence lit swift the forehead up,
And locked the mouth fast, like a castle braved,—
O human faces, hath it spilt, my cup?
What did ye give me that I have not saved?
Nor will I say I have not dreamed (how well!)
Of going—I, in each new picture,—forth,
As, making new hearts beat and bosoms swell,

PICTOR IGNOTUS § Subsequent placement: 1863: MW § 3| *1849:* soothes!— *1863:* soothes! 4| *1845:* Never *1863:* —Never 6| *1845:* would this flesh *1849:* would my flesh 7| *1845:* seconding that soul *1849:* seconding my soul 8| *1845:* to Heaven *1863:* heaven 9| *1845:* centre of an instant, or *1849:* centre, of an instant; or 10| *1845:* Sent calmly and inquisitive to *1849:* Turned calmly and inquisitive, to 11| *1845:* license *1863:* licence 12| *1845:* to Truth <> Man. *1868:* truth <> man. 14| *1845:* canvass *1863:* canvas 19| *1845:* eyes as *1849:* eyes, as 20| *1845:* place, *1863:* place; 23| *1845:* Men, women, children, hath *1849:* O Human faces, hath *1863:* human 27| *1845:* And making *1849:* As,

To Pope or Kaiser, East, West, South, or North,
Bound for the calmly-satisfied great State,
Or glad aspiring little burgh, it went,
Flowers cast upon the car which bore the freight,
Through old streets named afresh from the event,
Till it reached home, where learned age should greet
My face, and youth, the star not yet distinct
Above his hair, lie learning at my feet!—
Oh, thus to live, I and my picture, linked
With love about, and praise, till life should end,
And then not go to heaven, but linger here,
Here on my earth, earth's every man my friend,—
The thought grew frightful, 'twas so wildly dear!
But a voice changed it. Glimpses of such sights
Have scared me, like the revels through a door
Of some strange house of idols at its rites!
This world seemed not the world it was before:
Mixed with my loving trusting ones, there trooped
. . . Who summoned those cold faces that begun
To press on me and judge me? Though I stooped
Shrinking, as from the soldiery a nun,
They drew me forth, and spite of me . . . enough!
These buy and sell our pictures, take and give,
Count them for garniture and household-stuff,
And where they live needs must our pictures live

---

making 28| *1845:* As still to Pope and Kaiser, South and North, *1849:* To Pope or Kaiser, East, West, South or North, *1888:* South, or 29| *1845:* calmly satisfied *1888:* calmly-satisfied 31| *1845:* freight *1849:* freight, 32| *1845:* from its event, *1868:* from the event, 33| *1845:* —Of reaching thus my home, where Age *1849:* Till it reached home, where learned Age *1868:* age 34| *1845:* and Youth <> star as yet *1849:* star not yet *1868:* youth 35| *1845:* feet,— *1849:* feet!— 36| *1845:* pictures *1849:* picture 38| *1845:* to Heaven but *1849:* to Heaven, but *1863:* heaven 39| *1845:* earth, its every *1849:* earth, earth's every 40| *1845:* Oh, that grows <> 'tis *1849:* The thought grew <> 'twas 41| *1845:* it! Glimpses *1868:* it. Glimpses 42| *1845:* thro' *1863:* through 43| *1845:* strange House of Idols <> rites; *1868:* house of idols <> rites! 44| *1845:* before! *1863:* before: 45| *1845:* loving ones there trooped—for what? *1849:* loving trusting ones <> trooped *1888:* ones, there 46| *1845:* Who <> faces which begun *1849:* . . . Who <> faces that begun 47| *1845:* judge me? As asquat *1849:* judge me? Tho' I stooped *1863:* Though 48| *1845:* And shrinking from *1849:* Shrinking, as from 49| *1845:* me . . enough! *1888:* me . . . enough! 52| *1845:* live our pictures needs must live, *1863:*

And see their faces, listen to their prate,
Partakers of their daily pettiness,
Discussed of,—"This I love, or this I hate,
This likes me more, and this affects me less!"
Wherefore I chose my portion. If at whiles
My heart sinks, as monotonous I paint
These endless cloisters and eternal aisles
With the same series, Virgin, Babe and Saint,
With the same cold calm beautiful regard,—
At least no merchant traffics in my heart;
The sanctuary's gloom at least shall ward
Vain tongues from where my pictures stand apart:
Only prayer breaks the silence of the shrine
While, blackening in the daily candle-smoke,
They moulder on the damp wall's travertine,
'Mid echoes the light footstep never woke.
So, die my pictures! surely, gently die!
O youth, men praise so,—holds their praise its worth?
Blown harshly, keeps the trump its golden cry?
Tastes sweet the water with such specks of earth?

---

must live *1868:* live needs must our pictures live 55| *1845:* love or *1849:* love, or 56| *1845:* more and *1849:* more, and 58| *1845:* sinks as *1849:* sinks, as 60| *1845:* series, Virgin, Babe, and *1863:* series, Virgin, Babe and 61| *1845:* cold, calm, beautiful regard, *1868:* cold calm beautiful regard,— 64| *1845:* apart; *1863:* apart: 66| *1845:* candle smoke, *1849:* candle-smoke, *1868:* While blackening *1888:* While, blackening 69| *1845:* So die, my pictures; surely *1868:* So, die my pictures! surely 70| *1845:* Oh youth men <> so, holds *1849:* Oh, youth, men <> so,—holds *1868:* O youth

THE ITALIAN IN ENGLAND

That second time they hunted me
From hill to plain, from shore to sea,
And Austria, hounding far and wide
Her blood-hounds thro' the country-side,
Breathed hot and instant on my trace,—
I made six days a hiding-place
Of that dry green old aqueduct
Where I and Charles, when boys, have plucked
The fire-flies from the roof above,
Bright creeping thro' the moss they love:
—How long it seems since Charles was lost!
Six days the soldiers crossed and crossed
The country in my very sight;
And when that peril ceased at night,
The sky broke out in red dismay
With signal fires; well, there I lay
Close covered o'er in my recess,
Up to the neck in ferns and cress,
Thinking on Metternich our friend,
And Charles's miserable end,
And much beside, two days; the third,
Hunger o'ercame me when I heard
The peasants from the village go
To work among the maize; you know,

THE ITALIAN IN ENGLAND § Subsequent placement: 1863: DR § Title/ *1845: ITALY IN ENGLAND* *1849: THE ITALIAN IN ENGLAND* 4| *1863:* through the country-side *1868:* thro' *1888:* country-side, 5| *1845:* trace, *1849:* trace,— 8| *1863:* boys have *1868:* boys, have 10| *1845:* love. *1868:* love: 16| *1845:*

With us in Lombardy, they bring
Provisions packed on mules, a string
With little bells that cheer their task,
And casks, and boughs on every cask
To keep the sun's heat from the wine;
These I let pass in jingling line,
And, close on them, dear noisy crew,
The peasants from the village, too;
For at the very rear would troop
Their wives and sisters in a group
To help, I knew. When these had passed,
I threw my glove to strike the last,
Taking the chance: she did not start,
Much less cry out, but stooped apart,
One instant rapidly glanced round,
And saw me beckon from the ground.
A wild bush grows and hides my crypt;
She picked my glove up while she stripped
A branch off, then rejoined the rest
With that; my glove lay in her breast.
Then I drew breath; they disappeared:
It was for Italy I feared.

An hour, and she returned alone
Exactly where my glove was thrown.
Meanwhile came many thoughts: on me
Rested the hopes of Italy.
I had devised a certain tale
Which, when 'twas told her, could not fail
Persuade a peasant of its truth;
I meant to call a freak of youth
This hiding, and give hopes of pay,
And no temptation to betray.
But when I saw that woman's face,
Its calm simplicity of grace,

---

signal-fires *1868:* signal fires [25]| *1845:* us, in *1863:* us in [35]| *1845:* knew; when *1888:* knew. When [38]| *1845:* apart *1868:* apart, [39]| *1845:* instant, rapidly *1868:* instant rapidly [40]| *1845:* ground: [44]| *1845:* breast: *1888:* breast. [45]| *1845:* breath: they *1868:* breath; they [49]| *1845:* thoughts; on *1888:* thoughts: on [50]| *1845:* Italy; *1888:* Italy. [54]| *1845:* This hiding was a <> youth; *1849:* I meant to call a <> youth [55]| *1845:* I meant to give her hopes

Our Italy's own attitude
In which she walked thus far, and stood,
Planting each naked foot so firm,
To crush the snake and spare the worm—
At first sight of her eyes, I said,
"I am that man upon whose head
They fix the price, because I hate
The Austrians over us: the State
Will give you gold—oh, gold so much!—
If you betray me to their clutch,
And be your death, for aught I know,
If once they find you saved their foe.
Now, you must bring me food and drink,
And also paper, pen and ink,
And carry safe what I shall write
To Padua, which you'll reach at night
Before the duomo shuts; go in,
And wait till Tenebræ begin;
Walk to the third confessional,
Between the pillar and the wall,
And kneeling whisper, *Whence comes peace?*
Say it a second time, then cease;
And if the voice inside returns,
From Christ and Freedom; what concerns
The cause of Peace?—for answer, slip
My letter where you placed your lip;
Then come back happy we have done
Our mother service—I, the son,
As you the daughter of our land!"

1849: This hiding, and give hopes 64| *1845:* that person on whose *1849:* that man upon whose 65| *1845:* price because *1849:* price, because 67| *1845:* much, *1868:* much!— 68| *1845:* clutch! *1863:* clutch *1868:* clutch, 72| *1845:* pen, and *1863:* pen and 75| *1845:* the Duomo *1868:* duomo 77| *1845:* the Third Confessional, *1868:* third confessional, 79| *1845:* whisper *whence* *1863:* whisper, *Whence* 80| *1845:* time; then *1863:* time, then 81| *1849:* returns *1863:*

Three mornings more, she took her stand
In the same place, with the same eyes:
I was no surer of sun-rise
Than of her coming. We conferred
Of her own prospects, and I heard
She had a lover—stout and tall,
She said—then let her eyelids fall,
"He could do much"—as if some doubt
Entered her heart,—then, passing out,
"She could not speak for others, who
Had other thoughts; herself she knew:"
And so she brought me drink and food.
After four days, the scouts pursued
Another path; at last arrived
The help my Paduan friends contrived
To furnish me: she brought the news.
For the first time I could not choose
But kiss her hand, and lay my own
Upon her head—"This faith was shown
To Italy, our mother; she
Uses my hand and blesses thee."
She followed down to the sea-shore;
I left and never saw her more.

How very long since I have thought
Concerning—much less wished for—aught
Beside the good of Italy,
For which I live and mean to die!
I never was in love; and since
Charles proved false, what shall now convince
My inmost heart I have a friend?
However, if I pleased to spend
Real wishes on myself—say, three—
I know at least what one should be.

---

returns, 91| *1845:* coming: we *1888:* coming. We 97| *1845:* others— who *1863:* others, who 101| *1845:* path: at *1863:* path; at 103| *1845:* news: *1863:* news. 105| *1845:* hand and *1863:* hand, and 107| *1845:* mother;—she *1863:* mother; she 108| *1845:* thee!" *1868:* thee." 113| *1845:* of Italy *1863:* of Italy, 115| *1845:* In love I never was; and *1849:* I never was in love; and 116| *1845:* false, nothing could convince *1868:* false, what shall now convince 117| *1845:* had a friend; *1863:* friend. *1868:* have a friend? 119| *1845:* say, Three— *1863:* three— 120| *1845:* be; *1868:* be.

I would grasp Metternich until
I felt his red wet throat distil
In blood thro' these two hands. And next,
—Nor much for that am I perplexed—
Charles, perjured traitor, for his part,
Should die slow of a broken heart
Under his new employers. Last
—Ah, there, what should I wish? For fast
Do I grow old and out of strength.
If I resolved to seek at length
My father's house again, how scared
They all would look, and unprepared!
My brothers live in Austria's pay
—Disowned me long ago, men say;
And all my early mates who used
To praise me so—perhaps induced
More than one early step of mine—
Are turning wise: while some opine
"Freedom grows license," some suspect
"Haste breeds delay," and recollect
They always said, such premature
Beginnings never could endure!
So, with a sullen "All's for best,"
The land seems settling to its rest.
I think then, I should wish to stand
This evening in that dear, lost land,
Over the sea the thousand miles,
And know if yet that woman smiles
With the calm smile; some little farm
She lives in there, no doubt: what harm

123| *1845:* hands: and *1868:* hands. And 127| *1845:* employers—last *1849:* employers: last *1868:* employers. Last 128| *1845:* should one wish *1849:* should I wish 129| *1845:* strength; *1849:* strength.— *1863:* strength. 138| *1845:* wise; while part opine *1849:* while some opine *1868:* wise: while 139| *1845:* grows License," part suspect *1849:* grows License," some suspect *1868:* license 140| *1845:* breeds Delay *1868:* delay 141| *1845:* said such *1849:* said, such 142| *1845:* endure: *1849:* endure! 145| *1845:* think, then *1868:* think then 149| *1845:* smile—some *1849:* smile; some 150| *1845:* doubt—what *1849:* doubt; what *1868:*

If I sat on the door-side bench,
And, while her spindle made a trench
Fantastically in the dust,
Inquired of all her fortunes—just
Her children's ages and their names,
And what may be the husband's aims
For each of them. I'd talk this out,
And sit there, for an hour about,
Then kiss her hand once more, and lay
Mine on her head, and go my way.

So much for idle wishing—how
It steals the time! To business now.

---

doubt: what 151| *1845:* sate *1863:* sat 157| *1845:* them—I'd *1863:* them. I'd 162| *1845:* now! *1868:* now.

THE ENGLISHMAN IN ITALY

PIANO DI SORRENTO

Fortù, Fortù, my beloved one,
Sit here by my side,
On my knees put up both little feet!
I was sure, if I tried,
I could make you laugh spite of Scirocco.
Now, open your eyes,
Let me keep you amused till he vanish
In black from the skies,
With telling my memories over
As you tell your beads;
All the Plain saw me gather, I garland
—The flowers or the weeds.

Time for rain! for your long hot dry Autumn
Had net-worked with brown
The white skin of each grape on the bunches,
Marked like a quail's crown,
Those creatures you make such account of,
Whose heads,—speckled white
Over brown like a great spider's back,
As I told you last night,—
Your mother bites off for her supper.
Red-ripe as could be,
Pomegranates were chapping and splitting
In halves on the tree:

THE ENGLISHMAN IN ITALY § Subsequent placement: 1863: DR § Title/ *1845: ENGLAND IN ITALY* *1849: THE ENGLISHMAN IN ITALY* 1| *1845:* loved *1849:* beloved 2| *1845:* Sit by *1849:* Sit here by 5| *1845:* Scirocco: *1863:* Scirocco. 6| *1845:* eyes— *1863:* eyes, 11| *1849:* the memories plucked at Sorrento *1863:* the Plain saw me gather, I garland 12| *1845:* —Flowers prove they, or weeds. *1849:* —The flowers, or the weeds. *1863:* flowers or 13| *1845:* 'Twas time, for *1849:* Time for rain! for 18| *1845:* heads,—specked with white *1868:* heads,—speckled white 21| *1845:* supper; *1863:* supper. 22| *1849:* be. *1863:*

And betwixt the loose walls of great flintstone,
Or in the thick dust
On the path, or straight out of the rock-side,
Wherever could thrust
Some burnt sprig of bold hardy rock-flower
Its yellow face up,
For the prize were great butterflies fighting,
Some five for one cup.
So, I guessed, ere I got up this morning,
What change was in store,
By the quick rustle-down of the quail-nets
Which woke me before
I could open my shutter, made fast
With a bough and a stone,
And look thro' the twisted dead vine-twigs,
Sole lattice that's known.
Quick and sharp rang the rings down the net-poles,
While, busy beneath,
Your priest and his brother tugged at them,
The rain in their teeth.
And out upon all the flat house-roofs
Where split figs lay drying,
The girls took the frails under cover:
Nor use seemed in trying
To get out the boats and go fishing,
For, under the cliff,
Fierce the black water frothed o'er the blind-rock.
No seeing our skiff
Arrive about noon from Amalfi,
—Our fisher arrive,
And pitch down his basket before us,
All trembling alive
With pink and grey jellies, your sea-fruit;
You touch the strange lumps,

---

be, [25]| *1845:* 'twixt *1849:* betwixt [27]| *1845:* rock side, *1863:* rock-side, [29]| *1845:* Some starved sprig *1849:* Some burnt sprig [32]| *1845:* cup: *1849:* cup. [33]| *1845:* So I *1849:* So, I [40]| *1845:* known; *1849:* known! *1863:* known. [41]| *1845:* Sharp rang <> down the bird-poles *1849:* Quick and sharp <> down the net-poles, [43]| *1845:* brother were working, *1849:* brother tugged at them, [44]| *1849:* teeth: *1863:* teeth. [50]| *1845:* For under the cliff *1849:* For, under the cliff, [51]| *1845:* blind-rock— *1849:* blind-rock. [57]| *1845:* sea-fruit, *1863:* sea-fruit; [58]| —Touch *1849:* —You touch *1863:* You

And mouths gape there, eyes open, all manner
Of horns and of humps,
Which only the fisher looks grave at,
While round him like imps
Cling screaming the children as naked
And brown as his shrimps;
Himself too as bare to the middle
—You see round his neck
The string and its brass coin suspended,
That saves him from wreck.
But to-day not a boat reached Salerno,
So back, to a man,
Came our friends, with whose help in the vineyards
Grape-harvest began.
In the vat, halfway up in our house-side,
Like blood the juice spins,
While your brother all bare-legged is dancing
Till breathless he grins
Dead-beaten in effort on effort
To keep the grapes under,
Since still when he seems all but master,
In pours the fresh plunder
From girls who keep coming and going
With basket on shoulder,
And eyes shut against the rain's driving;
Your girls that are older,—
For under the hedges of aloe,
And where, on its bed
Of the orchard's black mould, the love-apple
Lies pulpy and red,
All the young ones are kneeling and filling
Their laps with the snails
Tempted out by this first rainy weather,—
Your best of regales,
As to-night will be proved to my sorrow,

64| *1845:* shrimps, *1849:* shrimps; 65| *1849:* middle— *1863:* middle
70| *1845:* back to a man *1863:* back, to a man, 72| *1845:* began: *1863:* began. 73| *1845:* vat half-way <> house-side. *1849:* vat, half-way <> house-side, *1863:* halfway 74| *1845:* spins *1849:* spins, 77| *1845:* Dead-beaten, in *1863:* Dead-beaten in 79| *1845:* For still <> master *1849:* Since still <> master,
83| *1845:* driving, *1863:* driving; 91| *1845:* by the first *1849:* by this first

When, supping in state,
We shall feast our grape-gleaners (two dozen,
Three over one plate)
With lasagne so tempting to swallow
In slippery ropes,
And gourds fried in great purple slices,
That colour of popes.
Meantime, see the grape bunch they've brought you:
The rain-water slips
O'er the heavy blue bloom on each globe
Which the wasp to your lips
Still follows with fretful persistence:
Nay, taste, while awake,
This half of a curd-white smooth cheese-ball
That peels, flake by flake,
Like an onion, each smoother and whiter;
Next, sip this weak wine
From the thin green glass flask, with its stopper,
A leaf of the vine;
And end with the prickly-pear's red flesh
That leaves thro' its juice
The stony black seeds on your pearl-teeth.
Scirocco is loose!
Hark, the quick, whistling pelt of the olives
Which, thick in one's track,
Tempt the stranger to pick up and bite them,
Tho' not yet half black!
How the old twisted olive trunks shudder,
The medlars let fall
Their hard fruit, and the brittle great fig-trees
Snap off, figs and all,

95| *1845:* grape-gleaners—two *1849:* grape-gleaners (two 96| *1845:* plate,— *1849:* plate) 97| *1845:* Maccaroni so *1849:* With lasagne so 98| *1845:* slippery strings, *1849:* slippery ropes, 100| *1845:* of kings,— *1849:* of popes.
101| *1845:* grape-bunch <> you,— *1863:* grape bunch <> you: 105| *1845:* persistence— *1863:* persistence: 106| *1845:* taste while *1849:* taste, while
107| *1845:* cheese-ball, *1863:* cheese-ball 109| *1845:* onion's <> whiter— *1849:* whiter; *1863:* onion 110| *1845:* Next sip *1849:* Next, sip 112| *1845:* vine,— *1863:* vine; 115| *1845:* pearl-teeth *1863:* pearl-teeth. 116| *1845:* . . . Scirocco *1849:* . . Scirocco *1863:* Scirocco 117| *1845:* Hark! the quick pelt *1849:* quick, whistling pelt *1868:* Hark, the 119| *1845:* them *1849:* them, 121| *1845:* And how their old twisted trunks shudder! *1849:* How the old twisted olive trunks *1868:* shudder, 123| *1845:* fruit—the *1849:* fruit, and the 124| *1849:* all,— *1863:*

For here comes the whole of the tempest!
    No refuge, but creep
Back again to my side and my shoulder,
    And listen or sleep.

O how will your country show next week,
    When all the vine-boughs
Have been stripped of their foliage to pasture
    The mules and the cows?
Last eve, I rode over the mountains;
    Your brother, my guide,
Soon left me, to feast on the myrtles
    That offered, each side,
Their fruit-balls, black, glossy and luscious,—
    Or strip from the sorbs
A treasure, or, rosy and wondrous,
    Those hairy gold orbs!
But my mule picked his sure sober path out,
    Just stopping to neigh
When he recognized down in the valley
    His mates on their way
With the faggots and barrels of water;
    And soon we emerged
From the plain, where the woods could scarce follow;
    And still as we urged
Our way, the woods wondered, and left us,
    As up still we trudged
Though the wild path grew wilder each instant,
    And place was e'en grudged
'Mid the rock-chasms and piles of loose stones
    Like the loose broken teeth
Of some monster which climbed there to die
    From the ocean beneath—

---

all, 126| *1845:* refuge but *1849:* refuge, but 133| *1845:* eve I <> mountains— *1849:* eve, I <> mountains; 135| *1845:* me to *1849:* me, to 137| *1845:* luscious, *1849:* luscious,— 139| *1845:* treasure, so rosy *1868:* treasure, or, rosy 140| *1845:* Of hairy *1868:* Those hairy 141| *1845:* sure, sober *1868:* sure sober 143| *1845:* recognised *1863:* recognized 145| *1845:* faggots, and *1868:* faggots and 147| *1845:* plain where <> follow *1849:* plain, where <> follow; 153| *1845:* rock-chasms, and *1863:* rock-chasms and 154| *1849:* (Like *1863:* Like 155| *1845:* monster, which *1863:* monster which 156| *1849:*

Place was grudged to the silver-grey fume-weed
That clung to the path,
And dark rosemary ever a-dying
That, 'spite the wind's wrath,
So loves the salt rock's face to seaward,
And lentisks as staunch
To the stone where they root and bear berries,
And . . . what shows a branch
Coral-coloured, transparent, with circlets
Of pale seagreen leaves;
Over all trod my mule with the caution
Of gleaners o'er sheaves,
Still, foot after foot like a lady,
Till, round after round,
He climbed to the top of Calvano,
And God's own profound
Was above me, and round me the mountains,
And under, the sea,
And within me my heart to bear witness
What was and shall be.
Oh, heaven and the terrible crystal!
No rampart excludes
Your eye from the life to be lived
In the blue solitudes.
Oh, those mountains, their infinite movement!
Still moving with you;
For, ever some new head and breast of them
Thrusts into view
To observe the intruder; you see it
If quickly you turn
And, before they escape you, surprise them.

---

beneath) *1863:* beneath— 159| *1845:* rosemary, ever a-dying, *1863:* rosemary ever a-dying 160| *1845:* Which, 'spite *1849:* That, 'spite 161| *1845:* seaward,— *1863:* seaward, 163| *1849:* berries,— *1863:* berries, 164| *1845:* And—what *1849:* And . . . what 166| *1845:* leaves— *1863:* leaves; 168| *1845:* sheaves: *1849:* sheaves, 169| *1845:* Foot after <> lady— *1849:* Still, foot after *1863:* lady: *1888:* lady, 170| *1845:* So, round after *1888:* Till, round after 175| *1845:* with me, my *1849:* within *1868:* me my 176| *1845:* be! *1868:* be. 177| *1845:* Oh heaven, and *1863:* Oh, heaven and 179| *1845:* The eye *1849:* Your eye 180| *1845:* solitudes! *1868:* solitudes. 182| *1845:* you— *1863:* you; 183| *1845:* For ever *1849:* For, ever 185| *1845:* intruder—you *1863:* intruder; you 187| *1845:* you, surprise them— *1863:* them: *1888:* you surprise them.

They grudge you should learn
How the soft plains they look on, lean over
And love (they pretend)
—Cower beneath them, the flat sea-pine crouches,
The wild fruit-trees bend,
E'en the myrtle-leaves curl, shrink and shut:
All is silent and grave:
'Tis a sensual and timorous beauty,
How fair! but a slave.
So, I turned to the sea; and there slumbered
As greenly as ever
Those isles of the siren, your Galli;
No ages can sever
The Three, nor enable their sister
To join them,—halfway
On the voyage, she looked at Ulysses—
No farther to-day,
Tho' the small one, just launched in the wave,
Watches breast-high and steady
From under the rock, her bold sister
Swum halfway already.
Fortù, shall we sail there together
And see from the sides
Quite new rocks show their faces, new haunts
Where the siren abides?
Shall we sail round and round them, close over
The rocks, tho' unseen,
That ruffle the grey glassy water
To glorious green?
Then scramble from splinter to splinter,
Reach land and explore,

189| *1845:* over, *1863:* over 190| *1845:* love, they pretend, *1849:* love (they pretend) 191| *1845:* them—the *1849:* them; the *1863:* them, the 193| *1845:* shut— *1863:* shut, *1868:* shut: 194| *1845:* grave— *1863:* grave, *1868:* grave: 195| *1845:* beauty— *1863:* beauty, 196| *1845:* fair, but a slave! *1863:* fair! but a slave. 197| *1845:* So I <> sea,—and *1849:* So, I *1863:* sea; and 199| *1845:* syren *1849:* siren 201| *1845:* The Three—nor *1849:* The Three, nor 202| *1845:* half way *1863:* halfway 204| *1849:* to-day; *1863:* further to-day, *1868:* farther 208| *1845:* half-way *1863:* halfway 209| *1845:* O when shall *1849:* Fortù, shall 211| *1845:* faces—new *1863:* faces, new 212| *1845:* syren *1849:* siren 213| *1845:* Oh, to sail *1849:* Shall we sail 215| *1849:* gray *1863:* grey 216| *1845:* green,— *1849:* green? 218| *1845:* explore *1849:*

On the largest, the strange square black turret
With never a door,
Just a loop to admit the quick lizards;
Then, stand there and hear
The birds' quiet singing, that tells us
What life is, so clear?
—The secret they sang to Ulysses
When, ages ago,
He heard and he knew this life's secret
I hear and I know.

Ah, see! The sun breaks o'er Calvano;
He strikes the great gloom
And flutters it o'er the mount's summit
In airy gold fume.
All is over. Look out, see the gipsy,
Our tinker and smith,
Has arrived, set up bellows and forge,
And down-squatted forthwith
To his hammering, under the wall there;
One eye keeps aloof
The urchins that itch to be putting
His jews'-harps to proof,
While the other, thro' locks of curled wire,
Is watching how sleek
Shines the hog, come to share in the windfall
—Chew, abbot's own cheek!
All is over. Wake up and come out now,
And down let us go,
And see the fine things got in order

---

explore, 220| *1845:* door— *1849:* door, 221| *1845:* loop that admits *1849:* loop to admit 222| *1845:* —To stand *1849:* Then, stand 224| *1845:* clear; *1849:* clear! *1863:* clear? 225| *1845:* The <> Ulysses, *1863:* —The <> Ulysses 226| *1845:* When ages ago *1849:* When, ages ago, 227| *1849:* secret, *1863:* secret 228| *1845:* know! *1868:* know. 229| *1845:* Ah see! O'er Calvano the sun breaks: *1849:* Ah, see! The sun breaks o'er Calvano— *1863:* o'er Calvano; 231| *1845:* over his summit *1849:* o'er the mount's summit 232| *1845:* fume! *1868:* fume. 233| *1845:* gypsy, *1849:* over! Look *1863:* gipsy, *1868:* over. Look 237| *1845:* hammering under *1849:* hammering, under 241| *1845:* other thro' <> wire *1849:* other, thro' <> wire, 243| *1845:* windfalls *1863:* windfall 244| *1845:* —An abbot's *1863:* cheek. *1888:* —Chew, abbot's own cheek! 245| *1845:* over! wake *1849:* over! Wake *1868:* over. Wake 247| *1845:* see all the <> things set

At church for the show
Of the Sacrament, set forth this evening.
To-morrow's the Feast
Of the Rosary's Virgin, by no means
Of Virgins the least,
As you'll hear in the off-hand discourse
Which (all nature, no art)
The Dominican brother, these three weeks,
Was getting by heart.
Not a pillar nor post but is dizened
With red and blue papers;
All the roof waves with ribbons, each altar
A-blaze with long tapers;
But the great masterpiece is the scaffold
Rigged glorious to hold
All the fiddlers and fifers and drummers
And trumpeters bold,
Not afraid of Bellini nor Auber,
Who, when the priest's hoarse,
Will strike us up something that's brisk
For the feast's second course.
And then will the flaxen-wigged Image
Be carried in pomp
Thro' the plain, while in gallant procession
The priests mean to stomp.
All round the glad church lie old bottles
With gunpowder stopped,
Which will be, when the Image re-enters,
Religiously popped;
And at night from the crest of Calvano
Great bonfires will hang,
On the plain will the trumpets join chorus,
And more poppers bang.

---

in *1849:* see the <> things got in 248| *1849:* At Church *1868:* church 249| *1845:* evening; *1888:* evening 252| *1845:* virgins the least— *1849:* Of Virgins *1863:* least, 253| *1845:* As we'll hear *1849:* As you'll hear 255| *1845:* brother these <> weeks *1849:* brother, these <> weeks, 257| *1845:* a post nor a pillar but's *1863:* a pillar nor post but is 259| *1845:* altar's *1849:* altar 263| *1845:* drummers, *1863:* drummers 273| *1845:* And all <> church stand old *1849:* church lie old *1868:* All round 276| *1845:* popped. *1868:* popped; 280| *1845:*

At all events, come—to the garden
 As far as the wall;
See me tap with a hoe on the plaster
 Till out there shall fall
A scorpion with wide angry nippers!

 —"Such trifles!" you say?
Fortù, in my England at home,
 Men meet gravely to-day
And debate, if abolishing Corn-laws
 Be righteous and wise
—If 'twere proper, Scirocco should vanish
 In black from the skies!

---

bang! *1868:* bang. 281| *1845:* garden, *1888:* garden 282| *1845:* wall, *1863:* wall; 286| *1845:* . . . "Such trifles" you *1849:* trifles"—you *1863:* —"Such trifles!" you 290| *1849:* Is *1863:* Be 291| *1845:* 'tis proper Scirocco *1849:* proper, Scirocco *1863:* 'twere

THE LOST LEADER

I

Just for a handful of silver he left us,
Just for a riband to stick in his coat—
Found the one gift of which fortune bereft us,
Lost all the others she lets us devote;
They, with the gold to give, doled him out silver,
So much was theirs who so little allowed:
How all our copper had gone for his service!
Rags—were they purple, his heart had been proud!
We that had loved him so, followed him, honoured him,
Lived in his mild and magnificent eye,
Learned his great language, caught his clear accents,
Made him our pattern to live and to die!
Shakespeare was of us, Milton was for us,
Burns, Shelley, were with us,—they watch from their graves!
He alone breaks from the van and the freemen,
—He alone sinks to the rear and the slaves!

II

We shall march prospering,—not thro' his presence;
Songs may inspirit us,—not from his lyre;
Deeds will be done,—while he boasts his quiescence,
Still bidding crouch whom the rest bade aspire:
Blot out his name, then, record one lost soul more,
One task more declined, one more footpath untrod,
One more devils'-triumph and sorrow for angels,

THE LOST LEADER § Subsequent placement: 1863: DL § 2| *1845:* ribband *1849:* riband 3| *1845:* Got the *1849:* Found the 6| *1845:* their's *1863:* theirs 8| *1845:* purple his *1849:* purple, his 16| *1845:* He *1888:* —He 18| *1845:* may excite us *1849:* may inspirit us 21| *1845:* then,—record *1863:* then, record 22| *1845:* task unaccepted, one footpath *1849:* task more declined, one more footpath 23| *1845:* sorrow to angels, *1849:* more triumph for devils, and sorrow for

One wrong more to man, one more insult to God!
Life's night begins: let him never come back to us!
There would be doubt, hesitation and pain,
Forced praise on our part—the glimmer of twilight,
Never glad confident morning again!
Best fight on well, for we taught him—strike gallantly,
Menace our heart ere we master his own;
Then let him receive the new knowledge and wait us,
Pardoned in heaven, the first by the throne!

---

angels, *1863:* devils and *1868:* more devils'-triumph and [29]| *1845:* him,—come gallantly, *1849:* him,—strike gallantly, *1868:* him—strike [30]| *1845:* Strike our face hard ere we shatter his *1849:* Aim at our heart ere we pierce through his *1863:* Menace our <> we master his [31]| *1845:* him get the *1849:* him receive the [32]| *1845:* in Heaven *1868:* heaven

THE LOST MISTRESS

I

All's over, then: does truth sound bitter
    As one at first believes?
Hark, 'tis the sparrows' good-night twitter
    About your cottage eaves!

II

And the leaf-buds on the vine are woolly,
    I noticed that, to-day;
One day more bursts them open fully
    —You know the red turns grey.

III

To-morrow we meet the same then, dearest?
    May I take your hand in mine?
Mere friends are we,—well, friends the merest
    Keep much that I resign:

IV

For each glance of the eye so bright and black,
    Though I keep with heart's endeavour,—
Your voice, when you wish the snowdrops back,
    Though it stay in my soul for ever!—

THE LOST MISTRESS § Subsequent placement: 1863: DL § 1| *1845:* then—does *1863:* then: does 4| *1845:* eaves. *1849:* eaves! 6| *1845:* that to-day; *1849:* that, to-day; 8| *1845:* gray. *1863:* grey. 12| *1845:* I'll *1868:* I 13| *1845:* For tho' no glance <> eyes so black *1849:* For each glance of that eye so bright and black, *1868:* of the eye 14| *1845:* But I *1849:* Though I 15| *1845:* If you only wish <> back *1849:* Your voice, when you wish <> back, 16| *1845:* That shall

V

Yet I will but say what mere friends say,
    Or only a thought stronger;
I will hold your hand but as long as all may,
    Or so very little longer!

stay *1849:* Though it stays *1863:* stay 17| *1845:* —Yet *1863:* Yet 19| *1845:* but so long *1849:* but as long

HOME-THOUGHTS, FROM ABROAD

I

Oh, to be in England
Now that April's there,
And whoever wakes in England
Sees, some morning, unaware,
That the lowest boughs and the brushwood sheaf
Round the elm-tree bole are in tiny leaf,
While the chaffinch sings on the orchard bough
In England—now!

II

And after April, when May follows,
And the whitethroat builds, and all the swallows!
Hark, where my blossomed pear-tree in the hedge
Leans to the field and scatters on the clover
Blossoms and dewdrops—at the bent spray's edge—
That's the wise thrush; he sings each song twice over,
Lest you should think he never could recapture
The first fine careless rapture!
And though the fields look rough with hoary dew
All will be gay when noontide wakes anew
The buttercups, the little children's dower
—Far brighter than this gaudy melon-flower!

HOME-THOUGHTS, FROM ABROAD § In 1845 the poems "Oh to be in England . . .", "Here's to Nelson's memory!" and "Nobly, nobly Cape St. Vincent . . ." were grouped under this title and designated I, II and III respectively. In 1849 the first poem alone became *HOME-THOUGHTS, FROM ABROAD*. "Here's to Nelson's Memory!" which was dropped in 1849 and became part of *Nationality in Drinks* in 1863 and subsequent editions, has been printed as part of that poem in order to maintain the integrity of the 1889 text. Subsequent placement: 1863: DL § 3| *1845:* who *1849:* whoever 5| *1845:* brush-wood *1888:* brushwood 8–9| *1845:* now! / § no stanza numeral but space § ¶ And *1849:* now! / II / And *1868:* § no ¶ § 10| *1845:* swallows— *1863:* swallows! 11| *1845:* Hark! where *1863:* Hark, where 14| *1845:* over *1849:* over, 17| *1845:* fields are rough <> dew, *1849:* fields look rough *1888:* dew 19| *1845:* dower, *1863:* dower

HOME-THOUGHTS, FROM THE SEA

Nobly, nobly Cape Saint Vincent to the North-west died away;
Sunset ran, one glorious blood-red, reeking into Cadiz Bay;
Bluish 'mid the burning water, full in face Trafalgar lay;
In the dimmest North-east distance dawned Gibraltar grand and gray;
"Here and here did England help me: how can I help England?—" say,
Whoso turns as I, this evening, turn to God to praise and pray,
While Jove's planet rises yonder, silent over Africa.

HOME-THOUGHTS, FROM THE SEA § This poem was first published without title in 1845 as Part III of *HOME-THOUGHTS, FROM ABROAD.* In 1849 the poem was given an independent position and the title *HOME-THOUGHTS, FROM THE SEA* which it retained. Subsequent placement: 1863: DL § 1| *1845:* Nobly Cape <> north-west *1849:* Nobly, nobly Cape *1863:* the North-West *1888:* the North-west 3| *1845:* mid *1868:* 'mid 4| *1845:* north-east distance, dawned *1863:* dimmest North-East *1868:* distance dawned *1888:* North-east 5| *1845:* me,—how *1863:* me: how 7| *1845:* Yonder where Jove's <> rises silent *1849:* While Jove's <> rises yonder, silent

THE BISHOP ORDERS HIS TOMB AT SAINT PRAXED'S CHURCH

ROME, 15—

Vanity, saith the preacher, vanity!
Draw round my bed: is Anselm keeping back?
Nephews—sons mine . . . ah God, I know not! Well—
She, men would have to be your mother once,
Old Gandolf envied me, so fair she was!
What's done is done, and she is dead beside,
Dead long ago, and I am Bishop since,
And as she died so must we die ourselves,
And thence ye may perceive the world's a dream.
Life, how and what is it? As here I lie
In this state-chamber, dying by degrees,
Hours and long hours in the dead night, I ask
"Do I live, am I dead?" Peace, peace seems all.
Saint Praxed's ever was the church for peace;
And so, about this tomb of mine. I fought
With tooth and nail to save my niche, ye know:
—Old Gandolf cozened me, despite my care;
Shrewd was that snatch from out the corner South
He graced his carrion with, God curse the same!

THE BISHOP ORDERS HIS TOMB AT SAINT PRAXED'S CHURCH § First published February 1845 in *Hood's Magazine* signed Robert Browning. This version indicated by 1845 H: Subsequent placement: 1863: MW § Title / *1845H:* THE TOMB AT ST. PRAXED'S *1849:* THE BISHOP ORDERS HIS TOMB AT ST. PRAXED'S CHURCH *1863:* SAINT 1| *1845 H:* the Preacher *1845:* preacher 7| *1845 H:* And long *1845:* Dead long 13| *1845 H:* all: *1849:* all. 14| *1845 H:* St. *1863:* Saint 17| *1845 H:*—Old Gandolf came me in, despite my care, *1845:*—Old Gandolf cozened me, despite my care; 18| *1845 H:* For a shrewd snatch out of the <> south *1845:* Shrewd was that snatch from out the <> South 19| *1845 H:* To grace *1845:* He

Yet still my niche is not so cramped but thence
One sees the pulpit o' the epistle-side,
And somewhat of the choir, those silent seats,
And up into the aery dome where live
The angels, and a sunbeam's sure to lurk:
And I shall fill my slab of basalt there,
And 'neath my tabernacle take my rest,
With those nine columns round me, two and two,
The odd one at my feet where Anselm stands:
Peach-blossom marble all, the rare, the ripe
As fresh-poured red wine of a mighty pulse.
—Old Gandolf with his paltry onion-stone,
Put me where I may look at him! True peach,
Rosy and flawless: how I earned the prize!
Draw close: that conflagration of my church
—What then? So much was saved if aught were missed!
My sons, ye would not be my death? Go dig
The white-grape vineyard where the oil-press stood,
Drop water gently till the surface sink,
And if ye find . . . Ah God, I know not, I! . . .
Bedded in store of rotten fig-leaves soft,
And corded up in a tight olive-frail,
Some lump, ah God, of *lapis lazuli*,
Big as a Jew's head cut off at the nape,
Blue as a vein o'er the Madonna's breast . . .
Sons, all have I bequeathed you, villas, all,
That brave Frascati villa with its bath,
So, let the blue lump poise between my knees,
Like God the Father's globe on both his hands

---

graced 20| *1845 H:* cramp'd *1849:* cramped 26| *1845 H:* rest *1849:* rest, 29| *1845 H:* Peachblossom-marble *1845:* Peach-blossom marble 30| *1845 H:* fresh-pour'd <> pulse *1845:* fresh-poured *1868:* pulse. 33| *1845 H:* earn'd *1845:* earned 35| *1845 H:* sav'd <> miss'd! *1845:* saved <> missed! 38| *1845 H:* sinks, *1868:* sink, 39| *1845 H:* find . . Ah, God I know *1868:* find . . Ah God, I know *1888:* find . . . Ah 40| *1845 H:* figleaves *1888:* fig-leaves 45| *1845 H:* bequeath'd *1845:* bequeathed 46| *1845 H:* Frescati *1845:* Frascati 47| *1845 H:* So let *1849:* So, let 48| *1863:* both His *1868:* his

Ye worship in the Jesu Church so gay,
For Gandolf shall not choose but see and burst!
Swift as a weaver's shuttle fleet our years:
Man goeth to the grave, and where is he?
Did I say basalt for my slab, sons? Black—
'Twas ever antique-black I meant! How else
Shall ye contrast my frieze to come beneath?
The bas-relief in bronze ye promised me,
Those Pans and Nymphs ye wot of, and perchance
Some tripod, thyrsus, with a vase or so,
The Saviour at his sermon on the mount,
Saint Praxed in a glory, and one Pan
Ready to twitch the Nymph's last garment off,
And Moses with the tables . . . but I know
Ye mark me not! What do they whisper thee,
Child of my bowels, Anselm? Ah, ye hope
To revel down my villas while I gasp
Bricked o'er with beggar's mouldy travertine
Which Gandolf from his tomb-top chuckles at!
Nay, boys, ye love me—all of jasper, then!
'Tis jasper ye stand pledged to, lest I grieve
My bath must needs be left behind, alas!
One block, pure green as a pistachio-nut,
There's plenty jasper somewhere in the world—
And have I not Saint Praxed's ear to pray
Horses for ye, and brown Greek manuscripts,
And mistresses with great smooth marbly limbs?
—That's if ye carve my epitaph aright,
Choice Latin, picked phrase, Tully's every word,
No gaudy ware like Gandolf's second line—
Tully, my masters? Ulpian serves his need!
And then how I shall lie through centuries,
And hear the blessed mutter of the mass,
And see God made and eaten all day long,
And feel the steady candle-flame, and taste

49| *1845 H:* church *1845:* the Jesu Church 56| *1845 H:* promis'd *1845:* promised 60| *1845 H:* St. *1863:* Saint 66| *1845 H:* Brick'd *1845:* Bricked 68| *1845 H:* jasper then! *1849:* jasper, then! 69| *1845 H:* pledg'd <> grieve *1845:* pledged *1888:* grieve. 73| *1845 H:* And I shall have St. *1845:* And have I not St. *1863:* Saint 75| *1845 H:* limbs *1845:* limbs? 78| *1845 H:* line *1845:* line— 79| *1845 H:*—Tully *1845:* Tully 80| *1845 H:* centuries *1845:*

Good strong thick stupefying incense-smoke!
For as I lie here, hours of the dead night,
Dying in state and by such slow degrees,
I fold my arms as if they clasped a crook,
And stretch my feet forth straight as stone can point,
And let the bedclothes, for a mortcloth, drop
Into great laps and folds of sculptor's-work:
And as yon tapers dwindle, and strange thoughts
Grow, with a certain humming in my ears,
About the life before I lived this life,
And this life too, popes, cardinals and priests,
Saint Praxed at his sermon on the mount,
Your tall pale mother with her talking eyes,
And new-found agate urns as fresh as day,
And marble's language, Latin pure, discreet,
—Aha, ELUCESCEBAT quoth our friend?
No Tully, said I, Ulpian at the best!
Evil and brief hath been my pilgrimage.
All *lapis*, all, sons! Else I give the Pope
My villas! Will ye ever eat my heart?
Ever your eyes were as a lizard's quick,
They glitter like your mother's for my soul,
Or ye would heighten my impoverished frieze,
Piece out its starved design, and fill my vase
With grapes, and add a vizor and a Term,
And to the tripod ye would tie a lynx
That in his struggle throws the thyrsus down,
To comfort me on my entablature
Whereon I am to lie till I must ask
"Do I live, am I dead?" There, leave me, there!
For ye have stabbed me with ingratitude

---

centuries, 87| *1845 H:* clasp'd *1845:* clasped 89| *1845 H:* bed-clothes for a mortcloth drop *1845:* bedclothes *1868:* bedclothes, for a mortcloth, drop 90| *1845 H:* sculptors'-work: *1845:* sculptor's-work: 93| *1845 H:* before this life I liv'd, *1845:* lived, *1849:* before I lived this life, 94| *1845 H:* too, Popes, Cardinals and Priests, *1868:* popes, cardinals and priests, 95| *1845 H:* St. *1863:* Saint 99| *1845 H:*—Aha, ELUCESCEBAT, quoth *1845:*—Aha, ELUCESCEBAT quoth 103| *1845 H:* villas: will *1868:* villas! Will 105–109| *1845: H:* soul, / Or to *1845:* soul, / Or ye would heighten my impoverished frieze, / Piece out its starved design, and fill my vase / With grapes, and add a vizor and a Term, / And to 114| *1845 H:* stabb'd *1845:* stabbed

To death—ye wish it—God, ye wish it! Stone—
Gritstone, a-crumble! Clammy squares which sweat
As if the corpse they keep were oozing through—
And no more *lapis* to delight the world!
Well go! I bless ye. Fewer tapers there,
But in a row: and, going, turn your backs
—Ay, like departing altar-ministrants,
And leave me in my church, the church for peace,
That I may watch at leisure if he leers—
Old Gandolf, at me, from his onion-stone,
As still he envied me, so fair she was!

1863: stabbed with *1868:* stabbed me with 119| *1845 H:* well, go *1868:* Well go

GARDEN FANCIES

I THE FLOWER'S NAME

I

Here's the garden she walked across,
Arm in my arm, such a short while since:
Hark, now I push its wicket, the moss
Hinders the hinges and makes them wince!
She must have reached this shrub ere she turned,
As back with that murmur the wicket swung;
For she laid the poor snail, my chance foot spurned,
To feed and forget it the leaves among.

II

Down this side of the gravel-walk
She went while her robe's edge brushed the box:
And here she paused in her gracious talk
To point me a moth on the milk-white phlox.
Roses, ranged in valiant row,
I will never think that she passed you by!
She loves you noble roses, I know;
But yonder, see, where the rock-plants lie!

GARDEN FANCIES § The two poems were first published July 1844 in *Hood's Magazine* signed Robert Browning. Subsequent placement: 1863: DL. In 1863 (only) *SOLILOQUY Of THE SPANISH CLOISTER* was listed in the table of contents as III under *GARDEN FANCIES*, but in the text it is set as a separate poem. In *Hood's Magazine* the stanzas are not numbered but spaced as in subsequent editions. § Title| *1844:* GARDEN-FANCIES *1863:* GARDEN FANCIES I. *THE FLOWER'S NAME* 10| *1844:* box: *1888:* box 12| *1844:* flox. *1863:* phlox. *1888:* phlox 14| *1844:* Think will I never she *1849:* I will never think that she 15| *1844:* loves noble *1849:* loves you noble 16| *1844:* But this—so surely this met her eye! *1845:* But yonder, see, where the rock-plants

III

This flower she stopped at, finger on lip,
Stooped over, in doubt, as settling its claim;
Till she gave me, with pride to make no slip,
Its soft meandering Spanish name:
What a name! Was it love or praise?
Speech half-asleep or song half-awake?
I must learn Spanish, one of these days,
Only for that slow sweet name's sake.

IV

Roses, if I live and do well,
I may bring her, one of these days,
To fix you fast with as fine a spell,
Fit you each with his Spanish phrase;
But do not detain me now; for she lingers
There, like sunshine over the ground,
And ever I see her soft white fingers
Searching after the bud she found.

V

Flower, you Spaniard, look that you grow not,
Stay as you are and be loved for ever!
Bud, if I kiss you 'tis that you blow not:
Mind, the shut pink mouth opens never!
For while it pouts, her fingers wrestle,
Twinkling the audacious leaves between,
Till round they turn and down they nestle—
Is not the dear mark still to be seen?

---

lie! 17| *1844:* lip; *1849:* lip, 18| *1844:* doubt, settling its claim, *1845:* doubt, as settling *1849:* claim; 20| *1849:* name. *1863:* name: 21| *1844:* love, or *1845:* was *1868:* name! Was it love or 22| *1844:* half-asleep, or *1868:* half-asleep or 23| *1844:* Spanish one *1849:* Spanish, one 28| phrase! *1863:* phrase; 33| *1844:* look you *1845:* look that you 35| *1844:* you, 'tis <> not, *1845:* you 'tis 36| *1844:* Mind the pink shut mouth *1845:* Mind that the pink mouth *1849:* Mind, the shut pink 37| *1844:* pouts thus, her *1845:* while thus it pouts, her *1868:*

VI

Where I find her not, beauties vanish;
Whither I follow her, beauties flee;
Is there no method to tell her in Spanish
June's twice June since she breathed it with me?
Come, bud, show me the least of her traces,
Treasure my lady's lightest footfall!
—Ah, you may flout and turn up your faces—
Roses, you are not so fair after all!

II SIBRANDUS SCHAFNABURGENSIS

I

Plague take all your pedants, say I!
He who wrote what I hold in my hand,
Centuries back was so good as to die,
Leaving this rubbish to cumber the land;
This, that was a book in its time,
Printed on paper and bound in leather,
Last month in the white of a matin-prime
Just when the birds sang all together.

II

Into the garden I brought it to read,
And under the arbute and laurustine
Read it, so help me grace in my need,
From title-page to closing line.
Chapter on chapter did I count,
As a curious traveller counts Stonehenge;
Added up the mortal amount;
And then proceeded to my revenge.

---

while it 46| *1844:* Tread in my <> foot-fall *1845:* Treasure my *1863:* footfall *1868:* footfall! 47| *1844:* faces! *1849:* faces— 48| *1844:* Roses, are you so <> all? *1845:* Roses, you are not so <> all. *1849:* all!

II. *SIBRANDUS SCHAFNABURGENSIS* 1| *1844:* all pedants *1849:* all your pedants 9| *1844:* read; *1849:* read, 10| *1844:* under these arbutes *1845:*

III

Yonder's a plum-tree with a crevice
An owl would build in, were he but sage;
For a lap of moss, like a fine pont-levis
In a castle of the Middle Age,
Joins to a lip of gum, pure amber;
When he'd be private, there might he spend
Hours alone in his lady's chamber:
Into this crevice I dropped our friend.

IV

Splash, went he, as under he ducked,
—At the bottom, I knew, rain-drippings stagnate:
Next, a handful of blossoms I plucked
To bury him with, my bookshelf's magnate;
Then I went in-doors, brought out a loaf,
Half a cheese, and a bottle of Chablis;
Lay on the grass and forgot the oaf
Over a jolly chapter of Rabelais.

V

Now, this morning, betwixt the moss
And gum that locked our friend in limbo,
A spider had spun his web across,
And sat in the midst with arms akimbo:
So, I took pity, for learning's sake,
And, *de profundis, accentibus lætis,*
Cantate! quoth I, as I got a rake;
And up I fished his delectable treatise.

---

under the arbute 17| *1844:* plum-tree, with *1863:* plum-tree with 20| *1844:* middle age, *1888:* the Middle Age, 26| *1844:*—I knew at the bottom rain-drippings *1845:* stagnate; *1868:* knew, at the bottom, rain-drippings *1888:*—At the bottom, I knew, rain-drippings stagnate: 27| *1844:* Next a *1888:* Next, a 28| *1844:* book-shelf's magnate: *1845:* bookshelf's magnate; 36| *1844:* sate <> a-kimbo: *1863:* sat <> akimbo: 37| *1844:* So I *1849:* So, I 39| *1844:*

VI

Here you have it, dry in the sun,
With all the binding all of a blister,
And great blue spots where the ink has run,
And reddish streaks that wink and glister
O'er the page so beautifully yellow:
Oh, well have the droppings played their tricks!
Did he guess how toadstools grow, this fellow?
Here's one stuck in his chapter six!

VII

How did he like it when the live creatures
Tickled and toused and browsed him all over,
And worm, slug, eft, with serious features,
Came in, each one, for his right of trover?
—When the water-beetle with great blind deaf face
Made of her eggs the stately deposit,
And the newt borrowed just so much of the preface
As tiled in the top of his black wife's closet?

VIII

All that life and fun and romping,
All that frisking and twisting and coupling,
While slowly our poor friend's leaves were swamping
And clasps were cracking and covers suppling!
As if you had carried sour John Knox
To the play-house at Paris, Vienna or Munich,
Fastened him into a front-row box,
And danced off the ballet with trousers and tunic.

Cantate, quoth <> rake, *1849: Cantate*! quoth *1888:* rake; 45| *1844:* yellow— *1863:* yellow: 46| *1844:* Oh, the droppings have played *1845:* Oh, well have the droppings played 52| *1844:* trover; *1863:* trover? 53| *1844:* When *1868:*—When 55| *1844:* borrowed so *1849:* borrowed just so 56| *1844:* closet. *1863:* closet? 57| *1844:* life, and fun, and *1863:* life and fun and 58| *1844:* frisking, and twisting, and *1863:* frisking and twisting and 59| *1844:* swamping, *1868:* swamping 60| *1844:* Clasps cracking, and *1845:* And clasps were *1863:* cracking and 62| *1844:* play at <> Vienna, or *1845:* play-house *1863:* at Paris, Vienna or 64| *1844:* the Ballet in trowsers *1845:* the Ballet with

IX

Come, old martyr! What, torment enough is it?
Back to my room shall you take your sweet self.
Good-bye, mother-beetle; husband-eft, *sufficit!*
See the snug niche I have made on my shelf!
A.'s book shall prop you up, B.'s shall cover you,
Here's C. to be grave with, or D. to be gay,
And with E. on each side, and F. right over you,
Dry-rot at ease till the Judgment-day!

---

trousers *1849:* tunic *1863:* ballet <> tunic. 65| *1844:* what *1845:* martyr! What 66| *1844:* self! *1868:* self. 68| *1844:* shelf. *1845:* shelf: *1863:* shelf. *1868:* shelf! 69| *1844:* A's <> B's *1845:* cover you *1849:* A's <> B.'s <> cover you, 70| *1844:* C <> D *1849:* C. <> D. 71| *1844:* E <> F *1849:* E. <> F. 72| *1844:* judgment-day! *1845:* the Judgment-day!

THE LABORATORY

ANCIEN RÉGIME.

I

Now that I, tying thy glass mask tightly,
May gaze thro' these faint smokes curling whitely,
As thou pliest thy trade in this devil's-smithy—
Which is the poison to poison her, prithee?

II

He is with her, and they know that I know
Where they are, what they do: they believe my tears flow
While they laugh, laugh at me, at me fled to the drear
Empty church, to pray God in, for them!—I am here.

III

Grind away, moisten and mash up thy paste,
Pound at thy powder,—I am not in haste!
Better sit thus, and observe thy strange things,
Than go where men wait me and dance at the King's.

THE LABORATORY § First published June 1844 in *Hood's Mdgazine* signed Robert Browning. In 1845 this and the following poem were brought together as *FRANCE AND SPAIN | I. THE LABORATORY* (Ancien Régime.) and *II.—SPAIN—THE CONFESSIONAL*. In 1849 they were separated and remained so. Subsequent placement: 1863: DL In 1844 stanzas are not numbered. § 1| *1844:* Now I have tied thy <> mask on tightly, *1845:* Now that I, tying thy <> mask tightly, 3| *1844:* devil's-smithy, *1845:* devil's-smithy— 5| *1844:* her; and *1868:* her, and 6| *1844:* are—what *1845:* are, what 7| *1844:* laugh—laugh at me—at *1845:* laugh, laugh at me, at 8| *1844:* church to <> in for *1849:* church, to <> in, for 10| *1844:* powder—am I in haste? *1845:* powder,—am *1849:* powder,—I am not in haste! 12| *1844:* me, and

IV

That in the mortar—you call it a gum?
Ah, the brave tree whence such gold oozings come!
And yonder soft phial, the exquisite blue,
Sure to taste sweetly,—is that poison too?

V

Had I but all of them, thee and thy treasures,
What a wild crowd of invisible pleasures!
To carry pure death in an earring, a casket,
A signet, a fan-mount, a filigree basket!

VI

Soon, at the King's, a mere lozenge to give,
And Pauline should have just thirty minutes to live!
But to light a pastile, and Elise, with her head
And her breast and her arms and her hands, should drop dead!

VII

Quick—is it finished? The colour's too grim!
Why not soft like the phial's, enticing and dim?
Let it brighten her drink, let her turn it and stir,
And try it and taste, ere she fix and prefer!

<> king's. *1845:* me and <> the King's. 13| *1844:* mortar—call you a *1845:* mortar—you call it a 14| *1844:* come! *1888:* come 15| *1844:* yon *1845:* yonder 16| *1844:* sweetly—is *1845:* sweetly,—is 17| *1844:* treasures— *1845:* treasures, 18| *1844:* pleasures— *1845:* pleasures! 19| *1844:* in a earring *1845:* in an earring 20| *1844:* filagree-basket! *1845:* fillagree-basket! *1863:* filigree-basket! *1888:* filigree basket! 21| *1844:* king's, but a lozenge *1845:* the King's <> give *1849:* the King's, a mere lozenge *1888:* give, 23| *1844:* To light a pastille <> head, *1849:* But to *1863:* head *1868:* pastile 24| *1844:* breast, and her arms, and *1863:* breast and her arms and 25| *1844:* grim; *1845:* grim! 26| *1844:* not like *1849:* not soft like 29| *1844:* little—no <> me; *1845:* little, no

VIII

What a drop! She's not little, no minion like me!
That's why she ensnared him: this never will free
The soul from those masculine eyes,—say, "no!"
To that pulse's magnificent come-and-go.

IX

For only last night, as they whispered, I brought
My own eyes to bear on her so, that I thought
Could I keep them one half minute fixed, she would fall
Shrivelled; she fell not; yet this does it all!

X

Not that I bid you spare her the pain;
Let death be felt and the proof remain:
Brand, burn up, bite into its grace—
He is sure to remember her dying face!

XI

Is it done? Take my mask off! Nay, be not morose;
It kills her, and this prevents seeing it close:
The delicate droplet, my whole fortune's fee!
If it hurts her, beside, can it ever hurt me?

XII

Now, take all my jewels, gorge gold to your fill,
You may kiss me, old man, on my mouth if you will!
But brush this dust off me, lest horror it brings
Ere I know it—next moment I dance at the King's!

<> me— *1868:* me! 31| *1844:* those strong, great eyes: say, "No!" *1845:* those masculine eyes,—say, "no!" *1849:* those strong, great eyes *1863:* those masculine eyes 34| *1844:* thought, *1845:* thought 35| *1844:* she'd *1845:* she would fall, *1868:* fall 36| *1844:* Shrivelled: she *1845:* Shrivelled; she 37| *1844:* her pain! *1845:* her the pain! *1868:* pain; 38| *1844:* remain; *1868:* remain: 41| *1844:* off! Be not morose! *1845:* off! Nay, be not morose, *1863:* morose *1868:* morose; 42| *1844:* close— *1849:* close: 43| *1844:* fee— *1868:* fee! 47| *1844:* horror there springs *1845:* horror it brings 48| *1844:* king's. *1845:* the King's. *1849:* the King's!

THE CONFESSIONAL

[*SPAIN*]

I

It is a lie—their Priests, their Pope,
Their Saints, their . . . all they fear or hope
Are lies, and lies—there! through my door
And ceiling, there! and walls and floor,
There, lies, they lie—shall still be hurled
Till spite of them I reach the world!

II

You think Priests just and holy men!
Before they put me in this den
I was a human creature too,
With flesh and blood like one of you,
A girl that laughed in beauty's pride
Like lilies in your world outside.

III

I had a lover—shame avaunt!
This poor wrenched body, grim and gaunt,
Was kissed all over till it burned,
By lips the truest, love e'er turned
His heart's own tint: one night they kissed
My soul out in a burning mist.

THE CONFESSIONAL § See editor's note to *THE LABORATORY*. Subsequent placement: 1863: DL § 3| *1845:* thro' *1863:* through 5| *1845:* lie, shall <> hurled, *1863:* lie—shall <> hurled 8| *1849:* den, *1863:* den 16| *1845:* truest love

IV

So, next day when the accustomed train
Of things grew round my sense again,
"That is a sin," I said: and slow
With downcast eyes to church I go,
And pass to the confession-chair,
And tell the old mild father there.

V

But when I falter Beltran's name,
"Ha?" quoth the father; "much I blame
The sin; yet wherefore idly grieve?
Despair not—strenuously retrieve!
Nay, I will turn this love of thine
To lawful love, almost divine;

VI

"For he is young, and led astray,
This Beltran, and he schemes, men say,
To change the laws of church and state;
So, thine shall be an angel's fate,
Who, ere the thunder breaks, should roll
Its cloud away and save his soul.

VII

"For, when he lies upon thy breast,
Thou mayst demand and be possessed
Of all his plans, and next day steal
To me, and all those plans reveal,
That I and every priest, to purge
His soul, may fast and use the scourge."

1849: truest, love 19| *1845:* So next *1849:* So, next 21| *1845:* said—and *1863:* said: and 25| *1845:* faulter *1863:* falter 26| *1845:* Ha? quoth <> father; much *1849:* "Ha?" quoth <> father; "much 28| *1845:* not,—strenuously *1868:* not—strenuously 30| *1845:* divine. *1868:* divine, *1888:* divine; 34| *1845:* So thine *1849:* So, thine 37| *1845:* For when <> breast *1849:* "For, when <> breast, 38| *1863:* may'st *1868:* mayst 40| *1845:* me and *1849:* me, and

VIII

That father's beard was long and white,
With love and truth his brow seemed bright;
I went back, all on fire with joy,
And, that same evening, bade the boy
Tell me, as lovers should, heart-free,
Something to prove his love of me.

IX

He told me what he would not tell
For hope of heaven or fear of hell;
And I lay listening in such pride!
And, soon as he had left my side,
Tripped to the church by morning-light
To save his soul in his despite.

X

I told the father all his schemes,
Who were his comrades, what their dreams;
"And now make haste," I said "to pray
The one spot from his soul away;
To-night he comes, but not the same
Will look!" At night he never came.

XI

Nor next night: on the after-morn,
I went forth with a strength new-born.
The church was empty; something drew
My steps into the street; I knew
It led me to the market-place:
Where, lo, on high, the father's face!

42| *1845:* scourge. *1849:* scourge." 46| *1845:* boy, *1888:* boy 50| *1845:* of Heaven or fear of Hell; *1868:* heaven <> hell; 51| *1845:* pride, *1863:* pride! 54| *1849:* despite *1863:* despite. 61| *1845:* after-morn *1849:* after-morn, 62| *1845:* new-born: *1863:* new-born. 63| *1845:* empty: something *1849:* empty; something 64| *1845:* street: I knew *1849:* street; I knew 65| *1845:* market-place— *1863:* market-place: 66| *1845:* And, lo,—on high—the *1849:*

XII

That horrible black scaffold dressed,
That stapled block . . . God sink the rest!
That head strapped back, that blinding vest,
Those knotted hands and naked breast,
Till near one busy hangman pressed,
And, on the neck these arms caressed . . .

XIII

No part in aught they hope or fear!
No heaven with them, no hell!—and here,
No earth, not so much space as pens
My body in their worst of dens
But shall bear God and man my cry,
Lies—lies, again—and still, they lie!

Where, lo *1863:* lo, on high, the 67| *1845:* drest— *1863:* drest, *1868:* dressed, 68| *1845:* The stapled block . . God *1863:* That stapled *1888:* block . . . God 70| *1845:* breast— *1863:* breast, 71| *1845:* pressed— *1863:* pressed, 72| *1845:* And—on <> caressed . . . . *1863:* And, on *1888:* caressed . . . 74| *1845:* No Heaven with them, no Hell,—and here *1849:* here, *1863:* them, no Hell!—and *1868:* heaven <> hell 75| *1845:* no Earth *1868:* earth 77| *1845:* and Man my cry— *1863:* cry, *1868:* man

THE FLIGHT OF THE DUCHESS

I

You're my friend:
        I was the man the Duke spoke to;
        I helped the Duchess to cast off his yoke, too;
So here's the tale from beginning to end,
My friend!

II

Ours is a great wild country:
        If you climb to our castle's top,
        I don't see where your eye can stop;
For when you've passed the cornfield country,
Where vineyards leave off, flocks are packed,
And sheep-range leads to cattle-tract,
And cattle-tract to open-chase,
And open-chase to the very base
Of the mountain where, at a funeral pace,
Round about, solemn and slow,
One by one, row after row,
Up and up the pine-trees go,
So, like black priests up, and so
Down the other side again
        To another greater, wilder country,
That's one vast red drear burnt-up plain,
Branched through and through with many a vein
Whence iron's dug, and copper's dealt;

THE FLIGHT OF THE DUCHESS § The first nine sections of the poem appeared in *Hood's Magazine* for April 1845 signed Robert Browning. The completed poem, in sixteen sections, was published in DRL in 1845. In 1849 the sixteenth section was subdivided after line 832 making seventeen sections. Subsequent placement: 1863: DR. In *Hood's Magazine* sections are not numbered but spaced as in subsequent editions. This version indicated by 1845 H. Indentations appearing in the 1889 text were introduced in 1888, except for lines 209 and 211 which were indented in all editions. § 1845 H: § First nine sections headed PART THE FIRST. § 3| *1845 H:* help'd *1845:* helped 4| *1849:* So, here's *1888:* So here's 9| *1845 H:* pass'd the cornfield-country, *1845:* corn-field country, *1849:* passed *1888:* cornfield 10| *1845 H:* pack'd, *1849:* packed, 14| *1849:* mountain, where *1868:* mountain where 16| *1845 H:* One after one *1845:* One by one 18| *1845 H:* So like *1845:* So, like 22| *1845 H:* Branch'd thro' and thro'

Look right, look left, look straight before,—
Beneath they mine, above they smelt,
Copper-ore and iron-ore,
And forge and furnace mould and melt,
And so on, more and ever more,
Till at the last, for a bounding belt,
Comes the salt sand hoar of the great sea-shore,
—And the whole is our Duke's country.

III

I was born the day this present Duke was—
(And O, says the song, ere I was old!)
In the castle where the other Duke was—
(When I was happy and young, not old!)
I in the kennel, he in the bower:
We are of like age to an hour.
My father was huntsman in that day;
Who has not heard my father say
That, when a boar was brought to bay,
Three times, four times out of five,
With his huntspear he'd contrive
To get the killing-place transfixed,
And pin him true, both eyes betwixt?
And that's why the old Duke would rather
He lost a salt-pit than my father,
And loved to have him ever in call;
That's why my father stood in the hall
When the old Duke brought his infant out

1849: Branched *1863:* through and through 24| *1845 H:* before, *1849:* before,— 29| *1845:* Till, at *1868:* Till at 30| *1845 H:* sea shore,— *1845:* sea shore, *1863:* sea-shore, 31| *1845 H:* And <> country! *1845:* —And *1868:* country. 35| *1849:* was hopeful and *1863:* was happy and 36| *1845:* I in the Kennel, he in the Bower: *1868:* kennel <> bower: 38| *1845:* was Huntsman *1868:* huntsman 40| *1845 H:* That when *1845:* that, when 41| *1845 H:* Three, four times *1849:* Three times, four 42| *1845 H:* hunt-spear *1845:* huntspear 43| *1845 H:* transfix'd, *1845:* transfixed, 44| *1845 H:* true both *1849:* true, both 45| *1845 H:* That's why <> old Duke had rather *1849:* And that's *1863:* old Duke would rather 46| *1845 H:* Lost a *1849:* Have lost *1863:* He lost 47| *1845 H:* lov'd <> call: *1845:* loved <> call; 48| *1845:* the Hall *1849:*

To show the people, and while they passed
The wondrous bantling round about,
Was first to start at the outside blast
As the Kaiser's courier blew his horn
Just a month after the babe was born.
"And," quoth the Kaiser's courier, "since
The Duke has got an heir, our Prince
Needs the Duke's self at his side:"
The Duke looked down and seemed to wince,
But he thought of wars o'er the world wide,
Castles a-fire, men on their march,
The toppling tower, the crashing arch;
And up he looked, and awhile he eyed
The row of crests and shields and banners
Of all achievements after all manners,
And "ay," said the Duke with a surly pride.
The more was his comfort when he died
At next year's end, in a velvet suit,
With a gilt glove on his hand, his foot
In a silken shoe for a leather boot,
Petticoated like a herald,
In a chamber next to an ante-room,
Where he breathed the breath of page and groom,
What he called stink, and they, perfume:
—They should have set him on red Berold
Mad with pride, like fire to manage!
They should have got his cheek fresh tannage
Such a day as to-day in the merry sunshine!
Had they stuck on his fist a rough-foot merlin!
(Hark, the wind's on the heath at its game!
Oh for a noble falcon-lanner
To flap each broad wing like a banner,

---

hall 50| *1845 H:* pass'd *1849:* passed 53| *1845 H:* horn, *1888:* horn 54| *1845 H:* Just one month <> born: *1845:* Just a month *1849:* born. 55| *1845:* "And" quoth *1868:* "And," quoth 56| *1845:* an Heir *1868:* heir 58| *1845 H:* look'd <> seem'd *1845:* seemed *1849:* looked 62| *1845 H:* look'd *1845:* looked 63| *1845 H:* crests, and shields, and banners, *1845:* crests and shields and *1868:* banners 65| *1845 H:* pride: *1849:* pride. 68| *1845 H:* hand, and his *1888:* hand, his 69| *1845 H:* silk *1849:* silken 71| *1845 H:* anteroom, *1845:* ante-room, 72| *1845 H:* breath'd <> groom, *1845:* breathed *1888:* groom 73| *1845 H:* call'd <> they perfume: *1845:* called stink and they, perfume: *1849:* stink, and 74| *1845 H:* Berold, *1868:* Berold 79| *1845 H:* —Hark <> game— *1845:* game! *1849:* —Hark *1863:* (Hark 80| *1845 H:* Oh! for *1845:* Oh for

And turn in the wind, and dance like flame!)
Had they broached a white-beer cask from Berlin
—Or if you incline to prescribe mere wine
Put to his lips, when they saw him pine,
A cup of our own Moldavia fine,
Cotnar for instance, green as May sorrel
And ropy with sweet,—we shall not quarrel.

IV

So, at home, the sick tall yellow Duchess
Was left with the infant in her clutches,
She being the daughter of God knows who:
　　And now was the time to revisit her tribe.
Abroad and afar they went, the two,
　　And let our people rail and gibe
At the empty hall and extinguished fire,
　　As loud as we liked, but ever in vain,
Till after long years we had our desire,
　　And back came the Duke and his mother again.

V

And he came back the pertest little ape
That ever affronted human shape;
Full of his travel, struck at himself.
　　You'd say, he despised our bluff old ways?
—Not he! For in Paris they told the elf
　　Our rough North land was the Land of Lays,
　　The one good thing left in evil days;

82| *1845 H:* flame! *1849:* flame!) 83| *1845 H:* broach'd a cask of white beer from *1845:* Berlin! *1849:* broached *1888:* a white-beer cask from Berlin 84| *1849:* wine— *1863:* wine 85| *1845 H:* lips when *1888:* lips, when 87| *1845 H:* Cotnar, for <> sorrel, *1868:* Cotnar for <> sorrel 89| *1845 H:* So at home the *1849:* So, at home, the 92| *1845 H:* tribe, *1868:* tribe. 93| *1845 H:* So abroad *1849:* So, abroad *1868:* Abroad and 94| *1845 H:* people curse and *1849:* people rail and 95| *1845:* empty Hall *1868:* hall 96| *1845 H:* Loud as we lik'd <> vain; *1845:* liked <> vain, *1849:* As loud 99| *1845 H:* pertest ape *1849:* pertest little ape 101| *1845 H:* himself— *1863:* himself. 102| *1845 H:* despis'd <> ways *1845:* despised *1863:* ways? 104| *1845 H:* That our *1888:* Our rough

Since the Mid-Age was the Heroic Time,
And only in wild nooks like ours
Could you taste of it yet as in its prime,
And see true castles, with proper towers,
Young-hearted women, old-minded men,
And manners now as manners were then.
So, all that the old Dukes had been, without knowing it,
This Duke would fain know he was, without being it;
'Twas not for the joy's self, but the joy of his showing it,
Nor for the pride's self, but the pride of our seeing it,
He revived all usages thoroughly worn-out,
The souls of them fumed-forth, the hearts of them torn-out:
And chief in the chase his neck he perilled
On a lathy horse, all legs and length,
With blood for bone, all speed, no strength;
—They should have set him on red Berold
With the red eye slow consuming in fire,
And the thin stiff ear like an abbey-spire!

VI

Well, such as he was, he must marry, we heard:
And out of a convent, at the word,
Came the lady, in time of spring.
—Oh, old thoughts they cling, they cling!
That day, I know, with a dozen oaths
I clad myself in thick hunting-clothes
Fit for the chase of urochs or buffle
In winter-time when you need to muffle.
But the Duke had a mind we should cut a figure,

106| *1845 H:* For the Mid-Age *1849:* Since the Mid-Age 109| *1845 H:* True castles, with *1845:* True Castles with proper Towers, *1849:* And see true castles <> towers, 112| *1845 H:* all the old dukes *1845:* old Dukes *1849:* all that the 115| *1845 H:* it. *1849:* it, 116| *1845 H:* reviv'd <> worn out, *1845:* revived <> worn-out, 117| *1845 H:* fum'd forth <> torn out: *1845:* fumed-forth <> torn-out: 118| *1845 H:* perill'd, *1849:* perilled, *1888:* perilled 121| *1845 H:* They *1845:* —They <> red Berold, *1868:* red Berold 123| *1845 H:* abbey spire! *1888:* abbey-spire! 126| *1845:* the Lady *1868:* lady 130| *1845 H:* urox *1888:* urochs 131| *1845 H:* winter-time, when <> muffle; *1845:* winter-time when *1863:*

And so we saw the lady arrive:
My friend, I have seen a white crane bigger!
She was the smallest lady alive,
Made in a piece of nature's madness,
Too small, almost, for the life and gladness
That over-filled her, as some hive
Out of the bears' reach on the high trees
Is crowded with its safe merry bees:
In truth, she was not hard to please!
Up she looked, down she looked, round at the mead,
Straight at the castle, that's best indeed
To look at from outside the walls:
As for us, styled the "serfs and thralls,"
She as much thanked me as if she had said it,
(With her eyes, do you understand?)
Because I patted her horse while I led it;
And Max, who rode on her other hand,
Said, no bird flew past but she inquired
What its true name was, nor ever seemed tired—
If that was an eagle she saw hover,
And the green and grey bird on the field was the plover.
When suddenly appeared the Duke:
And as down she sprung, the small foot pointed
On to my hand,—as with a rebuke,
And as if his backbone were not jointed,
The Duke stepped rather aside than forward,
And welcomed her with his grandest smile;
And, mind you, his mother all the while
Chilled in the rear, like a wind to Nor'ward;

---

muffle. 133| *1845:* the Lady *1868:* lady 135| *1845:* smallest Lady *1849:* lady 136| *1845 H:* Made, in *1845:* of Nature's *1868:* Made in <> nature's 138| *1845 H:* over-fill'd *1845:* over-filled 140| *1845 H:* bees— *1849:* bees: 141| *1845 H:* truth she *1849:* truth, she 142| *1845 H:* look'd <> look'd *1849:* looked <> looked 143| *1845:* the Castle *1849:* castle 146| *1845 H:* thank'd *1845:* thanked 147| *1845 H:* eye *1849:* eyes 149| *1845 H:* who went on *1845:* who rode on 150| *1845 H:* enquir'd *1845:* enquired *1863:* inquired 151| *1845 H:* seem'd tir'd— *1845:* seemed tired— 152| *1849:* hover,— *1863:* hover, 153| *1845 H:* gray <> plover? *1849:* If the green <> plover. *1863:* And the green and grey 154| *1845 H:* appear'd the Duke, *1845:* appeared *1863:* the Duke: 157| *1845 H:* back-bone *1845:* backbone 158| *1845 H:* stepp'd *1845:* stepped 159| *1845 H:* welcom'd *1845:* welcomed 161| *1845 H:* Chill'd <>

And up, like a weary yawn, with its pullies
Went, in a shriek, the rusty portcullis;
And, like a glad sky the north-wind sullies,
The lady's face stopped its play,
As if her first hair had grown grey;
For such things must begin some one day.

VII

In a day or two she was well again;
As who should say, "You labour in vain!
This is all a jest against God, who meant
I should ever be, as I am, content
And glad in his sight; therefore, glad I will be."
So, smiling as at first went she.

VIII

She was active, stirring, all fire—
Could not rest, could not tire—
To a stone she might have given life!
        (I myself loved once, in my day)
—For a shepherd's, miner's, huntsman's wife,
        (I had a wife, I know what I say)
Never in all the world such an one!
And here was plenty to be done,
And she that could do it, great or small,
She was to do nothing at all.
There was already this man in his post,
        This in his station, and that in his office,
And the Duke's plan admitted a wife, at most,
        To meet his eye, with the other trophies,

nor'ward; *1845:* Chilled <> to Nor'ward; 163| *1845 H:* portcullis, *1849:* portcullis; 165| *1845 H:* stopp'd *1845:* The Lady's <> stopped *1868:* lady's 166| *1845 H:* grey— *1868:* grey; 167| *1845 H:* day! *1868:* day. 172| *1845 H:* be!" *1863:* in His *1868:* his <> be." 173| *1845 H:* So smiling *1849:* So, smiling 176| *1845 H:* she had given *1863:* she might have 177| *1845 H:* lov'd <> day), *1845:* loved <> day,) *1863:* day) 178| *1845:* a Shepherd's, Miner's, Huntsman's *1868:* shepherd's, miner's, huntsman's 179| *1845 H:* say,) *1863:*

Now outside the hall, now in it,
    To sit thus, stand thus, see and be seen,
At the proper place in the proper minute,
    And die away the life between.
And it was amusing enough, each infraction
    Of rule—(but for after-sadness that came)
To hear the consummate self-satisfaction
    With which the young Duke and the old dame
Would let her advice, and criticise,
And, being a fool, instruct the wise,
    And, child-like, parcel out praise or blame:
They bore it all in complacent guise,
As though an artificer, after contriving
A wheel-work image as if it were living,
Should find with delight it could motion to strike him!
So found the Duke, and his mother like him:
The lady hardly got a rebuff—
That had not been contemptuous enough,
With his cursed smirk, as he nodded applause,
And kept off the old mother-cat's claws.

IX

So, the little lady grew silent and thin,
    Paling and ever paling,
As the way is with a hid chagrin;
    And the Duke perceived that she was ailing,
And said in his heart, " 'Tis done to spite me,
But I shall find in my power to right me!"
Don't swear, friend! The old one, many a year,
Is in hell, and the Duke's self . . . you shall hear.

---

say) 188| *1845:* the Hall *1868:* hall 191| *1845 H:* between: *1849:* between. 193| *1845 H:* came)— *1849:* rule (but <> came— *1863:* came) *1868:* rule—(but 195| *1845:* old Dame *1868:* dame 197| *1845 H:* wise; *1845:* wise, 198| *1845 H:* blame. *1845:* blame: 200| *1845 H:* tho' an artificer, having contriv'd *1845:* artificer, after contriving *1863:* though 201| *1845 H:* it liv'd, *1845:* it were living, 203| *1845 H:* him— *1845:* him,-- *1863:* him: 204| *1845:* The Lady *1868:* lady 208| *1845 H:* So the *1845:* little Lady *1849:* So, the *1868:* lady 211| *1845 H:* perceiv'd *1845:* perceived 213| *1845 H:* me." *1845:* me!" 214| *1845 H:* friend,—the *1845:* friend—the Old One *1868:* friend! The old one 215| *1845:* in Hell *1868:* hell § The first nine stanzas only appeared in *Hood's*

x

Well, early in autumn, at first winter-warning,
When the stag had to break with his foot, of a morning,
A drinking-hole out of the fresh tender ice
That covered the pond till the sun, in a trice,
Loosening it, let out a ripple of gold,
        And another and another, and faster and faster,
Till, dimpling to blindness, the wide water rolled:
        Then it so chanced that the Duke our master
Asked himself what were the pleasures in season,
        And found, since the calendar bade him be hearty,
He should do the Middle Age no treason
        In resolving on a hunting-party.
Always provided, old books showed the way of it!
        What meant old poets by their strictures?
And when old poets had said their say of it,
        How taught old painters in their pictures?
We must revert to the proper channels,
Workings in tapestry, paintings on panels,
And gather up woodcraft's authentic traditions:
Here was food for our various ambitions,
As on each case, exactly stated—
        To encourage your dog, now, the properest chirrup,
        Or best prayer to Saint Hubert on mounting your stirrup—
We of the household took thought and debated.
Blessed was he whose back ached with the jerkin
His sire was wont to do forest-work in;
Blesseder he who nobly sunk "ohs"
And "ahs" while he tugged on his grandsire's trunk-hose;
What signified hats if they had no rims on,
        Each slouching before and behind like the scallop,
        And able to serve at sea for a shallop,
Loaded with lacquer and looped with crimson?
So that the deer now, to make a short rhyme on't,
        What with our Venerers, Prickers and Verderers,

Magazine in 1844 and concluded with END OF PART THE FIRST. § 218| *1863:* ice, *1888:* ice 233| *1845:* pannels, *1863:* panels, 234| *1845:* up Woodcraft's *1868:* woodcraft's 236| *1845:* stated, *1868:* stated— 237| *1845:* —To *1868:* To 243| *1845:* trunkhose; *1868:* trunk-hose; 249| *1845:* our Venerers, Prickers,

Might hope for real hunters at length and not murderers,
And oh the Duke's tailor, he had a hot time on't!

XI

Now you must know that when the first dizziness
Of flap-hats and buff-coats and jack-boots subsided,
The Duke put this question, "The Duke's part provided,
Had not the Duchess some share in the business?"
For out of the mouth of two or three witnesses
Did he establish all fit-or-unfitnesses:
And, after much laying of heads together,
Somebody's cap got a notable feather
By the announcement with proper unction
That he had discovered the lady's function;
Since ancient authors gave this tenet,
"When horns wind a mort and the deer is at siege,
Let the dame of the castle prick forth on her jennet,
And, with water to wash the hands of her liege
In a clean ewer with a fair toweling,
Let her preside at the disemboweling."
Now, my friend, if you had so little religion
As to catch a hawk, some falcon-lanner,
And thrust her broad wings like a banner
Into a coop for a vulgar pigeon;
And if day by day and week by week
You cut her claws, and sealed her eyes,
And clipped her wings, and tied her beak,
Would it cause you any great surprise

---

and *1868:* our Venerers, Prickers and 250| *1845:* length, and *1868:* length and 251| *1845:* tailor—he *1849:* oh, the *1868:* oh the <> tailor, he 252| *1845:* know, that *1868:* know that 253| *1845:* buff coats and jackboots *1849:* buff-coats *1868:* jack-boots 256| *1845:* witnesses, *1863:* witnesses 262| *1845:* authors held this *1863:* authors gave this 264| *1845:* of the Castle *1868:* castle 265| *1845:* And with *1868:* And, with 267| *1845:* her superintend the *1849:* her preside at the 272| *1845:* by day, and week by week, *1868:* by day and week

If, when you decided to give her an airing,
You found she needed a little preparing?
—I say, should you be such a curmudgeon,
If she clung to the perch, as to take it in dudgeon?
Yet when the Duke to his lady signified,
Just a day before, as he judged most dignified,
In what a pleasure she was to participate,—
And, instead of leaping wide in flashes,
Her eyes just lifted their long lashes,
As if pressed by fatigue even he could not dissipate,
And duly acknowledged the Duke's forethought,
But spoke of her health, if her health were worth aught,
Of the weight by day and the watch by night,
And much wrong now that used to be right,
So, thanking him, declined the hunting,—
Was conduct ever more affronting?
With all the ceremony settled—
With the towel ready, and the sewer
Polishing up his oldest ewer,
And the jennet pitched upon, a piebald,
Black-barred, cream-coated and pink eye-balled,—
No wonder if the Duke was nettled!
And when she persisted nevertheless,—
Well, I suppose here's the time to confess
That there ran half round our lady's chamber
A balcony none of the hardest to clamber;
And that Jacynth the tire-woman, ready in waiting,
Stayed in call outside, what need of relating?
And since Jacynth was like a June rose, why, a fervent
Adorer of Jacynth of course was your servant;
And if she had the habit to peep through the casement,
How could I keep at any vast distance?
And so, as I say, on the lady's persistence,
The Duke, dumb-stricken with amazement,
Stood for a while in a sultry smother,
And then, with a smile that partook of the awful,
Turned her over to his yellow mother

---

by week 276| *1845:* If when <> airing *1863:* If, when <> airing, 296| *1845:* eye-ball'd,— *1868:* eye-balled,— 300| *1845:* our Lady's *1868:* lady's 301| *1845:* clamber, *1849:* clamber; 305| *1845:* of Jacynth, of course, was *1868:* of Jacynth of course was 308| *1845:* the Lady's *1868:* lady's 309| *1845:* dumb

To learn what was held decorous and lawful;
And the mother smelt blood with a cat-like instinct,
As her cheek quick whitened thro' all its quince-tinct.
Oh, but the lady heard the whole truth at once!
What meant she?—Who was she?—Her duty and station,
The wisdom of age and the folly of youth, at once,
Its decent regard and its fitting relation—
In brief, my friend, set all the devils in hell free
And turn them out to carouse in a belfry
And treat the priests to a fifty-part canon,
And then you may guess how that tongue of hers ran on!
Well, somehow or other it ended at last
And, licking her whiskers, out she passed;
And after her,—making (he hoped) a face
Like Emperor Nero or Sultan Saladin,
Stalked the Duke's self with the austere grace
Of ancient hero or modern paladin,
From door to staircase—oh such a solemn
Unbending of the vertebral column!

XII

However, at sunrise our company mustered;
And here was the huntsman bidding unkennel,
And there 'neath his bonnet the pricker blustered,
With feather dank as a bough of wet fennel;
For the court-yard walls were filled with fog
You might have cut as an axe chops a log—
Like so much wool for colour and bulkiness;
And out rode the Duke in a perfect sulkiness,
Since, before breakfast, a man feels but queasily,
And a sinking at the lower abdomen
Begins the day with indifferent omen.

---

stricken *1888:* dumb-stricken 313| *1845:* was decorous *1888:* was held decorous 315| *1845:* quince-tinct— *1863:* quince-tinct. 316| *1845:* the Lady *1868:* lady 321| *1845:* belfry, *1868:* belfry 328| *1845:* with all the grace *1849:* with the austere grace 329| *1845:* paladin,— *1863:* paladin, 330| *1845:* oh, such *1868:* oh such 332| *1845:* mustered, *1863:* mustered; 336| *1845:* court-yard's four walls *1868:* court-yard walls 337| *1845:* might cut <> log, *1849:* log. *1868:* log— *1888:* might have cut 340| *1845:* Since before *1863:* Since, before 341| *1845:* sinking of the *1849:* sinking at the 342| *1845:* omen: *1863:*

And lo, as he looked around uneasily,
The sun ploughed the fog up and drove it asunder
This way and that from the valley under;
　　And, looking through the court-yard arch,
Down in the valley, what should meet him
　　But a troop of Gipsies on their march?
No doubt with the annual gifts to greet him.

XIII

Now, in your land, Gipsies reach you, only
　　After reaching all lands beside;
North they go, South they go, trooping or lonely,
　　And still, as they travel far and wide,
Catch they and keep now a trace here, a trace there,
That puts you in mind of a place here, a place there.
But with us, I believe they rise out of the ground,
And nowhere else, I take it, are found
With the earth-tint yet so freshly embrowned:
Born, no doubt, like insects which breed on
The very fruit they are meant to feed on.
For the earth—not a use to which they don't turn it,
　　The ore that grows in the mountain's womb,
　　Or the sand in the pits like a honeycomb,
They sift and soften it, bake it and burn it—
Whether they weld you, for instance, a snaffle
With side-bars never a brute can baffle;
Or a lock that's a puzzle of wards within wards;
Or, if your colt's fore-foot inclines to curve inwards,
Horseshoes they hammer which turn on a swivel
And won't allow the hoof to shrivel.
Then they cast bells like the shell of the winkle

---

omen. 343| *1845:* around, uneasily, *1849:* around uneasily, 346| *1845:* thro' *1863:* through 347| *1845:* valley what *1849:* valley, what 348| *1845:* of Gypsies <> march, *1863:* of Gipsies *1868:* march? 350| *1845:* Now in this land, Gypsies <> you only *1849:* Now, in your land <> you, only *1863:* land, Gipsies 352| *1845:* south *1863:* go, South 355| *1845:* there: *1863:* there. 356| *1845:* us I *1849:* us, I 358| *1845:* embrowned; *1888:* embrowned: 360| *1845:* on: *1863:* on. 362| *1845:* mountains' *1849:* mountain's 369| *1845:* they'll *1868:* they 370| *1845:* shrivel; *1863:* shrivel. 371| *1845:* winkle, *1868:*

That keep a stout heart in the ram with their tinkle;
But the sand—they pinch and pound it like otters;
Commend me to Gipsy glass-makers and potters!
Glasses they'll blow you, crystal-clear,
Where just a faint cloud of rose shall appear,
As if in pure water you dropped and let die
A bruised black-blooded mulberry;
And that other sort, their crowning pride,
With long white threads distinct inside,
Like the lake-flower's fibrous roots which dangle
Loose such a length and never tangle,
Where the bold sword-lily cuts the clear waters,
And the cup-lily couches with all the white daughters:
Such are the works they put their hand to,
The uses they turn and twist iron and sand to.
And these made the troop, which our Duke saw sally
Toward his castle from out of the valley,
Men and women, like new-hatched spiders,
Come out with the morning to greet our riders.
And up they wound till they reached the ditch,
Whereat all stopped save one, a witch
That I knew, as she hobbled from the group,
By her gait directly and her stoop,
I, whom Jacynth was used to importune
To let that same witch tell us our fortune,
The oldest Gipsy then above ground;
And, sure as the autumn season came round,
She paid us a visit for profit or pastime,
And every time, as she swore, for the last time.
And presently she was seen to sidle
Up to the Duke till she touched his bridle,
So that the horse of a sudden reared up
As under its nose the old witch peered up
With her worn-out eyes, or rather eye-holes

---

winkle 372| *1845:* tinkle: *1863:* tinkle; 374| *1845:* to Gypsy *1863:* to Gipsy 377| *1845:* in water one dropped *1849:* in pure water you dropped 378| *1863:* bruise *1868:* bruised 386| *1845:* And the *1868:* The uses 387| *1845:* troop which *1863:* troop, which 388| *1845:* Towards *1868:* Toward 390| *1845:* riders; *1863:* riders. 392| *1845:* witch, *1868:* witch 394| *1845:* gait, directly, and *1868:* gait directly and 396| *1845:* fortune, *1849:* fortune. 397| *1845:* oldest Gypsy *1863:* oldest Gipsy 398| *1845:* And, so sure

Of no use now but to gather brine,
And began a kind of level whine
Such as they used to sing to their viols
When their ditties they go grinding
Up and down with nobody minding:
And then, as of old, at the end of the humming
Her usual presents were forthcoming
—A dog-whistle blowing the fiercest of trebles,
(Just a sea-shore stone holding a dozen fine pebbles,)
Or a porcelain mouth-piece to screw on a pipe-end,—
And so she awaited her annual stipend.
But this time, the Duke would scarcely vouchsafe
A word in reply; and in vain she felt
With twitching fingers at her belt
For the purse of sleek pine-martin pelt,
Ready to put what he gave in her pouch safe,—
Till, either to quicken his apprehension,
Or possibly with an after-intention,
She was come, she said, to pay her duty
To the new Duchess, the youthful beauty.
No sooner had she named his lady,
Than a shine lit up the face so shady,
And its smirk returned with a novel meaning—
For it struck him, the babe just wanted weaning;
If one gave her a taste of what life was and sorrow,
She, foolish to-day, would be wiser to-morrow;
And who so fit a teacher of trouble
As this sordid crone bent well-nigh double?
So, glancing at her wolf-skin vesture,
(If such it was, for they grow so hirsute
That their own fleece serves for natural fur-suit)
He was contrasting, 'twas plain from his gesture,
The life of the lady so flower-like and delicate
With the loathsome squalor of this helicat.
I, in brief, was the man the Duke beckoned

1868: And, sure 408| *1845:* use *1849:* used *1868:* use *1888:* used 411| *1845:* And, then as *1868:* And then, as 415| *1845:* mouthpiece *1849:* mouth-piece 425| *1845:* beauty: *1849:* beauty. 426| *1845:* his Lady, *1868:* lady, 427| *1845:* shady *1849:* shady, 430| *1845:* is *1849:* was 433| *1845:* well nigh *1863:* wellnigh *1888:* well-nigh 436| *1845:* fur suit) *1863:* fur-suit) 437| *1845:* contrasted *1849:* was contrasting 438| *1863:* of the Lady *1868:*

From out of the throng, and while I drew near
He told the crone—as I since have reckoned
By the way he went and spoke into her ear
With circumspection and mystery—
The main of the lady's history,
Her frowardness and ingratitude:
And for all the crone's submissive attitude
I could see round her mouth the loose plaits tightening,
And her brow with assenting intelligence brightening,
As though she engaged with hearty goodwill
Whatever he now might enjoin to fulfil,
And promised the lady a thorough frightening.
And so, just giving her a glimpse
Of a purse, with the air of a man who imps
The wing of the hawk that shall fetch the hernshaw,
He bade me take the Gipsy mother
And set her telling some story or other
Of hill or dale, oak-wood or fernshaw,
To wile away a weary hour
For the lady left alone in her bower,
Whose mind and body craved exertion
And yet shrank from all better diversion.

XIV

Then clapping heel to his horse, the mere curveter,
Out rode the Duke, and after his hollo
Horses and hounds swept, huntsman and servitor,
And back I turned and bade the crone follow.
And what makes me confident what's to be told you
Had all along been of this crone's devising,
Is, that, on looking round sharply, behold you,
There was a novelty quick as surprising:
For first, she had shot up a full head in stature,

---

lady 442| *1845:* crone, as *1868:* crone—as 444| *1845:* mystery, *1868:* mystery— 445| *1845:* of the Lady's *1868:* lady's 446| *1845:* ingratitude; *1888:* ingratitude: 449| *1845:* brightening *1849:* brightening, 450| *1845:* tho' <> good will *1863:* though, she <> goodwill *1868:* though she 452| *1845:* the Lady *1849:* lady *1863:* the Lady *1868:* lady 453| *1845:* so just *1849:* so, just 456| *1845:* gypsy *1863:* the Gipsy 459| *1849:* while *1868:* wile 460| *1845:* the Lady *1868:* lady 463| *1845:* curvetter, *1863:* curveter,

And her step kept pace with mine nor faltered,
As if age had foregone its usurpature,
And the ignoble mien was wholly altered,
And the face looked quite of another nature,
And the change reached too, whatever the change meant,
Her shaggy wolf-skin cloak's arrangement:
For where its tatters hung loose like sedges,
Gold coins were glittering on the edges,
Like the band-roll strung with tomans
Which proves the veil a Persian woman's:
And under her brow, like a snail's horns newly
Come out as after the rain he paces,
Two unmistakeable eye-points duly
Live and aware looked out of their places.
So, we went and found Jacynth at the entry
Of the lady's chamber standing sentry;
I told the command and produced my companion,
And Jacynth rejoiced to admit any one,
For since last night, by the same token,
Not a single word had the lady spoken:
They went in both to the presence together,
While I in the balcony watched the weather.

XV

And now, what took place at the very first of all,
I cannot tell, as I never could learn it:
Jacynth constantly wished a curse to fall
On that little head of hers and burn it
If she knew how she came to drop so soundly
Asleep of a sudden and there continue
The whole time sleeping as profoundly
As one of the boars my father would pin you
'Twixt the eyes where life holds garrison,
—Jacynth forgive me the comparison!

472| *1845:* faultered, *1863:* faltered, 475| *1845:* looked of quite another *1849:* looked quite of another 477| *1845:* arrangement, *1863:* arrangement: 486| *1845:* So we *1863:* So, we 487| *1845:* the Lady's *1868:* lady's 491| *1845:* the Lady *1868:* lady 492| *1845:* So they *1863:* They went 495| *1845:* tell as *1849:* tell, as 497| *1849:* it, *1868:* it 502| *1845:* where the life *1868:* where

But where I begin my own narration
Is a little after I took my station
To breathe the fresh air from the balcony,
And, having in those days a falcon eye,
To follow the hunt thro' the open country,
    From where the bushes thinlier crested
The hillocks, to a plain where's not one tree:—
    When, in a moment, my ear was arrested
By—was it singing, or was it saying,
Or a strange musical instrument playing
In the chamber?—and to be certain
I pushed the lattice, pulled the curtain,
And there lay Jacynth asleep,
Yet as if a watch she tried to keep,
In a rosy sleep along the floor
With her head against the door;
While in the midst, on the seat of state,
Was a queen—the Gipsy woman late,
With head and face downbent
On the lady's head and face intent:
For, coiled at her feet like a child at ease,
The lady sat between her knees
And o'er them the lady's clasped hands met,
And on those hands her chin was set,
And her upturned face met the face of the crone
Wherein the eyes had grown and grown
As if she could double and quadruple
At pleasure the play of either pupil
    —Very like, by her hands' slow fanning,
As up and down like a gor-crow's flappers
They moved to measure, or bell-clappers.
    I said "Is it blessing, is it banning,
Do they applaud you or burlesque you—

---

life 504| *1845:* own relation *1849:* own narration 510| *1845:* tree:— *1863:* tree. 518| *1845:* sleep on the *1849:* sleep along the 520| *1845:* And in *1849:* While in 521| *1845:* Like a queen the gypsy woman sate, *1849:* the Gypsy *1863:* Was a queen—the Gipsy woman late, 523| *1845:* the Lady's <> intent, *1863:* intent: *1868:* lady's 525| *1845:* sate *1849:* The Lady *1863:* sat *1868:* lady <> knees, *1888:* knees 526| *1845:* the Lady's *1868:* lady's 532| *1845:* like by her hands *1863:* like, by her hands, slow *1868:* hands' slow 534| *1845:* measure like bell clappers *1863:* measure, or bell clappers. *1888:* bell-clappers. 535| *1845:* —I said, is *1863:* I *1888:* said "Is 536| *1845:* burlesque you? *1863:* burlesque you—

Those hands and fingers with no flesh on?"
But, just as I thought to spring in to the rescue,
At once I was stopped by the lady's expression:
For it was life her eyes were drinking
From the crone's wide pair above unwinking,
—Life's pure fire received without shrinking,
Into the heart and breast whose heaving
Told you no single drop they were leaving,
—Life, that filling her, passed redundant
Into her very hair, back swerving
Over each shoulder, loose and abundant,
As her head thrown back showed the white throat curving;
And the very tresses shared in the pleasure,
Moving to the mystic measure,
Bounding as the bosom bounded.
I stopped short, more and more confounded,
As still her cheeks burned and eyes glistened,
As she listened and she listened:
When all at once a hand detained me,
The selfsame contagion gained me,
And I kept time to the wondrous chime,
Making out words and prose and rhyme,
Till it seemed that the music furled
Its wings like a task fulfilled, and dropped
From under the words it first had propped,
And left them midway in the world:
Word took word as hand takes hand,
I could hear at last, and understand,
And when I held the unbroken thread,
The Gipsy said:—

537| *1845:* on? *1888:* on?" 538| *1845:* When, just *1863:* But, just 539| *1845:* the Lady's *1868:* lady's 541| *1845:* crones' wide pair unwinking, *1849:* crone's wide pair above unwinking, 542| *1845:* Life's *1863:* —Life's 544| *1845:* leaving— *1863:* leaving, 545| *1845:* Life <> past *1863:* —Life <> passed 548| *1845:* curving, *1888:* curving; 552| *1845:* stopped, more and *1849:* stopped short, more and 554| *1845:* and she listened,— *1863:* and she listened: 556| *1845:* And the *1868:* The 562| *1845:* world, *1888:* world: 563| *1845:* And word took *1868:* Word took 566| *1845:* The Gypsy *1863:* The Gipsy 567| *1845:* And <>

"And so at last we find my tribe,
And so I set thee in the midst,
And to one and all of them describe
What thou saidst and what thou didst,
Our long and terrible journey through,
And all thou art ready to say and do
In the trials that remain:
I trace them the vein and the other vein
That meet on thy brow and part again,
Making our rapid mystic mark;
And I bid my people prove and probe
Each eye's profound and glorious globe
Till they detect the kindred spark
In those depths so dear and dark,
Like the spots that snap and burst and flee,
Circling over the midnight sea.
And on that round young cheek of thine
I make them recognize the tinge,
As when of the costly scarlet wine
They drip so much as will impinge
And spread in a thinnest scale afloat
One thick gold drop from the olive's coat
Over a silver plate whose sheen
Still thro' the mixture shall be seen.
For so I prove thee, to one and all,
Fit, when my people ope their breast,
To see the sign, and hear the call,
And take the vow, and stand the test
Which adds one more child to the rest—
When the breast is bare and the arms are wide,
And the world is left outside.
For there is probation to decree,
And many and long must the trials be
Thou shalt victoriously endure,
If that brow is true and those eyes are sure;
Like a jewel-finder's fierce assay
Of the prize he dug from its mountain-tomb—

---

tribe, *1849:* "And *1888:* tribe. 571| *1845:* thro', *1863:* through, 581| *1845:* snap, and burst, and *1863:* snap and burst and 583| *1845:* that young round cheek *1863:* that round young cheek 584| *1845:* recognise *1888:* recognize 591| *1845:* For, so *1863:* For so 603| *1845:* mountain tomb,— *1888:* mountain-tomb—

Let once the vindicating ray
Leap out amid the anxious gloom,
And steel and fire have done their part
And the prize falls on its finder's heart;
So, trial after trial past,
Wilt thou fall at the very last
Breathless, half in trance
With the thrill of the great deliverance,
Into our arms for evermore;
And thou shalt know, those arms once curled
About thee, what we knew before,
How love is the only good in the world.
Henceforth be loved as heart can love,
Or brain devise, or hand approve!
Stand up, look below,
It is our life at thy feet we throw
To step with into light and joy;
Not a power of life but we employ
To satisfy thy nature's want;
Art thou the tree that props the plant,
Or the climbing plant that seeks the tree—
Canst thou help us, must we help thee?
If any two creatures grew into one,
They would do more than the world has done:
Though each apart were never so weak,
Ye vainly through the world should seek
For the knowledge and the might
Which in such union grew their right:
So, to approach at least that end,
And blend,—as much as may be, blend
Thee with us or us with thee,—
As climbing plant or propping tree,
Shall some one deck thee, over and down
Up and about, with blossoms and leaves?

621| *1845:* we'll *1868:* we 624| *1845:* that takes the *1849:* that seeks the 627| *1845:* done; *1888:* done 628| *1845:* Tho' *1863:* Though 629| *1845:* Yet vainly thro' <> should ye seek *1863:* through *1868:* Ye vainly <> should seek 632| *1845:* approach, at least, that *1868:* approach at least that 634| *1845:* or us with thee, *1868:* or us with thee,— 635| *1845:* climbing-plant or propping-tree, *1863:* climbing plant *1888:* propping tree, 636| *1845:* down, *1888:* down

Fix his heart's fruit for thy garland-crown,
    Cling with his soul as the gourd-vine cleaves,
Die on thy boughs and disappear
While not a leaf of thine is sere?
Or is the other fate in store,
And art thou fitted to adore,
To give thy wondrous self away,
And take a stronger nature's sway?
I foresee and could foretell
Thy future portion, sure and well:
But those passionate eyes speak true, speak true,
Let them say what thou shalt do!
Only be sure thy daily life,
In its peace or in its strife,
Never shall be unobserved;
    We pursue thy whole career,
    And hope for it, or doubt, or fear,—
Lo, hast thou kept thy path or swerved,
We are beside thee in all thy ways,
With our blame, with our praise,
Our shame to feel, our pride to show,
Glad, angry—but indifferent, no!
Whether it be thy lot to go,
For the good of us all, where the haters meet
In the crowded city's horrible street;
Or thou step alone through the morass
Where never sound yet was
Save the dry quick clap of the stork's bill,
For the air is still, and the water still,
When the blue breast of the dipping coot
Dives under, and all is mute.
So, at the last shall come old age,
Decrepit as befits that stage;
How else wouldst thou retire apart
With the hoarded memories of thy heart,

638| *1845:* garland crown, *1888:* garland-crown, 646| *1845:* and I could *1868:* and could 647| *1845:* well— *1868:* well: 649| *1845:* And let *1868:* Let 650| *1845:* Only, be *1868:* Only be 651| *1845:* peace, or *1868:* peace or 654| *1845:* fear, *1849:* fear,— 656| *1845:* thee, in *1868:* thee in 659| *1845:* Glad, sorry—but *1863:* Glad, angry—but 660| *1845:* is *1868:* be 663| *1845:* thro' *1863:* through 665| *1845:* dry clap <> stork's quick bill, *1849:* dry quick clap <> stork's bill, 668| *1849:* all again is *1863:* all is 669| *1845:* So at *1868:* So,

And gather all to the very least
Of the fragments of life's earlier feast,
Let fall through eagerness to find
The crowning dainties yet behind?
Ponder on the entire past
Laid together thus at last,
When the twilight helps to fuse
The first fresh with the faded hues,
And the outline of the whole,
As round eve's shades their framework roll,
Grandly fronts for once thy soul.
And then as, 'mid the dark, a gleam
Of yet another morning breaks,
And like the hand which ends a dream,
Death, with the might of his sunbeam,
Touches the flesh and the soul awakes,
Then——"
Ay, then indeed something would happen!
But what? For here her voice changed like a bird's;
There grew more of the music and less of the words;
Had Jacynth only been by me to clap pen
To paper and put you down every syllable
With those clever clerkly fingers,
All I've forgotten as well as what lingers
In this old brain of mine that's but ill able
To give you even this poor version
Of the speech I spoil, as it were, with stammering
—More fault of those who had the hammering
Of prosody into me and syntax,
And did it, not with hobnails but tintacks!
But to return from this excursion,—
Just, do you mark, when the song was sweetest,
The peace most deep and the charm completest,
There came, shall I say, a snap—
And the charm vanished!
And my sense returned, so strangely banished,

---

at 677| *1863:* entire Past *1868:* past 680| *1845:* fresh, with *1868:* fresh with 682| *1845:* eve-shades *1849:* eve's shades 683| *1845:* soul: *1863:* soul. 687| *1845:* sunbeam *1868:* sunbeam, 689| *1845:* Then— ¶ Ay, then, indeed, something *1849:* Then—" ¶ Ay *1868:* then indeed something *1888:* Then——" ¶ Ay 693| *1845:* syllable, *1863:* syllable 695| *1845:* What I've *1849:* All that

And, starting as from a nap,
I knew the crone was bewitching my lady,
With Jacynth asleep; and but one spring made I
Down from the casement, round to the portal,
Another minute and I had entered,—
When the door opened, and more than mortal
Stood, with a face where to my mind centred
All beauties I ever saw or shall see,
The Duchess: I stopped as if struck by palsy.
She was so different, happy and beautiful,
I felt at once that all was best,
And that I had nothing to do, for the rest,
But wait her commands, obey and be dutiful.
Not that, in fact, there was any commanding;
I saw the glory of her eye,
And the brow's height and the breast's expanding,
And I was hers to live or to die.
As for finding what she wanted,
You know God Almighty granted
Such little signs should serve wild creatures
To tell one another all their desires,
So that each knows what his friend requires,
And does its bidding without teachers.
I preceded her; the crone
Followed silent and alone;
I spoke to her, but she merely jabbered
In the old style; both her eyes had slunk
Back to their pits; her stature shrunk;
In short, the soul in its body sunk
Like a blade sent home to its scabbard.
We descended, I preceding;
Crossed the court with nobody heeding;
All the world was at the chase,

I've *1868:* All I've 710| *1849:* I, *1868:* I 711| *1845:* casement round *1849:* casement, round 712| *1845:* entered, *1863:* entered,— 716| *1845:* The Duchess—I *1868:* The Duchess: I 720| *1845:* dutiful: *1849:* dutiful. 721| *1845:* commanding, *1868:* commanding; 722| *1845:* —I *1868:* I 724| *1845:* die: *1849:* die. 727| *1845:* serve his wild *1868:* serve wild 729| *1845:* what its friend *1888:* what his friend 737| *1845:* scabbard; *1849:* scabbard. 738| *1845:* preceding, *1849:* preceding; 739| *1845:* heeding, *1849:*

The courtyard like a desert-place,
The stable emptied of its small fry;
I saddled myself the very palfrey
I remember patting while it carried her,
The day she arrived and the Duke married her.
And, do you know, though it's easy deceiving
Oneself in such matters, I can't help believing
The lady had not forgotten it either,
And knew the poor devil so much beneath her
Would have been only too glad for her service
To dance on hot ploughshares like a Turk dervise,
But, unable to pay proper duty where owing it,
Was reduced to that pitiful method of showing it:
For though the moment I began setting
His saddle on my own nag of Berold's begetting,
(Not that I meant to be obtrusive)
        She stopped me, while his rug was shifting,
        By a single rapid finger's lifting,
And, with a gesture kind but conclusive,
And a little shake of the head, refused me,—
I say, although she never used me,
Yet when she was mounted, the Gipsy behind her,
And I ventured to remind her,
I suppose with a voice of less steadiness
        Than usual, for my feeling exceeded me,
—Something to the effect that I was in readiness
        Whenever God should please she needed me,—
Then, do you know, her face looked down on me
With a look that placed a crown on me,
And she felt in her bosom,—mark, her bosom—
And, as a flower-tree drops its blossom,
Dropped me . . . ah, had it been a purse
Of silver, my friend, or gold that's worse,
Why, you see, as soon as I found myself
        So understood,—that a true heart so may gain
        Such a reward,—I should have gone home again,
Kissed Jacynth, and soberly drowned myself!

---

heeding; 741| *1845:* court-yard *1888:* courtyard 745| *1845:* her; *1849:* her. 748| *1863:* The Lady *1868:* lady 752| *1845:* But unable <> it *1868:* But, unable <> it, 753| *1868:* it. *1888:* it: 754| *1845:* tho' *1849:* though 762| *1845:* gypsy *1863:* the Gipsy 772| *1845:* me—ah *1863:* me . .

It was a little plait of hair
      Such as friends in a convent make
      To wear, each for the other's sake,—
This, see, which at my breast I wear,
Ever did (rather to Jacynth's grudgment),
And ever shall, till the Day of Judgment.
And then,—and then,—to cut short,—this is idle,
      These are feelings it is not good to foster,—
I pushed the gate wide, she shook the bridle,
      And the palfrey bounded,—and so we lost her.

XVI

When the liquor's out why clink the cannikin?
I did think to describe you the panic in
The redoubtable breast of our master the mannikin,
And what was the pitch of his mother's yellowness,
      How she turned as a shark to snap the spare-rib
      Clean off, sailors say, from a pearl-diving Carib,
When she heard, what she called the flight of the feloness
—But it seems such child's play,
What they said and did with the lady away!
And to dance on, when we've lost the music,
Always made me—and no doubt makes you—sick.
Nay, to my mind, the world's face looked so stern
As that sweet form disappeared through the postern,
She that kept it in constant good humour,
It ought to have stopped; there seemed nothing to do more.
But the world thought otherwise and went on,
And my head's one that its spite was spent on:
Thirty years are fled since that morning,
And with them all my head's adorning.
Nor did the old Duchess die outright,
As you expect, of suppressed spite,
The natural end of every adder
Not suffered to empty its poison-bladder:

---

ah *1888:* me . . . ah 787| *1845:* her! *1863:* her. 788| *1845:* out, why <> cannakin? *1868:* out why <> cannikin? 794| *1845:* heard what <> feloness— *1849:* heard, what she called, the flight *1863:* feloness *1868:* called the flight 795| *1845:* But <> play *1863:* —But <> play, 796| *1845:* away, *1849:* away! *1863:* the Lady *1868:* lady 799| *1845:* And, to *1849:* Nay, to 800| *1845:*

But she and her son agreed, I take it,
That no one should touch on the story to wake it,
For the wound in the Duke's pride rankled fiery,
So, they made no search and small inquiry—
And when fresh Gipsies have paid us a visit, I've
Noticed the couple were never inquisitive,
But told them they're folks the Duke don't want here,
And bade them make haste and cross the frontier.
Brief, the Duchess was gone and the Duke was glad of it,
        And the old one was in the young one's stead,
        And took, in her place, the household's head,
And a blessed time the household had of it!
And were I not, as a man may say, cautious
How I trench, more than needs, on the nauseous,
I could favour you with sundry touches
Of the paint-smutches with which the Duchess
Heightened the mellowness of her cheek's yellowness
(To get on faster) until at last her
Cheek grew to be one master-plaster
Of mucus and fucus from mere use of ceruse:
In short, she grew from scalp to udder
Just the object to make you shudder.

XVII

You're my friend—
What a thing friendship is, world without end!
How it gives the heart and soul a stir-up
        As if somebody broached you a glorious runlet,
        And poured out, all lovelily, sparklingly, sunlit,
Our green Moldavia, the streaky syrup,
Cotnar as old as the time of the Druids—
Friendship may match with that monarch of fluids;
Each supples a dry brain, fills you its ins-and-outs,

---

thro' *1863:* through 814| *1845:* So they *1863:* So, they 815| *1845:* gypsies *1863:* fresh Gipsies 819| *1845:* The Duchess *1849:* Brief, the Duchess <> it *1863:* it, *1868:* it *1888:* it, 830| *1845:* ceruse *1863:* ceruse: 831| *1845:* Till in short she *1863:* In short, she 832–833| *1845:* § No stanza break § shudder! / You're *1849:* shudder! / XVII / You're *1863:* shudder. 835| *1845:* stir-up, *1863:* stir-up 837| *1845:* out all <> sparkling, and sunlit, *1863:* out, all <> sparklingly, sunlit, 840| *1845:* Friendship's as good as that <> fluids *1863:* Friendship may match with that <> fluids; 841| *1845:* To supple <> fill <> ins-and-outs,— *1863:* Each supples

Gives your life's hour-glass a shake when the thin sand doubts
Whether to run on or stop short, and guarantees
Age is not all made of stark sloth and arrant ease.
I have seen my little lady once more,
Jacynth, the Gipsy, Berold, and the rest of it,
For to me spoke the Duke, as I told you before;
I always wanted to make a clean breast of it:
And now it is made—why, my heart's blood, that went trickle,
Trickle, but anon, in such muddy driblets,
Is pumped up brisk now, through the main ventricle,
And genially floats me about the giblets.
I'll tell you what I intend to do:
I must see this fellow his sad life through—
He is our Duke, after all,
And I, as he says, but a serf and thrall.
My father was born here, and I inherit
His fame, a chain he bound his son with;
Could I pay in a lump I should prefer it,
But there's no mine to blow up and get done with:
So, I must stay till the end of the chapter.
For, as to our middle-age-manners-adapter,
Be it a thing to be glad on or sorry on,
Some day or other, his head in a morion
And breast in a hauberk, his heels he'll kick up,
Slain by an onslaught fierce of hiccup.
And then, when red doth the sword of our Duke rust,
And its leathern sheath lie o'ergrown with a blue crust,
Then I shall scrape together my earnings;

<> fills <> ins-and-outs, 842| *1845:* your Life's *1863:* life's 844| *1845:* ease! *1863:* ease. 845| *1845:* my Lady *1849:* my little Lady *1868:* lady 846| *1845:* the Gypsy *1863:* the Gipsy 848| *1845:* it, *1863:* it: 849| *1845:* why the heart's-blood *1849:* why, my heart's-blood *1868:* heart's blood 850| *1845:* dribblets, *1888:* driblets, 851| *1845:* thro' *1863:* through 852| *1845:* giblets! *1863:* giblets. 853| *1845:* what I shall do: *1849:* what I intend to do: 854| *1845:* thro' *1863:* through— 855| *1845:* —He <> Duke after *1863:* He <> Duke, after 856| *1845:* thrall; *1863:* thrall. 857| *1845:* here and *1863:* here, and 858| *1845:* with,— *1863:* with: *1868:* with; 860| *1845:* with, *1868:* with: 861| *1845:* So I <> chapter: *1863:* So, I <> chapter. 862| *1845:* middle-age manners adapter, *1849:* middle-age-manners-adapter, 864| *1845:* One day <> morion, *1863:* Some day *1868:* morion 865| *1845:* up *1863:* up, 866| *1845:* by some onslaught <> hiccup: *1849:* hiccup. *1863:* by an onslaught 868| *1845:* sheath is o'ergrown *1849:* sheath lies o'ergrown *1863:* lie 869| *1849:*

For, you see, in the churchyard Jacynth reposes,
And our children all went the way of the roses:
It's a long lane that knows no turnings.
One needs but little tackle to travel in;
So, just one stout cloak shall I indue:
And for a staff, what beats the javelin
With which his boars my father pinned you?
And then, for a purpose you shall hear presently,
Taking some Cotnar, a tight plump skinful,
I shall go journeying, who but I, pleasantly!
Sorrow is vain and despondency sinful.
What's a man's age? He must hurry more, that's all;
Cram in a day, what his youth took a year to hold:
When we mind labour, then only, we're too old—
What age had Methusalem when he begat Saul?
And at last, as its haven some buffeted ship sees,
(Come all the way from the north-parts with sperm oil)
I hope to get safely out of the turmoil
And arrive one day at the land of the Gipsies,
And find my lady, or hear the last news of her
From some old thief and son of Lucifer,
His forehead chapleted green with wreathy hop,
Sunburned all over like an Æthiop.
And when my Cotnar begins to operate
And the tongue of the rogue to run at a proper rate,
And our wine-skin, tight once, shows each flaccid dent,
I shall drop in with—as if by accident—
"You never knew, then, how it all ended,
What fortune good or bad attended

Then, I *1868:* Then I 870| *1845:* the Churchyard *1863:* churchyard 871| *1845:* roses— *1863:* roses: 872| *1845:* turnings— *1863:* turnings. 873| *1845:* in, *1863:* in; 874| *1845:* one cloak <> indue, *1849:* one stout cloak *1863:* indue: 878| *1845:* skinfull, *1888:* skinful, 879| *1845:* pleasantly? *1863:* pleasantly! 880| *1845:* sinful: *1849:* sinful. 882| *1845:* what youth takes <> hold; *1849:* what his youth took *1863:* hold: 886| *1845:* north parts *1849:* north-parts 887| *1845:* I shall get *1863:* I hope to get 888| *1845:* gypsies *1863:* of the Gipsies, 889| *1845:* lady or *1849:* lady, or *1863:* my Lady *1868:* lady 891| *1845:* chapletted *1863:* chapleted 892| *1845:* an Æthiop: *1863:* an Æthiop. 895| *1845:* wine skin *1849:* wine-skin 897| *1845:* knew then how *1849:* then, how *1888:* knew, then 898| *1845:* fortunes *1868:* fortune

The little lady your Queen befriended?"
—And when that's told me, what's remaining?
This world's too hard for my explaining.
The same wise judge of matters equine
Who still preferred some slim four-year-old
To the big-boned stock of mighty Berold,
And, for strong Cotnar, drank French weak wine,
He also must be such a lady's scorner!
Smooth Jacob still robs homely Esau:
Now up, now down, the world's one see-saw.
—So, I shall find out some snug corner
Under a hedge, like Orson the wood-knight,
Turn myself round and bid the world good night;
And sleep a sound sleep till the trumpet's blowing
Wakes me (unless priests cheat us laymen)
To a world where will be no further throwing
Pearls before swine that can't value them. Amen!

899| *1863:* little Lady *1868:* lady 901| *1845:* explaining— *1863:* explaining. 903| *1845:* some hot four-year-old *1849:* some slim four-year-old 905| *1845:* And for <> Cotnar drank *1863:* And, for <> Cotnar, drank 906| *1845:* a Lady's *1868:* lady's 907| *1845:* homely Esau, *1863:* homely Esau: 908| *1845:* up now <> see-saw! *1849:* up, now *1863:* see-saw. 909| *1845:* —So I *1849:* —So, I 910| *1845:* wood knight, *1849:* wood-knight, 911| *1845:* night, *1849:* night; 912| *1845:* blowing, *1849:* blowing 914| *1845:* where's to be *1863:* where will be 915| *1845:* them: Amen. *1849:* them. Amen!

EARTH'S IMMORTALITIES

FAME

See, as the prettiest graves will do in time,
Our poet's wants the freshness of its prime;
Spite of the sexton's browsing horse, the sods
Have struggled through its binding osier rods;
Headstone and half-sunk footstone lean awry,
Wanting the brick-work promised by-and-by;
How the minute grey lichens, plate o'er plate,
Have softened down the crisp-cut name and date!

LOVE

So, the year's done with!
        (*Love me for ever!*)
All March begun with,
        April's endeavour;
May-wreaths that bound me
        June needs must sever;
Now snows fall round me,
        Quenching June's fever—
        (*Love me for ever!*)

EARTH'S IMMORTALITIES § In 1845 the two parts of the poem were designated I and II, but were replaced by the subtitles *Fame* and *Love* in 1849. Subsequent placement: 1863: DL § 4| *1845:* thro' *1863:* through 6| *1845:* by and by; *1863:* by-and-by; 13| *1845:* May-wreathes *1849:* May-wreaths 14| *1845:* sever! *1863:* sever;

SONG

I

Nay but you, who do not love her,
    Is she not pure gold, my mistress?
Holds earth aught—speak truth—above her?
    Aught like this tress, see, and this tress,
And this last fairest tress of all,
So fair, see, ere I let it fall?

II

Because, you spend your lives in praising;
    To praise, you search the wide world over:
Then why not witness, calmly gazing,
    If earth holds aught—speak truth—above her?
Above this tress, and this, I touch
But cannot praise, I love so much!

SONG § Subsequent placement: 1863: DL § 5| *1845:* this one last tress *1849:* this last fairest tress 6| *1845:* fall! *1863:* fall? 7| *1845:* Because you *1849:* Because, you 8| *1845:* over; *1863:* over: 9| *1845:* So why *1849:* So, why *1868:* Then why 11| *1845:* and this I *1868:* and this, I

THE BOY AND THE ANGEL

Morning, evening, noon and night,
"Praise God!" sang Theocrite.

Then to his poor trade he turned,
Whereby the daily meal was earned.

Hard he laboured, long and well;
O'er his work the boy's curls fell.

But ever, at each period,
He stopped and sang, "Praise God!"

Then back again his curls he threw,
And cheerful turned to work anew.

Said Blaise, the listening monk, "Well done;
I doubt not thou art heard, my son:

"As well as if thy voice to-day
Were praising God, the Pope's great way.

"This Easter Day, the Pope at Rome
Praises God from Peter's dome."

Said Theocrite, "Would God that I
Might praise him, that great way, and die!"

THE BOY AND THE ANGEL § First published August 1844 in *Hood's Magazine* signed Robert Browning. Subsequent placement: 1863: DR § [1]| *1844:* Morning, noon, eve, and *1845:* Morning, evening, noon, and *1863:* noon and [2]| *1844:* God," sang Theocrite; *1845:* Theocrite. *1868:* God!" sang [3]| *1844:* turn'd, *1845:* turned *1849:* turned, [4]| *1844:* By which the <> earn'd. *1845:* earned. *1868:* Whereby the [5]| *1844:* labour'd <> well, *1845:* laboured <> well; [6]| *1844:* O'er the work his boy's <> fell; *1849:* O'er his work the boy's <> fell: *1868:* fell. [8]| *1844:* stopp'd <> God;" *1845:* stopped <> God:" *1849:* God." *1868:* God!" [10]| *1844:* turn'd *1845:* turned [11]| *1845:* well *1849:* monk," Well [12]| *1844:* son; *1845:* son: [13]| *1844:* As if *1845:* As well as if [14]| *1844:* praising God the <> way; *1845:* way. *1849:* praising God, the [16]| *1844:* from Peter's Dome." *1845:* dome." [17]| *1845:* would *1849:* said Theocrite, "Would [18]| *1844:* praise

Night passed, day shone,
And Theocrite was gone.

With God a day endures alway,
A thousand years are but a day.

God said in heaven, "Nor day nor night
Now brings the voice of my delight."

Then Gabriel, like a rainbow's birth,
Spread his wings and sank to earth;

Entered, in flesh, the empty cell,
Lived there, and played the craftsman well;

And morning, evening, noon and night,
Praised God in place of Theocrite.

And from a boy, to youth he grew:
The man put off the stripling's hue:

The man matured and fell away
Into the season of decay:

And ever o'er the trade he bent,
And ever lived on earth content.

(He did God's will; to him, all one
If on the earth or in the sun.)

God said, "A praise is in mine ear;
There is no doubt in it, no fear:

Him *1868:* him 19| *1844:* pass'd *1845:* passed 22| *1844:* are as a day: *1845:* are but a day. 23| *1844:* In Heaven God said, "Nor *1845:* God said in Heaven, "Nor *1868:* heaven 24| *1844:* Brings one voice *1845:* Now brings the voice 26| *1844:* earth, *1845:* earth; 27| *1844:* Enter'd the *1845:* Entered in flesh, the *1868:* Entered, in 28| *1844:* And play'd <> well, *1845:* Lived there, and played <> well: *1863:* well; 29| *1844:* morn, noon, eve, and *1845:* morning, evening, noon, and *1863:* noon and 30| *1844:* Prais'd *1845:* Praised 31| *1844:* boy to <> grew; *1845:* boy, to <> grew: 32| *1844:* hue; *1845:* the Man put off the Stripling's hue: *1849:* man <> stripling's 33| *1844:* matured, and *1845:* matured and 34| *1844:* decay; *1845:* decay: 35| *1844:* Yet ever *1845:* And ever <> bent *1849:* bent, 36–39| *1844:* lived content. / God *1845:* lived on earth content. *1849:* content.

"So sing old worlds, and so
New worlds that from my footstool go.

"Clearer loves sound other ways:
I miss my little human praise."

Then forth sprang Gabriel's wings, off fell
The flesh disguise, remained the cell.

'Twas Easter Day: he flew to Rome,
And paused above Saint Peter's dome.

In the tiring-room close by
The great outer gallery,

With his holy vestments dight,
Stood the new Pope, Theocrite:

And all his past career
Came back upon him clear,

Since when, a boy, he plied his trade,
Till on his life the sickness weighed;

And in his cell, when death drew near,
An angel in a dream brought cheer:

And rising from the sickness drear
He grew a priest, and now stood here.

To the East with praise he turned,
And on his sight the angel burned.

/ (He did God's will; to him, all one / If on the earth or in the sun.) / God   42| *1844:* go; *1845:* go.   43| *1844:* ways; *1845:* ways: 46| *1844:* flesh, remain'd *1845:* flesh disguise, remained   48| *1844:* above the dome. *1845:* above Saint Peter's dome.   49| *1844:* tiring-room, close *1845:* tiring-room close   52| *1844:* pope, Theocrite, *1845:* new Pope, Theocrite: *1888:* Theocrite   54–59| *1844:* clear—/ How rising *1845:* clear. / Since when, a boy, he plied his trade / Till on his life the sickness weighed: / And in his cell when death drew near / An angel in a dream brought cheer: / And rising *1849:* clear, / Since <> trade, / Till <> cell, when <> near,   60| *1844:* priest and *1845:* priest, and   61| *1844:* east <> turn'd, *1845:* the East <> turned *1849:* turned,   62–65| *1844:* And in the Angel burn'd:—/ "Vainly <> my sphere, *1845:*

"I bore thee from thy craftsman's cell
And set thee here; I did not well.

"Vainly I left my angel-sphere,
Vain was thy dream of many a year.
"Thy voice's praise seemed weak; it dropped—
Creation's chorus stopped!

"Go back and praise again
The early way, while I remain.

"With that weak voice of our disdain,
Take up creation's pausing strain.

"Back to the cell and poor employ:
Resume the craftsman and the boy!"

Theocrite grew old at home;
A new Pope dwelt in Peter's dome.

One vanished as the other died:
They sought God side by side.

And on his sight the angel burned. / I bore thee from thy craftsman's cell, / And set thee here; I did not well. / "Vainly <> my angel's-sphere, 63| *1888:* cell 65| *1863:* angel-sphere, 66–69| *1844:* Vainly hast thou lived many a year; / "Go back, and *1845:* Vain was thy dream of many a year. / Thy voice's praise seemed weak; it dropped— / Creation's chorus stopped! / "Go back and *1888:* year / Thy 70–73| *1844:* remain; / "Be again the boy all curl'd; *1845:* way—while I remain. / With that weak voice of our disdain, / Take up Creation's pausing strain. / "Back to the cell and poor employ: 70| *1863:* way, while 72| *1868:* creation's 74| *1844:* I will finish with the world." *1845:* Become the craftsman and the boy!" *1868:* Resume the craftsman 75| *1844:* home, *1845:* home; 76| *1844:* Gabriel dwelt <> dome: *1845:* A new Pope dwelt in Peter's Dome. *1868:* dome. 77| *1844:* vanish'd <> died; *1845:* vanished <> died:

MEETING AT NIGHT

I

The grey sea and the long black land;
And the yellow half-moon large and low;
And the startled little waves that leap
In fiery ringlets from their sleep,
As I gain the cove with pushing prow,
And quench its speed i' the slushy sand.

II

Then a mile of warm sea-scented beach;
Three fields to cross till a farm appears;
A tap at the pane, the quick sharp scratch
And blue spurt of a lighted match,
And a voice less loud, thro' its joys and fears,
Than the two hearts beating each to each!

PARTING AT MORNING

Round the cape of a sudden came the sea,
And the sun looked over the mountain's rim:
And straight was a path of gold for him,
And the need of a world of men for me.

MEETING AT NIGHT § In 1845 this and the following poem, *PARTING AT MORNING*, were grouped under the title *NIGHT AND MORNING* as *I.—NIGHT* and *II.—MORNING*, respectively. In 1849 the poems were separated and given their present titles. Subsequent placement: 1863: DL § 6| *1845:* in *1888:* i'

PARTING AT MORNING § For earlier title and subsequent placement see note to *MEETING AT NIGHT*. § 2| *1845:* rim— *1863:* rim:

NATIONALITY IN DRINKS

I

My heart sank with our Claret-flask,
Just now, beneath the heavy sedges
That serve this pond's black face for mask;
And still at yonder broken edges
O' the hole, where up the bubbles glisten,
After my heart I look and listen.

II

Our laughing little flask, compelled
Thro' depth to depth more bleak and shady;
As when, both arms beside her held,
Feet straightened out, some gay French lady
Is caught up from life's light and motion,
And dropped into death's silent ocean!

Up jumped Tokay on our table,
Like a pygmy castle-warder,
Dwarfish to see, but stout and able,
Arms and accoutrements all in order;
And fierce he looked North, then, wheeling South,
Blew with his bugle a challenge to Drouth,
Cocked his flap-hat with the tosspot-feather,
Twisted his thumb in his red moustache,
Jingled his huge brass spurs together,

NATIONALITY IN DRINKS § First published in June 1844 in *Hood's Magazine* as *CLARET AND TOKAY* signed Robert Browning. Reprinted 1845 in DRL but omitted in 1849. In 1863 the two poems were joined by a third, "Here's to Nelson's memory!" which had been printed in 1845 as part *II* of *HOME-THOUGHTS, FROM ABROAD,* q.v., but dropped in 1849. At the same time the title of the group was changed from *CLARET AND TOKAY* to *NATIONALITY IN DRINKS.* Title and arrangement remained the same in subsequent editions. In order to maintain the integrity of the 1889 text of "Nationality in Drinks" "Here's to Nelson's Memory!" has been placed here, though this is necessarily a violation of the 1845 order. Subsequent placement: 1863: DL § 1| *1844:* sunk <> claret-flask, *1845:* our Claret-flask, *1863:* sank 5| *1844:* Of *1888:* O' 7| *1845:* compell'd *1868:* compelled 8| *1844:* Through *1845:* Thro' 11| *1845:* from Life's *1863:* life's 12| *1845:* into Death's *1863:* death's 14| *1844:* pigmy *1845:* pygmy 17| *1844:* north; then <> south, *1845:* north, then *1863:* looked North <> wheeling South, 21| *1844:*

Tightened his waist with its Buda sash,
And then, with an impudence nought could abash,
Shrugged his hump-shoulder, to tell the beholder,
For twenty such knaves he should laugh but the bolder:
And so, with his sword-hilt gallantly jutting,
And dexter-hand on his haunch abutting,
Went the little man, Sir Ausbruch, strutting!

Here's to Nelson's memory!
'Tis the second time that I, at sea,
Right off Cape Trafalgar here,
Have drunk it deep in British Beer.
Nelson for ever—any time
Am I his to command in prose or rhyme!
Give me of Nelson only a touch,
And I save it, be it little or much:
Here's one our Captain gives, and so
Down at the word, by George, shall it go!
He says that at Greenwich they point the beholder
To Nelson's coat, "still with tar on the shoulder:
For he used to lean with one shoulder digging,
Jigging, as it were, and zig-zag-zigging
Up against the mizen-rigging!"

Gingled *1863:* Jingled 23| *1844:* then with <> naught *1845;* nought *1863:* then, with 24| *1844:* hump-shoulder, / To *1863:* hump-shoulder, to 25| *1844:* bolder; *1845:* bolder, *1863:* bolder: 26| *1845:* so with *1863:* so, with 27| *1844:* dexter hand *1845:* dexter-hand 28| *1844:* man from Ausbruch *1863:* man, Sir Ausbruch 32| *1845:* beer: *1863:* in British Beer. 36| *1845:* And I guard it <> much; *1863:* And I save it <> much: 37| *1845:* one the Captain *1863:* one our Captain 39| *1845:* they show the *1863:* they point the 40| *1845:* Nelson's coat <> shoulder, *1863:* To Nelson's *1888:* shoulder: 42| *1845:* zig-zag-zigging, *1863:* zig-zag-zigging 43| *1845:* mizen rigging!" *1863:* mizen-rigging!"

SAUL

I

Said Abner, "At last thou art come! Ere I tell, ere thou speak,
Kiss my cheek, wish me well!" Then I wished it, and did kiss his cheek.
And he, "Since the King, O my friend, for thy countenance sent,
Neither drunken nor eaten have we; nor until from his tent
Thou return with the joyful assurance the King liveth yet,
Shall our lip with the honey be bright, with the water be wet.
For out of the black mid-tent's silence, a space of three days,
Not a sound hath escaped to thy servants, of prayer nor of praise,
To betoken that Saul and the Spirit have ended their strife,
And that, faint in his triumph, the monarch sinks back upon life.

II

"Yet now my heart leaps, O beloved! God's child with his dew
On thy gracious gold hair, and those lilies still living and blue
Just broken to twine round thy harp-strings, as if no wild heat
Were now raging to torture the desert!"

SAUL § The first nine sections were published as eight sections in 1845 and 1849. Both versions were in half-lines with alternate lines indented; the sections were not numbered. In 1855 ten new sections were added and the complete poem was published in its present form, however sections were numbered in arabic numerals. Although the second part of *Saul* does not belong to DRL it has been printed here to preserve the unity of the poem. Changes in spacing of sections (at lines 6, 14 and 68) have been recorded as variants. Subsequent placement: *1863:* DL § 1| *1845:* come! / Ere <> speak,— *1855:* come! Ere <> speak, 2| *1845:* it, / And <> cheek: *1855:* it, and <> cheek. 3| *1845:* the King, oh my friend, / For *1855:* the King, O my friend, for 4| *1845:* Nor drunken <> we; / Nor, until *1855:* Neither drunken <> we; nor until 5| *1845:* assurance / The king *1855:* assurance the King 6–7| *1845:* brightened, / —The water, be wet. / § New section § For <> silence, / A *1855:* bright, with the water be wet. / § No new section § For <> silence, a 8| *1845:* No sound <> servants, / Of *1855:* Not a sound <> servants, of 9–11| *1845:* the Spirit / Have gone their dread ways. / § New section § "Yet <> beloved! / God's child, with *1849:* the Spirit / Have ended their strife, / And that faint in his triumph the monarch / Sinks back upon life. / § New section § "Yet *1855:* the Spirit have <> / And that, faint <> triumph, the monarch sinks <> / 2 / "Yet <> beloved! God's *1863:* < // > with His *1868:* his 12| *1845:* lilies / Still *1855:* lilies still 13| *1845:* As thou brak'st them to <> harp-strings, / As *1855:* Just broken to <> harp-strings, as 14| *1845:* Were raging <> desert!" / § No new section § Then *1855:* Were now raging <> desert!" / 3 /

III

Then I, as was meet,
Knelt down to the God of my fathers, and rose on my feet,
And ran o'er the sand burnt to powder. The tent was unlooped;
I pulled up the spear that obstructed, and under I stooped;
Hands and knees on the slippery grass-patch, all withered and gone,
That extends to the second enclosure, I groped my way on
Till I felt where the foldskirts fly open. Then once more I prayed,
And opened the foldskirts and entered, and was not afraid
But spoke, "Here is David, thy servant!" And no voice replied.
At the first I saw nought but the blackness; but soon I descried
A something more black than the blackness—the vast, the upright
Main prop which sustains the pavilion: and slow into sight
Grew a figure against it, gigantic and blackest of all.
Then a sunbeam, that burst thro' the tent-roof, showed Saul.

IV

He stood as erect as that tent-prop, both arms stretched out wide
On the great cross-support in the centre, that goes to each side;
He relaxed not a muscle, but hung there as, caught in his pangs
And waiting his change, the king-serpent all heavily hangs,
Far away from his kind, in the pine, till deliverance come
With the spring-time,—so agonized Saul, drear and stark, blind and dumb.

---

§ New section § Then 15| *1845:* fathers, / And *1855:* fathers, and 16| *1845:* powder. / The *1855:* powder. The 17| *1845:* obstructed, / And *1855:* obstructed, and 18| *1845:* knees o'er the <> grass-patch—/ All <> gone— *1855:* knees on the <> grass-patch, all <> gone, 19| *1845:* That leads to <> enclosure, / I <> on, *1855:* That extends to <> enclosure, I <> on 20| *1845:* open; / Then *1855:* open. Then 21| *1845:* entered, / And <> afraid; *1855:* entered, and <> afraid, *1868:* afraid 22| *1845:* And spoke <> servant!" / And <> replied; *1855:* But spoke <> servant!" And <> replied. 23| *1845:* And first <> blackness; / But *1855:* At the first <> blackness; but 24| *1845:* blackness / —the vast *1855:* blackness—the vast the *1868:* vast, the 25| *1845:* Main-prop <> pavilion,— / And *1855:* Main prop <> pavilion: and 26| *1845:* figure, gigantic, against it, / And <> all;— *1855:* figure against it, gigantic and *1863:* all: *1868:* all. 27| *1845:* tent-roof, / Showed *1855:* tent-roof,—showed *1863:* tent-roof, showed 28| *1845:* tent-prop; / Both *1855:* tent-prop; both *1868:* tent-prop, both 29| *1845:* centre / That <> side: *1855:* centre, that *1863:* side; 30| *1845:* So he bent not a muscle but <> there / As *1849:* muscle, but *1855:* He relaxed not <> there,—as *1863:* there, as *1868:* there as 31| *1845:* change the king-serpent / All *1849:* change, the *1855:* change the king-serpent all *1863:* change, the 32| *1845:* the Pine, / Till *1849:* pine *1855:* pine, till 33| *1845:* the Spring-time <> Saul, / Drear and black, blind *1849:* and stark, blind *1855:*

V

Then I tuned my harp,—took off the lilies we twine round its chords
Lest they snap 'neath the stress of the noontide—those sunbeams like
swords!
swords!
And I first played the tune all our sheep know, as, one after one,
So docile they come to the pen-door till folding be done.
They are white and untorn by the bushes, for lo, they have fed
Where the long grasses stifle the water within the stream's bed;
And now one after one seeks its lodging, as star follows star
Into eve and the blue far above us,—so blue and so far!

VI

—Then the tune, for which quails on the cornland will each leave his
mate
To fly after the player; then, what makes the crickets elate
Till for boldness they fight one another: and then, what has weight
To set the quick jerboa a-musing outside his sand house—
There are none such as he for a wonder, half bird and half mouse!
God made all the creatures and gave them our love and our fear,
To give sign, we and they are his children, one family here.

---

spring-time <> Saul, drear 34| *1845:* lilies / We *1855:* lilies we 35| *1845:* noontide / —Those *1855:* noontide—those 36| *1845:* know, / As *1855:* know, as 37| *1845:* pen-door / Till <> done *1849:* done; *1855:* pen-door, till <> done. *1868:* pen-door till 38| *1845:* —They <> bushes, / For *1855:* They <> bushes, for 39| *1845:* water / Within *1855:* water within 40| *1845:* How one after <> lodging, / As *1855:* And now one after <> lodging, as 41| *1845:* us, / —So *1855:* us,—so 42| *1845:* Then the tune for <> cornland / Will leave each his *1855:* —Then the tune, for <> cornland will each leave his 43| *1845:* To follow the player <> makes / The *1855:* To fly after the player <> makes the <> elate, *1868:* elate 44| *1845:* another: / And *1855:* another: and 45| *1845:* a-musing / Outside <> house *1855:* a-musing outside <> house— 46| *1845:* —There <> wonder— / Half bird *1855:* There <> wonder, half bird <> mouse!— *1863:* mouse! 47| *1845:* —God <> them / Our *1855:* God <> them our 48| *1845:* To show, we <> children, / One *1855:* To give sign, we <> children, one *1863:* are His *1868:* his

VII

Then I played the help-tune of our reapers, their wine-song, when hand
Grasps at hand, eye lights eye in good friendship, and great hearts expand
And grow one in the sense of this world's life.—And then, the last song
When the dead man is praised on his journey—"Bear, bear him along
With his few faults shut up like dead flowerets! Are balm-seeds not here
To console us? The land has none left such as he on the bier.
Oh, would we might keep thee, my brother!"—And then, the glad chaunt
Of the marriage,—first go the young maidens, next, she whom we vaunt
As the beauty, the pride of our dwelling.—And then, the great march
Wherein man runs to man to assist him and buttress an arch
Nought can break; who shall harm them, our friends?—Then, the chorus intoned
As the Levites go up to the altar in glory enthroned.
But I stopped here: for here in the darkness Saul groaned.

49| *1845:* our Reapers, / Their *1849:* reapers, *1855:* reapers, their 50| *1845:* Grasps hand <> friendship, / And <> expand, *1855:* Grasps at hand <> friendship, and <> expand 51| *1845:* life; / And <> the low song *1855:* life.—And <> the last song 52| *1845:* journey— / "Bear *1855:* journey—"Bear 53| *1845:* flowrets; / Are *1855:* flowerets! are *1868:* flowerets! Are balm seeds *1888:* balm-seeds 54| *1845:* land has got none such / As <> bier— *1849:* land is left none *1855:* land has none left, such as <> bier. *1863:* left such 55| *1845:* brother!" / And *1855:* brother!"—And 56| *1845:* maidens— / Next *1849:* maidens, / Next *1855:* maidens, next 57| *1845:* dwelling: / And *1855:* dwelling.—And 58| *1845:* When man runs <> him / And *1849:* him, / And *1855:* Wherein man runs <> him and 59| *1845:* break . . who <> our brothers? / Then *1849:* our friends? / Then *1855:* break; who <> friends?—Then 60| *1845:* altar / In <> enthroned— *1855:* altar in <>

VIII

And I paused, held my breath in such silence, and listened apart;
And the tent shook, for mighty Saul shuddered: and sparkles 'gan
dart
From the jewels that woke in his turban, at once with a start,
All its lordly male-sapphires, and rubies courageous at heart.
So the head: but the body still moved not, still hung there erect.
And I bent once again to my playing, pursued it unchecked,
As I sang,—

IX

"Oh, our manhood's prime vigour! No spirit feels waste,
Not a muscle is stopped in its playing nor sinew unbraced.
Oh, the wild joys of living! the leaping from rock up to rock,
The strong rending of boughs from the fir-tree, the cool silver shock
Of the plunge in a pool's living water, the hunt of the bear,
And the sultriness showing the lion is couched in his lair.
And the meal, the rich dates yellowed over with gold dust divine,
And the locust-flesh steeped in the pitcher, the full draught of wine,
And the sleep in the dried river-channel where bulrushes tell
That the water was wont to go warbling so softly and well.

---

enthroned . . . *1863:* enthroned. *1868:* levites *1888:* the Levites 61| *1845:* here—for here, in the darkness, / Saul groaned: *1849:* groaned. *1855:* for here in the darkness, Saul *1868:* here: for <> darkness Saul 62| *1845:* silence! / And <> apart— *1849:* apart; *1855:* silence, and 63| *1845:* shuddered,—/ And *1855:* shuddered,—and *1863:* shuddered—and *1868:* shuddered: and 64| *1845:* turban / —At <> start *1855:* turban at <> start— *1868:* start, *1888:* turban, at 65| *1845:* rubies / Courageous at heart; *1855:* rubies courageous at heart. 66| *1845:* head, but <> not,—/ Still *1849:* head—but <> not, / Still *1855:* not, still *1868:* head: but 67| *1845:* playing, / Pursued *1855:* playing, pursued 68| *1845:* sang, "Oh <> vigour! / —No *1855:* sang,—/ 9 / "Oh <> vigour! no *1868:* vigour! No 69| *1845:* No muscle <> playing / No sinew unbraced,— *1849:* playing, / No <> unbraced;— *1855:* Not a muscle <> playing, nor sinew unbraced. *1868:* playing nor 70| *1845:* And the wild <> The leaping / From <> to rock— *1855:* Oh, the wild <> the leaping from *1868:* to rock, 71| *1845:* The rending their boughs from the palm-trees,—/ The *1855:* The strong rending of boughs from the fir-tree,—the *1868:* fir-tree, the 72| *1845:* Of a plunge in the pool's <> water—/ The hunt *1849:* haunt *1855:* Of the plunge in a pool's <> water,—the hunt *1868:* water, the 73| *1845:* lion / Is <> lair: *1855:* shewing the lion is <> lair. *1863:* showing 74| *1845:* meal—the rich dates—yellowed over / With *1855:* over with *1863:* dates yellowed *1868:* meal, the 75| *1845:* locust's-flesh <> pitcher—/ The *1849:* pitcher, / The *1855:* pitcher; the *1863:* pitcher! the *1868:* locust-flesh <> pitcher, the 76| *1845:* river channel / Where tall rushes tell *1855:* river-channel where bullrushes tell *1863:* bulrushes 77| *1845:* The water <> warbling / So <> well,— *1855:* That the

How good is man's life, the mere living! how fit to employ
All the heart and the soul and the senses for ever in joy!
Hast thou loved the white locks of thy father, whose sword thou didst
guard
When he trusted thee forth with the armies, for glorious reward?
Didst thou see the thin hands of thy mother, held up as men sung
The low song of the nearly-departed, and hear her faint tongue
Joining in while it could to the witness, 'Let one more attest,
I have lived, seen God's hand thro' a lifetime, and all was for best'?
Then they sung thro' their tears in strong triumph, not much, but the
rest.
And thy brothers, the help and the contest, the working whence grew
Such result as, from seething grape-bundles, the spirit strained true:
And the friends of thy boyhood—that boyhood of wonder and hope,
Present promise and wealth of the future beyond the eye's scope,—
Till lo, thou art grown to a monarch; a people is thine;
And all gifts, which the world offers singly, on one head combine!
On one head, all the beauty and strength, love and rage (like the throe
That, a-work in the rock, helps its labour and lets the gold go)
High ambition and deeds which surpass it, fame crowning them,—all
Brought to blaze on the head of one creature—King Saul!"

<> warbling so <> well. 78| *1845:* life here, mere living! / How *1855:* life, the mere living! how 79| *1845:* The heart <> senses / For *1855:* All the heart <> senses, for *1868:* senses for 80| *1845:* father / Whose *1855:* father, whose 81| *1845:* forth to the wolf hunt / For *1855:* forth with the armies, for 82| *1845:* mother / Held up, as *1855:* mother, held up as 83| *1845:* The song <> nearly-departed, / And heard *1855:* The low song <> nearly-departed, and *1868:* hear 84| *1845:* witness / "Let *1855:* witness, "Let 85| *1845:* thro' that life-time, / And <> best . . ." *1855:* thro' a lifetime, and <> best . . ." *1863:* best!" *1888:* best"? 86| *1845:* tears, in <> triumph, / Not much,—but the rest! *1855:* tears in <> triumph, not <> rest. *1863:* much—but *1868:* much, but 87| *1845:* brothers—the help <> contest, / The *1855:* brothers, the help <> contest, the 88| *1845:* result, as from <> grape-bundles / The spirit so true— *1849:* true: *1855:* result as from <> grape-bundles, the spirit strained true! *1863:* as, from *1868:* true: 89| *1845:* that boyhood / With wonder *1855:* that boyhood of wonder 90| *1845:* And the promise and wealth in the future,— / The eye's eagle scope,— *1849:* Present promise, and *1855:* wealth of the future beyond the eye's scope,— *1868:* promise and 91| *1845:* monarch, / A <> thine! *1855:* monarch; a <> thine; *1888:* hine; 92| *1845:* Oh all, all the <> singly, / On <> combine, *1849:* Oh all gifts the *1855:* And all gifts which the <> singly, on <> combine! *1863:* gifts, which 93| *1845:* head the joy and the pride, / Even rage like *1855:* head, all the beauty and strength, love and rage, like *1863:* rage (like 94| *1845:* That opes the <> its glad labour, / And <> go— *1855:* That, a-work in the <> its labour, and <> go: *1863:* labour and <> go) 95| *1845:* And ambition that sees a sun lead it / Oh, all of these—all *1849:* it— / Oh *1855:* High ambition and deeds which surpass it, fame crowning it,—all *1868:* crowning them,—all 96| *1845:* Combine to

X

And lo, with that leap of my spirit,—heart, hand, harp and voice,
Each lifting Saul's name out of sorrow, each bidding rejoice
Saul's fame in the light it was made for—as when, dare I say,
The Lord's army, in rapture of service, strains through its array,
And upsoareth the cherubim-chariot—"Saul!" cried I, and stopped,
And waited the thing that should follow. Then Saul, who hung propped
By the tent's cross-support in the centre, was struck by his name.
Have ye seen when Spring's arrowy summons goes right to the aim,
And some mountain, the last to withstand her, that held (he alone,
While the vale laughed in freedom and flowers) on a broad bust of stone
A year's snow bound about for a breastplate,—leaves grasp of the sheet?
Fold on fold all at once it crowds thunderously down to his feet,
And there fronts you, stark, black, but alive yet, your mountain of old,
With his rents, the successive bequeathings of ages untold—
Yea, each harm got in fighting your battles, each furrow and scar
Of his head thrust 'twixt you and the tempest—all hail, there they are!
—Now again to be softened with verdure, again hold the nest
Of the dove, tempt the goat and its young to the green on his crest
For their food in the ardours of summer. One long shudder thrilled
All the tent till the very air tingled, then sank and was stilled
At the King's self left standing before me, released and aware.
What was gone, what remained? All to traverse, 'twixt hope and despair;
Death was past, life not come: so he waited. Awhile his right hand
Held the brow, helped the eyes left too vacant forthwith to remand
To their place what new objects should enter: 'twas Saul as before.
I looked up and dared gaze at those eyes, nor was hurt any more
Than by slow pallid sunsets in autumn, ye watch from the shore,

---

unite in one creature / —Saul! *1855:* Brought to blaze on the head of one creature—King Saul!" *1845, 1849:* § The first nine sections terminated by END OF PART THE FIRST § 97| *1855:* spirit, heart *1863:* spirit,—heart 100| *1855:* army in *1863:* army, in 102| *1855:* propt *1863:* propped 105| *1855:* held, (he *1863:* held (he 109| *1855:* black but *1863:* black, but 113| *1855:* Now *1868:* —Now 114| *1855:* on its crest *1868:* on his crest 115| *1855:* summer! One *1868:* summer. One 116| *1855:* stilled, *1863:* stilled 118| *1855:* all to traverse 'twixt <> despair— *1863:* despair; *1868:* remained? All <> despair. *1888:* traverse, 'twixt <> despair; 119| *1855:* come—so *1863:* come: so 123| *1855:* shore

At their sad level gaze o'er the ocean—a sun's slow decline
Over hills which, resolved in stern silence, o'erlap and entwine
Base with base to knit strength more intensely: so, arm folded arm
O'er the chest whose slow heavings subsided.

XI

What spell or what charm,
(For, awhile there was trouble within me) what next should I urge
To sustain him where song had restored him?—Song filled to the verge
His cup with the wine of this life, pressing all that it yields
Of mere fruitage, the strength and the beauty: beyond, on what fields,
Glean a vintage more potent and perfect to brighten the eye
And bring blood to the lip, and commend them the cup they put by?
He saith, "It is good;" still he drinks not: he lets me praise life,
Gives assent, yet would die for his own part.

XII

Then fancies grew rife
Which had come long ago on the pasture, when round me the sheep
Fed in silence—above, the one eagle wheeled slow as in sleep;
And I lay in my hollow and mused on the world that might lie
'Neath his ken, though I saw but the strip 'twixt the hill and the sky:
And I laughed—"Since my days are ordained to be passed with my flocks,
Let me people at least, with my fancies, the plains and the rocks,
Dream the life I am never to mix with, and image the show
Of mankind as they live in those fashions I hardly shall know!
Schemes of life, its best rules and right uses, the courage that gains,
And the prudence that keeps what men strive for." And now these old trains
Of vague thought came again; I grew surer; so, once more the string
Of my harp made response to my spirit, as thus—

1863: shore, 126| *1855:* intense <> folded in arm *1868:* intensely <> folded arm 131| *1855:* beauty! Beyond *1868:* beauty: beyond 134| *1855:* not—he *1863:* not: he 136| *1855:* pastures *1868:* pasture 137| *1855:* sleep, *1863:* sleep; 138| *1855:* hollow, and *1868:* hollow and 141| *1855:* least with *1863:* least, with 146| *1855:* so once *1863:* so, once 147| *1855:* king," *1863:* my

XIII

"Yea, my King,"
I began—"thou dost well in rejecting mere comforts that spring
From the mere mortal life held in common by man and by brute:
In our flesh grows the branch of this life, in our soul it bears fruit.
Thou hast marked the slow rise of the tree,—how its stem trembled first
Till it passed the kid's lip, the stag's antler; then safely outburst
The fan-branches all round; and thou mindest when these too, in turn
Broke a-bloom and the palm-tree seemed perfect: yet more was to learn,
E'en the good that comes in with the palm-fruit. Our dates shall we slight,
When their juice brings a cure for all sorrow? or care for the plight
Of the palm's self whose slow growth produced them? Not so! stem and branch
Shall decay, nor be known in their place, while the palm-wine shall staunch
Every wound of man's spirit in winter. I pour thee such wine.
Leave the flesh to the fate it was fit for! the spirit be thine!
By the spirit, when age shall o'ercome thee, thou still shalt enjoy
More indeed, than at first when inconscious, the life of a boy.
Crush that life, and behold its wine running! Each deed thou hast done
Dies, revives, goes to work in the world; until e'en as the sun
Looking down on the earth, though clouds spoil him, though tempests efface,
Can find nothing his own deed produced not, must everywhere trace
The results of his past summer-prime,—so, each ray of thy will,
Every flash of thy passion and prowess, long over, shall thrill
Thy whole people, the countless, with ardour, till they too give forth
A like cheer to their sons, who in turn, fill the South and the North
With the radiance thy deed was the germ of. Carouse in the past!
But the license of age has its limit; thou diest at last:
As the lion when age dims his eyeball, the rose at her height,

---

King," 153| *1855:* mindedst *1888:* mindest 154| *1855:* perfect; yet *1863:* perfect: yet 155| *1855:* Ev'n *1868:* E'en 163| *1855:* each *1868:* running! Each 169| *1855:* people the *1888:* people, the 170| *1855:* south <> north *1863:* the South and the North 171| *1855:* past. *1863:* in the Past! *1868:* past! 172| *1855:* last. *1863:* last: 173| *1855:* eye-ball <> height, *1863:* eyeball *1888:*

So with man—so his power and his beauty for ever take flight.
No! Again a long draught of my soul-wine! Look forth o'er the years!
Thou hast done now with eyes for the actual; begin with the seer's!
Is Saul dead? In the depth of the vale make his tomb—bid arise
A grey mountain of marble heaped four-square, till, built to the skies,
Let it mark where the great First King slumbers: whose fame would ye know?
Up above see the rock's naked face, where the record shall go
In great characters cut by the scribe,—Such was Saul, so he did;
With the sages directing the work, by the populace chid,—
For not half, they'll affirm, is comprised there! Which fault to amend,
In the grove with his kind grows the cedar, whereon they shall spend
(See, in tablets 'tis level before them) their praise, and record
With the gold of the graver, Saul's story,—the statesman's great word
Side by side with the poet's sweet comment. The river's a-wave
With smooth paper-reeds grazing each other when prophet-winds rave:
So the pen gives unborn generations their due and their part
In thy being! Then, first of the mighty, thank God that thou art!"

XIV

And behold while I sang . . . but O Thou who didst grant me that day,
And before it not seldom hast granted thy help to essay,
Carry on and complete an adventure,—my shield and my sword
In that act where my soul was thy servant, thy word was my word,—
Still be with me, who then at the summit of human endeavour
And scaling the highest, man's thought could, gazed hopeless as ever
On the new stretch of heaven above me—till, mighty to save,
Just one lift of thy hand cleared that distance—God's throne from man's grave!

---

height 175| *1855:* again <> look <> years— *1868:* No! Again <> Look <> years! 177| *1855:* in *1868:* dead? In 178| *1855:* till built <> skies. *1863:* till, built <> skies, 179| *1855:* slumbers—whose *1863:* slumbers: whose
188| *1855:* prophet winds *1863:* prophet-winds 190| *1855:* art." *1863:* art!"
191| *1855:* sang . . But *1868:* but *1888:* sang . . . but 192| *1855:* granted, thy <> essay *1863:* granted Thy *1868:* thy <> essay, 193| *1855:* my Shield and my Sword *1868:* shield <> sword 194| *1863:* was Thy servant, Thy *1868:* thy <> thy 196| *1855:* highest man's *1863:* highest, man's 197| *1855:* of Heaven <> till, Mighty *1863:* mighty *1868:* heaven 198| *1863:* of Thy *1868:* thy

Let me tell out my tale to its ending—my voice to my heart
Which can scarce dare believe in what marvels last night I took part,
As this morning I gather the fragments, alone with my sheep,
And still fear lest the terrible glory evanish like sleep!
For I wake in the grey dewy covert, while Hebron upheaves
The dawn struggling with night on his shoulder, and Kidron retrieves
Slow the damage of yesterday's sunshine.

XV

I say then,—my song
While I sang thus, assuring the monarch, and ever more strong
Made a proffer of good to console him—he slowly resumed
His old motions and habitudes kingly. The right-hand replumed
His black locks to their wonted composure, adjusted the swathes
Of his turban, and see—the huge sweat that his countenance bathes,
He wipes off with the robe; and he girds now his loins as of yore,
And feels slow for the armlets of price, with the clasp set before.
He is Saul, ye remember in glory,—ere error had bent
The broad brow from the daily communion; and still, though much spent
Be the life and the bearing that front you, the same, God did choose,
To receive what a man may waste, desecrate, never quite lose.
So sank he along by the tent-prop till, stayed by the pile
Of his armour and war-cloak and garments, he leaned there awhile,
And sat out my singing,—one arm round the tent-prop, to raise
His bent head, and the other hung slack—till I touched on the praise
I foresaw from all men in all time, to the man patient there;
And thus ended, the harp falling forward. Then first I was 'ware
That he sat, as I say, with my head just above his vast knees
Which were thrust out on each side around me, like oak-roots which please
To encircle a lamb when it slumbers. I looked up to know
If the best I could do had brought solace: he spoke not, but slow
Lifted up the hand slack at his side, till he laid it with care
Soft and grave, but in mild settled will, on my brow: thro' my hair

---

199| *1855:* heart, *1863:* heart 200| *1855:* marvels that night *1863:* marvels last night 208| *1855:* right hand *1888:* right-hand 217| *1855:* tent-prop, till *1863:* tent-prop till 219| *1855:* And so sat *1868:* And sat 221| *1855:* times <> there, *1863:* there; *1868:* time 224| *1855:* oak-roots *1863:* oak roots *1888:*

The large fingers were pushed, and he bent back my head, with kind power—
All my face back, intent to peruse it, as men do a flower.
Thus held he me there with his great eyes that scrutinized mine—
And oh, all my heart how it loved him! but where was the sign?
I yearned—"Could I help thee, my father, inventing a bliss,
I would add, to that life of the past, both the future and this;
I would give thee new life altogether, as good, ages hence,
As this moment,—had love but the warrant, love's heart to dispense!"

XVI

Then the truth came upon me. No harp more—no song more! outbroke—

XVII

"I have gone the whole round of creation: I saw and I spoke:
I, a work of God's hand for that purpose, received in my brain
And pronounced on the rest of his handwork—returned him again
His creation's approval or censure: I spoke as I saw:
I report, as a man may of God's work—all's love, yet all's law.
Now I lay down the judgeship he lent me. Each faculty tasked
To perceive him, has gained an abyss, where a dewdrop was asked.
Have I knowledge? confounded it shrivels at Wisdom laid bare.
Have I forethought? how purblind, how blank, to the Infinite Care!
Do I task any faculty highest, to image success?
I but open my eyes,—and perfection, no more and no less,
In the kind I imagined, full-fronts me, and God is seen God
In the star, in the stone, in the flesh, in the soul and the clod.
And thus looking within and around me, I ever renew
(With that stoop of the soul which in bending upraises it too)
The submission of man's nothing-perfect to God's all-complete,
As by each new obeisance in spirit, I climb to his feet.

---

oak-roots 231| *1855:* scrutinised *1863:* scrutinized 234| *1855:* add to <> this. *1863:* the Past <> Future and this; *1868:* add, to <> past <> future 237| *1855:* out-broke— *1888:* outbroke— 238| *1855:* of Creation <> spoke! *1868:* creation <> spoke: 240| *1863:* of His <> Him *1868:* his <> him 241| *1855:* saw. *1888:* saw: 242| *1855:* law! *1868:* law. 243| *1863:* judgeship He *1868:* he 244| *1863:* perceive Him *1868:* him 245| *1855:* wisdom *1863:* at Wisdom 246| *1855:* care! *1863:* the Infinite Care! 253| *1855:* of Man's <> All-Complete, *1868:* man's <> all-complete, 254| *1855:*

Yet with all this abounding experience, this deity known,
I shall dare to discover some province, some gift of my own.
There's a faculty pleasant to exercise, hard to hoodwink,
I am fain to keep still in abeyance, (I laugh as I think)
Lest, insisting to claim and parade in it, wot ye, I worst
E'en the Giver in one gift.—Behold, I could love if I durst!
But I sink the pretension as fearing a man may o'ertake
God's own speed in the one way of love: I abstain for love's sake.
—What, my soul? see thus far and no farther? when doors great and small,
Nine-and-ninety flew ope at our touch, should the hundredth appal?
In the least things have faith, yet distrust in the greatest of all?
Do I find love so full in my nature, God's ultimate gift,
That I doubt his own love can compete with it? Here, the parts shift?
Here, the creature surpass the Creator,—the end, what Began?
Would I fain in my impotent yearning do all for this man,
And dare doubt he alone shall not help him, who yet alone can?
Would it ever have entered my mind, the bare will, much less power,
To bestow on this Saul what I sang of, the marvellous dower
Of the life he was gifted and filled with? to make such a soul,
Such a body, and then such an earth for insphering the whole?
And doth it not enter my mind (as my warm tears attest)
These good things being given, to go on, and give one more, the best?
Ay, to save and redeem and restore him, maintain at the height
This perfection,—succeed with life's dayspring, death's minute of night?
Interpose at the difficult minute, snatch Saul the mistake,
Saul the failure, the ruin he seems now,—and bid him awake
From the dream, the probation, the prelude, to find himself set
Clear and safe in new light and new life,—a new harmony yet
To be run, and continued, and ended—who knows?—or endure!
The man taught enough, by life's dream, of the rest to make sure;
By the pain-throb, triumphantly winning intensified bliss,
And the next world's reward and repose, by the struggles in this.

---

feet! *1863:* to His *1868:* his feet. 255| *1855:* experience, this Deity *1868:* deity 257| *1855:* There's one faculty *1863:* There's a faculty 260| *1855:* gift.—Behold! I *1868:* gift.—Behold, I 262| *1855:* abstain, for <> sake! *1863:* abstain for <> sake. 265| *1855:* things, have *1868:* things have 267| *1855:* here *1863:* doubt His *1868:* his <> it? Here 268| *1855:* surpass the Creator, the <> what Began?— *1868:* surpass the Creator,—the <> Began? 270| *1855:* doubt He *1868:* he 279| *1855:* snatch Saul, the *1888:* snatch Saul the 280| *1855:* Saul, the failure *1888:* Saul the failure 284| *1855:* enough by <> sure. *1863:*

"I believe it! 'Tis thou, God, that givest, 'tis I who receive:
In the first is the last, in thy will is my power to believe.
All's one gift: thou canst grant it moreover, as prompt to my prayer
As I breathe out this breath, as I open these arms to the air.
From thy will, stream the worlds, life and nature, thy dread Sabaoth:
I will?—the mere atoms despise me! Why am I not loth
To look that, even that in the face too? Why is it I dare
Think but lightly of such impuissance? What stops my despair?
This;—'tis not what man Does which exalts him, but what man Would do!
See the King—I would help him but cannot, the wishes fall through.
Could I wrestle to raise him from sorrow, grow poor to enrich,
To fill up his life, starve my own out, I would—knowing which,
I know that my service is perfect. Oh, speak through me now!
Would I suffer for him that I love? So wouldst thou—so wilt thou!
So shall crown thee the topmost, ineffablest, uttermost crown—
And thy love fill infinitude wholly, nor leave up nor down
One spot for the creature to stand in! It is by no breath,
Turn of eye, wave of hand, that salvation joins issue with death!
As thy Love is discovered almighty, almighty be proved
Thy power, that exists with and for it, of being Beloved!
He who did most, shall bear most; the strongest shall stand the most weak.
'Tis the weakness in strength, that I cry for! my flesh, that I seek
In the Godhead! I seek and I find it. O Saul, it shall be
A Face like my face that receives thee; a Man like to me,
Thou shalt love and be loved by, for ever: a Hand like this hand
Shall throw open the gates of new life to thee! See the Christ stand!"

---

sure; *1888:* enough, by 286| *1855:* struggle *1863:* struggles 287| *1855:* 'tis Thou *1868:* it! 'Tis thou 288| *1863:* last, in Thy *1868:* thy 289| *1863:* gift: Thou *1868:* thou 291| *1863:* From Thy *1868:* thy 292| *1855:* me! and why am I loth *1863:* me! why am I not loth *1868:* me! Why 293| *1855:* why *1868:* too? Why 294| *1855:* what *1868:* impuissance? What 296| *1855:* king *1863:* the King 299| *1855:* perfect.—Oh *1863:* perfect. Oh 300| *1855:* love? So wilt Thou <> Thou! *1863:* love? So wouldst Thou—so *1868:* thou <> thou! 301| *1855:* uttermost Crown— *1863:* crown Thee <> crown— *1868:* thee 302| *1863:* and Thy *1868:* thy 304| *1855:* that Salvation *1863:* salvation 305| *1855:* As Thy *1868:* thy 306| *1855:* of Being beloved! *1863:* being Beloved! 308| *1855:* strength that I cry *1863:* strength, that I cry 310| *1855:* thee: a *1863:* thee; a

XIX

I know not too well how I found my way home in the night.
There were witnesses, cohorts about me, to left and to right,
Angels, powers, the unuttered, unseen, the alive, the aware:
I repressed, I got through them as hardly, as strugglingly there,
As a runner beset by the populace famished for news—
Life or death. The whole earth was awakened, hell loosed with her crews;
And the stars of night beat with emotion, and tingled and shot
Out in fire the strong pain of pent knowledge: but I fainted not,
For the Hand still impelled me at once and supported, suppressed
All the tumult, and quenched it with quiet, and holy behest,
Till the rapture was shut in itself, and the earth sank to rest.
Anon at the dawn, all that trouble had withered from earth—
Not so much, but I saw it die out in the day's tender birth;
In the gathered intensity brought to the grey of the hills;
In the shuddering forests' held breath; in the sudden wind-thrills;
In the startled wild beasts that bore off, each with eye sidling still
Though averted with wonder and dread; in the birds stiff and chill
That rose heavily, as I approached them, made stupid with awe:
E'en the serpent that slid away silent,—he felt the new law.
The same stared in the white humid faces upturned by the flowers;
The same worked in the heart of the cedar and moved the vine-bowers:
And the little brooks witnessing murmured, persistent and low,
With their obstinate, all but hushed voices—"E'en so, it is so!"

311| *1855:* ever! a *1863:* ever: a 315| *1855:* alive—the aware— *1863:* alive, the *1868:* aware: 320| *1855:* not. *1863:* not, 321| *1855:* supported—suppressed *1863:* supported, suppressed 327| *1855:* forests' new awe; in *1868:* forests' held breath; in 328| *1888:* bore oft, each 329| *1855:* Tho' averted, in wonder and dread; and the *1863:* Though averted with wonder and dread; in the 330| *1855:* awe! *1868:* awe: 331| *1855:* new Law. *1868:* law.
333| *1855:* cedar, and <> vine-bowers. *1863:* vine-bowers: *1868:* cedar and
335| *1855:* voices—E'en so! it is so. *1863:* voices—"E'en so, it is so!"

TIME'S REVENGES

I've a Friend, over the sea;
I like him, but he loves me.
It all grew out of the books I write;
They find such favour in his sight
That he slaughters you with savage looks
Because you don't admire my books.
He does himself though,—and if some vein
Were to snap to-night in this heavy brain,
To-morrow month, if I lived to try,
Round should I just turn quietly,
Or out of the bedclothes stretch my hand
Till I found him, come from his foreign land
To be my nurse in this poor place,
And make my broth and wash my face
And light my fire and, all the while,
Bear with his old good-humoured smile
That I told him "Better have kept away
Than come and kill me, night and day,
With, worse than fever throbs and shoots,
The creaking of his clumsy boots."
I am as sure that this he would do,
As that Saint Paul's is striking two.
And I think I rather . . . woe is me!
—Yes, rather would see him than not see,
If lifting a hand could seat him there
Before me in the empty chair
To-night, when my head aches indeed,
And I can neither think nor read
Nor make these purple fingers hold
The pen; this garret's freezing cold!

TIME'S REVENGES § Subsequent placement *1863:* DR § 2| *1845:* me; *1863:* me. 6| *1845:* books: *1868:* books. 12| *1863:* land, *1868:* land 14| *1845:* make me broth, and <> face, *1863:* make my broth and <> face 15| *1845:* fire, and *1868:* fire and 19| *1845:* With worse <> fever's *1863:* With, worse *1888:* fever 20| *1845:* At the *1863:* The creaking 21| *1845:* do *1849:* do, 22| *1845:* striking Two: *1863:* striking Two. *1868:* two. 23| *1845:* think I had rather . . woe *1863:* rather . . . woe *1868:* think I rather 24| *1845:* rather see *1868:* rather should see *1888:* rather would see 25| *1845:* would *1888:* could 28| *1845:* think, nor read, *1863:* think nor read 29| *1845:* And these blue fingers will

And I've a Lady—there he wakes,
The laughing fiend and prince of snakes
Within me, at her name, to pray
Fate send some creature in the way
Of my love for her, to be down-torn,
Upthrust and outward-borne,
So I might prove myself that sea
Of passion which I needs must be!
Call my thoughts false and my fancies quaint
And my style infirm and its figures faint,
All the critics say, and more blame yet,
And not one angry word you get.
But, please you, wonder I would put
My cheek beneath that lady's foot
Rather than trample under mine
The laurels of the Florentine,
And you shall see how the devil spends
A fire God gave for other ends!
I tell you, I stride up and down
This garret, crowned with love's best crown,
And feasted with love's perfect feast,
To think I kill for her, at least,
Body and soul and peace and fame,
Alike youth's end and manhood's aim,
—So is my spirit, as flesh with sin,
Filled full, eaten out and in
With the face of her, the eyes of her,

---

not hold *1863:* Nor make these purple fingers hold 31| *1845:* a Lady—There *1849:* wakes *1863:* wakes, *1868:* there he wakes *1888:* wakes, 35| *1845:* down-torn *1868:* down-torn, 36| *1845:* onward borne *1863:* outward-borne *1868:* outward-borne, 39| *1845:* quaint, *1863:* quaint 40| *1845:* infirm, and *1863:* infirm and 42| *1845:* get! *1868:* get. 44| *1845:* that Lady's *1868:* lady's 47| *1845:* the Devil *1868:* devil 48| *1845:* The fire *1849:* A fire 50| *1845:* with Love's *1849:* love's 51| *1845:* with Love's *1849:* love's 54–55| *1845:* aim, / As all my genius, all my learning / Leave me, where there's no returning, /

The lips, the little chin, the stir
Of shadow round her mouth; and she
—I'll tell you,—calmly would decree
That I should roast at a slow fire,
If that would compass her desire
And make her one whom they invite
To the famous ball to-morrow night.

There may be heaven; there must be hell;
Meantime, there is our earth here—well!

—So *1849:* aim, / —So 58| *1845:* lips and little *1863:* lips, the little 61| *1845:* fire *1849:* fire, 65| *1845:* be a Heaven <> be a Hell; *1849:* be Heaven <> be Hell; *1868:* heaven <> hell; 66| *1845:* our Earth *1868:* earth

THE GLOVE

(*PETER RONSARD loquitur*)

"Heigho!" yawned one day King Francis,
"Distance all value enhances!
When a man's busy, why, leisure
Strikes him as wonderful pleasure:
'Faith, and at leisure once is he?
Straightway he wants to be busy.
Here we've got peace; and aghast I'm
Caught thinking war the true pastime.
Is there a reason in metre?
Give us your speech, master Peter!"
I who, if mortal dare say so,
Ne'er am at loss with my Naso,
"Sire," I replied, "joys prove cloudlets:
Men are the merest Ixions"—
Here the King whistled aloud, "Let's
—Heigho—go look at our lions!"
Such are the sorrowful chances
If you talk fine to King Francis.

And so, to the courtyard proceeding,
Our company, Francis was leading,
Increased by new followers tenfold
Before he arrived at the penfold;
Lords, ladies, like clouds which bedizen
At sunset the western horizon.
And Sir De Lorge pressed 'mid the foremost

THE GLOVE § Subsequent placement: 1863: DR § 1| *1845:* "Heigho," yawned *1888:* "Heigho!" yawned 3| *1845:* why leisure *1849:* why, leisure 4| *1845:* pleasure,— *1863:* pleasure: 5| *1845:* he— *1849:* he? 8| *1845:* pastime! *1868:* pastime. 16| *1845:* ˙˙Heigho . . go *1849:* . , Heigho *1863:* . . . Heigho . . . go *1888:* —Heigho-go 20| *1845:* company Francis was leading *1849:* company, Francis was leading, *1868:* leading. *1888:* leading, 24| *1845:* horizon, *1849:*

With the dame he professed to adore most.
Oh, what a face! One by fits eyed
Her, and the horrible pitside;
For the penfold surrounded a hollow
Which led where the eye scarce dared follow,
And shelved to the chamber secluded
Where Bluebeard, the great lion, brooded.
The King hailed his keeper, an Arab
As glossy and black as a scarab,
And bade him make sport and at once stir
Up and out of his den the old monster.
They opened a hole in the wire-work
Across it, and dropped there a firework,
And fled: one's heart's beating redoubled;
A pause, while the pit's mouth was troubled,
The blackness and silence so utter,
By the firework's slow sparkling and sputter;
Then earth in a sudden contortion
Gave out to our gaze her abortion.
Such a brute! Were I friend Clement Marot
(Whose experience of nature's but narrow,
And whose faculties move in no small mist
When he versifies David the Psalmist)
I should study that brute to describe you
Illum Juda Leonem de Tribu.
One's whole blood grew curdling and creepy
To see the black mane, vast and heapy,
The tail in the air stiff and straining,
The wide eyes, nor waxing nor waning,
As over the barrier which bounded
His platform, and us who surrounded
The barrier, they reached and they rested

---

horizon. 26| *1845:* the Dame <> most— *1849:* dame *1888:* most. 32| *1845:* Where Bluebeard the <> lion brooded. *1849:* Where Bluebeard, the <> lion, brooded. 39| *1845:* fled; one's *1863:* fled: one's 44| *1845:* abortion! *1868:* abortion. 45| *1845:* . . Such <> were *1849:* Such <> Were 50| *1845: de*

On space that might stand him in best stead:
For who knew, he thought, what the amazement,
The eruption of clatter and blaze meant,
And if, in this minute of wonder,
No outlet, 'mid lightning and thunder,
Lay broad, and, his shackles all shivered,
The lion at last was delivered?
Ay, that was the open sky o'erhead!
And you saw by the flash on his forehead,
By the hope in those eyes wide and steady,
He was leagues in the desert already,
Driving the flocks up the mountain,
Or catlike couched hard by the fountain
To waylay the date-gathering negress:
So guarded he entrance or egress.
"How he stands!" quoth the King: "we may well swear,
(No novice, we've won our spurs elsewhere
And so can afford the confession,)
We exercise wholesome discretion
In keeping aloof from his threshold,
Once hold you, those jaws want no fresh hold,
Their first would too pleasantly purloin
The visitor's brisket or surloin:
But who's he would prove so fool-hardy?
Not the best man of Marignan, pardie!"

The sentence no sooner was uttered,
Than over the rails a glove fluttered,
Fell close to the lion, and rested:
The dame 'twas, who flung it and jested
With life so, De Lorge had been wooing
For months past; he sat there pursuing
His suit, weighing out with nonchalance
Fine speeches like gold from a balance.

Sound the trumpet, no true knight's a tarrier!
De Lorge made one leap at the barrier,

Tribu! *1868: de Tribu.* 58| *1845:* On the space *1888:* On space 65| *1845:* o'erhead; *1849:* o'erhead! 74| *1845:* No <> elsewhere, *1863:* (No *1868:* elsewhere 75| *1845:* confession *1849:* confession, *1863:* confession,) 77| *1845:* threshold; *1888:* threshold, 88| *1845:* sate *1863:* sat 92| *1845:* one

Walked straight to the glove,—while the lion
Ne'er moved, kept his far-reaching eye on
The palm-tree-edged desert-spring's sapphire,
And the musky oiled skin of the Kaffir,—
Picked it up, and as calmly retreated,
Leaped back where the lady was seated,
And full in the face of its owner
Flung the glove.
"Your heart's queen, you dethrone her?
So should I!"—cried the King—"'twas mere vanity,
Not love, set that task to humanity!"
Lords and ladies alike turned with loathing
From such a proved wolf in sheep's clothing.

No so, I; for I caught an expression
In her brow's undisturbed self-possession
Amid the Court's scoffing and merriment,—
As if from no pleasing experiment
She rose, yet of pain not much heedful
So long as the process was needful,—
As if she had tried in a crucible,
To what "speeches like gold" were reducible,
And, finding the finest prove copper,
Felt the smoke in her face was but proper;
To know what she had *not* to trust to,
Was worth all the ashes and dust too.
She went out 'mid hooting and laughter;
Clement Marot stayed: I followed after,
And asked, as a grace, what it all meant?
If she wished not the rash deed's recalment?
"For I"—so I spoke—"am a poet:
Human nature,—behoves that I know it!"

She told me, "Too long had I heard
Of the deed proved alone by the word:
For my love—what De Lorge would not dare!

---

spring at *1849:* one leap at 96| *1845:* Caffre,— *1849:* Kaffir,— 98| *1845:* Sprang back *1849:* Leaped back 100| *1845:* glove— *1863:* glove. 102| *1845:* set the task *1849:* set that task 107| *1845:* merriment, *1849:* merriment,— 110| *1845:* needful— *1863:* needful,— 111| *1845:* crucible *1849:* crucible, 116| *1845:* ashes, and *1863:* ashes and 119| *1845:* meant— *1863:* meant? 121| *1845:* a Poet: *1868:* poet: 125| *1845:* love,—what *1863:* love—what

With my scorn—what De Lorge could compare!
And the endless descriptions of death
He would brave when my lip formed a breath,
I must reckon as braved, or, of course,
Doubt his word—and moreover, perforce,
For such gifts as no lady could spurn,
Must offer my love in return.
When I looked on your lion, it brought
All the dangers at once to my thought,
Encountered by all sorts of men,
Before he was lodged in his den,—
From the poor slave whose club or bare hands
Dug the trap, set the snare on the sands,
With no King and no Court to applaud,
By no shame, should he shrink, overawed,
Yet to capture the creature made shift,
That his rude boys might laugh at the gift,
—To the page who last leaped o'er the fence
Of the pit, on no greater pretence
Than to get back the bonnet he dropped,
Lest his pay for a week should be stopped.
So, wiser I judged it to make
One trial what 'death for my sake'
Really meant, while the power was yet mine,
Than to wait until time should define
Such a phrase not so simply as I,
Who took it to mean just 'to die.'
The blow a glove gives is but weak:
Does the mark yet discolour my cheek?
But when the heart suffers a blow,
Will the pain pass so soon, do you know?"

I looked, as away she was sweeping,
And saw a youth eagerly keeping

133| *1845:* on the lion *1849:* on your lion 135| *1845:* men *1849:* men, 141| *1845:* shift *1849:* shift, 142| *1845:* gift,— *1849:* gift, 143| *1845:* To *1863:* —To 145| *1845:* Than recover the <> dropped *1849:* Than to get back the <> dropped, 146| *1845:* stopped— *1863:* stopped. 150| *1845:* Than defer it till time *1849:* Than to wait until time 153| *1845:* weak— *1863:* weak:

As close as he dared to the doorway.
No doubt that a noble should more weigh
His life than befits a plebeian;
And yet, had our brute been Nemean—
(I judge by a certain calm fervour
The youth stepped with, forward to serve her)
—He'd have scarce thought you did him the worst turn
If you whispered "Friend, what you'd get, first earn!"
And when, shortly after, she carried
Her shame from the Court, and they married,
To that marriage some happiness, maugre
The voice of the Court, I dared augur.

For De Lorge, he made women with men vie,
Those in wonder and praise, these in envy;
And in short stood so plain a head taller
That he wooed and won . . . how do you call her?
The beauty, that rose in the sequel
To the King's love, who loved her a week well.
And 'twas noticed he never would honour
De Lorge (who looked daggers upon her)
With the easy commission of stretching
His legs in the service, and fetching
His wife, from her chamber, those straying
Sad gloves she was always mislaying,
While the King took the closet to chat in,—
But of course this adventure came pat in.
And never the King told the story,
How bringing a glove brought such glory,
But the wife smiled—"His nerves are grown firmer:
Mine he brings now and utters no murmur."

Venienti occurrite morbo!
With which moral I drop my theorbo.

159| *1845:* doorway: *1863:* doorway; *1868:* doorway. 163| *1845:* fervor *1863:* fervour 172| *1845:* These <> those *1849:* Those <> these 174| *1845:* won . . How *1863:* won . . . how 175| *1863:* The Beauty *1868:* beauty 176| *1845:* well; *1863:* well. 180| *1845:* service and *1849:* service, and 181| *1845:* wife from her chamber those *1849:* wife, from her chamber, those 184| *1845:* in; *1849:* in: *1863:* in. 185| *1845:* never he finished the *1849:* never the King told the 186| *1845:* bringing the glove *1849:* bringing a glove 187| *1845:* firmer— *1863:* firmer: 188| *1845:* murmur!" *1868:* murmur."

BY THE SAME AUTHOR.

I.

PARACELSUS. A POEM.

Price 6*s*. *boards*.

II.

SORDELLO. A POEM.

Price 6*s*. 6*d*. *boards*.

III.

BELLS AND POMEGRANATES.

No. I.—PIPPA PASSES. *Price* 1*s*.

No. II.—KING VICTOR AND KING CHARLES. *Price* 1*s*.

No. III.—DRAMATIC LYRICS. *Price* 1*s*.

No. IV.—THE RETURN OF THE DRUSES. *Price* 1*s*.

No. V.—A BLOT IN THE 'SCUTCHEON. *Price* 1*s*.

No. VI.—COLOMBE'S BIRTHDAY. *Price* 1*s*.

Nearly ready.

No. VIII.—A SOUL'S TRAGEDY. LURIA.

§ In 1844 only §

BELLS AND POMEGRANATES, NO. VIII. AND LAST

LURIA

Edited by Morse Peckham

LURIA:

A TRAGEDY.

1846: Bells and Pomegranates. / No. VIII and Last. / Luria; / and / A Soul's Tragedy. / By Robert Browning, / Author of "Paracelsus." *1849:* Luria; / A Tragedy. *1863:* § on page with dedication and persons § *1868:* § on page with dedication § *1888:* § on separate page § Luria; A

I DEDICATE THIS LAST ATTEMPT FOR THE PRESENT AT DRAMATIC POETRY TO A GREAT DRAMATIC POET; "WISHING WHAT I WRITE MAY BE READ BY HIS LIGHT:" IF A PHRASE ORIGINALLY ADDRESSED, BY NOT THE LEAST WORTHY OF HIS CONTEMPORARIES, TO SHAKESPEARE, MAY BE APPLIED HERE, BY ONE WHOSE SOLE PRIVILEGE IS IN A GRATEFUL ADMIRATION, TO WALTER SAVAGE LANDOR.

LONDON: 1846.

1846: dedicate these last attempts <> light:"—if *1849:* dedicate this last attempt <> Landor. *1868:* § on page with title § light:" if *1888:* § on separate page §

PERSONS.

LURIA, *a Moor, Commander of the Florentine Forces.*

HUSAIN, *a Moor, his friend.*

PUCCIO, *the old Florentine Commander, now Luria's chief officer.*

BRACCIO, *Commissary of the Republic of Florence.*

JACOPO (LAPO), *his secretary.*

TIBURZIO, *Commander of the Pisans.*

DOMIZIA, *a noble Florentine lady.*

SCENE. *Luria's camp between Florence and Pisa.*

TIME. 14—

1846: § on page with title § *1849:* § top of first page of text § *1863:* § on page with title and persons § *1868:* § on separate page §

LURIA

1846

ACT I

MORNING

BRACCIO, *as dictating to his* SECRETARY; PUCCIO *standing by.*

BRACCIO [*to* PUCCIO.] Then, you join battle in an hour?
PUCCIO   Not I;
Luria, the captain.
BRACCIO [*to the* Secretary.] "In an hour, the battle."
[*To* PUCCIO.] Sir, let your eye run o'er this loose digest,
And see if very much of your report
Have slipped away through my civilian phrase.
Does this instruct the Signory aright
How army stands with army?
PUCCIO [*taking the paper.*]   All seems here:
—That Luria, seizing with our city's force
The several points of vantage, hill and plain,
Shuts Pisa safe from help on every side,
And, baffling the Lucchese arrived too late,
Must, in the battle he delivers now,
Beat her best troops and first of chiefs.
BRACCIO   So sure?
Tiburzio's a consummate captain too!
PUCCIO Luria holds Pisa's fortune in his hand.
BRACCIO [*to the* Secretary.] "The Signory hold Pisa in their hand."
Your own proved soldiership's our warrant, sir:

§ Ed. 1846, 1849, 1863, 1868, 1888, 1889. No known MS. §   1| *1846:* Then you *1849:* Then, you   2| *1846:* the Captain *1868:* captain   5| *1888:* phrase   8| *1846:* our City's *1863:* city's   11| *1846:* And baffling *1863:* And, baffling   16| *1846:* hand:" *1849:* hand!" *1863:* hand."   17| *1846:* sir. *1849:*

So, while my secretary ends his task,
Have out two horsemen, by the open roads,
To post with it to Florence!
PUCCIO [*returning the paper.*] All seems here;
Unless . . . Ser Braccio, 'tis my last report!
Since Pisa's outbreak, and my overthrow,
And Luria's hastening at the city's call
To save her, as he only could, no doubt;
Till now that she is saved or sure to be,—
Whatever you tell Florence, I tell you:
Each day's note you, her Commissary, make
Of Luria's movements, I myself supply.
No youngster am I longer, to my cost;
Therefore while Florence gloried in her choice
And vaunted Luria, whom but Luria, still,
As if zeal, courage, prudence, conduct, faith,
Had never met in any man before,
I saw no pressing need to swell the cry.
But now, this last report and I have done:
So, ere to-night comes with its roar of praise,
'Twere not amiss if some one old i' the trade
Subscribed with, "True, for once rash counsel's best.
This Moor of the bad faith and doubtful race,
This boy to whose untried sagacity,
Raw valour, Florence trusts without reserve
The charge to save her,—justifies her choice;
In no point has this stranger failed his friends.
Now praise!" I say this, and it is not here.
BRACCIO [*to the* Secretary.] Write, "Puccio, superseded in the charge,
By Luria, bears full witness to his worth,
And no reward our Signory can give
Their champion but he'll back it cheerfully."
Aught more? Five minutes hence, both messengers! [PUCCIO *goes.*]

---

sir: 18| *1846:* You, while *1849:* So, while 22| *1846:* outbreak and *1849:* outbreak, and 24| *1846:* her as *1849:* her, as 31| *1846:* but Luria still, *1849:* but Luria, still, 32| *1846:* As courage <> conduct, zeal and faith *1849:* As if zeal, courage <> conduct, faith, 34| *1846:* cry: *1849:* cry. 35| *1846:* done— *1888:* done: 38| *1846:* best; *1863:* best. 42| *1846:* her, justifies *1863:* her,—justifies 43| *1846:* friends; *1863:* friends: *1888:* friends. 45| *1846:*

BRACCIO [*after a pause, and while he slowly tears the paper into shreds.*]
I think . . . (pray God, I hold in fit contempt
This warfare's noble art and ordering,
And,—once the brace of prizers fairly matched,
Poleaxe with poleaxe, knife with knife as good,—
Spit properly at what men term their skill!—)
Yet here I think our fighter has the odds.
With Pisa's strength diminished thus and thus,
Such points of vantage in our hands and such,
Lucca still off the stage, too,—all's assured:
Luria must win this battle. Write the Court,
That Luria's trial end and sentence pass!
SECRETARY Patron,—
BRACCIO Ay, Lapo?
SECRETARY If you trip, I fall;
'Tis in self-interest I speak—
BRACCIO Nay, nay,
You overshoot the mark, my Lapo! Nay!
When did I say pure love's impossible?
I make you daily write those red cheeks thin,
Load your young brow with what concerns it least,
And, when we visit Florence, let you pace
The Piazza by my side as if we talked,
Where all your old acquaintances may see:
You'd die for me, I should not be surprised.
Now then!
SECRETARY Sir, look about and love yourself!
Step after step, the Signory and you
Tread gay till this tremendous point's to pass;
Which pass not, pass not, ere you ask yourself,—
Bears the brain steadily such draughts of fire,
Or too delicious may not prove the pride

---

charge *1863:* charge, 50| *1846:* think . . . pray God I *1849:* pray God, I *1863:* think . . . (pray 54| *1846:* skill . . . *1863:* skill!—) 55| *1846:* odds; *1863:* odds. 58| *1846:* With Lucca off *1863:* Lucca still off 59| *1846:* battle Write the Court *1849:* battle. Write the Court, 61| *1846:* BRACCIO Aye *1863:* BRACCIO Ay 70| *1846:* surprised! *1868:* surprised. 72| *1846:* after step the *1863:* after step, the 74| *1846:* Which, pass not, pass not ere <> yourself *1849:* yourself, *1863:* yourself,—

Of this long secret trial you dared plan,
Dare execute, you solitary here,
With the grey-headed toothless fools at home,
Who think themselves your lords, such slaves are they?
If they pronounce this sentence as you bid,
Declare the treason, claim its penalty,—
And sudden out of all the blaze of life,
On the best minute of his brightest day,
From that adoring army at his back,
Thro' Florence' joyous crowds before his face,
Into the dark you beckon Luria. . . .

BRACCIO Then—
Why, Lapo, when the fighting-people vaunt,
We of the other craft and mystery,
May we not smile demure, the danger past?

SECRETARY Sir, no, no, no,—the danger, and your spirit
At watch and ward? Where's danger on your part,
With that thin flitting instantaneous steel
'Gainst the blind bull-front of a brute-force world?
If Luria, that's to perish sure as fate,
Should have been really guiltless after all?

BRACCIO Ah, you have thought that?

SECRETARY Here I sit, your scribe,
And in and out goes Luria, days and nights;
This Puccio comes; the Moor his other friend,
Husain; they talk—that's all feigned easily;
He speaks (I would not listen if I could),
Reads, orders, counsels:—but he rests sometimes,—
I see him stand and eat, sleep stretched an hour
On the lynx-skins yonder; hold his bared black arms
Into the sun from the tent-opening; laugh
When his horse drops the forage from his teeth
And neighs to hear him hum his Moorish songs.
That man believes in Florence, as the saint

1888: Which pass not, pass not, ere 77| *1846:* secret Trial *1868:* trial 80| *1846:* lords, they are such slaves? *1868:* lords, such slaves are they? 87| *1846:* beckon Luria . . . BRACCIO *1888:* beckon Luria . . . . BRACCIO 92| *1846:* part *1849:* part, 93| *1849:* steel, *1868:* steel 100| *1846:* talk—all that's feigned 101| *1846:* could) *1868:* could), 102| *1846:* counsels;—but *1863:* counsels:—but 107| *1846:* songs: *1849:* songs, *1863:* songs. 108| *1846:* in

Tied to the wheel believes in God.

BRACCIO How strange!
You too have thought that!

SECRETARY Do but you think too,
And all is saved! I only have to write,
"The man seemed false awhile, proves true at last,
Bury it"—so I write the Signory—
"Bury this trial in your breast for ever,
Blot it from things or done or dreamed about!
So Luria shall receive his meed to-day
With no suspicion what reverse was near,—
As if no meteoric finger hushed
The doom-word just on the destroyer's lip,
Motioned him off, and let life's sun fall straight."

BRACCIO [*looks to the wall of the ten.*] Did he draw that?

SECRETARY With charcoal, when the watch
Made the report at midnight; Lady Domizia
Spoke of the unfinished Duomo, you remember;
That is his fancy how a Moorish front
Might join to, and complete, the body,—a sketch,—
And again where the cloak hangs, yonder in the shadow.

BRACCIO He loves that woman.

SECRETARY She is sent the spy
Of Florence,—spies on you as you on him:
Florence, if only for Domizia's sake,
Is surely safe. What shall I write?

BRACCIO I see—
A Moorish front, nor of such ill design!
Lapo, there's one thing plain and positive;
Man seeks his own good at the whole world's cost.
What? If to lead our troops, stand forth our chiefs,
And hold our fate, and see us at their beck,

Florence as the Saint *1849:* in Florence, as *1863:* saint 109| *1846:* in God! BRACCIO *1868:* in God. BRACCIO 112| *1846:* The *1863:* "The 113| *1846:* it . . . so I write to the Signory . . . *1863:* it" . . . so *1868:* write the *1888:* it"—so <> Signory— 114| *1846:* Bury this Trial <> breasts *1863:* "Bury *1868:* trial <> breast 115| *1846:* about, *1863:* about: *1868:* about! 120| *1846:* straight. *1863:* straight." 130| *1846:* Were surely *1849:* Is surely 134| *1846:* chief, *1849:*

Yet render up the charge when peace return,
Have ever proved too much for Florentines,
Even for the best and bravest of ourselves—
If in the struggle when the soldier's sword
Should sink its point before the statist's pen,
And the calm head replace the violent hand,
Virtue on virtue still have fallen away
Before ambition with unvarying fate,
Till Florence' self at last in bitterness
Be forced to own such falls the natural end,
And, sparing further to expose her sons
To a vain strife and profitless disgrace,
Declare, "The foreigner, one not my child,
Shall henceforth lead my troops, reach height by height
The glory, then descend into the shame;
So shall rebellion be less guilt in him,
And punishment the easier task for me:"
—If on the best of us such brand she set,
Can I suppose an utter alien here,
This Luria, our inevitable foe,
Confessed a mercenary and a Moor,
Born free from many ties that bind the rest
Of common faith in Heaven or hope on earth,
No past with us, no future,—such a spirit
Shall hold the path from which our staunchest broke,
Stand firm where every famed precursor fell?
My Lapo, I will frankly say, these proofs
So duly noted of the man's intent,
Are for the doting fools at home, not me.
The charges here, they may be true or false:
—What is set down? Errors and oversights,

---

chiefs, 136| *1846:* returned, *1868:* return, 140| *1846:* Before <> pen should <> point, *1849:* Should <> point before <> pen, 141| *1846:* And to the <> head yield the *1849:* And the <> head replace the 143| *1846:* unvarying fortune, *1849:* unvarying fate, 145| *1846:* own defeat the *1849:* own such falls the 148| *1846:* Have said "The Foreigner, no child of mine, *1849:* Declare "The Foreigner, one not my child, *1863:* Declare, "The *1868:* foreigner 152| *1846:* me" *1863:* me:" 153| *1846:* us this brand she sets, *1849:* set, *1863:* us such brand 157| *1846:* from any ties *1868:* from many ties 158| *1846:* on Earth, *1863:* earth, 159| *1846:* No Past <> no Future <>a Spirit *1863:* spirit *1868:* past <> future 162| *1846:* say these *1849:* say, these 164| *1888:* me 165| *1846:* false, *1868:* false:

A dallying interchange of courtesies
With Pisa's General,—all that, hour by hour,
Puccio's pale discontent has furnished us,
Of petulant speeches, inconsiderate acts,
Now overhazard, overcaution now;
Even that he loves this lady who believes
She outwits Florence, and whom Florence posted
By my procurement here, to spy on me,
Lest I one minute lose her from my sight—
She who remembering her whole House's fall,
That nest of traitors strangled in the birth,
Now labours to make Luria (poor device
As plain) the instrument of her revenge
—That she is ever at his ear to prompt
Inordinate conceptions of his worth,
Exorbitant belief in worth's reward,
And after, when sure disappointment follows,
Proportionable rage at such a wrong—
Why, all these reasons, while I urge them most,
Weigh with me less than least—as nothing weigh.
Upon that broad man's-heart of his, I go:
On what I know must be, yet, while I live,
Shall never be, because I live and know.
Brute-force shall not rule Florence! Intellect
May rule her, bad or good as chance supplies:
But intellect it shall be, pure if bad,
And intellect's tradition so kept up
Till the good come—'twas intellect that ruled,

167| *1846:* This dallying *1863:* A dallying 168| *1846:* With Pisa's General, all that hour by hour *1849:* With Pisa's General,—all that, hour by hour, 169| *1846:* us *1849:* us, 172| *1846:* this Lady *1863:* lady 178| *1846:* make Luria . . . poor *1868:* make Luria (poor 179| *1846:* plain . . . the <> revenge! *1868:* plain) the *1888:* revenge 182| *1846:* in its reward, *1888:* in worth's reward 186| *1846:* least; as <> weigh! *1868:* weigh. *1888:* least—as 187| *1846:* broad Man's heart <> go! *1863:* broad Man's-heart *1868:* man's-heart <> go: 188| *1846:* yet while I live 189| *1846:* Will never <> know! *1863:* Shall never *1868:* know.
191| *1846:* supplies,— *1888:* supplies: 192| *1846:* But Intellect *1868:* intellect 193| *1846:* And Intellect's *1868:* intellect's <> up! *1888:* up.
194| *1846:* comes—*'twas* Intellect *1868:* come—'twas intellect

Not brute-force bringing from the battle-field
The attributes of wisdom, foresight's graces
We lent it there to lure its grossness on;
All which it took for earnest and kept safe
To show against us in our market-place,
Just as the plumes and tags and swordsman's-gear
(Fetched from the camp where, at their foolish best,
When all was done they frightened nobody)
Perk in our faces in the street, forsooth,
With our own warrant and allowance. No!
The whole procedure's overcharged,—its end
In too strict keeping with the bad first step.
To conquer Pisa was sheer inspiration?
Well then, to perish for a single fault,
Let that be simple justice! There, my Lapo!
A Moorish front ill suits our Duomo's body:
Blot it out—and bid Luria's sentence come!

[LURIA, *who, with* DOMIZIA, *has entered unobserved at the close of the last phrase, now advances.*]

LURIA And Luria, Luria, what of Luria now?
BRACCIO Ah, you so close, sir? Lady Domizia too?
I said it needs must be a busy moment
For one like you: that you were now i' the thick
Of your duties, doubtless, while we idlers sat . . .
LURIA No—in that paper,—it was in that paper
What you were saying!
BRACCIO Oh—my day's despatch!
I censure you to Florence: will you see?
LURIA See your despatch, your last, for the first time?
Well, if I should, now? For in truth, Domizia,
He would be forced to set about another,
In his sly cool way, the true Florentine,
To mention that important circumstance.

195| *1846:* Not Brute-force *1868:* brute-force 201| *1846:* where at <> best *1863:* where, at <> best, 207| *1846:* inspiration! *1849:* inspiration? 209| *1846:* justice!—There *1888:* justice! There 210| *1846:* The Moorish <> body— *1849:* A Moorish *1868:* body: 213| *1846:* close, Sir *1863:* sir 215| *1846:* you—that *1868:* you; that *1888:* you: that 216| *1846:* sate . . . *1863:* sat . . . 218| *1846:* dispatch! *1888:* despatch! 220| *1846:* dispatch *1888:* despatch 221| *1846:* Why, if I should now *1849:* Well, if I should, now 222| *1846:* another *1849:* another, 224| *1846:* circumstance; *1868:*

So, while he wrote I should gain time, such time!
Do not send this!

BRACCIO And wherefore?

LURIA These Lucchese
Are not arrived—they never will arrive!
And I must fight to-day, arrived or not,
And I shall beat Tiburzio, that is sure:
And then will be arriving his Lucchese,
But slowly, oh so slowly, just in time
To look upon my battle from the hills,
Like a late moon, of use to nobody!
And I must break my battle up, send forth,
Surround on this side, hold in check on that.
Then comes to-morrow, we negotiate,
You make me send for fresh instructions home,
—Incompleteness, incompleteness!

BRACCIO Ah, we scribes!
Why, I had registered that very point,
The non-appearance of our foes' ally,
As a most happy fortune; both at once
Were formidable: singly faced, each falls.

LURIA So, no great battle for my Florentines!
No crowning deed, decisive and complete,
For all of them, the simple as the wise,
Old, young, alike, that do not understand
Our wearisome pedantic art of war,
By which we prove retreat may be success,
Delay—best speed,—half loss, at times,—whole gain:
They want results: as if it were their fault!
And you, with warmest wish to be my friend,
Will not be able now to simply say
"Your servant has performed his task—enough!
You ordered, he has executed: good!
Now walk the streets in holiday attire,
Congratulate your friends, till noon strikes fierce,

---

circumstance. 225| *1846:* So while *1863:* So, while 228| *1849:* not; *1888:* not, 229| *1846:* sure, *1849:* sure: 230| *1846:* arriving my Lucchese, *1863:* arriving his Lucchese, 233| *1846:* nobody,— *1849:* nobody! 235| *1846:* that! *1849:* that— *1868:* that. 242| *1846:* formidable—singly *1868:* formidable: singly 243| *1846:* And so no battle *1849:* So no great battle *1863:* So, no 249| *1846:* gain— *1849:* gain: 250| *1846:* results . . . as *1849:* results—as *1888:*

Then form bright groups beneath the Duomo's shade!"
No, you will have to argue and explain,
Persuade them, all is not so ill in the end,
Tease, tire them out! Arrive, arrive, Lucchese!
DOMIZIA Well, you will triumph for the past enough,
Whatever be the present chance; no service
Falls to the ground with Florence: she awaits
Her saviour, will receive him fittingly.
LURIA Ah Braccio, you know Florence! Will she, think you,
Receive one . . . what means "fittingly receive"?
—Receive compatriots, doubtless—I am none:
And yet Domizia promises so much!
BRACCIO Kind women still give men a woman's prize.
I know not o'er which gate most boughs will arch,
Nor if the Square will wave red flags or blue.
I should have judged, the fullest of rewards
Our state gave Luria, when she made him chief
Of her whole force, in her best captain's place.
LURIA That, my reward? Florence on my account
Relieved Ser Puccio?—mark you, my reward!
And Puccio's having all the fight's true joy—
Goes here and there, gets close, may fight, himself,
While I must order, stand aloof, o'ersee.
That was my calling, there was my true place!
I should have felt, in some one over me,
Florence impersonate, my visible head,
As I am over Puccio,—taking life
Directly from her eye! They give me you:
But do you cross me, set me half to work?
I enjoy nothing—though I will, for once!
Decide, shall we join battle? may I wait?

---

results: as 258| *1846:* No ! you *1868:* No, you 259| *1846:* them all *1863:* them, all 261| *1846:* the Past *1868:* past 262| *1846:* the Present's chance—no *1863:* chance; no *1868:* present 263| *1846:* with Florence; she *1863:* with Florence: she 265| *1846:* know Florence.. . will *1849:* Ah, Braccio *1863:* know Florence! will *1868:* Ah Braccio, you know Florence! Will 266| *1846:* fittingly receive?" *1863:* fittingly receive"? 271| *1846:* blue— *1863:* blue: *1868:* blue. 273| *1846:* Our State *1888:* state 274| *1846:* best Captain's *1863:* captain's 275| *1846:* That my *1863:* That, my 278| *1846:* there, directs, may fight himself, *1863:* there, gets close, may fight, himself, 280| *1846:* calling—there *1868:* calling, there 282| *1846:* visible Head, *1868:* head, 284| *1846:* eye!— They <> you! *1863:* eye! They <> you: 286| *1846:* nothing—but I

BRACCIO Let us compound the matter; wait till noon:
Then, no arrival,—
LURIA Ah, noon comes too fast!
I wonder, do you guess why I delay
Involuntarily the final blow
As long as possible? Peace follows it!
Florence at peace, and the calm studious heads
Come out again, the penetrating eyes;
As if a spell broke, all's resumed, each art
You boast, more vivid that it slept awhile.
'Gainst the glad heaven, o'er the white palace-front
The interrupted scaffold climbs anew;
The walls are peopled by the painter's brush;
The statue to its niche ascends to dwell.
The present noise and trouble have retired
And left the eternal past to rule once more;
You speak its speech and read its records plain,
Greece lives with you, each Roman breathes your friend:
But Luria—where will then be Luria's place?
DOMIZIA Highest in honour, for that past's own sake,
Of which his actions, sealing up the sum
By saving all that went before from wreck,
Will range as part, with which be worshipped too.
LURIA Then I may walk and watch you in your streets,
Lead the smooth life my rough life helps no more,
So different, so new, so beautiful—
Nor fear that you will tire to see parade
The club that slew the lion, now that crooks
And shepherd-pipes come into use again?
For very lone and silent seems my East
In its drear vastness: still it spreads, and still
No Braccios, no Domizias anywhere—
Not ever more! Well, well, to-day is ours!

1868: nothing—though I 288| *1846:* noon; *1863:* noon: 295| *1868:* all *1888:* all's 296| *1846:* awhile! *1863:* awhile. 299| *1846:* the Painter's *1863:* painter's 300| *1846:* The Statue <> dwell; *1863:* statue <> dwell. 301| *1846:* The Present's *1868:* present 302| *1846:* eternal Past <> more.— *1863:* more;— *1868:* past *1888:* more; 304| *1846:* friend, *1863:* friend: 305| *1846:*—But Luria,—where *1849:*—But Luria —where *1868:* But 306| *1846:* that Past's *1868:* past's 310| *1846:* streets *1868:* streets, 311| *1846:* Leading the life *1868:* Lead the smooth life 317| *1846:* vastness—still *1863:* vastness: still 319| *1846:* more!—Well, well *1888:*

DOMIZIA [*to* BRACCIO.] Should he not have been one of us?

LURIA Oh, no!

Not one of you, and so escape the thrill
Of coming into you, of changing thus,—
Feeling a soul grow on me that restricts
The boundless unrest of the savage heart!
The sea heaves up, hangs loaded o'er the land,
Breaks there and buries its tumultuous strength;
Horror, and silence, and a pause awhile:
Lo, inland glides the gulf-stream, miles away,
In rapture of assent, subdued and still,
'Neath those strange banks, those unimagined skies.
Well, 'tis not sure the quiet lasts for ever!
Your placid heads still find rough hands new work;
Some minute's chance—there comes the need of mine:
And, all resolved on, I too hear at last.
Oh, you must find some use for me, Ser Braccio!
You hold my strength; 'twere best dispose of it:
What you created, see that you find food for—
I shall be dangerous else!

BRACCIO How dangerous, sir?

LURIA There are so many ways, Domizia warns me,
And one with half the power that I possess,
—Grows very formidable. Do you doubt?
Why, first, who holds the army . . .

DOMIZIA While we talk,
Morn wears; we keep you from your proper place,
The field.

LURIA Nay, to the field I move no more;
My part is done, and Puccio's may begin:
I cannot trench upon his province longer
With any face.—You think yourselves so safe?

---

more! Well, well 327| *1846:* awhile; *1863:* awhile: 330| *1846:* skies! *1868:* skies. 332| *1846:* find our hands *1863:* find rough hands 333| *1846:* mine— *1868:* mine: 336| *1846:* it! *1868:* it: 338| *1846:* BRACCIO How dangerous, Sir? *1868:* sir? 339| *1846:* Oh, there are many *1868:* There are so many
341| *1846:* Grows <> formidable! Do *1888:*—Grows <> formidable. Do
343| *1846:* wears, we <> place *1863:* wears; we *1868:* place,
344| *1846:* In the field!—LURIA <> more!— *1849:* more! *1863:* field. LURIA <> more: *1868:* The field <> more; 345| *1846:* begin! *1863:*

Why, see—in concert with Tiburzio, now—
One could . . .

DOMIZIA A trumpet!

LURIA My Lucchese at last!
Arrived, as sure as Florence stands! Your leave! [*Springs out.*]

DOMIZIA How plainly is true greatness charactered
By such unconscious sport as Luria's here,
Strength sharing least the secret of itself!
Be it with head that schemes or hand that acts,
Such save the world which none but they could save,
Yet think whate'er they did, that world could do.

BRACCIO Yes: and how worthy note, that these same great ones
In hand or head, with such unconsciousness
And all its due entailed humility,
Should never shrink, so far as I perceive,
From taking up whatever tool there be
Effects the whole world's safety or mishap,
Into their mild hands as a thing of course!
The statist finds it natural to lead
The mob who might as easily lead him—
The captain marshals troops born skilled in war—
Statist and captain verily believe!
While we poor scribes . . . you catch me thinking now,
That I shall in this very letter write
What none of you are able! To it, Lapo! [DOMIZIA *goes.*]
This last worst all-affected childish fit
Of Luria's, this be-praised unconsciousness,
Convinces me; the past was no child's play:
It was a man beat Pisa,—not a child.
All's mere dissimulation—to remove

---

begin. *1868:* begin: 348| *1846:* Why see *1888:* Why, see 352| *1846:* unconsciousness as *1868:* unconscious sport as 353| *1846:* And sharing *1863:* Strength sharing 357| *1846:* those *1863:* these 361| *1846:* whatever offices *1868:* whatever tool there be 362| *1846:* Involve the *1868:* Effects the 364| *1846:* The Statist *1863:* statist 366| *1846:* The Soldier marshals men who know as much— *1863:* soldier *1868:* The captain marshals troops born skilled in war— 367| *1846:* and Soldier verily *1863:* soldier *1868:* and captain verily 368| *1846:* thinking, now, *1868:* thinking now, 371–373| *1846:* last, worst, all affected <> fit / Convinces me: the Past <> play; *1849:* fit / Of Luria's, this be-praised unconsciousness, / Convinces *1863:* me; the <> play: *1868:* past *1888:* last worst all-affected 375| *1846:* 'Tis

The fear, he best knows we should entertain.
The utmost danger was at hand. Is't written?
Now make a duplicate, lest this should fail,
And speak your fullest on the other side.
SECRETARY I noticed he was busily repairing
My half-effacement of his Duomo sketch,
And, while he spoke of Florence, turned to it,
As the Mage Negro king to Christ the babe.
I judge his childishness the mere relapse
To boyhood of a man who has worked lately,
And presently will work, so, meantime, plays:
Whence, more than ever I believe in him.
BRACCIO [*after a pause.*] The sword! At best, the soldier, as he says,
In Florence—the black face, the barbarous name,
For Italy to boast her show of the age,
Her man of men! To Florence with each letter!

---

mere *1849:* All's mere 377| *1846:* hand. 'Tis *1849:* hand. Is't 378| *1846:* make the duplicate *1849:* make a duplicate 382| *1846:* And to it, while <> turned *1849:* And, while <> turned to it, 383| *1846:* the Mage Negro King <> the Babe.— *1863:* the Mage Negro turns to *1868:* the Mage Negro king to <> babe.— *1888:* babe. 384| *1846:* the true relapse *1863:* the mere relapse 387| *1846:* Whence more *1868:* Whence, more 391| *1846:* men!—To *1888:* men! To

ACT II

NOON

DOMIZIA Well, Florence, shall I reach thee, pierce thy heart
Thro' all its safeguards? Hate is said to help—
Quicken the eye, invigorate the arm;
And this my hate, made up of many hates,
Might stand in scorn of visible instrument,
And will thee dead: yet do I trust it not.
Nor man's devices nor Heaven's memory
Of wickedness forgot on earth so soon,
But thy own nature,—hell and thee I trust,
To keep thee constant in that wickedness,
Where my revenge may meet thee. Turn aside
A single step, for gratitude or shame,—
Grace but this Luria,—this wild mass of rage
I have prepared to launch against thee now,—
With other payment than thy noblest found,—
Give his desert for once its due reward,—
And past thee would my sure destruction roll.
But thou, who mad'st our House thy sacrifice,
It cannot be thou wilt except this Moor

3| *1846:* arm, *1863:* arm; 4| *1846:* of so many *1849:* of many 6| *1846:* dead . . . yet <> not; *1849:* dead:—yet <> not. *1868:* dead: yet 7| *1846:* Nor Man's devices, nor *1868:* man's devices nor 8| *1846:* on Earth *1868:* earth 9| *1846:* nature,—Hell *1868:* hell 11| *1846:* thee: turn *1863:* thee. Turn 12| *1846:* For gratitude a <> step, or *1849:* A <> step, for gratitude, or *1868:* gratitude or 13| *1846:* Grace thou this Luria, this *1849:* Grace but this *1863:* this Luria,—this 14| *1846:* That I prepare <> now, *1863:* now,— *1868:* I have prepared 18| *1846:* thou who *1849:* thou, who 19| *1846:* thou dost except *1849:* thou wilt except

From the accustomed fate of zeal and truth:
Thou wilt deny his looked-for recompense,
And then—I reach thee. Old and trained, my sire
Could bow down on his quiet broken heart,
Die awe-struck and submissive, when at last
The strange blow came for the expected wreath,
And Porzio passed in blind bewilderment
To exile, never to return,—they say,
Perplexed in his frank simple honest soul,
As if some natural law had changed,—how else
Could Florence, on plain fact pronouncing thus,
Judge Porzio's actions worthy such reward?
But Berto, with the ever-passionate pulse,
—Oh that long night, its dreadful hour on hour,
In which no way of getting his fair fame
From their inexplicable charges free,
Was found, save pouring forth the impatient blood
To show its colour whether false or no!
My brothers never had a friend like me
Close in their need to watch the time, then speak,
—Burst with a wakening laughter on their dream,
Cry, "Florence was all falseness, so, false here!"
And show them what a simple task remained—
To leave dreams, rise, and punish in God's name
The city wedded to the wickedness.
None stood by them as I by Luria stand.
So, when the stranger cheated of his due
Turns on thee as his rapid nature bids,
Then, Florence, think, a hireling at thy throat
For the first outrage, think who bore thy last,
Yet mutely in forlorn obedience died!
He comes—his friend—black faces in the camp
Where moved those peerless brows and eyes of old.

20| *1849:* truth; *1863:* truth: 22| *1846:* thee! Old *1863:* thee. Old 25| *1846:* wreath; 28| *1846:* soul *1849:* soul, 31| *1846:* such an end? *1868:* such reward? 36| *1846:* found save to pour forth *1849:* found, save pouring forth 37| *1846:* And show *1849:* To show 41| *1846:* Say, Florence was one falsehood, so false here,— *1849:* was all falseness, so *1863:* Cry, Florence <> so, false *1868:* Cry, "Florence <> here!" 44| 1846: The City <> to its wickedness— *1863:* city <> wickedness. *1868:* to the wickedness. 45| *1846:* stand! *1868:* stand. 51| *1846:* comes . . his friend . . black *1863:* comes—his friend—black 52| *1846:* old! *1888:*

Enter LURIA *and* HUSAIN.

DOMIZIA Well, and the movement—is it as you hope?
'Tis Lucca?
LURIA Ah, the Pisan trumpet merely!
Tiburzio's envoy, I must needs receive.
DOMIZIA Whom I withdraw before; tho' if I lingered
You could not wonder, for my time fleets fast.
The overtaking night brings such reward!
And where will then be room for me? Yet, praised,
Remember who was first to promise praise,
And envy those who also can perform! [*Goes.*]
LURIA This trumpet from the Pisans?—
HUSAIN In the camp;
A very noble presence—Braccio's visage
On Puccio's body—calm and fixed and good;
A man I seem as I had seen before:
Most like, it was some statue had the face.
LURIA Admit him! This will prove the last delay.
HUSAIN Ay, friend, go on, and die thou going on!
Thou heardst what the grave woman said but now:
To-night rewards thee. That is well to hear;
But stop not therefore: hear it, and go on!
LURIA Oh, their reward and triumph and the rest
They round me in the ears with, all day long?
All that, I never take for earnest, friend!
Well would it suit us,—their triumphal arch
Or storied pillar,—thee and me, the Moors!
But gratitude in those Italian eyes—
That, we shall get?
HUSAIN It is too cold an air.

---

old. 55| *1846:* envoy I <> receive— *1849:* envoy, I *1863:* receive. 56| *1846:* before; yet if *1863:* before; tho' if 57| *1846:* fast; *1863:* fast. 58| *1846:* brings Florence' praise *1849:* brings such reward!— *1863:* reward! 59| *1846:* for mine? Yet still *1849:* for me? Yet *1863:*—And *1868:* And <> me? Yet, praised, 60| *1846:* promise it, *1868:* promise praise, 61| *1846:* envies *1863:* envied *1868:* envy 65| *1846:* before— *1863:* before: 66| *1846:* like it *1849:* like, it 67| *1846:* delay! *1863:* delay. 69| *1846:* heard'st *1863:* heardst 70| *1846:* thee! That <> hear! *1863:* thee. That <> hear; 71| *1846:* therefore; hear *1863:* therefore: hear 74| *1846:* But that <> took *1849:* All that <> take 76| pillar, thee *1849:* pillar,—thee 77| *1846:* Just gratitude *1849:* But gratitude 78| *1846:*

Our sun rose out of yonder mound of mist:
Where is he now? So, I trust none of them.
LURIA Truly?
HUSAIN I doubt and fear. There stands a wall
'Twixt our expansive and explosive race
And those absorbing, concentrating men.
They use thee.
LURIA And I feel it, Husain! yes,
And care not—yes, an alien force like mine
Is only called to play its part outside
Their different nature; where its sole use seems
To fight with and keep off an adverse force,
As alien,—which repelled, mine too withdraws:
Inside, they know not what to do with me.
Thus I have told them laughingly and oft,
But long since am prepared to learn the worst.
HUSAIN What is the worst?
LURIA I will forestall them, Husain,
Will speak the destiny they dare not speak—
Banish myself before they find the heart.
I will be first to say, "The work rewards!
I know, for all your praise, my use is over,
So may it prove!—meanwhile 'tis best I go,
Go carry safe my memories of you all
To other scenes of action, newer lands,"—
Thus leaving them confirmed in their belief
They would not easily have tired of me.
You think this hard to say?
HUSAIN Say or not say,
So thou but go, so they but let thee go!
This hating people, that hate each the other,
And in one blandness to us Moors unite—

---

air— *1863:* air. 79| *1846:* mist— *1863:* mist: 80| *1846:* now? So I *1863:* now? So, I 83| *1846:* men! *1868:* men. 84| *1846:* thee! LURIA <> Husain; yes, *1868:* thee. LURIA <> Husain! yes, 88| *1846:* force *1888:* force, 89| *1846:* repelled, ours too withdraws; *1849:* repelled, mine to *1863:* withdraws: 90| *1846:* me; *1863:* me. 91| *1846:* So I *1863:* Thus I 92| *1846:* since I prepared *1863:* since was prepared *1868:* since am prepared 93| *1863:* forestal *1888:* forestall 94| *1846:* And speak my destiny *1849:* destiny, they *1868:* Will speak the destiny they 95| *1846:* heart! *1863:* heart. 96| *1846:* say, "the *1863:* say, "The 98| *1846:* it be!—meanwhile *1863:* it prove!—meanwhile 99| *1846:* And carry *1868:* Go carry 100| *1846:* lands,"— *1863:* lands."— 102| *1846:* me! *1863:* me. 103| *1846:* HUSAIN Say it or not, *1868:*

Locked each to each like slippery snakes, I say,
Which still in all their tangles, hissing tongue
And threatening tail, ne'er do each other harm;
While any creature of a better blood,
They seem to fight for, while they circle safe
And never touch it,—pines without a wound,
Withers away beside their eyes and breath.
See thou, if Puccio come not safely out
Of Braccio's grasp, this Braccio sworn his foe,
As Braccio safely from Domizia's toils
Who hates him most! But thou, the friend of all,
. . . Come out of them!

LURIA The Pisan trumpet now!

HUSAIN Breathe free—it is an enemy, no friend! [*Goes.*]

LURIA He keeps his instincts, no new culture mars
Their perfect use in him; just so the brutes
Rest not, are anxious without visible cause,
When change is in the elements at work,
Which man's trained senses fail to apprehend.
But here,—he takes the distant chariot wheel
For thunder, festal flame for lightning's flash,
The finer traits of cultivated life
For treachery and malevolence: I see!

Enter TIBURZIO.

LURIA Quick, sir, your message! I but wait your message
To sound the charge. You bring no overture
For truce? I would not, for your General's sake,
You spoke of truce: a time to fight is come,
And, whatso'er the fight's event, he keeps
His honest soldier's-name to beat me with,

HUSAIN Say or not say, 109| *1846:* At threatening *1849:* And threatening 113| *1846:* away before their *1863:* away beside their 114| *1846:* thou if *1849:* thou, if 115| *1846:* grasp, the Braccio *1849:* grasp, this Braccio 116| *1846:* And Braccio *1849:* As Braccio 117| *1846:* most!—But *1868:* most! But 118| *1846:* . . Come *1888:* . . . Come 121| *1846:* him; and so *1849:* him; just so 123| *1846:* work *1849:* work, 125| *1846:* here . . he <> chariot-wheels *1849:* here,—he *1868:* chariot-wheel 126| *1846:* festal fire for <> flash, . . *1849:* flash, *1868:* festal flame for 128| *1846:* see. *1849:* see! 129| *1846:* message. I *1863:* message! I 130| *1846:* bring not overtures *1868:* bring no overture 131| *1846:* truce?—I *1888:* truce? I 132| *1846:* truce—a *1868:* truce: a 133| *1846:* And whatsoe'er *1863:* And, whatsoe'er *1888:* whatso'er 134| *1846:* soldier's name *1888:*

Or leaves me all himself to beat, I trust!
TIBURZIO I am Tiburzio.
LURIA   You? 'Tis—yes . . . Tiburzio!
You were the last to keep the ford i' the valley
From Puccio, when I threw in succours there!
Why, I was on the heights—through the defile
Ten minutes after, when the prey was lost!
You wore an open skull-cap with a twist
Of water-reeds—the plume being hewn away;
While I drove down my battle from the heights,
I saw with my own eyes!
TIBURZIO   And you are Luria
Who sent my cohort, that laid down its arms
In error of the battle-signal's sense,
Back safely to me at the critical time—
One of a hundred deeds. I know you. Therefore
To none but you could I . . .
LURIA   No truce, Tiburzio!
TIBURZIO Luria, you know the peril imminent
On Pisa,—that you have us in the toils,
Us her last safeguard, all that intercepts
The rage of her implacablest of foes
From Pisa: if we fall to-day, she falls.
Tho' Lucca will arrive, yet, 'tis too late.
You have so plainly here the best of it,
That you must feel, brave soldier as you are,
How dangerous we grow in this extreme,
How truly formidable by despair.
Still, probabilities should have their weight:
The extreme chance is ours, but, that chance failing,
You win this battle. Wherefore say I this?
To be well apprehended when I add,

---

soldier's-name 136| *1846:* LURIA You? Ah, yes . . Tiburzio! *1849:* LURIA You? 'Tis—yes *1888:* yes . . . Tiburzio! 139| *1846:* thro' *1863:* through 140| *1849:* lost; *1863:* lost! 141| *1846:* scull-cap *1863:* skull-cap 144| *1846:*—I *1868:* I 148| *1846:* deeds—I <> you! Therefore *1868:* deeds. I *1888:* you. Therefore 150| *1846:* peril's *1863:* peril 152| *1888:* safeguard all 154| *1846:* From Pisa,—if *1888:* From Pisa: if 156| *1846:* it *1849:* it, 157| *1846:* soldier that you *1849:* soldier as you 159| *1846:* despair: *1849:* despair. 160| *1849:* Still probabilities <> weight— *1849:* Still, probabilities *1868:* weight: 161| *1846:* extremest <> ours; but that *1849:* ours, but, that *1868:* extreme 162| *1846:* battle: wherefore *1849:* battle. Wherefore 163| *1849:*

This danger absolutely comes from you.
Were you, who threaten thus, a Florentine . . .
LURIA Sir, I am nearer Florence than her sons.
I can, and have perhaps obliged the State,
Nor paid a mere son's duty.
TIBURZIO Even so.
Were you the son of Florence, yet endued
With all your present nobleness of soul,
No question, what I must communicate
Would not detach you from her.
LURIA Me, detach?
TIBURZIO Time urges. You will ruin presently
Pisa, you never knew, for Florence' sake
You think you know. I have from time to time
Made prize of certain secret missives sent
From Braccio here, the Commissary, home:
And knowing Florence otherwise, I piece
The entire chain out, from these its scattered links.
Your trial occupies the Signory;
They sit in judgment on your conduct now.
When men at home inquire into the acts
Which in the field e'en foes appreciate . . .
Brief, they are Florentines! You, saving them,
Seek but the sure destruction saviours find.
LURIA Tiburzio!
TIBURZIO All the wonder is of course.
I am not here to teach you, nor direct,
Only to loyally apprise—scarce that.
This is the latest letter, sealed and safe,
As it left here an hour ago. One way
Of two thought free to Florence, I command.
The duplicate is on its road, but this,—
Read it, and then I shall have more to say.
LURIA Florence!
TIBURZIO Now, were yourself a Florentine,

---

add *1849:* add, 168| *1846:* so! *1868:* so. 172| *1846:* LURIA Me detach? *1849:* LURIA Me, detach? 173| *1846:* urges: you *1868:* urges. You 177| *1846:* home— *1868:* home: 178| *1846:* otherwise, can piece *1849:* otherwise, I piece 179| *1846:* out from these scattered links. *1849:* out, from these its scattered *1888:* links 180| *1846:* Your Trial *1849:* trial 181| *1846:* now! *1863:* now. 185| *1846:* Will seek the *1868:* Seek but the 186| *1846:* Tiburzio— TIBURZIO *1868:* Tiburzio! TIBURZIO 187| *1846:* or *1849:* nor 192| *1846:* road:

This letter, let it hold the worst it can,
Would be no reason you should fall away.
The mother city is the mother still,
And recognition of the children's service
Her own affair; reward—there's no reward!
But you are bound by quite another tie.
Nor nature shows, nor reason, why at first
A foreigner, born friend to all alike,
Should give himself to any special State
More than another, stand by Florence' side
Rather than Pisa; 'tis as fair a city
You war against as that you fight for—famed
As well as she in story, graced no less
With noble heads and patriotic hearts:
Nor to a stranger's eye would either cause,
Stripped of the cumulative loves and hates
Which take importance from familiar view,
Stand as the right and sole to be upheld.
Therefore, should the preponderating gift
Of love and trust, Florence was first to throw,
Which made you hers, not Pisa's, void the scale,—
Old ties dissolving, things resume their place
And all begins again. Break seal and read!
At least let Pisa offer for you now!
And I, as a good Pisan, shall rejoice—
Though for myself I lose, in gaining you,
This last fight and its opportunity;
The chance it brings of saving Pisa yet,
Or in the turn of battle dying so
That shame should want its extreme bitterness.
LURIA Tiburzio, you that fight for Pisa now
As I for Florence . . . say my chance were yours!

---

but *1863:* road; but *1888:* road, but 196| *1846:* away— *1863:* away.
197| *1846:* The Mother *1863:* mother 198| *1868:* service, *1888:* service
199| *1846:* reward . . there's *1849:* reward—there's 200| *1846:* tie; *1868:* tie.
201| *1846:* Nor Nature <> nor Reason *1863:* nature <> reason 204| *1846:* Florence' *1888:* Florence § Ohio text emended § 205| *1846:* than Pisa's—'tis *1863:* than Pisa's; 'tis *1868:* Pisa 206| *1846:* against, as 208| *1846:* hearts,— *1863:* hearts: 212| *1846:* the Right, and Sole *1863:* right <> sole *1868:* right and
214| *1846:* trust Florence *1849:* trust, Florence 215| *1846:* hers not *1868:* hers, not 220| *1846:* Tho' *1863:* Though 226| *1846:* for Florence . . say *1888:* for

You read this letter, and you find . . . no, no!
Too mad!
TIBURZIO I read the letter, find they purpose
When I have crushed their foe, to crush me: well?
LURIA You, being their captain, what is it you do?
TIBURZIO Why, as it is, all cities are alike;
As Florence pays you, Pisa will pay me.
I shall be as belied, whate'er the event,
As you, or more: my weak head, they will say,
Prompted this last expedient, my faint heart
Entailed on them indelible disgrace,
Both which defects ask proper punishment.
Another tenure of obedience, mine!
You are no son of Pisa's: break and read!
LURIA And act on what I read? What act were fit?
If the firm-fixed foundation of my faith
In Florence, who to me stands for mankind,
—If that break up and, disimprisoning
From the abyss . . . Ah friend, it cannot be!
You may be very sage, yet—all the world
Having to fail, or your sagacity,
You do not wish to find yourself alone!
What would the world be worth? Whose love be sure?
The world remains: you are deceived!
TIBURZIO Your hand!
I lead the vanguard.—If you fall, beside,
The better: I am left to speak! For me,
This was my duty, nor would I rejoice

Florence . . . say 227| *1846:* find . . no, no! *1888:* find . . . no, no! 230| *1846:* And you, their *1849:* You, being their 231–233| *1846:* Why as <> alike—/ I *1849:* alike—/ Pisa will pay me much as Florence you; / I *1868:* alike; / As Florence pays you, Pisa <> me. / I *1888:* Why, as 240| *1846:* what *1849:* read? What 242| *1846:* for Mankind, *1849:* In Florence, which to *1863:* mankind, *1868:* In Florence, who to 243| *1846:* breaks <> disemprisoning *1863:* disimprisoning *1868:* break 245| *1846:* yet . . all *1863:* yet—all 247| *1849:* alone *1863:* alone! 249| *1846:* remains—you *1868:* remains: you 251| *1846:* better—I *1868:* better: I

If I could help, it misses its effect;
And after all you will look gallantly
Found dead here with that letter in your breast.
LURIA Tiburzio—I would see these people once
And test them ere I answer finally!
At your arrival let the trumpet sound:
If mine return not then the wonted cry
It means that I believe—am Pisa's!
TIBURZIO Well! [*Goes.*]
LURIA My heart will have it he speaks true! My blood
Beats close to this Tiburzio as a friend.
If he had stept into my watch-tent, night
And the wild desert full of foes around,
I should have broke the bread and given the salt
Secure, and, when my hour of watch was done,
Taken my turn to sleep between his knees,
Safe in the untroubled brow and honest cheek.
Oh world, where all things pass and nought abides,
Oh life, the long mutation—is it so?
Is it with life as with the body's change?
—Where, e'en tho' better follow, good must pass,
Nor manhood's strength can mate with boyhood's grace,
Nor age's wisdom, in its turn, find strength,
But silently the first gift dies away,
And though the new stays, never both at once.
Life's time of savage instinct o'er with me,
It fades and dies away, past trusting more,
As if to punish the ingratitude
With which I turned to grow in these new lights,
And learned to look with European eyes.
Yet it is better, this cold certain way,
Where Braccio's brow tells nothing, Puccio's mouth,

253| *1846:* effect: *1863:* effect; 255| *1846:* breast! *1863:* breast. 259| *1846:* cry, *1868:* cry 262| *1846:* friend; *1849:* friend. 264| *1846:* the wide desert *1849:* the wild desert 266| *1846:* and when <> done *1849:* and, when <> done, 267| *1846:* knees *1849:* knees, 268| *1846:* the unclouded brow *1849:* the untroubled brow 269| *1846:* Oh, world where *1849:* world, where *1868:* Oh world 270| *1846:* Oh, life the *1868:* Oh life, the 273| *1888:* grace 274| *1846:* wisdom in its turn find *1849:* wisdom, in its turn, find 276| *1846:* tho' <> stays—never <> once! *1849:* stays, never *1863:* though *1868:* once. 277| *1846:* instinct's *1863:* instinct 280| *1846:* lights *1849:* lights, 283| *1846:* nothing,—Puccio's *1868:*

Domizia's eyes reject the searcher: yes!
For on their calm sagacity I lean,
Their sense of right, deliberate choice of good,
Sure, as they know my deeds, they deal with me.
Yes, that is better—that is best of all!
Such faith stays when mere wild belief would go.
Yes—when the desert creature's heart, at fault
Amid the scattering tempest's pillared sands,
Betrays its step into the pathless drift—
The calm instructed eye of man holds fast
By the sole bearing of the visible star,
Sure that when slow the whirling wreck subside,
The boundaries, lost now, shall be found again,—
The palm-trees and the pyramid over all.
Yes: I trust Florence: Pisa is deceived.

Enter BRACCIO, PUCCIO, *and* DOMIZIA.

BRACCIO Noon's at an end: no Lucca? You must fight.
LURIA Do you remember ever, gentle friends,
I am no Florentine?
DOMIZIA It is yourself
Who still are forcing us, importunately,
To bear in mind what else we should forget.
LURIA For loss!—for what I lose in being none!
No shrewd man, such as you yourselves respect,
But would remind you of the stranger's loss
In natural friends and advocates at home,
Hereditary loves, even rivalships
With precedent for honour and reward.
Still, there's a gain, too! If you take it so,

---

nothing, Puccio's 284| *1846:* searcher . . yes . . *1849:* searcher—yes— *1863:* yes! *1868:* searcher: yes! 287| *1846:* That as <> deeds they *1849:* Sure, as <> deeds, they 288| *1846:* better . . that *1849:* better—that 289| *1846:* when the wild <> go! *1849:* when mere wild *1868:* go. 291| *1846:* tempest and its sands, *1849:* tempest's pillared sands, 295| *1846:* subsides, *1868:* subside, 297| *1846:* all! *1849:* all. 298| *1846:* trust Florence—Pisa *1849:* deceived! *1863:* trust Florence: Pisa is deceived. 302| *1846:* us importunately, *1868:* us, importunately, 303| *1888:* forget 304| *1846:* loss!—For *1868:* for 308| *1846:* loves, or rivalships, *1849:* loves, even rivalships, *1868:* rivalships 309| *1846:* precedents for honor *1863:* honour *1868:* precedent 310| *1846:* you

The stranger's lot has special gain as well.
Do you forget there was my own far East
I might have given away myself to, once,
As now to Florence, and for such a gift,
Stood there like a descended deity?
There, worship waits us: what is it waits here? [*Shows the letter.*]
See! Chance has put into my hand the means
Of knowing what I earn, before I work.
Should I fight better, should I fight the worse,
With payment palpably before me? See!
Here lies my whole reward! Best learn it now
Or keep it for the end's entire delight?
BRACCIO If you serve Florence as the vulgar serve,
For swordsman's-pay alone,—break seal and read!
In that case, you will find your full desert.
LURIA Give me my one last happy moment, friends!
You need me now, and all the graciousness
This letter can contain will hardly balance
The after-feeling that you need no more.
This moment . . . oh, the East has use with you!
Its sword still flashes—is not flung aside
With the past praise, in a dark corner yet!
How say you? 'Tis not so with Florentines,
Captains of yours: for them, the ended war
Is but a first step to the peace begun:
He who did well in war, just earns the right

---

recollect, *1849:* you take it so, 311| *1846:* well! *1868:* well. 315| *1846:* descended Deity? *1863:* deity? 316| *1846:* worship greets us! what do I get here? *1868:* worship waits us: what is it waits here? 318| *1846:* work! *1868:* work. 320| *1846:* With the crown palpably *1849:* With your crown *1868:* With payment palpably 321| *1846:* reward! Best know it now? *1849:* now, *1868:* reward! Best learn it now 324| *1846:* swordsman's pay *1863:* swordsman's-pay 325| *1846:* desert! *1868:* desert. 327| *1846:* the gratitude *1868:* the graciousness 328| *1846:* letter may contain would never balance *1849:* letter can contain will never *1868:* will hardly balance 329| *1846:* that your need's at end! *1868:* after feeling that you need no more. *1888:* after-feeling 330| *1846:* moment . . Oh the *1849:* moment . . Oh, the *1868:* oh *1888:* moment . . . oh 331| *1846:* flashes . . is *1849:* flashes—is 332| *1846:* praise in *1849:* praise, in 333| *1846:* with Florentines— *1888:* with Florentines, 334| *1846:* yours—for *1888:* yours: for 335| *1846:* begun *1868:* begun: 336| *1846:*—He <> war just *1849:* war, just

To begin doing well in peace, you know:
And certain my precursors,—would not such
Look to themselves in such a chance as mine,
Secure the ground they trod upon, perhaps?
For I have heard, by fits, or seemed to hear,
Of strange mishap, mistake, ingratitude,
Treachery even. Say that one of you
Surmised this letter carried what might turn
To harm hereafter, cause him prejudice:
What would he do?
DOMIZIA [*hastily.*] Thank God and take revenge!
Hurl her own force against the city straight!
And, even at the moment when the foe
Sounded defiance . . . [TIBURZIO's *trumpet sounds in the distance.*]
LURIA Ah, you Florentines!
So would you do? Wisely for you, no doubt.
My simple Moorish instinct bids me clench
The obligation you relieve me from,
Still deeper! [*To* PUCCIO.] Sound our answer, I should say,
And thus:—[*tearing the paper.*]—The battle! That solves every doubt.

1868: He 337| *1846:* know! *1868:* know: 338| *1846:* Now, certain *1849:* And certain 339| *1846:* as this, *1868:* as mine, 342| *1846:* strange occurrences, ingratitude, *1868:* strange mishap, mistake, ingratitude, 343| *1846:* even,—say *1868:* even. Say 345| *1846:* prejudice— *1868:* prejudice: 347| *1846:* Turn her <> straight, *1868:* Hurl her <> straight! 348| *1846:* And even *1868:* And, even 350| *1846:* doubt! *1888:* doubt. 351| *1846:* instinct leads to sink *1849:* instinct bids me *1868:* me clench 352| *1846:* relieved *1849:* relieve 353| *1846:* say! *1868:* say, 354| *1846:* thus!—[*tearing* <> doubt! / [*As the Trumpet answers, the scene shuts.*] *1849:* thus:—[*tearing* <> doubt! § SD dropped § *1868:* doubt. *1888:* doubt

ACT III

AFTERNOON

PUCCIO, *as making a report to* JACOPO.

PUCCIO And here, your captain must report the rest;
For, as I say, the main engagement over
And Luria's special part in it performed,
How could a subaltern like me expect
Leisure or leave to occupy the field
And glean what dropped from his wide harvesting?
I thought, when Lucca at the battle's end
Came up, just as the Pisan centre broke,
That Luria would detach me and prevent
The flying Pisans seeking what they found,
Friends in the rear, a point to rally by.
But no, more honourable proved my post!
I had the august captive to escort
Safe to our camp; some other could pursue,
Fight, and be famous; gentler chance was mine—
Tiburzio's wounded spirit must be soothed!
He's in the tent there.
JACOPO Is the substance down?
I write—"The vanguard beaten and both wings
In full retreat, Tiburzio prisoner"—
And now,—"That they fell back and formed again
On Lucca's coming." Why then, after all,
'Tis half a victory, no conclusive one?

1| *1846:* your Captain *1868:* captain 2| *1846:* over, *1868:* over 4| *1846:* could subalterns like myself expect *1868:* subaltern *1888:* could a subaltern like me expect 7| *1846:* thought when *1849:* thought, when 11| *1846:* by: *1863:* by. 12| *1846:* no—more *1868:* no, more 14| *1846:* camp—some *1868:* camp; some 19| *1846:* retreat—Tiburzio *1868:* retreat, Tiburzio 20| *1846:* fall <> form *1849:* fell <> formed 21| *1846:* coming."—Why *1868:* coming." Why

PUCCIO Two operations where a sole had served.
JACOPO And Luria's fault was—?
PUCCIO Oh, for fault—not much!
He led the attack, a thought impetuously,
—There's commonly more prudence; now, he seemed
To hurry measures, otherwise well judged.
By over-concentrating strength at first
Against the enemy's van, both wings escaped:
That's reparable, yet it is a fault.

Enter BRACCIO.

JACOPO As good as a full victory to Florence,
With the advantage of a fault beside—
What is it, Puccio?—that by pressing forward
With too impetuous . . .
BRACCIO The report anon!
Thanks, sir—you have elsewhere a charge, I know. [PUCCIO *goes.*]
There's nothing done but I would do again;
Yet, Lapo, it may be the past proves nothing,
And Luria has kept faithful to the close.
JACOPO I was for waiting.
BRACCIO Yes: so was not I.
He could not choose but tear that letter—true!
Still, certain of his tones, I mind, and looks:—
You saw, too, with a fresher soul than I.
So, Porzio seemed an injured man, they say!
Well, I have gone upon the broad, sure ground.

Enter LURIA, PUCCIO, *and* DOMIZIA.

LURIA [*to* PUCCIO.] Say, at his pleasure I will see Tiburzio!

24| *1846:* fault . . . not *1868:* fault—not 25| *1846:* attack a *1849:* attack, a 27| *1846:* well-judged; *1868:* well-judged. *1888:* well judged. § Ohio text emended § 28| *1846:* over concentrating strength, at *1849:* strength at *1863:* over-concentrating 29| *1846:* both sides escaped: *1868:* both wings escaped: 30| *1846:* reparable—yet *1868:* reparable, yet 35| *1846:* Thanks, Sir <> know *1849:* know. *1868:* sir 37| *1846:* the Past *1868:* past 38| *1846:* the end! *1863:* end. *1868:* the close. 39| *1846:* not I! *1863:* not I. 41| *1846:* looks— *1868:* looks: *1888:* looks:— 43| *1846:* So Porzio *1849:* So, Porzio 45| *1846:* see

All's at his pleasure.
DOMIZIA [*to* LURIA.] Were I not forewarned
You would reject, as you do constantly,
Praise,—I might tell you how you have deserved
Of Florence by this last and crowning feat:
But words offend.
LURIA Nay, you may praise me now.
I want instruction every hour, I find,
On points where once I saw least need of it;
And praise, I have been used to slight perhaps,
Seems scarce so easily dispensed with now.
After a battle half one's strength is gone;
The glorious passion in us once appeased,
Our reason's calm cold dreadful voice begins.
All justice, power and beauty scarce appear
Monopolized by Florence, as of late,
To me, the stranger: you, no doubt, may know
Why Pisa needs must bear her rival's yoke.
And peradventure I grow nearer you,
For I, too, want to know and be assured.
When a cause ceases to reward itself,
Its friend seeks fresh sustainments; praise is one,
And here stand you—you, lady, praise me well.
But yours—(your pardon)—is unlearned praise.
To the motive, the endeavour, the heart's self,
Your quick sense looks: you crown and call aright

Tiburzio: *1868:* see Tiburzio! 46| *1846:* not so sure *1868:* not forewarned
48| *1846:* you what you *1868:* you how you 50| *1846:* words are vain! LURIA <> now! *1863:* vain. LURIA *1868:* words offend. LURIA <> now. 53| *1846:* to do without, *1868:* to slight perhaps, 54| *1846:* Seems not so easy to dispense with now: *1849:* now, *1863:* now: *1868:* Seems scarce so easily dispensed with now.
55–58| *1846:* gone—/ All *1849:* gone—/ And glorious passion in us once appeased, / Our reason's calm cold dreadful voice begins. / All *1868:* gone; / The glorious 60| *1846:* stranger; you *1863:* stranger: you 61| *1846:* must give her rival place; *1863:* place. *1868:* must bear her rival's yoke. 62| *1846:* And I am growing nearer you, perhaps, *1868:* And peradventure I grow nearer you, 63| *1846:* assured: *1849:* assured, *1863:* assured. 64| *1846:* So, when a cause does not reward *1849:* When a cause ceases to reward 65| *1846:* friend needs fresh *1868:* friend seeks fresh
66| *1846:* you—you, Lady <> well! *1863:* well. *1868:* lady 67| *1846:* yours—your pardon—is <> praise: *1849:* yours—(your pardon)—is *1868:* praise. 68| *1846:* endeavour,—the <> self— *1849:* endeavour, the <> self, 69| *1846:* looks; you

The soul o' the purpose, ere 'tis shaped as act,
Takes flesh i' the world, and clothes itself a king.
But when the act comes, stands for what 'tis worth,
—Here's Puccio, the skilled soldier, he's my judge!
Was all well, Puccio?

PUCCIO All was . . . must be well:
If we beat Lucca presently, as doubtless . . .
—No, there's no doubt, we must—all was well done.

LURIA In truth? Still you are of the trade, my Puccio!
You have the fellow-craftsman's sympathy.
There's none cares, like a fellow of the craft,
For the all-unestimated sum of pains
That go to a success the world can see:
They praise then, but the best they never know
—While you know! So, if envy mix with it,
Hate even, still the bottom-praise of all,
Whatever be the dregs, that drop's pure gold!
—For nothing's like it; nothing else records
Those daily, nightly drippings in the dark
Of the heart's blood, the world lets drop away
For ever—so, pure gold that praise must be!
And I have yours, my soldier! yet the best
Is still to come. There's one looks on apart
Whom all refers to, failure or success;
What's done might be our best, our utmost work,
And yet inadequate to serve his need.
Here's Braccio now, for Florence—here's our service—
Well done for us, seems it well done for him?
His chosen engine, tasked to its full strength
Answers the end? Should he have chosen higher?

1863: looks: you 71| *1846:* king; *1863:* king. 73| *1849:* soldier; he's *1863:* soldier, he's 74| *1846:* was . . must *1849:* was . . . must 76| *1846:* must—All *1863:* all 77| *1846:* truth? But you *1868:* truth? Still, you *1888:* truth? Still you 78| *1846:* sympathy! *1863:* sympathy. 79| *1846:* none knows like <> craft *1849:* craft, *1868:* none cares, like 80| *1846:* The all unestimated *1863:* all-unestimated *1868:* For the 81| *1846:* see; *1863:* see: 82| *1846:* know: *1863:* know 83| *1846:*—But you know!—Oh, if *1863:*—While you *1868:* know! So, if 84| *1846:* bottom praise *1863:* bottom-praise 88| *1846:* blood the *1849:* blood, the 89| *1846:* ever . . So *1863:* ever—so 90| *1846:* soldier; yet *1849:* soldier: yet *1863:* soldier! yet 91| *1846:* come—there's *1868:* come. There's 94| *1846:* need: *1863:* need. 96| *1846:* us, is it *1868:* us, seems it 97| *1846:* The chosen *1849:* His chosen 98| *1846:* end?—Should *1849:* Answers his end

Do we help Florence, now our best is wrought?
BRACCIO This battle, with the foregone services,
Saves Florence.
LURIA Why then, all is very well!
Here am I in the middle of my friends,
Who know me and who love me, one and all.
And yet . . . 'tis like . . . this instant while I speak
Is like the turning-moment of a dream
When . . . Ah, you are not foreigners like me!
Well then, one always dreams of friends at home;
And always comes, I say, the turning-point
When something changes in the friendly eyes
That love and look on you . . . so slight, so slight . . .
And yet it tells you they are dead and gone,
Or changed and enemies, for all their words,
And all is mockery and a maddening show.
You now, so kind here, all you Florentines,
What is it in your eyes . . . those lips, those brows . . .
Nobody spoke it, yet I know it well!
Come now—this battle saves you, all's at end,
Your use of me is o'er, for good, for ill,—
Come now, what's done against me, while I speak,
In Florence? Come! I feel it in my blood,
My eyes, my hair, a voice is in my ears
That spite of all this smiling and soft speech
You are betraying me. What is it you do?
Have it your way, and think my use is over—
Think you are saved and may throw off the mask—
Have it my way, and think more work remains
Which I could do,—so, show you fear me not!
Or prudent be, or daring, as you choose,

1863: end? Should *1868:* Answers the end 99| *1846:* is done? *1868:* is wrought? 103| *1846:* all! *1888:* all. 104| *1846:* yet . . 'tis like . . this *1888:* yet . . . 'tis like . . . this 107| *1846:* home, *1863:* home; 108| *1846:* turning point *1863:* turning-point 110| *1846:* you . . so slight, so slight . . *1888:* you . . . so slight, so slight . . . 112| *1846:* enemies for *1849:* enemies, for 113| *1846:* mockery, and <> show! *1863:* mockery and <> show. 114| *1846:* You, now *1868:* You now 115| *1846:* eyes . . those lips, those brows . . *1888:* eyes . . . those lips, those brows . . . 116| *1846:* it . . yet <> well!— *1868:* it, yet *1888:* well! 118| *1846:* good, for evil,— *1868:* good, for ill,— 121| *1846:* ear *1868:* ears 122| *1846:* and kind speech *1868:* and soft speech 123| *1846:* me! What *1888:* me. What 124| *1846:* over; *1863:* over— 125| *1846:* That you *1868:* Think you 127| *1846:* so show *1863:* so, show 128| *1846:* be, or generous, as *1868:* be, or daring,

But tell me—tell what I refused to know
At noon, lest heart should fail me! Well? That letter?
My fate is sealed at Florence! What is it?
BRACCIO Sir, I shall not deny what you divine.
It is no novelty for innocence
To be suspected, but a privilege:
Then after certain compensation comes.
Charges, I say not whether false or true,
Have been preferred against you some time since,
Which Florence was bound, plainly, to receive,
And which are therefore undergoing now
The due investigation. That is all.
I doubt not but your innocence will prove
Apparent and illustrious, as to me,
To them this evening, when the trial ends.
LURIA My trial?
DOMIZIA Florence, Florence to the end,
My whole heart thanks thee!
PUCCIO [*to* BRACCIO.] What is "trial," sir?
It was not for a trial—surely, no—
I furnished you those notes from time to time?
I held myself aggrieved—I am a man—
And I might speak,—ay, and speak mere truth, too,
And yet not mean at bottom of my heart
What should assist a—trial, do you say?
You should have told me!
DOMIZIA Nay, go on, go on!
His sentence! Do they sentence him? What is it?
The block—wheel?
BRACCIO Sentence there is none as yet,
Nor shall I give my own opinion now

---

as 130| *1846:* noon lest heart might fail *1849:* noon, lest heart should fail 131| *1846:* is known at *1868:* is sealed at 132| *1846:* not conceal what you divine; *1849:* divine: *1863:* divine. *1868:* not deny what 138| *1846:* bound plainly to *1849:* bound, plainly, to 141| *1846:* will shine *1863:* will prove 143| *1846:* evening when *1849:* evening, when <> ends *1863:* ends. 145| *1846:* is "Trial," Sir? *1863:* sir? *1868:* trial 146| *1846:* a Trial—surely no— *1849:* trial—surely, no— 149| *1846:* ay, and the mere *1849:* ay, and speak mere 151| *1846:* a—Trial *1868:* trial 153| *1846:* sentence? What *1849:* sentence him? What 154| *1846:* block? Wheel *1868:* block—wheel 155| *1846:* opinion here *1868:* opinion now

Of what it should be, or is like to be.
When it is passed, applaud or disapprove!
Up to that point, what is there to impugn?
LURIA They are right, then, to try me?
BRACCIO I assert,
Maintain and justify the absolute right
Of Florence to do all she can have done
In this procedure,—standing on her guard,
Receiving even services like yours
With utmost fit suspicious wariness.
In other matters, keep the mummery up!
Take all the experiences of all the world,
Each knowledge that broke through a heart to life,
Each reasoning which, to reach, burnt out a brain,
—In other cases, know these, warrant these,
And then dispense with these—'tis very well!
Let friend trust friend, and love demand love's like,
And gratitude be claimed for benefits,—
There's grace in that,—and when the fresh heart breaks,
The new brain proves a ruin, what of them?
Where is the matter of one moth the more
Singed in the candle, at a summer's end?
But Florence is no simple John or James
To have his toy, his fancy, his conceit
That he's the one excepted man by fate,
And, when fate shows him he's mistaken there,
Die with all good men's praise, and yield his place
To Paul and George intent to try their chance!
Florence exists because these pass away.
She's a contrivance to supply a type
Of man, which men's deficiencies refuse;

156| *1846:* to be: *1849:* to be, *1863:* to be. 158| *1846:* point what *1849:* point, what 159| *1846:* assert *1849:* assert, 160| *1849:* Maintain, and *1868:* maintain and 165| *1846:* matters—keep *1863:* matters, keep 166| *1846:* of the whole world, *1868:* of all the world, 167| *1846:* thro' *1863:* through 168| *1846:* which to work out cost a *1849:* which, to <> out, cost *1868:* to reach, burnt out a 170| *1846:* with them—'tis *1868:* with these—'tis 171| *1846:* demand its like, *1868:* demand love's like, 173| *1846:* that—and <> breaks *1849:* breaks, *1868:* that,—and 174| *1846:* a martyr, what of it? *1863:* of them? *1868:* a ruin, what 176| *1846:* candle at *1849:* candle, at 178| *1846:* conceit, *1868:* conceit 182| *1846:* chance: *1863:* chance! 183| *1846:* away; *1868:* away. 185| *1846:* Of Man which mens' *1849:* Of Man, which men's *1868:*

She binds so many, that she grows out of them—
Stands steady o'er their numbers, though they change
And pass away—there's always what upholds,
Always enough to fashion the great show.
As see, yon hanging city, in the sun,
Of shapely cloud substantially the same!
A thousand vapours rise and sink again,
Are interfused, and live their life and die,—
Yet ever hangs the steady show i' the air,
Under the sun's straight influence: that is well,
That is worth heaven should hold, and God should bless!
And so is Florence,—the unseen sun above,
Which draws and holds suspended all of us,
Binds transient vapours into a single cloud
Differing from each and better than they all.
And shall she dare to stake this permanence
On any one man's faith? Man's heart is weak,
And its temptations many: let her prove
Each servant to the very uttermost
Before she grant him her reward, I say!
DOMIZIA And as for hearts she chances to mistake,
Wrongëd hearts, not destined to receive reward,
Though they deserve it, did she only know,
—What should she do for these?
BRACCIO What does she not?
Say, that she gives them but herself to serve!
Here's Luria—what had profited his strength,
When half an hour of sober fancying
Had shown him step by step the uselessness
Of strength exerted for strength's proper sake?
But the truth is, she did create that strength,
Draw to the end the corresponding means.

---

man 186| *1846:* many, she *1849:* many, that she 187| *1846:* tho' *1863:* though 188| *1846:* away . . there's *1849:* away—there's 189| *1846:* show! *1863:* show. 190| *1846:* city in the sun *1849:* city, in the sun, 194| *1846:* air *1868:* air, 195| *1846:* well! *1868:* well, 196| *1846:* worth Heaven to hold, and God to bless! *1863:* heaven *1888:* heaven should hold, and God should bless! 198| *1846:* That draws <> us— *1849:* Which draws *1863:* us,— *1868:* us, 199| *1846:* transient mists and vapours into one *1849:* one, *1868:* transient vapours into a single cloud 207–209| *1846:* That are not <> reward, / What *1846:* reward / Tho' they deserve it, did she only know! / —What *1863:* Wronged hearts, not <> / Though *1888:* know, 210| *1846:* Say that *1849:* Say, that 214| *1846:* for its proper *1868:* for strength's proper 215| *1846:* is she *1849:* is, she 216| *1846:* Drew

The world is wide—are we the only men?
Oh, for the time, the social purpose' sake,
Use words agreed on, bandy epithets,
Call any man the sole great wise and good!
But shall we therefore, standing by ourselves,
Insult our souls and God with the same speech?
There, swarm the ignoble thousands under him:
What marks us from the hundreds and the tens?
Florence took up, turned all one way the soul
Of Luria with its fires, and here he glows!
She takes me out of all the world as him,
Fixing my coldness till like ice it checks
The fire! So, Braccio, Luria, which is best?
LURIA Ah, brave me? And is this indeed the way
To gain your good word and sincere esteem?
Am I the baited animal that must turn
And fight his baiters to deserve their praise?
Obedience is mistake then? Be it so!
Do you indeed remember I stand here
The captain of the conquering army,—mine—
With all your tokens, praise and promise, ready
To show for what their names meant when you gave,
Not what you style them now you take away?
If I call in my troops to arbitrate,
And dash the first enthusiastic thrill
Of victory with this you menace now—
Commend to the instinctive popular sense,
My story first, your comment afterward,—
Will they take, think you, part with you or me?
If I say—I, the labourer they saw work,

1868: Draw 217| *1846:* wide . . are *1849:* wide—are 220| *1846:* man, sole Great and Wise and Good! *1863:* sole great and wise and good! *1868:* man the sole great wise 221| *1846:* we, therefore *1868:* we therefore 223| *1846:* under Him— *1868:* him: 226| *1846:* he stands! *1868:* he glows! 228| *1846:* it stays *1863:* it checks 232| *1846:* baited tiger that *1868:* baited animal that 234| *1846:* Obedience has no fruit then?—Be *1868:* Obedience is mistake then? Be 236| *1846:* The Captain *1868:* captain 238| *1846:* names were when *1868:* names meant when 241| *1846:* And in their first *1868:* And dash the first 242| *1846:* victory, tell them how you menace me— *1868:* victory with this you menace now— 243| *1846:* Commending to their plain instinctive sense, *1868:* Commend to the instinctive popular sense, 244| *1846:* well-judged. *1888:* well judged. 246| *1846:* When I say simply, I, the man they know, *1868:* If I say, I the labourer they saw work,

Ending my work, ask pay, and find my lords
Have all this while provided silently
Against the day of pay and proving faith,
By what you call my sentence that's to come—
Will friends advise I wait complacently?
If I meet Florence half way at their head,
What will you do, my mild antagonist?
BRACCIO I will rise up like fire, proud and triumphant
That Florence knew you thoroughly and by me,
And so was saved. "See, Italy," I'll say,
"The crown of our precautions! Here's a man
Was far advanced, just touched on the belief
Less subtle cities had accorded long;
But we were wiser: at the end comes this!"
And from that minute, where is Luria? Lost!
The very stones of Florence cry against
The all-exacting, nought-enduring fool
Who thus resents her first probation, flouts
As if he, only, shone and cast no shade,
He, only, walked the earth with privilege
Against suspicion, free where angels fear:
He, for the first inquisitive mother's-word,
Must turn, and stand on his defence, forsooth!
Reward? You will not be worth punishment!
LURIA And Florence knew me thus! Thus I have lived,—
And thus you, with the clear fine intellect,

1888: say—I 247| *1846:* ask payment and find Florence *1849:* payment, and *1868:* ask pay, and find my lords 248| *1846:* Has *1868:* Have 249| *1846:* proving words, *1868:* proving faith, 251| *1846:* Will they sit waiting it complacently? *1868:* Will friends advise I wait complacently? 252| *1846:* When I resist that sentence at *1868:* If I meet Florence half way at 254| *1846:* Then I <> rise like *1849:* I <> rise up like 256| *1846:* saved: "See *1863:* saved. "See 257| *1846:* The need of our precautions—here's *1863:* precautions! here's *1868:* The crown of our precautions! Here's 258| *1846:* the reward *1868:* the belief 259| *1846:* accorded him— *1863:* him; *1868:* accorded long; 260| *1846:* wiser; at *1863:* wiser: at 261| *1846:* minute all your strength will go— *1863:* go. *1868:* minute, where is Luria? Lost! 263| *1846:* all-exacting, unenduring Luria, *1868:* all-exacting, nought-enduring fool, *1888:* fool 264| *1846:* Resenting her first slight probation thus *1849:* thus, *1863:* thus; *1868:* Who thus resents her first probation, flouts 265| *1846:* he only shone *1849:* he, only, shone 266| *1846:* He only walked *1849:* He, only, walked 267| *1846:* free from causing fear— *1863:* fear: *1868:* free where angels fear: 268| *1846:* So, for *1868:* He, for 269–270| *1846:* Turned round and stood on <> forsooth! / And you will sink into the savage back. / Reward? you *1849:* He turned, and <> forsooth! / Reward? You *1868:* Must turn,

Braccio, the cold acute instructed mind,
Out of the stir, so calm and unconfused,
Reported me—how could you otherwise!
Ay?—and what dropped from you, just now, moreover?
Your information, Puccio?—Did your skill,
Your understanding sympathy approve
Such a report of me? Was this the end?
Or is even this the end? Can I stop here?
You, lady, with the woman's stand apart,
The heart to see with, past man's brain and eyes,
. . . I cannot fathom why you should destroy
The unoffending one, you call your friend—
Still, lessoned by the good examples here
Of friendship, 'tis but natural I ask—
Had you a further aim, in aught you urged,
Than your friend's profit—in all those instances
Of perfidy, all Florence wrought of wrong—
All I remember now for the first time?
DOMIZIA I am a daughter of the Traversari,
Sister of Porzio and of Berto both,
So, have foreseen all that has come to pass.
I knew the Florence that could doubt their faith,
Must needs mistrust a stranger's—dealing them
Punishment, would deny him his reward.
And I believed, the shame they bore and died,
He would not bear, but live and fight against—

---

and stand on 273| *1846:* mind *1849:* mind, 276| *1846: you* *1868:* you 277| *1846:* skill *1863:* did *1868:* information, Puccio?—Did <> skill, 278| *1846:* And understanding *1868:* Your understanding 280| *1846:* is this the end even? Can I stop? *1849:* is even this the end? Can I stop here— *1863:* here? 281| *1846:* You, Lady *1868:* lady 282| *1846:* with, not those learned eyes, *1863:* not man's learned *1868:* with, past man's brain and eyes, 283–286| . . I <> you would destroy me,—/ It is but natural, therefore, I should ask *1849:* should destroy / The unoffending man, you call your friend—/ So, looking at the good examples here / Of friendship, 'tis but natural I ask 283| *1888:* . . . I 284| *1863:* unoffending one, you 285| *1868:* Still, lessoned by the 286| *1863:* ask— 287–290| *1846:* further end in all you spoke, / All *1849:* end, in <> spoke, / Than profit to me, in those instances / Of perfidy from Florence to her chiefs—/ All 287| *1868:* further aim, in aught your urged, 288| *1868:* Than your friend's profit—in all those 289| *1868:* perfidy, all Florence wrought of wrong— 292| *1846:* both. *1868:* both: *1888:* both, 293| *1846:* I have <> pass: *1849:* pass. *1868:* So, have 295| *1846:* stranger's—holding back *1868:* stranger's—dealing them 296| *1846:* Reward from them, must hold back his *1868:* Punishment, would deny him his 297| *1846:* believed, that shame *1849:* believed, the shame

Seeing he was of other stuff than they.
LURIA Hear them! All these against one foreigner!
And all this while, where is, in the whole world,
To his good faith a single witness?
TIBURZIO [*who has entered unseen during the preceding dialogue.*]
Here!
Thus I bear witness, not in word but deed.
I live for Pisa; she's not lost to-day
By many chances—much prevents from that!
Her army has been beaten, I am here,
But Lucca comes at last, one happy chance!
I rather would see Pisa three times lost
Than saved by any traitor, even by you;
The example of a traitor's happy fortune
Would bring more evil in the end than good;—
Pisa rejects the traitor, craves yourself!
I, in her name, resign forthwith to you
My charge,—the highest office, sword and shield!
You shall not, by my counsel, turn on Florence
Your army, give her calumny that ground—
Nor bring one soldier: be you all we gain!
And all she'll lose,—a head to deck some bridge,
And save the cost o' the crown should deck the head.
Leave her to perish in her perfidy,
Plague-stricken and stripped naked to all eyes,
A proverb and by-word in all mouths!
Go you to Pisa! Florence is my place—

300| *1846:* one Foreigner! *1863:* foreigner! 301| *1846:* while where is in <> world *1849:* while, where *1888:* is, in <> world, 302| *1846: entered during* *1868: entered unseen during* 303| *1846:* witness to it, not in word *1868:* witness, not in word but deed. 304| *1846:* But deed. I <> lost *1868:* I <> lost to-day 305| *1846:* chances,—much *1849:* chances—much 307| *1846:* one chance exists. *1868:* one happy chance! 308| *1846:* rather had see *1863:* rather would see 309| *1846:* even you. *1849:* even by you. *1863:* you; 311| *1846:* good. *1863:* good;— 312| *1846:* rejects such: save yourself and her! *1868:* rejects the traitor, craves yourself! 314| *1846:* highest of her offices. *1868:* highest office, sword and shield! 316| *1846:* Her army *1868:* Your army 317| *1846:* bring it with you: you are all we gain, *1849:* you; be you all *1863:* gain! *1868:* bring one soldier: be 318| *1846:* lose, a *1863:* lose,—a 319| *1846:* crown's cost that should *1868:* the cost o' the crown should 322| *1846:* and a bye word in men's mouths! *1849:* bye-word in all mouths! *1888:* and by-word 323| *1846:* to Pisa—Florence *1863:* to Pisa!

Leave me to tell her of the rectitude,
I, from the first, told Pisa, knowing it.
To Pisa!

DOMIZIA Ah my Braccio, are you caught?

BRACCIO Puccio, good soldier and good citizen,
Whom I have ever kept beneath my eye,
Ready as fit, to serve in this event
Florence, who clear foretold it from the first—
Through me, she gives you the command and charge
She takes, through me, from him who held it late!
A painful trial, very sore, was yours:
All that could draw out, marshal in array
The selfish passions 'gainst the public good—
Slights, scorns, neglects, were heaped on you to bear:
And ever you did bear and bow the head!
It had been sorry trial, to precede
Your feet, hold up the promise of reward
For luring gleam; your footsteps kept the track
Thro' dark and doubt: take all the light at once!
Trial is over, consummation shines;
Well have you served, as well henceforth command!

PUCCIO No, no . . . I dare not! I am grateful, glad;
But Luria—you shall understand he's wronged:
And he's my captain: this is not the way
We soldiers climb to fortune: think again!
The sentence is not even passed, beside!
I dare not: where's the soldier could?

LURIA Now, Florence—
Is it to be? You will know all the strength
O' the savage—to your neck the proof must go?
You will prove the brute nature? Ah, I see!

Florence 324| *1846:* rectitude *1849:* rectitude, 325| *1846:* I from the first told *1849:* I, from the first, told 327| *1846:* and selected man, *1868:* and good citizen *1888:* citizen, 328| *1846:* eye *1849:* eye, 329| *1846:* fit to *1846:* Ready, as fit, to *1868:* Ready as 331| *1846:* Thro' me she *1849:* me, she *1863:* Through 332| *1846:* thro' *1863:* through 338| *1846:* trial to *1849:* trial, to 341| *1863:* Through *1868:* Thro' 344| *1846:* No. no . . I <> not . . I *1849:* No, no *1863:* not! I *1888:* No, no . . . I dare 345| *1846:* wronged— *1888:* wronged: 346| *1846:* my Captain—this *1868:* captain *1888:* captain: this 349| *1846:* not . . where's *1888:* not: where's 350| *1846:* be?—You *1888:* be? You *1846:* Of *1888:* O'

The savage plainly is impassible:
He keeps his calm way through insulting words,
Sarcastic looks, sharp gestures—one of which
Would stop you, fatal to your finer sense,
But if he stolidly advance, march mute
Without a mark upon his callous hide,
Through the mere brushwood you grow angry with,
And leave the tatters of your flesh upon,
—You have to learn that when the true bar comes,
The murk mid-forest, the grand obstacle,
Which when you reach, you give the labour up,
Nor dash on, but lie down composed before,
—He goes against it, like the brute he is:
It falls before him, or he dies in his course.
I kept my course through past ingratitude:
I saw—it does seem, now, as if I saw,
Could not but see, those insults as they fell,
—Ay, let them glance from off me, very like,
Laughing, perhaps, to think the quality
You grew so bold on, while you so despised
The Moor's dull mute inapprehensive mood,
Was saving you: I bore and kept my course.
Now real wrong fronts me: see if I succumb!
Florence withstands me? I will punish her.

At night my sentence will arrive, you say.
Till then I cannot, if I would, rebel

353| *1846:* impassible— *1888:* impassible: 354| *1846:* thro' *1863:* through 355| *1846:* Cold looks <> gestures—any one *1849:* Sarcastic looks <> gestures—one 356| *1846:* you and offend your <> sense: *1849:* you, fatal to your *1868:* sense. *1888:* sense, 357| *1846:* he steadily pursues the path *1849:* steadily advances, still *1868:* stolidly advance, march mute 358| *1846:* hide *1849:* hide, 359| *1846:* Thro' *1863:* Through 362| *1846:* The thick mid forest, the real obstacle, *1863:* mid-forest *1868:* The murk mid-forest, the grand obstacle, 365| *1846:* is! *1868:* is: 366| *1846:* course! *1868:* course. 367| *1846:* thro' <> ingratitude— *1863:* through *1868:* ingratitude: 368| *1846:* saw . . it <> seem now as *1849:* saw—it <> seem, now, as 371| *1846:* Laughing perhaps to *1849:* Laughing, perhaps, to 372| *1846:* on while <> despised, *1849:* on, while <> despised 373| *1846:* moor's *1849:* The Moor's 374| *1846:* you; I <> course: *1863:* you. I <> course. *1868:* you: I 375| *1846:* me—see *1868:* me: see 376| *1846:* me?—I <> her! *1868:* her. *1888:* me? I 377| *1846:* say! *1868:*

—Unauthorized to lay my office down,
Retaining my full power to will and do:
After—it is to see. Tiburzio, thanks!
Go; you are free: join Lucca! I suspend
All further operations till to-night.
Thank you, and for the silence most of all!
[*To* BRACCIO.] Let my complacent bland accuser go
Carry his self-approving head and heart
Safe through the army which would trample him
Dead in a moment at my word or sign!
Go, sir, to Florence; tell friends what I say—
That while I wait my sentence, theirs waits them!
[*To* DOMIZIA.] You, lady,—you have black Italian eyes!
I would be generous if I might: oh, yes—
For I remember how so oft you seemed
Inclined at heart to break the barrier down
Which Florence finds God built between us both.
Alas, for generosity! this hour
Asks retribution: bear it as you may,
I must—the Moor—the savage,—pardon you!
Puccio, my trusty soldier, see them forth!

---

say. 378–380| *1846:* rebel—/ Retaining *1849:* rebel—/—Unauthorised to lay my office down, / Retaining *1863:* rebel / —Unauthorized 382| *1846:* Go—you are free—join Lucca. I *1863:* Go; you are free: join *1868:* join Lucca! I 383| *1846:* till the night. *1849:* till to-night. 385–387| *1846:* my self-justified accuser go / Safe thro' *1849:* my complacent bland accuser go, / And carry his self-approving head and heart / Safe *1863:* through *1868:* Carry *1888:* go 389| *1846:* Go, Sir *1863:* sir 390| *1846:* wait their sentence <> them. *1849:* them! *1868:* wait my sentence 391| *1846:* You . . Lady, you have dark Italian *1849:* You, Lady,—you have black Italian *1868:* lady 392| *1846:* might . . Oh, yes *1849:* yes— *1868:* oh *1888:* might: oh 393| *1846:* When I <> oft it seemed *1849:* For I <> oft you seemed 394| *1846:* You were inclined to *1849:* Inclined at heart to 395| *1846:* And lift me to you . . all that praise of old! *1849:* Which Florence makes God build between us both. *1863:* Which Florence finds God built 396| *1846:* Alas for generosity—this *1849:* Alas, for generosity! this 397| *1846:* Demands strict justice—bear <> may! *1863:* justice: bear *1868:* Asks retribution: bear <> may, 398| *1846:* the Moor,—the Savage *1863:* you. *1868:* the Moor—the savage <> you! 399| *1846:* [*To Puccio.*] Puccio <> forth!— *1863:* forth! *1868:* Puccio

ACT IV

EVENING

Enter Puccio *and* Jacopo.

PUCCIO What Luria will do? Ah, 'tis yours, fair sir,
Your and your subtle-witted master's part,
To tell me that; I tell you what he can.
JACOPO Friend, you mistake my station: I observe
The game, watch how my betters play, no more.
PUCCIO But mankind are not pieces—there's your fault!
You cannot push them, and, the first move made,
Lean back and study what the next shall be,
In confidence that, when 'tis fixed upon,
You find just where you left them, blacks and whites:
Men go on moving when your hand's away.
You build, I notice, firm on Luria's faith
This whole time,—firmlier than I choose to build,
Who never doubted it—of old, that is—
With Luria in his ordinary mind.
But now, oppression makes the wise man mad:
How do I know he will not turn and stand
And hold his own against you, as he may?
Suppose he but withdraw to Pisa—well,—
Then, even if all happen to your wish,
Which is a chance . . .
JACOPO Nay—'twas an oversight,

1| *1846:* fair Sir, *1849:* *will* *1863:* sir, *1868:* will 2| *1868:* You *1888:* Your and 4| *1846:* station! I *1863:* station: I 6| *1846:* pieces . . there's *1849:* pieces—there's 7| *1846:* them and *1849:* them, and 8| *1846:* back to study <> should *1868:* back and study <> shall 9| *1846:* that when 'tis fixed at length, *1849:* fixed upon, *1863:* that, when 10| *1846:* You'll find *1868:* You find 15| *1846:* mind: *1868:* mind. 16| *1846:* mad— *1863:* mad. *1888:* mad: 19| *1846:* But say that he withdraws *1849:* Suppose that he withdraws *1863:* Suppose he but withdraws *1868:* withdraw 20| *1846:* happens *1868:* happen 21| *1849:* oversight

Not waiting till the proper warrant came:
You could not take what was not ours to give.
But when at night the sentence really comes,
Our city authorizes past dispute
Luria's removal and transfers the charge,
You will perceive your duty and accept?
PUCCIO Accept what? muster-rolls of soldiers' names?
An army upon paper? I want men,
The hearts as well as hands—and where's a heart
But beats with Luria, in the multitude
I come from walking through by Luria's side?
You gave them Luria, set him thus to grow,
Head-like, upon their trunk; one heart feeds both,
They feel him there, live twice, and well know why.
—For they do know, if you are ignorant,
Who kept his own place and respected theirs,
Managed their sweat, yet never spared his blood.
All was your act: another might have served—
There's peradventure no such dearth of heads—
But you chose Luria: so, they grew one flesh,
And now, for nothing they can understand,
Luria removed, off is to roll the head;
The body's mine—much I shall do with it!
JACOPO That's at the worst.
PUCCIO   No—at the best, it is!
Best, do you hear? I saw them by his side.
Only we two with Luria in the camp
Are left that keep the secret? You think that?

1849: oversight, 25| *1846:* And Florence authorizes *1868:* Our city authorizes 26| *1846:* and your own advance, *1868:* and transfers the charge, 29| *1846:* paper?—I *1888:* paper? I 30| *1846:* Their hearts *1868:* The hearts 31| *1846:* That's not with Luria in *1849:* with Luria, in *1868:* But beats with 32| *1846:* thro' *1868:* through 33| *1846:* gave him to them, set him on to grow *1849:* grow, *1863:* gave them Luria, set *1868:* him thus to 34| *1846:* A head upon <> trunk, one blood feeds *1849:* Head-like, upon *1868:* trunk; one heart feeds 35| *1846:* there and live and live and <> why *1849:* there, and live, and <> why! *1868:* there, live twice, and <> why. 37| *1846:* and kept theirs alike,— *1849:* and respected theirs, 38| *1846:* their ease yet <> his own: *1849:* ease, yet <> own. *1868:* their sweat, yet <> his blood. 39| *1846:* your deed: another *1868:* your act: another 40| *1846:* of men— *1868:* of heads— 41| *1846:* chose Luria—so they grew to him: *1863:* so, they <> him. *1868:* grew one flesh. *1888:* chose Luria: so <> flesh, 43| *1846:* Luria's <> head— *1868:* Luria <> head; 45| *1846:* best it *1849:* best, it 46| *1846:* side: *1849:* side; *1863:* side. 48| *1846:* that know the secret? That you think? *1849:*

Hear what I know: from rear to van, no heart
But felt the quiet patient hero there
Was wronged, nor in the moveless ranks an eye
But glancing told its fellow the whole story
Of that convicted silent knot of spies
Who passed thro' them to Florence; they might pass—
No breast but gladlier beat when free of such!
Our troops will catch up Luria, close him round,
Bear him to Florence as their natural lord,
Partake his fortune, live or die with him.
JACOPO And by mistake catch up along with him
Puccio, no doubt, compelled in self despite
To still continue second in command!
PUCCIO No, sir, no second nor so fortunate!
Your tricks succeed with me too well for that!
I am as you have made me, live and die
To serve your end—a mere trained fighting-hack,
With words, you laugh at while they leave your mouth,
For my life's rule and ordinance of God!
I have to do my duty, keep my faith,
And earn my praise, and guard against my blame,
As I was trained. I shall accept your charge,
And fight against one better than myself,
Spite of my heart's conviction of his worth—
That, you may count on!—just as hitherto
I have gone on, persuaded I was wronged,
Slighted, insulted, terms we learn by rote,—
All because Luria superseded me—
Because the better nature, fresh-inspired,

---

secret? You think that? *1868:* that keep the 49| *1846:* what I saw: from <> van no *1849:* van, no *1868:* what I know: from 54| *1846:* to Florence—they *1849:* to Florence; they 55| *1846:* of them! *1863:* of such! 57| *1846:* Lead him *1868:* Bear him 58| *1846:* fortunes <> him! *1863:* him. 60| *1846:* self-despite *1888:* self despite 61| *1846:* continue Second in Command! *1868:* second in command! 62| *1846:* No, Sir *1868:* sir 64| *1846:* me, and shall die *1868:* me, live and die 65| *1846:* A <> fighting hack to <> end; *1863:* fighting-hack *1868:* To <> end; a <> fighting-hack *1888:* fighting-hack, *1888:* end—a 66| *1846:* mouth, *1888:* mouth 67| *1846:* rules *1868:* rule 68| *1846:* Duty have I to do, and faith to keep, *1849:* I have to do my duty, keep my faith, 69| *1846:* And praise to earn, and blame to guard against, *1849:* And earn my praise, and guard against my blame, 72| *1846:* And my own heart's <> his wrongs— *1849:* his worth— *1863:* Spite of my heart's *1868:* worth. *1888:* worth— 73| *1846:* That you *1849:* That, you 74| *1846:* Have I gone <> was slighted, *1849:* I have gone <> was wronged, 75–77| *1846:* Degraded, all the terms <> rote,— / Because *1849:* Slighted,

Mounted above me to its proper place!
What mattered all the kindly graciousness,
The cordial brother's-bearing? This was clear—
I, once the captain, now was subaltern,
And so must keep complaining like a fool!
Go, take the curse of a lost soul, I say!
You neither play your puppets to the end,
Nor treat the real man,—for his realness' sake
Thrust rudely in their place,—with such regard
As might console them for their altered rank.
Me, the mere steady soldier, you depose
For Luria, and here's all your pet deserves!
Of what account, then, is your laughing-stock?
One word for all: whatever Luria does,
—If backed by his indignant troops he turn,
Revenge himself, and Florence go to ground,—
Or, for a signal everlasting shame,
He pardon you, simply seek better friends,
Side with the Pisans and Lucchese for change
—And if I, pledged to ingrates past belief,
Dare fight against a man such fools call false,
Who, inasmuch as he was true, fights me,—
Whichever way he win, he wins for worth,
For every soldier, for all true and good!

---

and all <> rote,—/ All because Luria superseded me—/ Because *1863:* Slighted, and moody, terms *1868:* Slighted, insulted, terms 78| *1846:* place: *1849:* place! 79| *1846:* graciousness *1849:* graciousness, 80| *1846:* And cordial brother's bearing *1863:* brother's-bearing *1868:* The cordial 81| *1846:* I was once captain, am subaltern now, *1849:* I, once the captain, was subaltern *1888:* captain, now was subaltern, 83| *1846:* So take <> lost man, I *1849:* Go, take *1868:* lost soul, I 89| *1846:* all that he deserves! *1863:* all your pet deserves! 90| *1846:* then, are my services? *1868:* then, is your laughing-stock? 92| *1846:* turns *1868:* turn, 93| *1846:* In self-defence and <> goes *1868:* Revenge himself, and <> go 94| *1846:* Or for a signal, everlasting shame *1849:* shame, *1868:* Or, for a signal everlasting 95| *1846:* pardons you, and simply seeks his friends *1863:* you, simply seeks better friends *1868:* pardon <> seek <> friends, 96| *1846:* And heads the Pisan and the Lucchese troops *1868:* Side with the Pisans and Lucchese for change 97| *1846:* if I, for you ingrates *1868:* if I, pledged to ingrates 98| *1846:* Resolve to fight against one false to us, *1849:* against a man called false, *1868:* Dare fight <> man such fools call 99| *1846:* is <> fights there— *1863:* was *1868:* fights me,— 100| *1846:* wins, he <> for me, *1863:* win, he *1868:* way we win <> for worth, *1888:* way he win, 101| *1846:* for the common good! *1863:* the true and good! *1868:* for all true

Sir, chronicling the rest, omit not this!

As they go, enter LURIA *and* HUSAIN.

HUSAIN Saw'st thou?—For they are gone! The world lies bare
Before thee, to be tasted, felt and seen
Like what it is, now Florence goes away!
Thou livest now, with men art man again!
Those Florentines were all to thee of old;
But Braccio, but Domizia, gone is each,
There lie beneath thee thine own multitudes!
Saw'st thou?
LURIA I saw.
HUSAIN Then, hold thy course, my king!
The years return. Let thy heart have its way:
Ah, they would play with thee as with all else,
Turn thee to use, and fashion thee anew,
Find out God's fault in thee as in the rest?
Oh watch, oh listen only to these fiends
Once at their occupation! Ere we know,
The free great heaven is shut, their stifling pall
Drops till it frets the very tingling hair,
So weighs it on our head,—and, for the earth,
Our common earth is tethered up and down,
Over and across—"here shalt thou move," they cry!
LURIA Ay, Husain?
HUSAIN So have they spoiled all beside!
So stands a man girt round with Florentines,
Priests, greybeards, Braccios, women, boys and spies,

102–103| *1846: Enter* *1849: As they go, enter* 107| *1846:* were eyes to *1868:* were all to 108| *1846:* each— *1863:* each: *1868:* each, 109| *1846:* multitudes— *1863:* multitudes. *1868:* multitudes! 110| *1846:* Sawest <> HUSAIN So hold <> my King! *1849:* HUSAIN Then, hold *1863:* Saw'st *1868:* king! 111| *1846:* return—Let <> way! *1849:* return. Let *1888:* way: 112| *1846:* else? *1868:* else, 115| *1846:* Oh, watch but, listen <> these men *1868:* Oh watch, but listen <> these fiends *1888:* watch, oh listen 116| *1846:* occupation! Ere ye know, *1888:* occupation! Ere we know, 118| *1846:* hair— *1863:* hair, 121| *1846:* across—here <> move, they say! *1863:* across—"here <> move," they *1868:* they

All in one tale, all singing the same song,
How thou must house, and live at bed and board,
Take pledge and give it, go their every way,
Breathe to their measure, make thy blood beat time
With theirs—or, all is nothing—thou art lost—
A savage, how shouldst thou perceive as they?
Feel glad to stand 'neath God's close naked hand!
Look up to it! Why, down they pull thy neck,
Lest it crush thee, who feel'st it and wouldst kiss,
Without their priests that needs must glove it first,
Lest peradventure flesh offend thy lip.
Love woman! Why, a very beast thou art!
Thou must . . .

LURIA Peace, Husain!

HUSAIN Ay but, spoiling all,
For all, else true things, substituting false,
That they should dare spoil, of all instincts, thine!
Should dare to take thee with thine instincts up,
Thy battle-ardours, like a ball of fire,
And class them and allow them place and play
So far, no farther—unabashed the while!
Thou with the soul that never can take rest—
Thou born to do, undo, and do again,
And never to be still,—wouldst thou make war?
Oh, that is commendable, just and right!
"Come over," say they, "have the honour due
In living out thy nature! Fight thy best:
It is to be for Florence, not thyself!

---

cry! 125| *1846:* tale, each singing *1868:* tale, all singing 129| *1846:* or—all *1863:* or, all 130| *1846:* savage . . how should such perceive *1849:* shouldst thou perceive *1868:* savage, how 132| *1846:* it! Why down <> neck *1849:* it! Why, down <> neck, *1868:* it! Why down *1888:* it! Why, down 133| *1846:* thee who feel it <> would *1849:* thee, who feel'st <> wouldst 134| *1846:* first *1849:* first, 135| *1846:* In mercy to thy lip it else will wound! *1849:* Lest peradventure it should wound thy lip! *1863:* it offend thy *1868:* peradventure flesh offend <> lip. 136| *1846:* Love Woman—why a *1849:* Love Woman! Why, a *1868:* woman 137| *1846:* HUSAIN Ay, but *1868:* HUSAIN Ay but 138| *1846:* all else <> things substituting *1849:* all, else true, things *1863:* else true things, substituting 146| *1846:* But never <> still,—thou wouldst make *1849:* still,—wouldst thou make *1863:* And never 148| *1846:* Come over, say they, have *1863:* "Come over," say they, "have 149| *1846:* best— *1863:* best: 150| *1846:* for Florence not *1863:* for Florence, not

For thee, it were a horror and a plague;
For us, when war is made for Florence, see,
How all is changed: the fire that fed on earth
Now towers to heaven!"—

LURIA And what sealed up so long
My Husain's mouth?

HUSAIN Oh friend, oh lord—for me,
What am I?—I was silent at thy side,
Who am a part of thee. It is thy hand,
Thy foot that glows when in the heart fresh blood
Boils up, thou heart of me! Now, live again,
Again love as thou likest, hate as free!
Turn to no Braccios nor Domizias now,
To ask, before thy very limbs dare move,
If Florence' welfare be concerned thereby!

LURIA So clear what Florence must expect of me?

HUSAIN Both armies against Florence! Take revenge!
Wide, deep—to live upon, in feeling now,—
And, after live, in memory, year by year—
And, with the dear conviction, die at last!
She lies now at thy pleasure: pleasure have!
Their vaunted intellect that gilds our sense,
And blends with life, to show it better by,
—How think'st thou?—I have turned that light on them!
They called our thirst of war a transient thing;
"The battle-element must pass away
From life," they said, "and leave a tranquil world."
—Master, I took their light and turned it full
On that dull turgid vein they said would burst

151| *1846:* thee it <> plague— *1849:* thee, it *1863:* plague; 153| *1846:* changed . . the *1849:* changed—the *1863:* changed: the 154| *1846:* heaven!— LURIA *1863:* heaven!"—LURIA 155| *1846:* HUSAIN Oh, friend, oh, lord *1868:* HUSAIN Oh friend, oh lord 156| *1846:* side *1849:* side, 157| *1846:* That am <> thee—It *1863:* Who am <> thee. It 159| *1846:* up as thine does! Thou wilt live *1849:* up, thou heart of me! Now live *1863:* me! Now, live 160| *1846:* freely, *1849:* free! 161| *1846:* now *1849:* now, 162| *1846:* limbs may move, *1849:* limbs dare move, 163| *1846:* be not touched therein! *1849:* be concerned thereby! 167| *1846:* And after, in remembrance, year by *1868:* And, after live, in memory, year by 168| *1846:* And, in the *1849:* And, with the 169| *1846:* pleasure—pleasure *1863:* pleasure: pleasure 171| *1846:* They blend <> life to *1849:* And blends <> life, to 174| *1846:* The battle element *1849:* battle-element *1863:* "The 175| *1846:* life, they said, and <> world: *1863:* life," they said, "and <>

And pass away; and as I looked on life,
Still everywhere I tracked this, though it hid
And shifted, lay so silent as it thought,
Changed shape and hue yet ever was the same.
Why, 'twas all fighting, all their nobler life!
All work was fighting, every harm—defeat,
And every joy obtained—a victory!
Be not their dupe!
Be not their dupe! —Their dupe? That hour is past!
Here stand'st thou in the glory and the calm:
All is determined. Silence for me now! [HUSAIN *goes.*]

LURIA Have I heard all?

DOMIZIA [*advancing from the background.*] No, Luria, I remain!
Not from the motives these have urged on thee,
Ignoble, insufficient, incomplete,
And pregnant each with sure seeds of decay,
As failing of sustainment from thyself,
—Neither from low revenge, nor selfishness,
Nor savage lust of power, nor one, nor all,
Shalt thou abolish Florence! I proclaim
The angel in thee, and reject the sprites
Which ineffectual crowd about his strength,
And mingle with his work and claim a share!
Inconsciously to the augustest end
Thou hast arisen: second not in rank
So much as time, to him who first ordained
That Florence, thou art to destroy, should be.
Yet him a star, too, guided, who broke first
The pride of lonely power, the life apart,
And made the eminences, each to each,
Lean o'er the level world and let it lie

---

world." 178| *1846:* on Life, *1863:* life, 181| *1846:* Changed oft the hue <> same: *1863:* same. *1868:* Changed shape and hue 186| *1846:* calm! *1888:* calm: 187| *1846:* determined! Silence *1888:* determined. Silence 188| *1846: background*]. No, Luria, I am here. *1849:* here! *1863: background*]. No, Luria, I remain! 191| *1846:* decay *1849:* decay, 196| *1846:* thee and <> the spirits *1849:* thee, and *1863:* the sprites 197| *1846:* strength *1849:* strength, 199| *1846:*—Inconsciously *1863:* Inconsciously 200| *1846:* not to him *1849:* not in rank 201| *1846:* In rank so <> time, who *1849:* So <> time, to him who 202| *1846:* The Florence thou <> be— *1849:* That Florence, thou *1863:* be.

Safe from the thunder henceforth 'neath their tops;
So the few famous men of old combined,
And let the multitude rise underneath,
And reach them and unite—so Florence grew:
Braccio speaks true, it was well worth the price.
But when the sheltered many grew in pride
And grudged the station of the elected ones,
Who, greater than their kind, are truly great
Only in voluntary servitude—
Time was for thee to rise, and thou art here.
Such plague possessed this Florence: who can tell
The mighty girth and greatness at the heart
Of those so perfect pillars of the grove
She pulled down in her envy? Who as I,
The light weak parasite born but to twine
Round each of them and, measuring them, live?
My light love keeps the matchless circle safe,
My slender life proves what has passed away.
I lived when they departed; lived to cling
To thee, the mighty stranger; thou wouldst rise
And burst the thraldom, and avenge, I knew.
I have done nothing; all was thy strong bole.
But a bird's weight can break the infant tree
Which after holds an aery in its arms,
And 'twas my care that nought should warp thy spire
From rising to the height; the roof is reached
O' the forest, break through, see extend the sky!
Go on to Florence, Luria! 'Tis man's cause!

207| *1846:* their arms— *1863:* their tops: 209| *1846:* underneath *1849:* underneath, 210| *1846:* them, and <> grew! *1863:* grew: *1868:* them and 211| *1846:* speaks well, it *1863:* speaks true, it 212| *1846:* sheltered Many *1863:* many 213| *1846:* grudged their station to the glorious ones, *1849:* grudged the station of the *1863:* the elected ones, 215–216| *1846:* servitude—/ Which they who, being less, would fain be more, / And so accept not, then are least of all—/ Time *1849:* servitude—/ Time 217| *1846:* this Florence—who *1863:* this Florence: who 220| *1846:* as I *1849:* as I, 222| *1846:* measuring them, so live? *1863:* measuring them, live? 224| *1846:* past away! *1863:* pass'd away. *1868:* passed 226| *1846:* would'st *1863:* wouldst 228| *1846:* nothing—all <> strong heart— *1849:* nothing; all <> heart: *1863:* heart. *1868:* strong bole. 229| *1846:* But as a <> weight breaks *1849:* But a <> weight can break 231| *1846:* So did I care *1849:* And 'twas my care 232| *1846:* reached— *1863:* reached: *1868:* reached 233| *1846:* Break through and there is all the sky above! *1863:* there extends the *1868:* O'

Fail thou, and thine own fall were least to dread:
Thou keepest Florence in her evil way,
Encouragest her sin so much the more—
And while the ignoble past is justified,
Thou all the surelier warp'st the future growth,
The chiefs to come, the Lurias yet unborn,
That, greater than thyself, are reached o'er thee
Who giv'st the vantage-ground their foes require
As o'er my prostrate House thyself wast reached.
Man calls thee, God requites thee! All is said,
The mission of my House fulfilled at last:
And the mere woman, speaking for herself,
Reserves speech—it is now no woman's time. [DOMIZIA *goes*.]
LURIA Thus at the last must figure Luria, then!
Doing the various work of all his friends,
And answering every purpose save his own.
No doubt, 'tis well for them to wish; but him—
After the exploit what were left? Perchance
A little pride upon the swarthy brow
At having brought successfully to bear
'Gainst Florence' self her own especial arms,—
Her craftiness, impelled by fiercer strength
From Moorish blood than feeds the northern wit:
But after!—once the easy vengeance willed,
Beautiful Florence at a word laid low
—(Not in her domes and towers and palaces,

---

the forest, break through, see extend the sky! 235| *1846:* But fail <> thy fall is <> dread! *1849:* Fail <> thine own fall *1868:* were <> dread: 238–239| *1846:* the bloody past is justified, / The murder of those gone before approved, / Thou <> surelier dost work against *1849:* justified, / Thou *1863:* bloody Past <> / <> dost the Future wrong, *1868:* the ignoble past <> / <> surelier warp'st the future growth, 240| *1846:* The men to *1863:* The chiefs to 241| *1849:* Who, greater *1863:* That, greater 242| *1849:* That giv'st *1863:* Who giv'st 243| *1846:* reached! *1849:* was't *1863:* wast *1888:* reached 244| *1846:* thee—God shall judge thee: all is said! *1849:* said, *1863:* thee, God requites thee. All *1868:* thee! All 245| *1846:* last! *1863:* last: 247| *1846:* speech; it *1863:* speech—it 248| *1846:* [*sol.*] So at <> Luria then! *1849:* So <> Luria, then! *1863:* Thus at 249| *1846:* friends *1849:* friends, 251| *1846:* to see; but *1849:* to wish; for him— *1863:* wish; but him— 252| *1846:* what remains? Perchance *1849:* what is left? Perchance *1863:* were 253| *1849:* brow, 255| *1846:* arms, *1849:* arms,— 256| *1846:* craftiness impelled *1849:* craftiness, impelled 257| *1846:* wit— *1868:* wit. *1888:* wit 260| *1846:* her Domes and Towers and Palaces, *1868:* domes and towers and

Not even in a dream, that outrage!)—low,
As shamed in her own eyes henceforth for ever,
Low, for the rival cities round to laugh,
Conquered and pardoned by a hireling Moor!
—For him, who did the irreparable wrong,
What would be left, his life's illusion fled,—
What hope or trust in the forlorn wide world?
How strange that Florence should mistake me so!
Whence grew this? What withdrew her faith from me?
Some cause! These fretful-blooded children talk
Against their mother,—they are wronged, they say—
Notable wrongs her smile makes up again!
So, taking fire at each supposed offence,
They may speak rashly, suffer for their speech:
But what could it have been in word or deed
Thus injured me? Some one word spoken more
Out of my heart, and all had changed perhaps.
My fault, it must have been,—for, what gain they?
Why risk the danger? See, what I could do!
And my fault, wherefore visit upon them,
My Florentines? The notable revenge
I meditated! To stay passively,
Attend their summons, be as they dispose!
Why, if my very soldiers keep the rank,
And if my chieftains acquiesce, what then?
I ruin Florence, teach her friends mistrust,

---

palaces, 261| *1846:* Not in <> outrage!)—but laid low *1849:* Not even in <> outrage!)—low, 263| *1846:* And for <> to see, *1849:* Low, for *1868:* to laugh, 265| *1846:* him who <> wrong *1849:* him, who <> wrong, 266| *1846:* left, the life's *1849:* left, his life's 267–268| *1846:* § space § *1849:* § end of page § *1863:* § no space § 269| *1846:* How grew *1863:* Whence grew 272| *1846:* wrongs a smile *1863:* wrongs her smile 274| *1846:* These may <> for rash speech— *1849:* They may *1863:* for their speech: 276| *1846:* That injured *1868:* Thus injured 277| *1846:* perhaps! *1868:* perhaps *1888:* perhaps. 278| *1846:* fault it <> for what *1849:* fault, it *1863:* for, what 279| *1846:* danger? See what *1849:* danger? See, what 280| *1846:* fault wherefore *1849:* fault, wherefore 281| *1846:* My Florentines? The generous revenge *1849:* revenge, *1868:* My Florentines? The notable revenge, *1888:* revenge 282| *1846:* meditate <> stay here passively, *1868:* meditated <> stay passively, 283| *1846:* Go at their <> dispose— *1868:* Attend their <> dispose! 284| *1846:* soldiers stop not that, *1849:* soldiers keep their ranks, *1868:* keep the rank, 285| *1846:* if I moderate my chiefs, what *1849:* if I pacify my *1868:* if my chieftains acquiesce, what 286| *1846:* ruin Florence—teach

Confirm her enemies in harsh belief,
And when she finds one day, as find she must,
The strange mistake, and how my heart was hers,
Shall it console me, that my Florentines
Walk with a sadder step, in graver guise,
Who took me with such frankness, praised me so,
At the glad outset? Had they loved me less,
They had less feared what seemed a change in me.
And after all, who did the harm? Not they!
How could they interpose with those old fools
I' the council? Suffer for those old fools' sake—
They, who made pictures of me, sang the songs
About my battles? Ah, we Moors get blind
Out of our proper world, where we can see!
The sun that guides is closer to us! There—
There, my own orb! He sinks from out the sky.
Why, there! a whole day has he blessed the land,
My land, our Florence all about the hills,
The fields and gardens, vineyards, olive-grounds,
All have been blest: and yet we Florentines
With souls intent upon our battle here,
Found that he rose too soon, or set too late,
Gave us no vantage, or gave Pisa much—
Therefore we wronged him! Does he turn in ire
To burn the earth that cannot understand?
Or drop out quietly, and leave the sky,
His task once ended? Night wipes blame away.
Another morning from my East shall spring
And find all eyes at leisure, all disposed

<> mistrust— *1863:* ruin Florence, teach <> mistrust, 287| *1846:* belief— *1863:* belief, 288| *1846:* as she must find, *1868:* as find she must, 290| *1846:* This shall console *1849:* Shall it console 291| *1846:* step, a graver face, *1868:* step, in graver guise, 293| *1846:* outset! Had they been less sure *1849:* they loved me less, *1863:* outset? Had 295| *1846:* And is it they who will have done the harm? *1849:* And after all, who did the harm? Not they! 297| *1846:* In <> sakes— *1868:* sakes *1888:* I' <> sake— 298| *1846:* me, turned the *1849:* me, sang the 300| *1846:* world where we are right! *1849:* we can see! *1888:* world, where 301| *1846:* us! See— *1849:* us! There— 302| *1846:* See, my <> sky! *1849:* There, my *1888:* sky. 303| *1846:* Why there *1849:* Why, there 306| *1846:* blest—and *1888:* blest: and 307| *1846:* With minds intent *1868:* With souls intent 308| *1846:* or rose too *1849:* or else too *1868:* or set too 309| *1846:* gave Pisa more— *1868:* gave Pisa much— 310| *1846:* And so we <> does *1849:* him! Does *1868:* Therefore we 311| *1849:* earth, that *1863:* earth that 313| *1846:* away: *1863:* away. 314| *1846:* shall rise *1863:* shall spring 315| *1849:* leisure, more disposed *1868:*

To watch and understand its work, no doubt.
So, praise the new sun, the successor praise,
Praise the new Luria and forget the old!
[*Taking a phial from his breast.*]
Strange! This is all I brought from my own land
To help me: Europe would supply the rest,
All needs beside, all other helps save one!
I thought of adverse fortune, battle lost,
The natural upbraiding of the loser,
And then this quiet remedy to seek
At end of the disastrous day. [*He drinks.*]
At end of the disastrous day. 'Tis sought!
This was my happy triumph-morning: Florence
Is saved: I drink this, and ere night,—die! Strange!

---

leisure, all disposed 316| *1846:* watch it and approve its every work. *1849:* its work, no doubt. *1863:* watch and understand its 317| *1846:* successor praise! *1863:* successor praise, 318| *1846:* new Luria, and *1868:* new Luria and 319| *1846:*—Strange <> own Land *1863:* land *1888:* Strange 320| *1846:* me—Europe *1863:* me: Europe 321| *1846:* save this! *1868:* save one! 322| *1846:* battles *1888:* battle 323| *1846:* upbraidings *1868:* upbraiding 325| *1846:* day—[*He* *1868:* day. [*He* 327| *1846:* die!—Strange! *1868:* die! Strange!

ACT V

NIGHT

LURIA *and* PUCCIO.

LURIA I thought to do this, not to talk this: well,
Such were my projects for the city's good,
To help her in attack or by defence.
Time, here as elsewhere, soon or late may take
Our foresight by surprise thro' chance and change;
But not a little we provide against
—If you see clear on every point.
PUCCIO Most clear.
LURIA Then all is said—not much, if you count words,
Yet to an understanding ear enough;
And all that my brief stay permits, beside.
Nor must you blame me, as I sought to teach
My elder in command, or threw a doubt
Upon the very skill, it comforts me
To know I leave,—your steady soldiership
Which never failed me: yet, because it seemed
A stranger's eye might haply note defect
That skill, through use and custom, overlooks—
I have gone into the old cares once more,
As if I had to come and save again
Florence—that May—that morning! 'Tis night now.

1| *1846:* well! *1863:* well, 2| *1846:* the City's *1863:* city's 3| *1846:* To save her *1849:* her from attack *1863:* To help her in attack 5| *1846:* With chance and change our <> surprise; *1849:* Our <> surprise with chance and change; *1863:* surprise thro' chance 8| *1846:* much, to count the words, *1849:* much, if you count words, 9| *1846:* Yet for an <> enough, *1863:* enough; *1868:* Yet to an 11| *1846:* me as *1849:* me, as 12| *1846:* command or *1849:* command, or 13| *1846:* skill it *1849:* skill, it 14| *1846:* leave,—that steady *1849:* leave,—your steady 15| *1849:* That never *1863:* Which never 16| *1849:* defect, *1863:* defect 17| *1846:* Which skill thro' <> custom overlooks, *1849:* skill, thro' <> custom, overlooks, *1863:* That skill, through *1888:* overlooks— 20| *1846:* Florence

Well—I broke off with? . . .
PUCCIO Of the past campaign
You spoke—of measures to be kept in mind
For future use.
LURIA True, so . . . but, time—no time!
As well end here: remember this, and me!
Farewell now!
PUCCIO Dare I speak?
LURIA South o' the river—
How is the second stream called . . . no,—the third?
PUCCIO Pesa.
LURIA And a stone's cast from the fording-place,
To the east,—the little mount's name?
PUCCIO Lupo.
LURIA Ay!
Ay—there the tower, and all that side is safe!
With San Romano, west of Evola,
San Miniato, Scala, Empoli,
Five towers in all,—forget not!
PUCCIO Fear not me!
LURIA —Nor to memorialize the Council now,
I' the easy hour, on those battalions' claim,
Who forced a pass by Staggia on the hills,
And kept the Sienese at check!
PUCCIO One word—
Sir, I must speak! That you submit yourself
To Florence' bidding, howsoe'er it prove,
And give up the command to me—is much,
Too much, perhaps: but what you tell me now,
Even will affect the other course you choose—
Poor as it may be, perils even that!
Refuge you seek at Pisa: yet these plans

. . that May . . that <> now— *1849:* Florence—that May—that *1863:* now. 25| *1846:* LURIA—The south <> river,— *1849:* river— *1863:* LURIA—The South *1868:* LURIA South 26| *1846:* called . . no *1888:* called . . . no 27| *1846:* fording place, *1863:* stone's-cast <> fording-place, *1888:* stone's cast 28| *1846:* the East *1868:* east 29| *1846:* tower and *1849:* tower, and 34| *1846:* claim *1868:* claim, 35| *1846:* On the other side, by *1868:* side by *1888:* Who forced a pass by 36| *1846:* That kept the Siennese *1863:* Who kept the Sienese *1888:* And kept 38| *1846:* bidding howsoe'er *1849:* bidding, howsoe'er 40| *1846:* now *1849:* now, 41| *1846:* Even affects <> course to choose— *1849:* Even will affect <> course you choose— 42| *1849:* peril *1868:* perils 43| *1846:* at Pisa—yet

All militate for Florence, all conclude
Your formidable work to make her queen
O' the country,—which her rivals rose against
When you began it,—which to interrupt,
Pisa would buy you off at any price!
You cannot mean to sue for Pisa's help,
With this made perfect and on record?

LURIA I—
At Pisa, and for refuge, do you say?

PUCCIO Where are you going, then? You must decide
On leaving us, a silent fugitive,
Alone, at night—you, stealing through our lines,
Who were this morning's Luria,—you escape
To painfully begin the world once more,
With such a past, as it had never been!
Where are you going?

LURIA Not so far, my Puccio,
But that I hope to hear, enjoy and praise
(If you mind praise from your old captain yet)
Each happy blow you strike for Florence.

PUCCIO Ay,—
But ere you gain your shelter, what may come?
For see—though nothing's surely known as yet,
Still—truth must out—I apprehend the worst.
If mere suspicion stood for certainty
Before, there's nothing can arrest the step
Of Florence toward your ruin, once on foot.
Forgive her fifty times, it matters not!
And having disbelieved your innocence,
How can she trust your magnanimity?
You may do harm to her—why then, you will!
And Florence is sagacious in pursuit.

1863: at Pisa: yet 45| *1846:* The formidable *1849:* Your formidable 46| *1846:* Of *1888:* O' 48| *1846:* off in any case! *1849:* off at any price! 49| *1846:* help *1849:* help, 52| *1846:* going? Then you *1849:* going, then? You 53| *1846:* To leave the camp a *1849:* On leaving us, a 54| *1846:* you stealing thro' our lines *1849:* you, stealing <> lines, *1863:* through 55| *1846:* you, escaped *1849:* you escape 57| *1846:* a Past *1868:* past 59| *1846:* But I shall get to hear and know and *1849:* But that I hope to hear, and know, and *1863:* hear, enjoy and 61| *1846:* for Florence! PUCCIO —Ay, *1868:* PUCCIO Ay, *1888:* for Florence. PUCCIO Ay,— 62| *1846:* come! *1849:* come? 63| *1846:* tho' *1863:* though 64| *1846:* Still . . truth <> out . . I *1863:* Still—truth <> out—I 66| *1846:* steps *1868:* step

Have you a friend to count on?
LURIA One sure friend.
PUCCIO Potent?
LURIA All-potent.
PUCCIO And he is apprised?
LURIA He waits me.
PUCCIO So!—Then I, put in your place,
Making my profit of all done by you,
Calling your labours mine, reaping their fruit,
To this, the State's gift, now add yours beside—
That I may take as my peculiar store
These your instructions to work Florence good.
And if, by putting some few happily
In practice, I should both advantage her
And draw down honour on myself,—what then?
LURIA Do it, my Puccio! I shall know and praise.
PUCCIO Though so, men say, "mark what we gain by change
—A Puccio for a Luria!"
LURIA Even so.
PUCCIO Then, not for fifty hundred Florences,
Would I accept one office save my own,
Fill any other than my rightful post
Here at your feet, my captain and my lord!
That such a cloud should break, such trouble be,
Ere a man settle, soul and body, down
Into his true place and take rest for ever!
Here were my wise eyes fixed on your right-hand,
And so the bad thoughts came and the worse words,
And all went wrong and painfully enough,—
No wonder,—till, the right spot stumbled on,

74| *1846:* LURIA All potent *1863:* LURIA All-potent 78| *1846:* this the <> gift now add this from you— *1849:* these, the <> gift, now add this of yours— *1868:* this <> add yours beside— 79| *1846:* take to my *1868:* take as my 80| *1846:* All these instructions to do Florence good, *1849:* All your instructions <> good; *1863:* good. *1868:* These your <> to work Florence 81| *1846:* if by *1849:* if, by 82| *1846:* practice I *1849:* practice, I 84| *1846:* praise! *1863:* praise *1868:* praise! *1888:* Then not <> Florences *1849:* Then, not <> Florences, 90| *1846:* my Captain and my Lord! *1868:* captain <> lord! 92| *1846:* settles soul and body down *1849:* settle *1863:* settle, soul and body, down 93| *1846:* takes *1849:* take 94| *1846:* There were <> right hand, *1849:* Here were *1863:* right-hand, 97| *1846:* wonder,

All the jar stops, and there is peace at once!
I am yours now,—a tool your right-hand wields!
God's love, that I should live, the man I am,
On orders, warrants, patents, and the like,
As if there were no glowing eye i' the world
To glance straight inspiration to my brain,
No glorious heart to give mine twice the beats!
For, see—my doubt, where is it?—fear? 'tis flown!
And Florence and her anger are a tale
To scare a child. Why, half-a-dozen words
Will tell her, spoken as I now can speak,
Her error, my past folly—and all's right,
And you are Luria, our great chief again!
Or at the worst—which worst were best of all—
To exile or to death I follow you.
LURIA Thanks, Puccio! Let me use the privilege
You grant me: if I still command you,—stay!
Remain here—my vicegerent, it shall be,
And not successor: let me, as of old,
Still serve the State, my spirit prompting yours—
Still triumph, one for both. There! Leave me now!
You cannot disobey my first command?
Remember what I spoke of Jacopo,
And what you promised to concert with him!
Send him to speak with me—nay, no farewell!
You shall be by me when the sentence comes. [PUCCIO *goes.*]
So, there's one Florentine returns again!
Out of the genial morning-company

till *1849:* wonder,—till 98| *1846:* stops and *1849:* stops, and 99| *1846:* right hand wields. *1849:* wields! *1863:* right-hand 101| *1846:* patents and *1888:* patents, and 102| *1849:* world, *1888:* world 105| *1846:* see,—the doubt <> it?—Fear *1849:* see—my doubt *1863:* fear 107| *1846:* child—Why, half a dozen *1849:* child! Why *1863:* half-a-dozen *1888:* child. Why 110| *1846:* are Luria, the great *1849:* are Luria, our great 112| *1849:* you! *1888:* you. 117| *1846:* yours; *1863:* yours— 118| *1846:* both—There *1863:* both. There 120| *1846:* of Jacopo *1849:* of Jacopo, 121| *1846:* him: *1849:* him! 122| *1846:* farewell— *1868:* farewell! 124| *1846:* So there's *1849:* So, there's 125| *1846:* morning company *1849:* morning company, *1863:* morning-company, *1888:*

One face is left to take into the night.

Enter JACOPO.

JACOPO I wait for your command, sir.
LURIA What, so soon?
I thank your ready presence and fair word.
I used to notice you in early days
As of the other species, so to speak,
Those watchers of the lives of us who act—
That weigh our motives, scrutinize our thoughts.
So, I propound this to your faculty
As you would tell me, were a town to take
. . . That is, of old. I am departing hence
Under these imputations; that is nought—
I leave no friend on whom they may rebound,
Hardly a name behind me in the land,
Being a stranger: all the more behoves
That I regard how altered were the case
With natives of the country, Florentines
On whom the like mischance should fall: the roots
O' the tree survive the ruin of the trunk—
No root of mine will throb, you understand.
But I had predecessors, Florentines,
Accused as I am now, and punished so—
The Traversari: you know more than I
How stigmatized they are and lost in shame.
Now Puccio, who succeeds me in command,
Both served them and succeeded, in due time;
He knows the way, holds proper documents,
And has the power to lay the simple truth

---

morning-company 127| *1846:* commands, Sir *1868:* command, sir 132| *1846:* thoughts; *1863:* thoughts. 133| *1846:* So I *1849:* So, I 134| *1846:* me were *1849:* me, were 135| *1846:* . . That *1888:* . . . That 136| *1846:* imputations: that *1863:* imputations; that 139| *1846:* stranger; all *1863:* stranger: all 141| *1846:* country, Florentines, *1868:* country, Florentines 142| *1846:* fall; the *1863:* fall: the 144| *1846:* throb . . you understand: *1849:* throb—you understand. *1888:* throb, you 146| *1846:* now and *1849:* now, and 147| *1846:* The Traversari—you *1863:* The Traversari: you 149| *1846:* Now, Puccio who <> command *1849:* Now, Puccio, who <> command, *1868:* Now Puccio 150| *1846:* succeeded in *1849:* succeeded, in 151| *1846:* way, and holds the documents, *1849:*

Before an active spirit, as I count yours:
And also there's Tiburzio, my new friend,
Will, at a word, confirm such evidence,
He being the great chivalric soul we know.
I put it to your tact, sir—were't not well,
—A grace, though but for contrast's sake, no more,—
If you who witness, and have borne a share
Involuntarily in my mischance,
Should, of your proper motion, set your skill
To indicate—that is, investigate
The right or wrong of what mischance befell
Those famous citizens, your countrymen?
Nay, you shall promise nothing: but reflect,
And if your sense of justice prompt you—good!
JACOPO And if, the trial past, their fame stand clear
To all men's eyes, as yours, my lord, to mine—
Their ghosts may sleep in quiet satisfied!
For me, a straw thrown up into the air,
My testimony goes for a straw's worth.
I used to hold by the instructed brain,
And move with Braccio as my master-wind;
The heart leads surelier: I must move with you—
As greatest now, who ever were the best.
So, let the last and humblest of your servants
Accept your charge, as Braccio's heretofore,
And tender homage by obeying you! [JACOPO *goes.*]
LURIA Another! Luria goes not poorly forth.
If we could wait! The only fault's with time;

---

way, holds proper documents, 153| *1846:* as I know yours: *1868:* as I count yours: 155| *1846:* Will at a word confirm *1849:* Will, at a word, confirm 156| *1846:* the chivalric *1868:* the great chivalric 157| *1846:* your instinct—were't *1868:* your tact, sir—were't 158| *1846:* more, *1849:* more,— 159| *1846:* witness and *1849:* witness, and 160| *1849:* Involuntarily, in *1868:* Involuntarily in 162| *1846:* indicate . . that *1863:* indicate—that 163| *1846:* The reason or the wrong of what befel *1863:* befell *1868:* The right or wrong of what mischance befell 164| *1846:* citizens your *1849:* citizens, your 165| *1846:* Nay—you <> nothing—but *1863:* Nay, you <> nothing: but 167| *1846:* stands white *1849:* stand clear 168| *1863:* my Lord *1868:* lord 171| *1846:* worth: *1849:* worth. 173| *1846:* as the master-wind; *1868:* as my master-wind; 176| *1846:* So let *1849:* So, let 177–179| *1846:* heretofore. [*Exit* JACOPO.] / Another!—Luria *1849:* heretofore, / And offer homage, by obeying you! [JACOPO *goes.*] / Another *1868:* And tender homage by *1888:* Another! Luria 180| *1846:* If one could <> Time: *1849:* If we

All men become good creatures: but so slow!

Enter DOMIZIA.

LURIA Ah, you once more?
DOMIZIA Domizia, whom you knew,
Performed her task, and died with it. 'Tis I,
Another woman, you have never known.
Let the past sleep now!
LURIA I have done with it.
DOMIZIA How inexhaustibly the spirit grows!
One object, she seemed erewhile born to reach
With her whole energies and die content,—
So like a wall at the world's edge it stood,
With nought beyond to live for,—is that reached?
Already are new undreamed energies
Outgrowing under, and extending farther
To a new object; there's another world.
See! I have told the purpose of my life;
'Tis gained: you are decided, well or ill—
You march on Florence, or submit to her—
My work is done with you, your brow declares.
But—leave you? More of you seems yet to reach:
I stay for what I just begin to see.
LURIA So that you turn not to the past!
DOMIZIA You trace
Nothing but ill in it—my selfish impulse,
Which sought its end and disregarded yours?

---

could *1863:* time: *1868:* time; 181| *1846:* creatures . . . but *1849:* creatures—but *1868:* creatures: but 182| *1846:* DOMIZIA Domizia, that you *1868:* DOMIZIA Domizia, whom you 183–185| *1846:* task and <> it—Tis I! / Let the Past <> now. LURIA *1849:* task, and <> I! / Another woman, you have never known. / Let *1868:* known, / <> past <> now! LURIA *1888:* known. 187| *1846:* object she *1849:* object, she 188| *1846:* content, *1863:* content,— 189| *1846:* world's end it *1868:* world's edge it 190| *1846:* for—is it reached, . . *1849:* for,—is it reached? *1868:* is that reached? 192| *1846:* under and <> further *1849:* under, and *1868:* farther 193| *1846:* object;—there's <> world! *1888:* object; there's <> world. 194| *1846:* See: I <> life,— *1849:* See! I *1863:* life: *1868:* life; 195–197| *1846:* gained—you <> ill—/ My <> declares: *1849:* ill—/ You march on Florence, or submit to her—/ My *1863:* declares. *1868:* gained: you 198| *1846:* reach! *1888:* reach: 200| *1846:* the Past *1868:* past 201| *1846:* impulse *1849:*

LURIA Speak not against your nature: best, each keep
His own—you, yours—most, now that I keep mine,
—At least, fall by it, having too weakly stood.
God's finger marks distinctions, all so fine,
We would confound: the lesser has its use,
Which, when it apes the greater, is forgone.
I, born a Moor, lived half a Florentine;
But, punished properly, can end, a Moor.
Beside, there's something makes me understand
Your nature: I have seen it.

DOMIZIA Aught like mine?

LURIA In my own East . . . if you would stoop and help
My barbarous illustration! It sounds ill;
Yet there's no wrong at bottom: rather, praise.

DOMIZIA Well?

LURIA We have creatures there, which if you saw
The first time, you would doubtless marvel at
For their surpassing beauty, craft and strength.
And though it were a lively moment's shock
When you first found the purpose of forked tongues
That seem innocuous in their lambent play,
Yet, once made know such grace requires such guard,
Your reason soon would acquiesce, I think,
In wisdom which made all things for the best—
So, take them, good with ill, contentedly,
The prominent beauty with the latent sting.

---

impulse, 203| *1846:* best each *1849:* best, each 204| *1846:* you yours—most now when I *1849:* you, yours—most, now, when *1868:* now that I 205| *1846:* At least fall <> having weakly *1849:* —At least, fall <> having too weakly 206| *1846:* distinctions all so fine *1849:* distinctions, all so fine, 207| *1846:* confound—the Lesser <> use *1846:* use, *1863:* confound:the lesser 208| *1846:* Which when <> the Greater, is foregone. *1849:* Which, when *1863:* greater 210| *1846:* can die a *1863:* can end, a 211| *1846:* Beside there is what makes *1849:* Beside, there *1868:* there's something makes 212| *1846:* nature . . I <> it— DOMIZIA One like *1863:* nature: I <> it. DOMIZIA Aught like 213| *1846:* own East . . if *1888:* own East . . . if 214| *1846:* illustration . . it <> ill *1849:* ill— *1863:* illustration! it *1868:* illustration! It <> ill; 215| *1846:* bottom—rather praise— *1849:* rather, praise— *1863:* praise. *1868:* bottom: rather 216| *1846:* there which *1849:* there, which 217| *1846:* at, *1868:* at 218| *1863:* craft, and *1868:* craft and 219| *1846:* tho' *1863:* though 220| *1846:* Wherein you found <> of their tongues *1849:* of those tongues *1868:* of forked tongues *1888:* When you first found 221| *1846:* seemed *1868:* seem 224| *1846:* In the Wisdom <> best, *1849:* best; *1863:* wisdom <> best— *1868:* In wisdom 225| *1846:* So take <> contentedly— *1863:* So, take <> contentedly, 226| *1846:* the secret sting. *1868:* the latent

I am glad to have seen you wondrous Florentines:
Yet . . .

DOMIZIA I am here to listen.

LURIA My own East!
How nearer God we were! He glows above
With scarce an intervention, presses close
And palpitatingly, his soul o'er ours:
We feel him, nor by painful reason know!
The everlasting minute of creation
Is felt there; now it is, as it was then;
All changes at his instantaneous will,
Not by the operation of a law
Whose maker is elsewhere at other work.
His hand is still engaged upon his world—
Man's praise can forward it, man's prayer suspend,
For is not God all-mighty? To recast
The world, erase old things and make them new,
What costs it him? So, man breathes nobly there.
And inasmuch as feeling, the East's gift,
Is quick and transient—comes, and lo, is gone—
While Northern thought is slow and durable,
Surely a mission was reserved for me,
Who, born with a perception of the power
And use of the North's thought for us of the East,
Should have remained, turned knowledge to account,
Giving thought's character and permanence
To the too transitory feeling there—
Writing God's message plain in mortal words.
Instead of which, I leave my fated field
For this where such a task is needed least,

---

sting. 227| *1846:* Florentines *1849:* Florentines, *1863:* Florentines: 228| *1846:* Yet . . DOMIZIA *1888:* Yet . . . DOMIZIA 231| *1846:* palpitatingly, His <> ours! *1868:* his *1888:* ours: 232| *1846:* feel Him *1868:* him 234| *1846:* there; *Now* <> was Then; *1863:* there; Now *1868:* now <> then; 235| *1846:* at His *1868:* his 237| *1846:* work! *1868:* work. 238| *1846:* His soul is *1863:* His hand is <> upon His *1868:* his 239| *1846:* it, Man's *1868:* man's 240| *1846:* all-mighty?—To *1868:* all-mighty? To 242| *1846:* it Him? So man <> there! *1849:* it Him? So, man *1868:* him *1888:* it Him <> there. 243| *1846:* as Feeling *1868:* feeling 245| *1846:* While Northern Thought *1868:* thought 246| *1846:* Oh, what a *1863:* Surely a 249| *1846:* have stayed there and turned it to *1868:* have remained and *1888:* remained, turned knowledge to 250| *1846:* Giving Thought's *1868:* thought's 251| *1846:* too-transitory Feelings *1863:* too-transitory Feeling *1868:* too transitory feeling 252| *1846:* words! *1868:* words.

Where all are born consummate in the art
I just perceive a chance of making mine,—
And then, deserting thus my early post,
I wonder that the men I come among
Mistake me! There, how all had understood,
Still brought fresh stuff for me to stamp and keep,
Fresh instinct to translate them into law!
Me, who . . .

DOMIZIA Who here the greater task achieve,
More needful even: who have brought fresh stuff
For us to mould, interpret and prove right,—
New feeling fresh from God, which, could we know
O' the instant, where had been our need of it?
—Whose life re-teaches us what life should be,
What faith is, loyalty and simpleness,
All, once revealed but taught us so long since
That, having mere tradition of the fact,—
Truth copied falteringly from copies faint,
The early traits all dropped away,—we said
On sight of faith like yours, "So looks not faith
We understand, described and praised before."
But still, the feat was dared; and though at first
It suffered from our haste, yet trace by trace
Old memories reappear, old truth returns,
Our slow thought does its work, and all's re-known.
Oh noble Luria! What you have decreed
I see not, but no animal revenge,
No brute-like punishment of bad by worse—
It cannot be, the gross and vulgar way
Traced for me by convention and mistake,
Has gained that calm approving eye and brow!

265| *1849:* feelings *1868:* feeling 266| *1846:* of them? *1868:* of it? 269| *1846:* All their revealment, taught *1849:* All, their revealment taught *1868:* All, once revealed but taught 270| *1846:* fact, *1863:* fact,— 273| *1846:* yours, so *1849:* yours, "so *1868:* yours, "So 274| *1846:* and taught before. *1849:* before." *1868:* and praised before." 275| *1846:* still the truth was shown; and tho' *1849:* still, the *1863:* though *1868:* the feat was dared; and 276| *1846:* suffer *1868:* suffered
277| *1846:* reappear, the likeness grows, *1868:* reappear, old truth returns,
278| *1846:* slow Thought <> all is known *1849:* all's re-known. *1868:* thought
279| *1846:* Oh, noble Luria! what *1868:* Oh noble Luria! What 280–282| *1846:* revenge, . . ./It <> be the *1849:* revenge,/No brute-like punishment of bad by woree—/It <> be, the 283| *1846:* mistake *1849:* mistake, 284| *1846:* brow. *1849:*

Spare Florence, after all! Let Luria trust
To his own soul, he whom I trust with mine!
LURIA In time!
DOMIZIA How, Luria?
LURIA It is midnight now,
And they arrive from Florence with my fate.
DOMIZIA I hear no step.
LURIA I feel one, as you say.

Enter HUSAIN.

HUSAIN The man returned from Florence!
LURIA As I knew.
HUSAIN He seeks thee.
LURIA And I only wait for him.
Aught else?
HUSAIN A movement of the Lucchese troops
Southward—
LURIA Toward Florence? Have out instantly . . .
Ah, old use clings! Puccio must care henceforth.
In—quick—'tis nearly midnight! Bid him come!

Enter TIBURZIO, BRACCIO, *and* PUCCIO.

Tiburzio?—not at Pisa?
TIBURZIO I return
From Florence: I serve Pisa, and must think
By such procedure I have served her best.
A people is but the attempt of many
To rise to the completer life of one;
And those who live as models for the mass
Are singly of more value than they all.
Such man are you, and such a time is this,
That your sole fate concerns a nation more

---

brow! 285| *1846:* Spare Florence after *1863:* Spare Florence, after 286| *1846:* soul, and I will trust to him! *1868:* trust him mine! *1888:* soul, he whom I trust with mine! 287| *1846:* now— *1863:* now, 289| *1846:* step . . LURIA I feel it, as *1849:* step. LURIA <> say. *1868:* feel one, as 293| *1846:* LURIA . . . Toward <> instantly . . . *1863:* LURIA Toward *1888:* instantly . . 294| *1846:* henceforth! *1868:* henceforth. 296| *1846:* Tiburzio,—not *1849:* Tiburzio?—not 300| *1846:* one— *1863:* one; 303| *1846:* this *1868:*

Than much apparent welfare: that to prove
Your rectitude, and duly crown the same,
Imports us far beyond to-day's event,
A battle's loss or gain: man's mass remains,—
Keep but God's model safe, new men will rise
To take its mould, and other days to prove
How great a good was Luria's glory. True—
I might go try my fortune as you urged,
And, joining Lucca, helped by your disgrace,
Repair our harm—so were to-day's work done;
But where leave Luria for our sons to see?
No, I look farther. I have testified
(Declaring my submission to your arms)
Her full success to Florence, making clear
Your probity, as none else could: I spoke,
And out it shone!

LURIA Ah—until Braccio spoke!

BRACCIO Till Braccio told in just a word the whole—
His lapse to error, his return to knowledge:
Which told . . . Nay, Luria, *I* should droop the head,
I whom shame rests with! Yet I dare look up,
Sure of your pardon now I sue for it,
Knowing you wholly. Let the midnight end!
'Tis morn approaches! Still you answer not?
Sunshine succeeds the shadow past away;

---

this, 305| *1846:* Than its immediate welfare; and to *1849:* its apparent welfare *1888:* Than much apparent welfare: that to 307–309| *1846:* Of consequence beyond the day's event. / Keep but the model *1849:* Imports it far beyond <> event, / Its battle's loss or gain—the mass remains, / Keep *1863:* gain: the <> remains,— *1868:* Imports us far <> / A battle's *1888:* today's <> / gain: man's mass <> / <> but God's model 310–312| *1846:* To study it, and many another day. / I <> you bade, *1849:* and other days to prove / How great a good was Luria's having lived. / I *1868:* To take its mould, and *1888:* was Luria's glory. True— / <> you urged, 313| *1846:* And joining *1888:* And, joining 314–316| *1846:* done: / But I *1849:* done; / But where were Luria for our sons to see? / No, I *1863:* where find Luria *1888:* where leave Luria 318| *1846:* Your full *1863:* Her full 319| *1846:* probity as <> spoke— *1849:* probity, as *1868:* spoke, 320| *1846:* And it shone clearly! LURIA Ah—till Braccio *1868:* And out it knowledge— *1863:* knowledge: *1868:* His lapse to error, his return 323| *1846:* told . . Nay <> head *1849:* head, *1888:* told . . . Nay 324| *1846:* Whom all shame <> with, yet *1849:* I, whom shame *1863:* with! yet *1868:* I whom <> with! Yet 326| *1846:* wholly—so let midnight *1868:* wholly. Let the midnight 327| *1846:* Sunrise will come next! Still *1863:* Sunrise approaches! Still *1868:* 'Tis morn approaches 328| *1846:* The shadow of the night is past away: *1863:* away; *1868:*

Our faces, which phantasmal grew and false,
Are all that felt it: they change round you, turn
Truly themselves now in its vanishing.
Speak, Luria! Here begins your true career:
Look up, advance! All now is possible,
Fact's grandeur, no false dreaming! Dare and do!
And every prophecy shall be fulfilled
Save one—(nay, now your word must come at last)
—That you would punish Florence!

HUSAIN [*pointing to* LURIA's *dead body.*] That is done.

Sunshine succeeds the shadow past 329| *1846:* The circling faces here 'mid which it rose *1849:* Our circling *1863:* it grew *1868:* Our faces, which phantasmal grew and false, 330| *1846:* it,—they close round you now *1863:* it: they *1868:* you, turn *1888:* they change round 331| *1846:* To witness its completest vanishing. *1868:* Themselves now in its complete *1888:* Truly themselves <> its vanishing.
332| *1846:* career— *1863:* career: 333| *1846:* up to it!—All <> possible— *1863:* it! All <> possible *1868:* possible, *1888:* up, advance! All 334| *1846:* The glory and the grandeur of each dream— *1863:* dream: *1868:* dream. *1888:* Fact's grandeur, no false dreaming! Dare and do! 336| *1846:* one . . (nay *1863:* one—(nay
337| *1846:* done!— / *Curtain falls.* *1849:* done!— *1863:* done.

BY THE SAME AUTHOR.

I.

PARACELSUS. A POEM.

Price 6*s*. *boards*.

II.

SORDELLO. A POEM.

Price 6*s*. 6*d*. *boards*.

III.

BELLS AND POMEGRANATES.

No. I.—PIPPA PASSES. *Price* 1*s*.

No. II.—KING VICTOR AND KING CHARLES. *Price* 1*s*.

No. III.—DRAMATIC LYRICS. *Price* 1*s*.

No. IV.—THE RETURN OF THE DRUSES. *Price* 1*s*.

No. V.—A BLOT IN THE 'SCUTCHEON. *Price* 1*s*.

No. VI.—COLOMBE'S BIRTHDAY. *Price* 1*s*.

No. VII.—DRAMATIC ROMANCES AND LYRICS. *Price* 2*s*.

Editorial Notes

A BLOT IN THE 'SCUTCHEON

Emendations to the Text

I, 2, l. 39 In 1889 punctuation following *loving* not clear. Emended in accordance with all prior texts to read *loving,*

I, 2, l. 43 In 1889 reads *Austin* followed by blank space. Obvious printer's error emended in accordance with all prior texts to read *Austin;*

I, 3, l. 55 In 1889 text reads *brother:* Obvious error based upon apparent defective type in 1888. Emended in accordance with all texts before 1888 to read *brother;*

III, 1, l. 64 In 1889 an illegible blot which might be interpreted as a defective period or comma at end of line is eliminated since no mark of punctuation appears in any prior edition or in the corrected Dykes Campbell copy of the 1889.

III, 2, l. 127 In 1889 type for punctuation at end of line is defective and might be mistaken for comma. Emended in accordance with all prior editions to a semicolon.

The Manuscript

The MS from which *A Blot in the 'Scutcheon* was printed is not extant. The earliest record of the play's composition is contained in a letter written at Hanover Cottage, Southampton Street, from B to William Charles Macready: " 'The luck of a third adventure' is proverbial. I have written a spick and span new Tragedy . . ." (Hood, p. 5). Although not specifically named in the letter, B was referring to *A Blot in the 'Scutcheon,* since it was his third attempt to present Macready with a drama suitable for the stage, the two rejected plays being *King Victor and King Charles* and the *Return of the Druses.* The available evidence suggests that the original MS of *A Blot in the 'Scutcheon* was completed sometime between 17 September 1840, the day B retrieved the *Druses* MS from Macready, and before the end of December 1840, the time at which, according to Griffin and Minchin, the

Browning family moved from Southampton Street, Camberwell, in Surrey. According to Edmund Gosse, B's friend and biographer, the play was written in the "space of five days" (*Robert Browning, Personalia* [New York: Houghton Mifflin Co., 1890], p. 61). Yale University, however, holds an early MS (hereafter referred to as the Yale MS), a copy of the original MS which B presented to Macready. A blank leaf in front in B's autograph reads: "This is the copy (in my sister's handwriting) which was altered for acting by Macready . . . (R.B. Oct. 20. '84.)." The only available document indicating when Macready received the Yale MS is B's letter of 1884 to Mr. Frank Hill, editor of the *Daily News*. The letter contains certain inaccuracies, but if B is correct he gave Macready the Yale MS sometime during the summer of 1841. B wrote to Hill that "Macready received and accepted the play, while he was engaged at the Haymarket, and retained it for Drury Lane, of which I was ignorant that he was about to become manager: he accepted it 'at the instigation' of nobody,—and Charles Dickens was not in England when he did so: it was read to him after his return, by Forster" (Orr, p. 171). Macready records in his diary that the last day of his Haymarket engagement was 7 December 1841. That Macready received the MS before this time is corroborated by his diary, in which he states that he read B's tragedy on 26 September 1841. B stated, however, that Dickens was not in England at the time, and if correct, B was alluding to Dickens's trip to Scotland, the only trip Dickens made outside of England in 1841, inferring that Macready accepted the Yale MS sometime between Dickens's departure for Scotland on 19 June1841 and his return on 29 July 1841. Obviously, the Yale MS remains an invaluable literary document, representing an early state of B's conception of the play, and elucidating the variance between B's and Macready's notions of stagecraft. Yet the information derived from a textual study of the Yale MS indicates that the MS used for printer's copy evolved independently from the Yale MS. Hence, the Yale MS does not form part of an ancestral series, in which each state of the text, from MS form through subsequent printed editions, is derived from its immediate predecessor. The number of variant readings obtained in collating the Yale MS with the first edition suggests that the Yale MS remained in Macready's possession while B made revisions in the original MS. Edward Moxon published *A Blot in the 'Scutcheon* on 11 February 1843, more than two years after its composition, and at least sixteen months after Macready received the Yale MS. Joseph W. Reed, Jr.'s article "Browning and Macready: The Final Quarrel," *PMLA* (1960): 597–603, contains some interesting speculations on the revisions made by B and Macready in the Yale MS. Since the Yale MS has a collateral rather than an ancestral relationship in the subsequent revisions of the text of *A Blot in the 'Scutcheon,* it is considered secondary rather than primary material. Variants obtained from a collation of the printed text and the Yale MS, including Macready's revisions, will appear as a supplement in Volume XIII of this edition. Variant readings in the Yale

MS which contribute to an elucidation of B's conception of the play will appear as annotations in this volume.

The Text

The first edition was published by Edward Moxon on the day of its presentation at Drury Lane, 11 February 1843. Printed in the form of a pamphlet of sixteen pages (eight unsigned leaves, 24.1 x 15.8 cm.) in a pale yellow wrapper, it was paid for by B's father at a cost of approximately £ 16, and sold for 1s per copy. The text consisted of a title page (p. 1), dramatis personae (p. 2) and the text (3–16). The text was printed in double columns, with running titles BELLS AND POMEGRANATES (verso) and A BLOT IN THE 'SCUTCHEON (recto). Page sixteen carries the imprint LONDON:/BRADBURY AND EVANS, PRINTERS, WHITEFRIARS. The play was included in the 1849 collected edition and all collected editions thereafter. (For the series title "Bells and Pomegranates," see Volume III, p. 343.) When in 1846 Moxon bound all the numbers of *Bells and Pomegranates* in one volume, he printed additional copies of *A Blot in the 'Scutcheon* with the words "Second Edition" printed above the publisher's imprint on the front wrapper and title page. It is a reimpression rather than a genuine second edition. The variant readings in this reimpression are all grammatical or stylistic changes and appear to be the kind that B made himself. These textual changes are recorded as variants in this volume under the designation 1843a.

Productions

A Blot in the 'Scutcheon initially was performed at Drury Lane under Macready's direction on 11, 13 and 15 February 1843. Playing to a capacity audience on the 11th, with receipts of £ 176, its run was terminated by lack of patronage, the receipts for the third performance having dwindled to £ 88. Samuel Phelps revived *A Blot in the 'Scutcheon* twice during his management of Sadler's Wells Theatre in Islington, performing it six times in late December and early November 1848, and twice in February 1849. Lawrence Barrett presented it in Washington, D.C. in 1884. The Browning Society of London revived it at St. George's Hall on 2 May 1885, and again at the Olympic Theatre on 15 May 1888, with Alma Murray acting the part of Mildred. In 1893 it was performed in Manchester. It opened at the Hudson Theatre, New York, with Mrs. Sarah LeMoyne's company in 1905. It was produced professionally at Ravinia Park, Illinois in 1907.

Theatre Royal] In Holborn, London, Drury Lane (originally a riding yard) was built by Thomas Killigrew under a Letter-Patent granted by Charles II in 1662 to Sir William Davenant, and opened on 7 May 1663. Partially destroyed by fire in 1674, it was rebuilt under the design of Sir Christopher Wren. David Garrick, Richard Brinsley Sheridan and John

Philip Kemble managed it at different times during the eighteenth century. Completely destroyed by fire in 1809, it was rebuilt under the design of Wyatt in 1812. In 1814 it was taken over by a committee including Lord Byron. Macready managed it from 1841–1843. It remains today as London's most famous and oldest surviving theatre.

Persons] Of the actors listed in the 1843 edition, the following achieved distinction on the stage:

Mr. Phelps Samuel Phelps (1804–1878), who played Thorold Tresham, first appeared in London in 1837 at the Haymarket under B. N. Webster. Engaged by Macready in late 1837, Phelps played Othello to Macready's Iago at Covent Garden. He had a considerable reputation as a tragedian. When the Theatres Act of 1843 licensed all theatres in London, he became manager of Sadler's Wells, where until his retirement in 1862 he produced 34 of Shakespeare's plays, acting the principal role in almost all of them. At Sadler's Wells he produced *A Blot in the 'Scutcheon* in 1848 and 1849. An advocate of traditional, respectable drama, he retired from the stage on 31 March 1878.

Miss Helen Faucit Helena Saville Faucit (1817–1898), the famous actress who played Mildred Tresham, also appeared as Lady Carlyle in *Strafford* (1837), and as Colombe in *Colombe's Birthday* (1853). Her friendship with B extended for more than fifty years, and after his demise she erected a plaque in his honor in Llanlysilio Church, Wales. Often playing opposite Macready and Phelps, she was best known for roles in Shakespeare's tragedies. She married Theodore Martin in 1851, and became known in society as Lady Martin when her husband was knighted in 1880. She authored one book, *On Some of Shakespere's Female Characters* (1885).

Mrs. Stirling Fanny Stirling [born Mary Anne Hehl] (1813–1895), who played Guendolen Tresham, first appeared at the East London in 1829 as Fanny Clifton. She married the actor-manager Edward Stirling in 1832, and frequently appeared under his management at the Adelphi. Not considered a good actress of tragedy (Macready said she acted "badly" in the first performance of *A Blot in the 'Scutcheon*), she had a celebrated career in comedy, her best roles being Juliet's Nurse and Mrs. Malaprop. She retired in 1870.

ACT I, scene i

4] *poursuivant* A follower of a herald, a herald being a junior officer at arms, the lowest degree of officer. The official dress of the poursuivant is flowered damask silk. In chivalric times nobles often had heralds and poursuivants attached to their house; the surcoats of the heralds and poursuivants bore the arms of the noble; their duties, however, were not armorial.

13] *bravery* Browning uses the word as described in *Johnson's Dictionary*: "Splendor; magnificence."
23] *congee* Congé; a ceremonious bow made in courtesy or obeisance.
42] *high days* A day of religious celebration; a solemn or feast day.
42] *holidays* A day on which ordinary occupations are suspended. The 1843 and 1849 versions read "holy days."
44] *cast of Swedish hawks* In falconry the number of hawks released together at one time—two. Continental hawks were considered to be superior to English hawks.
45] *a leash of greyhounds* Originally in sporting, a set of three held in line by a single leash or thong.
46] *logman* As in *Johnson's Dictionary*: "One whose business is to carry logs."
46] *supporter* In the heraldic sense; supporters are figures emblazoned on each side of the shield as if to support it; usually two in number, but single supporters are found occasionally. Granted only to the nobility or Knights of the Grand Cross.
59] *proper* Browning uses the word as described in *Johnson's Dictionary*: "Tall; lusty; handsome with bulk. A low word."
72] *rosette* An ornament comprised of a bunch or knot of ribbons or leather strips concentrically arranged to resemble a rose. Worn as a decoration or badge of office.
92] *such square by rule* As in the phrase "by the square," referring to a square rule, an implement or tool for determining or measuring right angles.
93] *no herald more* In the heraldic sense; an officer whose duties included organizing processions, making proclamations, ordering cavalcades and ceremonies.

ACT I, scene ii

16] *he's the king's* An idiom for "in the service of the king"—in the army.
59] *thicks* Archaic for thickets.
60] *eyass* Or eyas; in falconry an eyas is a hawk taken from the nest (eyrie) when fully fledged, but as yet flightless, for the purpose of training. An eyas is thought to be slightly inferior to a mature hawk caught for training.
125] *Here's Thorold. Tell him so!* See I, ii, 133n.
128] *The mercy stroke* A coup de grâce.
130] *blazon* [ME] Properly, a concise and complete verbal description of a coat of arms according to the formula invented by Gerard Legh in the sixteenth century; this system is in use today. Tresham here loosely employs the term blazon to refer to a coat of arms.
133] *Mildred is fourteen* Much has been written about the influence of Shakespeare's *Romeo and Juliet* and *Much Ado About Nothing* on Brown-

ing's *A Blot in the 'Scutcheon.* See especially G.R. Elliott's "Shakespeare's Significance for Browning," *Anglia* 32 (1909): 134–137. In the Yale MS Macready substituted "eighteen" for "fourteen."

ACT I, scene iii

25] *the Conqueror* William I, The Conqueror (c. 1028–1087), Duke of Normandy and King of England, also surnamed "the Bastard," son of Duke Robert I (d. 1035) of Normandy and his mistress Arlette, daughter of a Falaise tanner. In 1066 his illegitimate cousin, Edward the Confessor, King of England from 1042–1066, died childless, after having earlier named William his heir and having appointed a Norman as Archbishop of Canterbury to facilitate William's succession. In absence of written documents, however, Harold II succeeded Edward on the throne, and William became king only after defeating Harold's army near Hastings. William was crowned King of England in Westminster Abbey on Christmas Day, 1066.

27] *bow-hand or arrow-hand's* For a right-handed person, the left hand holds the bow while the right hand sets the arrow, and vice versa for a left-handed person.

46] *paladins* Latin palā-tīn-us; of or belonging to the palace; a palatine. In modern versions of the romances of Charlemagne, one of the Twelve Peers or famous warriors of the Court; sometimes transferred to signify a knight of Arthur's Round Table. Figuratively, a knightly hero, a renowned champion.

67–68] *to that fair dame/Whose garter slipped down at the famous dance* According to popular legends the Countess of Salisbury is said to have been in love with King Edward III (1312–1377). During a dance at the Court she is supposed to have dropped her garter. When some of the courtiers joked about it, Edward picked it up, put it on his knee, admonishing the courtiers with the words "Honi Soit qui Mal Y Pense" (Dishonor to him who thinks evil of it). When Edward instituted the Knights of the Garter (c. 1347), fulfilling a promise made in 1344 to establish a Round Table at Windsor Castle after the fashion of King Arthur, he used the same phrase as the motto for an incentive for chivalry among his knights. The garter is considered the principal ensign of the order; it is worn on the left leg below the knee. Accounts of this incident are found in Polydore Vergil, Jean Froissart, Holinshed and others.

90–91] The Yale MS contains the following lines omitted from the printed text: "her—/That to soothe of her caprices—one—her least whim, pettiest fancy,/She might ravage me unwitting as she'd tear to shreads a pansy/I"

91–92] The rendering of these lines in the Yale MS is: "I may enter at her portal, seek that woman's inmost bower,/Calmly breathe my passion, clasping fearlessly her hand, the flower."

92] *slouched hat* A hat of soft or unstiffened felt, or some similar material, with a broad brim which hangs down over the face.

151–152] *some cursed fount/That should spirt water, and spouts blood* Shakespeare's *Julius Caesar,* II, ii, 75–79:

> Calpurnia here, my wife stays me at home.
> She dreamt tonight she saw my statue,
> Which like a fountain with a hundred spouts
> Did run pure blood, and many lusty Romans
> Came smiling and did bathe their hands in it.

171–172] *pluck it off/And cast it from me!* Matthew 5: 27–30.
187] *diamond scales* Sensitive scales, like those employed in weighing expensive stones.
217] *Crest* Literally the summit, the crest is the highest part among the charges in a coat of arms. Worn upon the helmet, encircled by a coronet or silken wreath, the crest may also be borne upon either the Chapeau or cap of estate. In pre-Tudor times the crest was restricted to the greater nobles, but later became regarded as a necessary adjunct to arms and was allowed freely. Women, with the exception of the sovereign, have no crest.
217] *fight-mark* A charge or favor worn in a warrior's crest, given as a mark of valor in battle. This form of the term is B's and not an official heraldic designation. A mark in heraldry is a small charge added to a coat of arms for distinction.
217] *device* [ME] An achievement of arms (i.e., the full armorial display including exterior design), or a single facet of arms; the armorial composition designed for a petitioner by a herald or poursuivant; properly called a charge. A device is often a motto, i.e. a word or phrase inserted in a scroll (the riband below the escutcheon), which most frequently alludes to the name of the bearer, sometimes a war cry. Mottoes are not granted by the Herald's College.
236] *Oh, I'll believe him every word* See I, ii, 133n.
240–241] The Yale MS contains the following lines omitted from the printed text: "beyond/Well, I have made him happy. Let me sleep—/No mother—God forgot me—and I fell./Surely"

ACT II

43] *pale* A stake, a fence made of stakes driven into the earth, or of perpendicular bars or strips attached to horizontal rails supported by posts; an area enclosed by a fence. In heraldry, a stripe in an escutcheon.
73] *hind* A servant; from "hineman"; Browning uses the word as described in *Johnson's Dictionary*: "[hine, *Saxon*] A servant; [hineman, *Saxon*] A peasant; a boor; a mean rustic."
102] *Avert, oh God, only this woe from me!* See Matthew 26: 39.
113] *'scutcheon* Escutcheon; in heraldry a term sometimes employed to express the entire coat of arms, sometimes only the field (i.e. the whole

surface of the shield or escutcheon, which is the ground upon which tinctures, furs, ordinaries and charges are presented), upon which the arms are emblazoned.

114] *Arthur's time* Presumably Arthur was an historical person, though his name probably was not Arthur, and more doubtful that he was a king. He may have been a Welsh or Roman military leader of the Celts in Wales against the Germanic invaders of the fifth century. There is no mention of Arthur in contemporary records of the Germanic invasions, but a Roman citizen, Gildas, who lived in Wales, states in his *De excido et conquesta Britanniae* (c.547) that at the battle of Mt. Badon (c.500) a valiant Roman, Ambrosius Aurelianus led the Britons in defeating the Saxons. Later accounts connect Arthur with this battle. The earliest extant reference to Arthur is in a Welsh poem *Y Gododdin* (c.600; edited in Welsh as *Canu Aneurin*), a lament for Briton warriors killed in battle. Of one of the warriors it is said that "he gutted black ravens on the rampart of the fort, though he was not Arthur." The Welsh historian Nennius in his *Historia Britonum* (c.800) records twelve victories of the Britons, the final one being Mt. Badon, in which he explicitly names Arthur, calling him a "dux bellorum." In the *Annales Cambriae* (c.955) there are two references to Arthur; one under the date 516 mentions the battle of Mt. Badon where Arthur wore a cross on his shield; the other reference is to the battle of Camlan (537) where Arthur and Medraut fell. Geoffrey of Monmouth in his *Historia Regum Brittanniae* (c.1136) adds much Arthurian material, stating that his source was an old Welsh book. Later augmentations of Arthurian matter include Wace's *Roman de Brut* (c.1154), the romances of Chrétien de Troyes (c.1300), and Layamon's *Brut* (c.1205). The Arthurian tradition reached its culmination in the Middle Ages with Malory's *Le Morte D'arthur* (printed 1485). Its fullest expression in the nineteenth century is Tennyson's *Idylls of the King*.

124] *that old Italian book* Ovid's *Metamorphoses* See II, 177n.

150–152] *That's Latin surely . . . "Love conquers all things"* Ovid, *Metamorphoses,* V, 365–368: "O son, both arms and hands to me, and source of all my power, take now those shafts, Cupid, with which you conquer all, and shoot your swift arrows into the heart of that god to whom the final lot of the triple kingdom fell" (Frank J. Miller, trans., Cambridge: Harvard University Press, 1936).

177] *Ovid* Publius Ovidius Naso (c.43 B.C.–A.D.18), Roman poet of the Augustine Age. Born at Sulmo (modern Sulmona) in the Abruzzi mountains, Italy, in March of 43 B.C., Ovid chronicles the main events of his life in chapter ten of his autobiographical poem *Tristia*. His father, a prominent and wealthy landowner, wanted his son to enter the legal profession, sending him to Rome to study under the two most prominent rhetoricians of his day, Porcius Latro and Arellius Fuscus. His education was completed by travels in Greece, Sicily and Asia Minor with the poet Aemilius Macer. Afterward he held some minor official post in government until he abandoned his legal career for poetry. In A.D. 8 emperor Augustus banished him to Tomis (near modern Constanta) on the Euxine (Black) Sea for unknown reasons. Ovid supplies two: his *Ars amatoria* (Art of Love), and an offense which he admits was an indiscretion, but not a crime. Some feel that his error was complicity in the adultery of the emperor's granddaughter, Julia, exiled at the same time as Ovid. Shortly before his exile he had written the *Metamorphoses*, a collection of Greek, Latin, and Eastern myths, all of which deal with fabulous transformations. A work comprising fifteen books written in the hexameter, totaling almost 12,000 lines, it traces the roughly chronological history of mythology from the transformation of Chaos into the universe of earth, sea and sky to the transformation of Julius Caesar into a star. Even though this final transformation was a tribute to Augustus, the adopted son of Caesar, Ovid was exiled. In *Tristia* (I,7) he states that he burned the *Metamorphoses*, but copies of his friends survived. Neither Augustus, nor his successor Tiberius, ever mitigated his sentence. He died at Tomis in A.D. 17 or 18.

180–181] *the turtles voice,/"Arise and come away!"* Song of Solomon, 2:12–13.

218–219] *Is there a gallant that has night by night/Admittance to your chamber?* See I, ii, 133n.

267] *Bacchant's mien* Roman Bacchae or Bacchantes, from the Greek maenads, the female followers of Dionysius (Roman Bacchus), god of wine and fertility. The tradition of the maenads arose from those who followed Dionysius when he traveled the earth in a frenzy of madness inspired by Hera. The maenads celebrated the festivals of Dionysius, at which they wore the nebris (fawnskin), chewed laurel leaves, and carried the ivy twined thyrsus with a pine cone tip. Their faces and arms were sometimes painted or tattooed as a disguise during their orgies in the mountains when they became the lovers of Pan. In a Dionysiac frenzy they assisted Agave in tearing her son Pentheus apart because he had doubted the divinity of Dionysius. At the instigation of Dionysius, they murdered their husbands, and then tore Orpheus to pieces, throwing his head into the Hebrus River. Dionysius saved them from the Erinyes by transforming them into oak trees.

303] *losels* In the etymological sense "one who is lost," a son of perdition. Browning uses the word as described in *Johnson's Dictionary*: "A scoundrel; a sorry worthless fellow."

315] *I curse her to her face* In the Yale MS Macready substituted "I cast her out from me."

352] *badge* A cognizance in heraldry; an adjunct to arms which may be displayed alone or in association with arms, but not an integral part of them, and subject of a grant by the king of arms. A badge, unlike the crest, is not worn upon a wreath of colors or other crest bearing matter. Originally the badge was used for designating property, and was also worn by the liveried dependents in the feudal forces and retinues. Since the sixteenth century, the badge is often loosely equated with the crest.There are three main types of badges: the breast badge, the simple charge, and the plant badge.

ACT III, scene i

23] *surcoat* A loose garment, commonly of rich material, worn over the armor of a knight, hence the designation coat armor. The coat usually was emblazoned with the armorial bearings of the wearer.
163] *Lowers me down the bloody slope to death* See Tennyson's "Dream of Fair Women": "Lower'd softly with a threefold cord of love/Down to a silent grave."
171] *And I tied down with grave clothes and the worm* See, I,ii, 133n.
221] *lets loose a Fury* Roman Furiae or Dirae, from the Greek Erinye: Female divinities, avengers of injustices, who live in Erelius and are older than Zeus and the Olympians. According to Hesiod they are daughters of Gaea, sprung from the blood of Uranus when he was mutilated by his son Cronus. In Aeschylus they are the daughters of the Night; in Sophocles of Darkness and Earth. Euripides spoke of them as three in number. The Erinyes are monstrous hags, with winged black bodies and dog heads from which serpents stream. They carry bronze scourges to punish offenders. Though not vindictive, the Erinyes are impersonal and impartial in their judgments, taking no account of mitigating circumstances in crimes or offenses that must be avenged to satisfy the spirits of the dead who have called on them for vengeance. Because Orestes slew his mother he is pursued by the Erinyes, even though his act was necessary to avenge his father. Later the number of Erinyes was reduced to three: Alecto, Megaera and Tisiphone. Also called the Eumenides, "the Kindly Ones," a name attributed to them by Orestes.

ACT III, scene ii

139] *masque* Originally a band of masked persons of the same sex, who, with torchbearers, would arrive at a social affair and dance and play dice with the guests. These disguisings or mummings were of a folk nature, but when adopted by the aristocracy they evolved into highly elaborate and costly spectacles which evolved into magnificent entertainments. In the masque the dramatic business was performed by professionals, while the masquers remained silent. Henry VII is said to have introduced the masque into England in 1512 on Twelfth Night, when he and eleven others disguised as Italian dominoes arrived at the banquet hall and invited the women to dance and talk with them. The masque reached its apotheosis in the reigns of James I and Charles I. In 1609 Ben Jonson introduced the antimasque in the *Masque of Queens*. Originally, the masque was little more than spectacle.

150] *gules* In heraldry, red; one of the seven colors used in painting or emblazoning a coat of arms. Its origin is French.
153] *Vengeance is God's, not man's* Romans 12: 19–20; On a blank sheet in the Yale MS, Macready substituted the following: "Within a convent's shade in stranger lands/Penance and Prayer shall wear my life away." Under these lines B wrote: "The above in Macready's handwriting, was the substitution for [what] he found written: this to avoid giving the piece the dignity of a Tragedy, and Mr. Phelps the distinction of playing in one! R. B. Oct. 20. '84."

Editorial Notes

COLOMBE'S BIRTHDAY

Emendations to the Text

The following emendations have been made in the 1889 text:
I, 175: B declared to Dr. Rolfe that the 1868 reading *crowding* was a misprint for *crowning* (P-C), of the 1844–1863 texts, but apparently failed to make the change in 1888. The 1844–1863 reading has been restored.
I, 208: the 1888 *path* has been restored to the 1844–1868 reading *path,* as syntactically superior.
I, 342: *mass-priest* is printed with the hyphen in 1844. In 1849, 1863, 1868, 1888, and 1889 *mass-* comes at the end of line so that one cannot tell how B intended it to be printed after 1844 from textual evidence. Since B usually preserves the hyphen, the 1844 reading is restored.
II, 198: The 1849–1868 reading *you, let* has been restored. In 1888–1889 the comma was apparently broken off.
III, 24: The two points (*once* . .) is an apparent typographical error in the 1888 printing. All previous editions read *once* . . . . The earlier reading is restored.
III, 80: The 1844–1868 reading *degree*—has been restored. The omission of the dash damages the sense.
IV, 210: The original reading *her:* has been restored, since the grammatical relationship of *fortune* (l. 210), *aim* (l. 211), and *prize* (l. 214) appear to require it.
V, 218: 1844–1868 reading *gifts,* has been restored as syntactically required.

Composition

Colombe's Birthday is the last work B wrote explicitly for the stage. Probably it was begun soon after February 11, 1843 (when B's working relations with Macready ended). One first hears of it in B's letter of May 15, 1843 to Domett. The play was completed between that day and March 9,

1844, when B read the text to the London actor-manager Charles Kean (who had advanced a sum to B for a new play) and to Kean's "charming wife" (for whom the part of Colombe undoubtedly was intended). Unfortunately Kean wanted to keep it "till 'Easter next year'—and unpublished all the time," (Hood *Ltrs*, pp. 9–10) and B, anxious to have something in print soon, could not wait; the play was dispatched at once to the publisher Edward Moxon of Dover Street in London. On or about April 20, 1844—when Moxon announced it as "just published"—a yellow paper-covered pamphlet of twenty pages appeared under the title: *Bells and Pomegranates. No. VI.—Colombe's Birthday. A Play, In Five Acts.* The Keans never acted the play. B had a chance to revise the text before its first presentation, and insisted that Helena Saville Faucit follow the corrections as they appear in the 1849 edition (in *Poems by Robert Browning*) as they were important to the sense. Miss Faucit, taking the part of Colombe, produced *Colombe's Birthday* at the Haymarket Theatre in London in April, 1853. After seven performances, she took her production to Manchester. The play was staged at Boston on February 16, 1854. The London Browning Society revived it on November 19, 1885, at St. George's Hall in London, with Alma Murray as Colombe.

The Manuscript

The MS is missing. This much is known about it. It has been described as a folio MS written upon thirty sheets of blue foolscap paper, on one side only, in B's neat hand. After Edward Moxon (presumably in 1844) returned the MS B's father had it bound. The book auctioneers of Leicester Square, Messrs. Puttick and Simpson, sold the MS to Bertram Dobell. In May or June, 1877, Dobell sold it to H. Buxton Forman. Next, the MS became Item 127 in the March 15, 1920 sale of the Forman papers by Anderson Galleries of New York City. An American dealer bought it. In 1933 Professor T. L. Hood indicated that the "present possessor" was "unwilling to disclose his identity" (Hood *Ltrs*, p. 364n.). Variant readings from the MS may one day be listed in an appendix to this edition.

Sources

B in the play departs freely from historical facts, but it is clear that he knew about the Contest of the Jülich Succession (of 1609–1614), which had been brought about by the extinction of the ducal house of Cleves. See *Persons*] *Colombe of Ravestein, Duchess of Juliers and Cleves* n. He may have consulted a history of the Duchy of Jülich such as Carl Friedrich von Wiebeking's *Beiträge zur Kurpfälzischen Staatengeschichte, vorzüglich in Rücksicht auf das Herzogthum Jülich and Berg* (Heidelberg, 1773), or, perhaps more likely, one of the later French accounts which uses Wiebeking. (The Succession Contest was important enough to be a contributing cause of the Thirty Years War of 1618–1648). Critics point out that Colombe is blithely unaware of Rhenish and European politics and that the play is essentially romantic and domestic. But many details in the text show that B knew something about—and altered for his own use—the power struggle that developed after March 25, 1609. The play's romantic elements seem to owe in part to the history of Marianne Pajot, the Duke of Lorraine, and the Marquis de Lassay (Armand Léon de Madaillan de Lesparre), which is recounted in de Lassay's *Recueil de differentes choses* (Lausanne, 1756), 1: 5–19. The importance of the latter work to B is treated in W. C. DeVane's *Browning's Parleyings: The Autobiography of a Mind* (New Haven, 1927 and 1964), pp. 50–91.

Epigraph

B takes three lines from the following poem, Sir John Hanmer's "Written After Reading Horace Walpole's Account of Castle Henningham," in *Fra Cipollo, and Other Poems* (London: Edward Moxon, 1839), p. 95:

> Dark looks the Jew at the noble's hall
> Blithely the peasant walks o'er the lea,
> He knows nothing of towers that fall
> Rent by the ivy so fair to see.
> Joy to the violet smelling so sweet
> Under the hedges his steps to greet.
>
> Ivy and Violet what do ye here,
> With blossom and shoot in the warm spring weather?
> Hiding the arms of Monchenci and Vere
> On the lonely gate ye are met together.
> 'Tis an old tale of the days gone by
> With the wind in the nettles for symphony.

Since ll. 7–9, which B quotes, refer to a sequence of episodes which link the historic names "Munchensi," "Vere," and "Valence" (the latter also being the name of B's hero), we draw attention to the following background. Castle Hedingham in Essex was a massive fortress completed about the time of the Norman Conquest. Its ruins remain. (Hanmer—who more than once took liberties with spelling—reflects in the poem's title the older spelling, "Heueningham in Esix," or Paston's "Henyngh'm" in a letter of c.1469.) It was the seat of the old and famous de Veres, Earls of Oxford since the twelfth century. Later de Veres became distinguished as soldiers ("the fighting Veres"), diplomats, and poets, and perhaps less often, as boisterous ne'er-do-wells. However, Hanmer's "towers that fall" (l. 3) refers to another castle besides the one at Hedingham. In 1289, fighting under Edmund, Earl of Cornwall, the rich and powerful baronial leader William de Munchensi was killed at the siege of Dyryslwyan in Wales by the fall of a wall which had been undermined. In the next twenty-five years his lands passed from the de Munchensis to the de Veres to the de Valences. The baron's daughter married Hugh de Vere (son of Robert de Vere, then Earl of Oxford). At her death without children in 1314, de Munchensi's old estate was inherited by Aymer de Valence, then Earl of Pembroke. De Valence had succeeded to his earldom in 1296. He saw military service in Scotland and Flanders, and acted as emissary to the pope. He was captured and held for ransom as a prisoner in Germany, for a time, on his way home from a mission to Rome in 1316. He died in 1324. Sir John Hanmer (1809–1881), liberal-minded M.P. over a span of forty years and author of poems on Italian and historical subjects, was a friend of B's. B conceived a new idea for his own poem, "The Flight of the Duchess," while staying at Hanmer's estate, Bettisfield Park in Flintshire in NE Wales, in September 1842. For T. S. Eliot's later use of the names "Ivy," "Violet," and "Monchensey," evidently adapted from B's epigraph for another play about a paradoxical birthday, *The Family Reunion*, see *Times Literary Supplement*, (12 December 1952), p. 819.

Dedication

Barry Cornwall Nom de plume (and casual anagram of the name) of Bryan Waller Procter (1787–1874), solicitor, poet, and friend of B's who led a jovial life in London, helping materially and encouraging many literary men. His tragedy *Mirandola* (aided by Charles Kemble as Procter's Guido) ran for sixteen nights at Covent Garden in 1821. In 1832, he was made a metropolitan commissioner in lunacy, "which seems to have been thought an eminently suitable appointment for a poet," comments Richard Garnett. B seems to have met him through John Forster in 1836. Procter wrote a verse epistle to B, and edited a selection of B's poetry. B continued in old age to attend the lively, gossipy "afternoons" of Procter's widow Anne, who had met John Keats and knew writers to achieve fame in the twentieth century.

Persons

Colombe of Ravestein, Duchess of Juliers and Cleves Colombe is not known to have an exact historical counterpart, but her ducal title, time ("16—"), locale, and predicament show that B played upon details in the Rhenish Contest (discussed below) for her dramatic situation. In French *colombe* means pigeon or dove (from Latin *columba*, "dove"), traditional symbol of gentleness and peace. Ravestein or Ravenstein is the name of a castle and its small town (population 4,124 in 1952) in the province of N Brabant in E Netherlands. Ravenstein figured in the Jülich Succession settlement of 1614, at which time it was in the mainly Flemish-speaking Duchy of Brabant which had been ruled for about two-hundred years by dukes of Burgundy. Juliers (in French *Juliers*; in German *Jülich*) and Cleves (French *Clèves*; German *Cleve* or *Kleve*), though almost totally destroyed by artillery and air attacks in 1944–1945, survive as towns in the *Land* or province of N Rhine-Westphalia, in W Germany. Jülich is on the Roer River about sixteen mi. NE of Aachen. It is said to have been founded by Julius Caesar, and to be the "Juliacum" of Roman days (mentioned in the *Antonini Itinerarium*). Kleve is situated on the old Spoy Canal, near the Rhine, about sixty-six miles W of Münster; it was the northern anchorage of the German Westwall (Siegfried Line) in World War II. Both Jülich and Cleves at about A.D. 1000 were Rhenish feudal strongholds, dominating large stretches of land around them. The estate of Cleves passed from the counts of Teisterbant, d'Anton, and La Mark or La Marck, until in the fifteenth century it was elevated to a duchy. At this time it consisted of a capital town with its castle (the Schwanenberg, or Swan's Castle, associated with the Lohengrin legend), and of about 850 sq. mi. of land on both banks of the lower Rhine. In 1521, the nearby southerly duchies of Jülich (W of the Rhine) and Berg (E of the Rhine) passed by marriage into control of the house of Cleves. However, on March 25, 1609 John William, Duke of Cleves, died childless. Charles V, Emperor of the Germans (the Holy Roman Emperor) had decreed in 1546 that in the absence of a male heir in the Rhenish ducal families, the right of inheritance might pass to a legitimate female one. Which of John William's three surviving sisters (or their descendants) had the best claim to his domain? This question might not have been difficult to settle in theory. In practice, the Holy Roman Emperor Rudolf II in 1609 lacked power to enforce political decisions in the German states which he nominally controlled. Some six eager competitors were drawn into the so-called Contest of the Jülich Succession. At stake were three duchies (Cleves, Jülich, and Berg) and two counties (Ravensberg and La Marck), altogether of strategic importance for their wealth, population, and situation in the delta of the Rhine at the entrance to Holland. Anna, the daughter of John William's eldest sister, had married the Elector of Brandenburg, John Sigismund; two other sisters, Anna and Madeline, had married powerful counts. King Henry IV of France interfered (until he was murdered in May 1610); Spanish troops were summoned by the Emperor from Holland; the duchies were invested and invaded; major powers of Europe aligned themselves in a tense and bitter rivalry during the next five years; see I, 45n. Partly through the intervention of England, a rather tentative pact was concluded at Xanten on November 12, 1614, according to which the administration of the duchies and counties was divided up. Wolfgang William of Neuburg received the Duchy of Cleves, as well as La Marck, Ravensberg, and Ravenstein. John Sigismund the Elector, husband of John William's niece Anna, received the duchies of Berg and Jülich. (But negotiations were to recommence after the end of the War of 1618–1648, with its own complicating territorial, dynastic, and religious issues.) P-C state that the plot of *Colombe's Birthday* is based on B's "supposition" that John William, Duke of Cleves, had shrewdly concealed a daughter in order "to shield her better and secure her reign." (There is no evidence that B believed that this happened in fact.) Certainly no daughter ever came forth. John William was senile, if not insane for some years before he died; and it is unlikely that he outwitted his three sisters and the monarchs of Europe after 1600 in any matter. In short, Colombe's situation relates to the real one of 1609–1614, tangentially and lightly. In history: a younger female relative—Anna—of the last Duke of Cleves did inherit the Duchy of Jülich in 1614; for five years there had been more than one "claimant"; the Pope and the Holy Roman Emperor interested themselves in the duchy's administration; and the question of who would control Jülich was tense and inflammatory. An earlier Anne of the Rhenish ducal families had entered English history. Anne of Cleves (1515–1557) became the fourth wife of King Henry VIII. Her father was a duke of Cleves, and one of her grandfathers, a duke of Jülich.

Sabyne, Adolf Sabina in Latin means "a Sabine woman" or one belonging to the Sabine race of ancient Italy; Sabina—in various spellings—as a Christian name honors the Roman matron St. Sabina, martyred under Hadrian in the second century. Adolf is the usual German form of the Old German *Athalwolf* from *athal*, noble and *wolfa*, "a wolf."

Guibert, Gaucelme, Maufroy, Clugnet Names with medieval suggestions. The French *Guibert* (like Gilbert) probably was formed from the popular medieval name *Gisilbert* (Old German *gisil*, "pledge" and *berhta*, "bright"). Gaucelme may relate to *Gauvain*, the name of the character who appears in French versions of the Arthurian cycle (usually in English: Gawayne). Gaucelm was the name of a Catharist Bishop of Toulouse. Maufroy is probably related to the Old German *frithu*, "peace," as in the Old French name *Geoffroi*; some French names beginning with "Mau" were formed from the French *Mauger* (from Old German *Malgar* from *malvjan*, "to grind" and *ger*, "spear"). Clugnet is French in spelling, but compare the German word *Klügler*, "wiseacre, would-be wit."

Valence, advocate of Cleves Advocate is a technical title, in districts retaining Roman law, for a professional pleader in a court of justice. The names Valence and Valentine alike derive from Latin *valens*, "strong, healthy." St. Valentine was the third-century Roman martyr whose feast day (February 14th) so nearly coincided with the festival of Juno Februata that the custom of drawing lots for lovers was transferred from the pagan to the Christian festival. Cf. also *valour* and the French *valeur*, "value, worth." For the possibility that B had Aymer de Valence in mind, see *Epigraph* n.

Prince Berthold, claimant of the Duchy A fictitious person, though B may have drawn upon the fact that one Jülich claimant offered a son in marriage to further his own interest; see *Colombe of Ravestein, Duchess of Juliers and Cleves* n. During the Contest of 1609–1614 the Count Palatine of Neuburg offered his son to the daughter of John Sigismund of Brandenburg (who later acquired the Duchy of Jülich) but the offer was rejected. The name of B's Prince derives from the Old German *berhta*, "bright" and *hildi*, "battle."

Melchior The name is Hebrew for "King of Light." Melchior (with Balthazar and Caspar) was one of the three kings whom medieval legend transformed into the Eastern wise men who visited Bethlehem. Cf. also the French *melchior*, "nickel silver."
Time, 16— The play relates fancifully and freely to Rhenish events of 1609–1614.

ACT I

Act I "You speak of *Colombe*. . . .all I heard of proposed adapting was that the theatres want the five to be made *three* acts. I bade them do so, by all means," B wrote John Forster on April 12, 1853, in the month of this play's first stage presentation. See *New Letters of Robert Browning*, ed. William Clyde DeVane and Kenneth Leslie Knickerbocker (New Haven, 1950), p. 61.
3–11] *the late Duke's true heiress. . .disclosed his child's retreat* In history the last Duke of Cleves in the seventeenth century had sisters, a niece, but no daughter; see *Persons* nn.
14–16] *Castle Ravestein. . .On the Meuse' quiet bank* The river Meuse rises in NE France and flows usually N for about five hundred mi. through Belgium and, in Holland, past the small town and medieval castle of Ravenstein to the N Sea. It forms a common delta with the Rhine.
19] *buckle's constant to his cap* Buckle is the boss or convex projection in the center of a shield or buckler. "He supports (or fights for) the party of his emblems or colors."
44] *the Pope* Pope Paul V in 1609 was interested in which party would inherit the duchies of Jülich, Cleves, and Berg. Throughout central Europe tensions were keen between Catholics and Protestants, who were about evenly matched in the three Rhenish duchies. But it is B's invention that a northern claimant (Berthold in the play) was a nephew to the Pope (in history, of the Borghese, a noble Roman family), as B's Melchior says at III, 54.
45] *The Emperor, the Kings of Spain and France* In B's play all three support one Juliers or Jülich claimant; in history they were divided. The clever but indolent and unpopular Rudolf II (1552–1612), Holy Roman Emperor from October 1576, opposed the claims of both Brandenburg and Neuburg from 1609 to 1611 and ordered Spanish and imperial troops to seize the contested Rhenish duchies. But his own rule collapsed in these years. By 1611 his brother Matthias had virtually succeeded him. Philip III (1578–1621), King of Spain from 1598 to 1621, had concluded a truce with the Dutch in 1609 and so was free to move troops from the Lowlands into the duchies at the imperial command; but his support of the Emperor was ineffectual. King Henry IV of France (1553–1610) supported both Brandenburg and Neuburg (who were awarded the duchies at last); it is thought that if Henry IV had not been assassinated in May 1610, he almost certainly

would have declared war on the Emperor. As it was, with the Duchy of Jülich's fate temporarily settled in 1614, a long and general European war was delayed until 1618.

72] *guilder* Probably not the gold, but the silver Dutch and Rhenish gulden, a coin worth about 3s. 6d. in English currency in 1617.

84] *Salic law* A collection of ancient customs codified into law in the early Middle Ages by the Salian Franks, a Germanic people, and probably not in force much later than the 11th century. Mainly the Law was a penal code. But it contained a chapter on private property which forbade daughters from inheriting land; and this was sometimes construed to exclude them from thrones.

132] *gratulation* Congratulation.

163] *pill and poll* To ruin by excessive taxation. Literally, to make bare of hair and skin.

218] *Pascal. . .Fabian* The guards have names used as Christian ones as early as medieval times; the first comes from *Pask,* Easter; the second honors the third-century Pope Fabian, venerated as a saint.

286] *Saint Paul* Ironically invoked in a narrow context of civic law or politics. The life and theology of Paul the Apostle, martyred about A.D. 62, display his zeal in studying and propagating what he believed to be the Law of God.

342] *sursum corda* The versicle meaning "Lift up your hearts" which is uttered by the priest as he prepares to consecrate bread and wine in the Mass or Communion.

353] *marcasite* Ornament made of crystallized iron pyrites which have a metallic luster. The natural color of pyrite itself (or "fool's gold") is pale brass-yellow.

ACT II

42] *Tristan* The name is very romantic and medieval. Tristan or Tristram, one of the most famous heroes of medieval legend, was supreme in the knightly arts from fencing and horsemanship to music, chess, and linguistics. He usually dies from a poisoned arrow, after which a sapling springs from his grave to reach the nearby one of Queen Iseult of Ireland whom he loved.

43] *Romuald* The name may be a form of the Norse name *Rögnvaldr* (to which Ronald and Reynold are related), but compare *Roâld* or *Rual,* in medieval legend the seneschal who reared Tristan after Tristan's father died in battle.

105] *unenjoyingly* Without gusto. (B forms the word from *unenjoying,* a word in use since the seventeenth century.)

122] *insuppressive* Incapable of suppression.

161] *circlet* Ducal crown.

207] *A lion crests him for a cognizance* The heraldic crest of the Duchy of

Jülich consisted of a black lion against a golden background, the exposed claws and tongue of the lion in red.

256] *carbine's* Firearm longer than the pistol and shorter than the musket. The shortness of the barrel made it popular with seventeenth-century cavalry, though it was still crude.

273] *manufacturers* Archaic, meaning workers, not owners.

290] *Chancellor's* First minister to the ducal crown. The chief minister of state in the Holy Roman Empire carried the title of Imperial Chancellor.

332–33] *a stage behind/At Aix* Jülich is about sixteen mi. from Aachen or Aix-la-Chapelle, which remains the main entry point into Germany from W Europe. With sulphur springs frequented since Roman times, Aix rose to prominence in the late eighth century as the favorite residence and northern capital of Charlemagne (whose tomb is in the cathedral he founded there). Aix was created a free imperial city in the thirteenth century and remained the coronation place of German kings until 1531.

341] *Marshal's* A chief functionary of the court, probably entrusted with the duchy's soldiery.

ACT III

2–4] *Juliers. . .Aix, Cologne, Frankfort,—Milan;—Rome* Political road map for becoming Holy Roman Emperor, the new Charlemagne, and the greatest temporal power on earth c. A.D. 1610. (Ambitious French and German politicians have entertained versions of B's Berthold's dream for a millennium.) Berthold, starting as Prince of Juliers or Jülich, would need nearby Aix (see II, 332–333n) for its associations with Charlemagne and to establish an important Rhenish political base. Cologne or Köln, the great cathedral city on the Rhine (110 mi. E of Brussels) and focal point of Rhenish culture, had been raised to an archdiocese by Charlemagne; its powerful archbishops were princes and electors of the Empire. With their help, Berthold might be crowned Holy Roman Emperor at Frankfurt am Main, one hundred mi. SE of Cologne; Frankfurt or Frankfort had been designated the scene of election (1356) and then of the coronation (1562) of the Emperor; and there, too, Charlemagne had built a residence and convoked assemblies. The Crown of Italy would be conferred at Milan or Milano, capital of Lombardy, three hundred mi. NW of Rome. Rome would be the final step. Charlemagne's control of Europe had been confirmed when Pope Leo III crowned him in A.D. 800; Rome had been under effective papal dominion since 1420; with papal endorsement—as total as that given by Leo III—Emperor Berthold's influence might conceivably extend over all western civilization.

10] *seneschal* Chief steward; entrusted with domestic arrangements in the palace.

44] *redoubtables* The formidable officials of Colombe's court.

54–55] *this Pope, your uncle— / Your cousin, the other King* The relations are B's inventions; see I, 44 and I, 45nn.
63] *oeconomy* Economy.
67] *Treves* Or Trier (anciently Augusta Treverorum), city on the Moselle River seventy-five mi. WSW of Mainz and near the Luxemburg border, in the former Prussian Rhine Province, W Germany. It was a residence of early western emperors. After it was raised to an archiepiscopal see in 815, its archbishops became powerful temporal princes. In the seventeenth century Treves was a major commercial center with a large wine trade, an important university, and a population of 50,000. (One of its old Romanesque cathedral's treasures is the Holy Coat of Treves, supposed to be the seamless coat of Jesus, and an object of pilgrimage.)
70–71] *this tough Platonist. . .Amelius* Third century ascetic, mystic, Neoplatonic philosopher, and pupil of Plotinus (who wrote the primary and classical document of Neoplatonism). Borrowing metaphysics from Plato, ethics from the Stoics, and philosophic method from Aristotle, the idealistic system of Plotinus and Amelius posits a supreme good lying beyond empirical experience and attempts to account for an ideal world and the soul, as well as the phenomenal world. Amelius, to an extent, Christianized the system of his teacher by putting value on the prologue to the Gospel of John.
108] *truncheon* Staff carried as symbol of authority.
175] *wands* Here: rods or switches for flogging.
258] *plash* Standing pool or puddle.
261] *pillared flame* Compare Exodus 13:22 and Numbers 14:14.

ACT IV

1] *this mine* The petty plot of the courtiers (P-C).
154] *Burgraves, Landgraves, Markgraves* German titles. A burgrave (Burgraf) is governor or hereditary ruler of a town or a castle with its adjacent domain. A landgrave (Landgraf) is a count with territorial jurisdiction and several inferior counts under him. Margrave (Margraf) was first given as a title to military governors, and later as an hereditary title to certain imperial princes.
157] *chrysoprase* Semiprecious apple green variety of quartz. But as late as the seventeenth century the term referred to a rarer stone supposed to shine in the dark. Probably it was a gold green variety of beryl. B may well have intended the latter.
181] *Luitpold* A duke honored by a bronze statue. No historic person seems intended by B.

ACT V

2] *Amelius* See III, 70–71n.
14] *King-cousin* B originally wrote "King Philip"; for Philip III, see I, 45n.

48] *King Philip* See I, 45n.
77] *Brabant* Flemish duchy containing Ravenstein (birth place B assigns to Colombe) in the seventeenth century. The area today is in S Netherlands and N Belgium.
117] *Charlemagne* The great lawgiver, founder of monasteries and bishoprics, conqueror of Europe and architect of the first ecclesiastical state, born c. 742 and died January 28, 814; he was crowned in 800 by Pope Leo III as the first Holy Roman Emperor.
236] *requisition's* Written demand that all parties acknowledge sovereign claims.
247] *The Empire has its old success* For the Carlovingian dream of B's Berthold see III, 2–4n. By the seventeenth century the Holy Roman Empire was in decline, though Emperors and would-be emperors thought of emulating the political and administrative success of Charlemagne. By the time that he commanded his son Louis to crown himself at Aix in 813, Charlemagne had so securely established an empire—extending N to Dania (Denmark), S to the Pyrenees and below Rome, and SE far into what became the Hungarian Kingdom—that it remained more or less intact for centuries even though its boundaries altered.
380] *Barnabite* Minor Roman Catholic order; founded at Milan in 1530 and taking its name from a monastery which honors St. Barnabas, who appears in Acts of the Apostles as a prophet, teacher, and co-worker with Paul.

DRAMATIC ROMANCES AND LYRICS

Emendations to the Text

The following emendations have been made to the 1889 text:

The Englishman in Italy, l. 187: A space in the large-paper copy of 1888, in the trade 1888, and in 1889 suggests a comma has dropped out. The 1845–1868 reading of *you, surprise* has been restored.

The Flight of the Duchess, l. 396: The 1845 reading of *fortune,* has been restored. The 1863–1889 reading isolates syntactically the following line.

The Flight of the Duchess, l. 510: The 1845–1849 reading of *tree:*—has been restored. The 1863–1889 reading of *tree.* obscures the dependency of the "When" clause on l. 505.

The Flight of the Duchess, l. 567: The 1855–1868 reading *tribe,* has been restored, since *find, sit,* and *describe* are syntactically parallel.

Saul, l. 173: The 1855–1868 reading *height,* has been restored. The 1888 reading of *heigh* was corrected by B in the Dykes Campbell copy. B entered the missing *t* and comma, but the 1888 added only the *t* but not the comma.

Text and Publication

Dramatic Romances and Lyrics was published on November 6, 1845, as Number VII of *Bells and Pomegranates.* (For an explanation of the series title see *Text* n. to *Bell* No. I, *Pippa Passes.*) Most of the poems appear to have been written in 1844 and 1845, but several cannot be dated with any certainty. As with the *Dramatic Lyrics,* their immediate publication was urged by B's publisher, Moxon, in hopes of extending the poet's audience (Domett, p.36). The twenty-four page pamphlet was dedicated to John Kenyon. The text, like that of the other *Bells,* was printed in double columns of fine type. Of the twenty-one poems listed in the "Contents" six—"The Laboratory," "Claret and Tokay," "Garden Fancies," "The Boy and the Angel," "The Tomb at St. Praxed's," and the first nine sections of "The Flight of the Duchess"—had appeared previously in *Hood's Magazine* between June, 1844 and April, 1845. They were given, despite B's dislike of periodical publication, as an assistance to Hood in his final illness. The whole group underwent considerable rearrangement in subsequent editions. In the collected edition of 1849 B printed the *Dramatic Lyrics* of 1842 together with these poems all under the general title *Dramatic Romances and Lyrics.* Both series retained their original order and no distinction was made between romances and lyrics; however two poems from the series of 1845—"Claret and Tokay" and "Home Thoughts, from Abroad, II" ("Here's to Nelson's memory!")—were dropped temporarily. In the edition of 1863 B "collected and redistributed" his shorter poems under descriptive heads: *Lyrics, Romances, Men, and Women*—drawn from titles of his three previous collections. In the distribution of 1863 "The Lost Leader," " 'How They Brought the Good News from Ghent to Aix,' " "Nationality in Drinks," "Garden Fancies," "The Laboratory," "The Confessional," "The Lost Mistress," "Earth's Immortalities," "Meeting at Night," "Parting at Morning," "Song," "Home Thoughts, from Abroad" ("Home Thoughts, from the Sea") and "Saul," were grouped under *Dramatic Lyrics.* "The Boy and the Angel," "The Glove," "Time's Revenges," "The Italian in England," "The Englishman in Italy," and "The Flight of the Duchess" appeared under *Dramatic Romances.* "Pictor Ignotus" and "The Bishop Orders his Tomb at Saint Praxed's Church" were shifted to *Men, and Women.* This distribution was retained in subsequent editions. (Details of title change, subsequent placement or internal rearrangement of individual poems are given with the variants to each poem.) All of the *Dramatic Romances and Lyrics* came under the scrutiny of EBB, whether in manuscript, proof or *Hood's Magazine, prior* to their publication in November, 1845. Many of her comments appear in the published letters of 1845–1846 (Kintner, RB-EBB, 1969); however some of this material has yet to be made fully available. In May 1913 a collection (56 pp. 8vo) of her critical letters, all relating to *Bells and Pomegranates* Nos. VII and VIII and written to Browning in 1845, was auctioned at Sotheby's. A defective typescript of fourteen of these letters was sent to Kenyon, who published a review and partial transcript of them in his *New Poems* (1914). These notes contain general appraisals or suggested stylistic emendations of twelve of the twenty-one *Dramatic Romances and Lyrics.* However one long critical letter devoted exclusively to "The Flight of the Duchess" was not sent to Kenyon and consequently remained unexamined until Snyder and Palmer summarized it in 1937 (see Edward Snyder and Frederick Palmer, Jr., "New Light on the Brownings," *QR* 269 [July, 1937] :48–63). Most illuminating is their conclusion that of the seventy-three changes EBB proposed for the "Duchess," only four were completely rejected (9 in B's MS are indeterminable). Her criticism must be reckoned, along with B's second Italian journey and his experience of courtship, as a considerable influence on this group of poems; for this reason a few examples of it have been introduced into the following notes to individual poems.

"HOW THEY BROUGHT THE GOOD NEWS FROM GHENT TO AIX" (16—)

Title] *Ghent* A city in NW Belgium, capital of E Flanders. *Aix* Aix-la-Chapelle, French name for what is now Aachen, a city in NW Germany. They are approximately one hundred miles apart by the most direct route. The route described is ten or fifteen miles farther. B had a general familiarity with Flanders, having traveled that way twice (in 1834 and 1838) before the poem was written, but his conception of the relationship of the towns mentioned and the distances between them is not precise.
(*16*—)] Though frequently queried on the subject, B always insisted that the incident of the poem was imaginary. On January 23, 1881 he wrote, "There is no sort of historical foundation about 'Good News from Ghent.' I wrote it under the bulwark of a vessel, off the African Coast, after I had been at sea long enough to appreciate even the fancy of home. It was written in pencil on the fly leaf of Bartoli's *Simboli*, I remember" (*Browning Society's Papers*, Chronological List of Browning's Works, I, 49). It has been suggested (P-C, p. 362) that the general historical setting for the poem might be "The Pacification of Ghent," a pact to oppose the tyranny of Philip II of Spain signed there by Holland, Zealand, and the southern Netherlands. But B's (16—) is then a discrepancy, for the Pacification was signed in 1576.
10] *pique* Pommel and spur have been proposed as meanings for this word. Charles D. Smith (*Explicator* 11 [1953]: Item 42) suggests that B made the noun from the French *piquer*, "to spur," and that adjusting his spur is the action a rider would logically take after tightening the girth and adjusting his stirrups.

14] *Lokeren* A town in Belgium twelve miles NE of Ghent.
15] *Boom* A town seventeen or eighteen miles E of Lokeren.
16] *Düffeld* Also Düffel; about six miles E of Boom and five miles N of Mechlin.
17] *Mecheln* Contraction of Mechelen, Flemish for Mechlin. The church-steeple is presumably the three hundred twenty-four foot tower of the Cathedral of St. Rombold, also noted for its chimes.
19] *Aerschot* The Belgian town of Aarschot, about sixteen miles SE of Düffel.
31] *Hasselt* A town about twenty-five miles E of Aerschot and nearly eighty miles from Ghent by the route taken.
38] *Looz. . .Tongres* These towns are about eight and eleven miles respectively from Hasselt. They are S of the more direct route to Aix (Aachen) which would be through Maastricht. By the route described Aix is nearly forty miles from Hasselt, bringing the total devious distance to nearly one hundred twenty miles.
41] *by Dalhem a dome-spire* Dalhem may be a village close to Aix. The dome-spire probably alludes to the dome of the "Octagon," the palace

chapel built at Aix by Charlemagne and, according to tradition, housing his tomb.

PICTOR IGNOTUS

Title] Literally, "Painter Unknown."
Florence, 15—] The date allows the speaker's career to overlap those of Leonardo (1452–1519), Michelangelo (1475–1564) and Raphael (1483–1520), but whether his conventionalism is the result merely of a self-deceiving timidity or a deliberate refusal of naturalism is open to question. For discussion see Paul F. Jamieson, "Browning's *Pictor Ignotus, Florence 15—*," *Explicator* 11 (1952): Item 8, and DeVane, p. 156.
1–2] *that youth's/Ye praise so* No specific referent can be assigned, of course, but only Raphael of the three great Florentines just noted would have been, strictly speaking, a "youth" in the sixteenth century.

THE ITALIAN IN ENGLAND

Title] The Italian, of course, is an imaginary patriot who has taken part in an unsuccessful revolt against Austrian control; however Sir Frederic Kenyon (*Centenary Edition*, III, xxxiv) has suggested, and DeVane agrees, that the poem was inspired by the brief insurrection led by Otillia and Emilio Bandiera against the Neapolitan coast in the summer of 1844. The Bandieras, sons of an Austrian admiral, renounced Austrian service, took up the cause of Young Italy in resisting Austrian oppression, and fled to Corfu. In June, 1844, with nineteen companions, they launched a raid against the coast near Naples in the hope of liberating political prisoners. After a month of guerilla activity they were betrayed from within, captured, and executed along with seven of their band. Each man shouted "Viva l'Italia!" as he died. The affair created a stir in the Neapolitan area which had not subsided when B arrived there in the fall of that year. It appears that the poem may have been conceived at that time, though probably not written until later. What is certain is that EBB had the MS. in a rather rough state on August 13, 1845 and suggested B change the lines "I would grasp Metternich until/I felt his throat and had my will" (*New Poems*, p. 151).
19] *Metternich* Klemens Wenzel Nepomuk Lothar, Prince von Metternich (1773–1859), distinguished Austrian diplomat and determined foe of Italian independence.
75] *duomo* The cathedral.
76] *Tenebræ* An office sung in the Roman Catholic churches on Wednesday, Thursday, and Friday of Holy Week. During the service candles are gradually extinguished until the church is in darkness, commemorating the darkness that covered the earth while Christ was crucified.

THE ENGLISHMAN IN ITALY

Subtitle] *PIANO DI SORRENTO* The Plain of Sorrento, adjoining the city of the same name in S Italy on the Bay of Naples.
5] *Scirocco* Also sirocco, a hot dry wind from Africa which blows frequently on the northern Mediterranean coast in autumn.
35] *quail-nets* "Nets spread to catch quails as they fly to or from the other side of the Mediterranean. They are slung by rings on to poles, and stand sufficiently high for the quails to fly into them" (Orr, *Hbk.*, 287n).
53] *Amalfi* A town near Naples on the Gulf of Salerno.
69] *Salerno* A port city ESE of Naples on the Gulf of Salerno, an inlet of the Tyrrhenian Sea.
87] *love-apple* Archaic for tomato.
97] *lasagne* B may mean a kind of spaghetti, as "slippery ropes" (l. 98) implies. Lasagne are wide flat noodles; the word is from the Latin *lasanum* (Gr. *lasanon*), cooking pot, originally "chamber pot."
162] *lentisks* The mastic tree, a small evergreen of the Mediterranean region.
171] *Calvano* It is unclear just which hill near Sorrento the speaker climbed. Possibly Monte Tore (540 ft.) or Monte Comune (877 ft.), both within a few miles of Sorrento and giving a prospect of the Galli on the S side of the peninsula. The whole ridge which divides the gulfs of Salerno and Naples is called *Le Tore* and a well-known path, the *via delle tore,* runs along it. *Calvano* may be a local place-name B picked up during his visit to Naples and vicinity in 1844. *Calvare,* an obsolete Italian verb, means to make bald; thus *Calvano* might mean something like "Bald Mt.," of which there are many in the area.
199] *isles of the siren, your Galli* Isole li Galli, islets off the coast near Crapolla, reputed to be those from which the sirens sang to Ulysses (*Odyssey* Bks. 12 and 23). For a description of them see N. Douglas, *Siren Land* (London, 1923), pp. 49–63.
219] *square black turret* A structure on the largest of the three Isles of the Sirens, the remains—actually a cistern—of a tower built there by Robert of Naples in 1330. B visited the Isles on October 4, 1844. EBB recommended the change from "tower" to "turret" (See Kintner, RB-EBB, i, 259–260).
250–51] *Feast/Of the Rosary's Virgin* The Feast of the Rosary is celebrated annually to commemorate the destruction of the Turkish fleet at Lepanto in 1571 by a Christian armada.
265] *Bellini nor Auber* Vincenzo Bellini (1801–1835), an Italian composer and Daniel François Auber (1782–1871), a French composer, both well known at the time.
288–89] *Men meet gravely to-day/. . .Corn Laws* On October 31, 1845, the British prime minister Sir Robert Peel asked his cabinet to repeal the Corn Laws, duties and restrictions on the grain trade which had been enacted in 1815 to protect the interests of landowners. Essentially a tax on food, these laws were oppressive to the common people and had been a cause of

political agitation in England for many years. The effort to repeal them stirred up a storm of opposition which reached its height in September, 1845. Letters exchanged between B and EBB indicate that this topical last section of the poem, ll. 286–292, was not in it when EBB first examined it on August 13, 1845, but was added before it went to press on October 13. She noted and praised B on the unifying value of this section when she saw the poem in proof on October 22 (See Kintner, RB-EBB, i, 155, 244).

THE LOST LEADER

1–2] *Just for a handful of silver. . . ,/Just for a riband* The genesis of the poem is usually taken to be Wordsworth's acceptance of the laureateship on April 4, 1843. The aging poet had also accepted a civil list pension of three hundred pounds on October 15, 1842. Presumably these awards are the *riband* and the *silver* alluded to; more deeply, however, these signalize the final sellout of a once-honored liberal. Later in life B appears to have regretted the partiality of this portrait. Mrs. Orr (*Life*, 191–192) quotes the following from a letter to Miss Lee on September 7, 1875: "I undoubtedly had Wordsworth in my mind—but simply as 'a model'; you know, an artist takes one or two striking traits in the features of his 'model' and uses them to start his fancy on a flight which may end far enough from the good man or woman who happens to be 'sitting' for nose and eye. . . . But once call my fancy-portrait *Wordsworth*—and how much more ought one to say—how much more would not I have attempted to say!" Earlier that year he had made the same point to Grosart (See Hood, pp. 166–167).

THE LOST MISTRESS

IV] When EBB read the poem in MS. she called this stanza "obscure." She continued to think so after the poem was published even though she noted that B has "changed a word" since she saw it (Kintner, RB-EBB, 244, 260).

HOME-THOUGHTS, FROM ABROAD

Title] In 1845 this title also included "Here's to Nelson's Memory!" and "Nobly, nobly Cape St. Vincent" in that order. The three poems were designated I, II, and III respectively. In a letter to B on October 4, 1845, EBB praised his "spring song" but objected to its being dropped on the reader without a title: "Now these fragments . . you mean to print them with a line between . . and not one word at the top of it . . now don't you!—And then people will read 'Oh, to be in England' and say to themselves . . 'Why who is this? . . who's out of England?' Which is an extreme case of course; but you will see what I mean . . and often I have observed how some of the very most beautiful of your lyrics have suffered just from your disdain of the usual tactics of writers in this one respect" (Kintner, RB-EBB, I, pp. 222). B replied that he would "devise titles."

"Here's To Nelson's Memory!"] (See NATIONALITY IN DRINKS, Part III.)

HOME-THOUGHTS, FROM THE SEA

Title] In 1845 this poem appeared without a title as Part III of "Home-Thoughts, from Abroad." It was given separate status and its present title in the collected edition of 1849.
1] *Cape Saint Vincent* The SW tip of Portugal off which in 1797 Nelson won a major naval victory over the Spanish.
2] *Cadiz Bay* On the SW coast of Spain, E of Cape St. Vincent, where the English fleet destroyed the second Spanish Armada in 1596 and in which the French and Spanish fleets were assembled for the Battle of Trafalgar.
3] *Trafalgar* A cape on the S coast of Spain E of Cadiz Bay, site of Nelson's great victory over Napoleon's fleets in 1805.
4] *Gibraltar* A peninsula on the S coast of Spain, dominated by the massive Rock of Gibraltar, elevation 1,396 feet. Gibraltar, which controls the strait of that name connecting the Mediterranean and the Atlantic, has been a British fortress since its capture in 1704.
7] *Jove's planet* Jupiter.

THE BISHOP ORDERS HIS TOMB AT SAINT PRAXED'S CHURCH

Title] *St. Praxed's Church* The church of Santa Prassede in Rome, just S of S. Maria Maggiore; named for the virgin daughter of Pudens, a Roman senator of the second century A.D., who used her wealth to assist poor Christians. The present structure, said to be on the site of her house, was built in 822 but has been much restored and rebuilt. Its apse, chancel, and particularly the famous chapel known as the "Garden of Paradise," are richly decorated with ninth-century Byzantine mosaics. The high altar is approached by steps cut into massive blocks of antique red marble; the canopy above it rests on four columns of prophyry. On the right (epistle) side near the high altar is the tomb of Mgr. G. B. Sanboni (d. 1592), said to be the first work of Bernini, and in a deep recess on the same side is the handsome tomb of Cardinal Alano (d. 1474) by Andrea Bregno. However the church has no "aery dome" and Barbara Melchiori (*Browning's Poetry of Reticence*, p. 20 [New York, 1967]) is substantially correct in saying "no tomb there resembles the one Browning's Bishop orders, either in position or structure." B visited this church among others in late October, 1844. DeVane believes that the poem was conceived at this time and finished later in the year when the poet returned home. His view is based on the date of B's visit to the church and the assumption that if B had written it earlier he would have published the poem with those which appeared in *Hood's* in the summer of 1844. EBB first saw the poem when it appeared in *Hood's* and had nothing but praise for it. In her letter to B on July 21, 1845 she wrote:

"But I leave my sins and yours gladly, to get into the *Hood* poems which have delighted me so—and first to the St. Praxed's which is of course the finest and most powerful .. and indeed full of the power of life .. and of death. It has impressed me very much." And in her letter of November 15, 1845 she assigned it first place among the *Dramatic Romances and Lyrics* (Kintner, RB-EBB, 130, 267). But the most famous appreciation of the poem is that of Ruskin, who urged it on his readers in *Modern Painters*, IV (1856): "I know of no other piece of modern English, prose or poetry, in which there is so much told, as in these lines, of the Renaissance spirit,—its worldliness, inconsistency, pride, hypocrisy, ignorance of self, love of art, of luxury, and of good Latin. It is nearly all that I said of the central Renaissance in thirty pages of the *Stones of Venice*, put into as many lines, Browning's being also the antecedent work" (*Works*, Library Edition, VI, p. 449). The question of whether B's bishop can be referred to a particular historical source has been much discussed and remains open. John D. Rea (SP, 29 [1932]:120–122) put forth Ireneo Affò's *Vita di Vaspasiano Gonzaga* as a possible source for both this poem and *My Last Duchess*. His argument has not been entirely discredited (see L. S. Friedland, ' "Ferrara and My Last Duchess," ' SP, 53 [1936]: 656–684 and B. Melchiori, *Browning's Poetry of Reticence*, pp. 21–23): Lionel Stevenson has advanced the theory—more plausibly, DeVane thinks—that B modeled the bishop on Cardinal Ippolito d'Este the Younger and the duke on his brother Ercole II, Duke of Ferrara from 1534 to 1559 ("The Pertinacious Victorian Poets," TQ, 21 [1952]: 232 ff.). Melchiori has argued persuasively that the materials and decorative motifs ordered were largely drawn from *The Art of Painting in All its Branches*, edition of 1778, by Gerard de Lairesse (see also DeVane, *Browning's Parleyings*, New Haven, 1927).

1] Vanity, *saith the preacher* Compare *Ecclesiastes* 1:2.

3] *Nephews—sons mine* A euphemism for illegitimate sons.

5,17] *Gandolf* The bishop's predecessor is, like the bishop, essentially an imaginary person though sources have been suggested. EBB objected to the reading of this line in *Hood's*: "Old Gandolf came me in, etc." "Is that 'came me in' a correct expression. . .or rather does it *express*?" (*New Poems*, 145).

21] *the epistle-side* The right-hand side looking toward the altar.

26] *tabernacle* The stone canopy, to be supported by the nine columns, under which the bishop's sculptured effigy would lie.

31] *onion-stone* Marble of an inferior grade that would flake away in layers.

41] *olive-frail* A rush basket for holding olives.

46] *Frascati* A suburb ten miles SE of Rome, a resort.

49] *Jesu Church* Il Gesù church in Rome, noted as the prototype of the so-called Jesuit style. Extremely ornate and lavishly decorated, the church was built by the Jesuits between 1558 and 1584, though interior elaboration continued until 1700. The reference to Il Gesù, designed to combat Protestantism by an open plan which would allow everyone to hear the preacher, does not seem to be coherent with the general tone of the poem which suggests a period prior to the Counter-Reformation.

51] *Swift as a weaver's shuttle* Compare *Job* 7:6.

54] *antique-black* A black marble, preferred to basalt.

58] *Some tripod, thyrsus* Tripod, a three-legged stool on which the oracles of Apollo at Delphi sat to make their prophecies. The thyrsus was a staff carried in processions in honor of Dionysius, god of fertility and wine.

60] *in a glory* That is, in a halo.

77] *Tully's* Familiar for Marcus Tullius Cicero, considered the exemplar, during the Renaissance, of classical Latin prose.

79] *Ulpian* Domitius Ulpianus, Roman jurist of the third century whose style was considered decadent.

89] *mortcloth* Costly cloth used as a funeral pall.

99] *ELUCESCEBAT* "He was illustrious" in the Latin of Ulpian. The Ciceronian form would have been *Elucebat*.

108] *a vizor and a Term* The visor is the front piece of a helmet, and was a common decorative motif in sculpture. A Term is a statue of Terminus, the Roman god of boundaries.

116] *Gritstone* Coarse sandstone such as is used for making grindstones.

GARDEN FANCIES

I. *The Flower's Name*

16] *But yonder, see, where the rock-plants lie!* EBB's objection to the "singular 'eye' " resulted in the complete revision of this line from its reading of "But this—so surely this met her eye!" in *Hood's* (*New Poems*, p. 141).

II. *Sibrandus Schafnaburgensis*

Title] DeVane says (p. 169) that B may have encountered Sibrandus of Aschafenburg in Nathaniel Wanley's *Wonders of the Little World* (1678), a favorite book in his father's library. B simply takes Sibrandus as the type of all scholastic pedantry.

10] *arbute and laurustine* Arbute, probably arbutus, a broad-leaved evergreen tree. Laurustine, an evergreen shrub of the honeysuckle family.

14] *Stonehenge* Ruin of a prehistoric ceremonial structure on Salisbury Plain in Wiltshire, England. It is a circular arrangement of massive upright stone slabs and lintels, like the chapters of Sibrandus.

19] *pont-levis* A drawbridge.

32] *Rabelais* The writings of François Rabelais (1494?–1553), the great French humanist, characterized by broad satire and earthy humor, would be a suitable antidote to a dose of Sibrandus.

38–39] *de profundis, accentibus lætis,/Cantate!* From the depths, with joyful accents, sing!

52] *trover* A common-law action to recover the value of property illegally withheld or converted to his own use by another.
61] *John Knox* The dour and earnest Scottish Calvinist preacher and reformer of the sixteenth century, author of, among other things, the *First Blast of the Trumpet against the Monstrous Regiment of Women* (1558).
67] *husband-eft, sufficit*! An eft is a newt, a species of lizard. *Sufficit* translates "enough."

THE LABORATORY

Title] In 1845 this poem and its companion piece "The Confessional" appeared under the general title *France and Spain*.
Subtitle] *Ancien Régime* Literally "former regime" indicating the political and social order existing in France before the Revolution of 1789. No definite source has been found for the poem. DeVane speculates that in setting the poem in the *ancien régime* B may have had in mind such a figure as Marie Madeleine Marguerite D'Aubray Brinvilliers (c. 1630–1676), an accomplished poisoner at the court of Louis XIV, who among others took off her father and two brothers. She was prevented from poisoning her husband when her lover and co-conspirator's glass mask fell off and he perished while preparing the poison.
1] *Now that I, tying thy glass mask tightly* In her letter to B on July 21, 1845, EBB objected strenuously to the rhythm of the first few lines and gave one of her most sweeping assessments of his style: "And the Laboratory is hideous as you meant to make it:—only I object a little to your tendency .. which is almost a habit .. and is very observable in this poem I think . . . of making lines difficult for the reader to read .. see the opening lines of this poem. Not that <you want> music is required everywhere, not in *them* certainly, but that the uncertainty of rhythm throws the reader's mind off the *rail* .. and interrupts his progress with you and your influence with him. Where we have not direct pleasure from rhythm, <we> and where no peculiar impression is to be produced by the changes in it, we sh^{d} be encouraged by the poet to *forget it altogether*; should we not?" (Kintner, RB-EBB, I, p. 131).

THE CONFESSIONAL

Subtitle] It should be noted that B does not specifically set this poem in the past as he does its companion-poem *The Laboratory*.

THE FLIGHT OF THE DUCHESS

Sources and Composition EBB's particular interest in the poem is evidenced by her letters. Her detailed criticism of it prior to the publication in *Bells and Pomegranates*, No. VII, has already been mentioned in the general note to these texts. Some readers have argued that her influence goes beneath the stylistic level; points of analogy between *The Flight of the Duchess* and that of the Browning's have been discussed, even the possibility that B used the voice of the Gypsy Queen to propose what had been forbidden to the letters (see F. M. Smith, "Elizabeth Barrett and 'The Flight of the Duchess,' " and "More Light on Elizabeth Barrett and Browning's 'The Flight of the Duchess,' " SP 39 [1942]: 102–117; 693–695). But the autobiographical case has been somewhat undercut by uncertainty as to just how much of the poem was written in 1845. It is impossible to come at a precise chronology of the poem's development from B's or EBB's references to it; however the work appears to have come into being in something like the following stages. The seed of it, as B explained to Furnivall in a letter of April 15, 1883, was "this one intelligible line" of a song the poet had heard as a boy: "Following the Queen of the Gypsies, O!" (DeVane, p. 172, suggests that the song was a version of the Scotch ballad of *The Gypsy Laddie*, which does contain the essential motif). In a letter to EBB on July 25, 1845 B gave an account of the work as first conceived, perhaps as early as the spring of 1842, his idea for a poem which "consisted entirely of the gipsy's description of the life the Lady was to lead with her future gipsy lover—a *real* life, not an unreal one like that with the Duke. . . ." Of this conception, B said, "not a line was written." However the letter to Furnivall just cited tells how the poem was begun and accidentally interrupted so that the overall conception was lost. DeVane, p. 179, assumes that this occurred in the summer of 1842 and that the first nine sections, setting the scene, remained unfinished in B's portfolio until March 1845 when, pressed to aid Hood in his emergency, he transcribed the fragment "at a day's notice" and sent it off. The same letter to Furnivall goes on to explain how the poem came to be completed: "Some time afterwards I was staying at Bettisfield Park in Wales, and a guest, speaking of early winter said, 'the deer had already to break the ice in the pond.' A fancy struck me, which on returning home, I worked up into what concludes the story. . . ." But when did this occur? A letter to Domett, (*Domett*, p. 44) refers to one visit to Bettisfield Park in 1842, but there may have been later ones, and the context here does imply that "some time after" means a point between the transcription of the fragment for *Hood's* in March 1845 and the delivery of the completed poem to EBB in mid-July, 1845. There is then a crucial question for biographical readers as to just how much of the poem was actually written during the courtship. F. M. Smith concludes, "there are no very good reasons for saying that any part of the poem was written before 1845. . . .There are good reasons for saying that no matter when the first two hundred lines were written the rest of the poem was written in 1845. One thing is most certain—much work was done on the poem in 1845" (SP 39 [1942]: 108). DeVane is more decisive. He believes sections ten through sixteen were written slowly between May and July of 1845 and "with Miss Barrett very much in mind" (DeVane, p. 175). Whatever may be the case for the view that the poem's true source is their relationship, EBB's special critical interest in the poem cannot be doubted. It is the poem most frequently referred to in the letters of 1845—twenty-two times as compared with eight for *Saul*, the poem next in prominence; in addition there is the twelve-page critical *Duchess* letter discovered in 1913 which is exclusively devoted to her recommended revisions to sections ten through sixteen *before* publication. (For a summary of its contents see E. Snyder and F. Palmer, Jr., "New Light on the Brownings" [QR 269 (1937):48–63].) Snyder and Palmer suggest that B obtained a verbal commitment from EBB to read the MS. of sections ten through sixteen with particular care, not merely for her editorial advice, but to make certain that she would perceive the special message for herself in the character of the liberated Duchess. The long letter is the fulfillment of her promise to scrutinize the new sections carefully. But if EBB did see herself in the poem her comments, perhaps quite naturally, do not reveal this. Nearly all of them refer directly to features of style—praising or mending details of rhythm or phrasing. For example, B had written "What meant a hat if it had no rims on" (l. 244). She objected: "Do you like '*what meant*'? I do not quite—and the connection is broken. . . .And then "the rims"—"a hat has only one rim ever—except for the rhyme of 'crimson.' So why not write. . . .'a hat where never a rim's on.' *That* wd. do—wouldn't it?—You are not to think that I have not a proper respect and admiration for all these new live rhymes and that I would not make every sacrifice in reason for them" (Snyder and Palmer, "New Light," p. 54). Here B kept his "rims" in although he did alter phrasing slightly; in all he accepted verbatim or in part sixty of her seventy-three proposed emendations. Apparently she permitted herself few generalized emotional responses to the poem, but to the climactic passage of the Gypsy's prophecy, ll. 618–649, she did exclaim: "But all this passage is quite exquisite—I mean down this page and the next and the next to the end of the prophecy—The figure 'shall some one deck thee' etc. a most beautiful, infinitely beautiful, revivification of what is old in the seed of it" (Snyder and Palmer, "New Light," p. 52).

78] *merlin* The pigeon hawk, a small falcon.
80] *falcon-lanner* The lanner is a species of falcon native to Africa and the Mediterranean region. The female of this species was once used in falconry.
86] *Moldavia* Moldavian wine. Until 1859 Moldavia was a principality in the eastern part of what is now Rumania. The Carpathian foothill zone of Moldavia has been a vineyard region for centuries.
87] *Cotnar* Wine from the region of Cotnari, a village and noted wine center in Moldavia.
119] *a lathy horse* A thin horse, like a lath.
130] *urochs or buffle* Urochs, an extinct species of wild boar; the name is also applied to the European bison, still extant in Lithuania. Buffle, buffalo.
238] *St. Hubert* The patron of hunters. According to legend Hubert (d. 727) was converted while hunting on Good Friday by the miraculous apparition of a stag bearing a cross between its horns.
249] *Venerers, Prickers and Verderers* Medieval terms for huntsmen,

mounted attendants at a hunt, and game wardens.
263] *a mort* A note sounded on a horn to announce a kill.
264] *jennet* A small Spanish horse.
269] *falcon-lanner* See note to l. 80.
293] *sewer* In medieval times, a servant of rank who supervised the serving of meals.
302] *tire-woman* A lady's maid.
322] *a fifty-part canon* "A canon in music," B explained, "is a piece wherein the subject is repeated, in various keys; and, being strictly obeyed in the repetition, becomes the 'canon'—the imperative *law*—to what follows. Fifty of such parts would be indeed a notable peal; to manage three is enough of an achievement for a good musician" (Berdoe, *Browning Cyclopedia*, p. 180).
334] *pricker* See note to l. 249.
420] *pine-marten pelt* Fur of the marten, sable.
439] *helicat* A hellcat. An evil or spiteful woman, a witch, a vixen.
454] *imps* To imp, in falconry, is to engraft feathers into the wing of a bird and thus restore or improve its flying power.
455] *hernshaw* Diminutive of heron.
458] *fernshaw* A thicket or brake of fern.
463] *mere curveter* The mere performer. A curvet is a leap in which the horse's hind legs spring up just before the forelegs are set down; also used generally for prancing or frolicking.
480] *tomans* Persian gold coins.
533] *gor-crow's flappers* A gor-crow is a carrion crow.
535] *banning* Cursing.
701] *tintacks* Tacks; light fastening compared to the thick-headed hobnails.
793] *Carib* A Caribbean; a member of the group of Indian peoples who occupied northern South America, and the Lesser Antilles when they were discovered by Europeans.
884] *Methasalem* Corruption of Methuselah, name of the Hebrew patriarch said to have lived nine hundred sixty-nine years.
907] *Smooth Jacob still robs homely Esau Genesis* 25:29–34 tells how famished Esau sold his birthright to his brother Jacob for a mess of pottage.
910] *Orson the wood-knight* According to legend the twin brothers Orson and Valentine were born in the forest near Orleans, but as a baby Orson was carried off and suckled by a bear while Valentine was found by King Pepin and brought up to be a knight. Orson grew up wild to become the terror of the French forests; eventually, however, he was conquered and domesticated by his brother Valentine. Their story is told in the early French *Romance of Valentine and Orson*.

EARTH'S IMMORTALITIES

Text and Composition] In her letter to B on October 29, 1845, EBB included this poem and the following, "Song," in her general praise for the "new poems" he had just sent her in proof: "You throw largesses out on all sides without counting the coins: how beautiful that 'Night and Morning' . . . and the 'Earth's Immortalities' . . . and the 'Song' too" (Kintner, RB-EBB, i, 252). In a letter of February 22, 1889 B spoke of the refrain "*Love me forever*!" as "a mournful comment on the short duration of the conventional 'For Ever!' " (*Macmillan Edition*, p. 1350).

SONG

Text] DeVane considers the poem impossible to date with any precision.

THE BOY AND THE ANGEL

Text] EBB criticized the poem between its first publication in *Hood's* for August, 1844 and its appearance in *Dramatic Romances and Lyrics* in November, 1845. During that interval five couplets (ll. 55–58, 63–64, 66–67, 71–72) were added and a new one was substituted for ll. 73–74.
2] *Theocrite* The incidents are imaginary; no Theocrite was ever made pope.

PARTING AT MORNING

3] *him* Answering a query put to him in 1889 about the meaning of this poem B wrote: "it is *his* confession of how fleeting is the belief (implied in the first part) that such raptures are self-sufficient and enduring—as for the time they appear" (*Macmillan Edition*, pp. 1350–51). "Him" in this line, then, is the sun.

NATIONALITY IN DRINKS

Title] These two poems first appeared in *Hood's Magazine* for June, 1844, under the title *Claret and Tokay*. The title was retained when they were reprinted in *Dramatic Romances and Lyrics* of 1845. They were omitted from the collected edition of 1849; however in 1863 they were reprinted and joined by "Here's to Nelson's memory!" (See variants to *Home-Thoughts from Abroad*). In 1863 the title of the group was changed to *Nationality in Drinks*. In her letter of July 21, 1845, EBB declared "Tokay" (presumably meaning both poems) "inferior to all" the *Hood's* poems (Kintner, RB-EBB, i, 131).
14] *pygmy castle-warder* It has been suggested that B is describing the figure on the ornate label of a Hungarian tokay bottle (see *Explicator* 20 [1961]: Item 54).
28] *Sir Ausbruch* E. C. McAleer's discussion, cited in the previous note, continues: "B first thought that this was a place name, for the poem originally read (in *Hood's Magazine* for June, 1844) 'the little man from Ausbruch.' Actually the word as applied to Hungarian wines is almost identical with the word Auslese as applied to German wines, and it means 'to break

off,' or, in the wine trade, to make a special picking of the grapes from each individual bunch and to press these grapes separately, producing a wine of particularly good quality."

31] *Cape Trafalgar* A cape on the S coast of Spain E of Cadiz Bay, site of Nelson's great victory over Napoleon's fleets in 1805.

40] *Nelson's coat* Nelson lost his right arm in his assault upon Santa Cruz de Tenerife on July 24, 1797. Relics of Nelson are kept at Greenwich Hospital, and it is likely that B had seen them many times, but there is no other corroboration of the Captain's anecdote except the tar on Nelson's coat (DeVane, 164).

SAUL

Sources and Composition] There has been considerable discussion of possible sources and influences; however this question is entwined with the problem of the poem's evolution, for there are really two "Saul's": the poem of 1845 and that of 1855. The ultimate source, of course, is the biblical account in I Samuel 16:14–23 which relates simply that David sang before Saul and rid him of an evil spirit from Jehovah that was troubling him. Beyond this, DeVane suggests that the catalog of earth's blessings in the first nine sections (1845) reflects the manner of Christopher Smart, especially in his *Song to David*, yet he points to no particular debts of structure or phrasing. James A. S. McPeek, in "The Shaping of *Saul*" (JEGP 44 [1945]:360–366), has attempted to show the influence of Sir Thomas Wyatt's *Seven Penitential Psalms* on the structure and texture of the poem. His case is stronger for the later parts of *Saul* and is troubled by the question of why, if B had the full structure of *Saul* from Wyatt in 1845, he waited a decade to complete, or at least to print, the poem. But this question merely leads to broader ones having to do with the place of the poem in B's religious and artistic development and with the spiritual influence of EBB (see A. W. Crawford, "Browning's *Saul*," QQ 34 [1927]: 448–454; H. B. Charlton, "Browning as Poet of Religion," *Bull. John Rylands Lib.*, 27 [1942–3]: 291–298; R. A. King, Jr., "Spiritual Dogmatics: *Saul*," *The Bow and the Lyre* [Ann Arbor, 1957], pp. 100–123; W. D. Shaw, "The Analogical Argument of Browning's *Saul*," VP 2 [1964]: 277–282; and W. Hellstrom, "Time and Type in Browning's *Saul*," ELH 33 [1966]: 370–389). It would be interesting to know whether B actually regarded the poem of 1845 as a fragment or whether EBB persuaded him to think of it as such. Her remarks on August 27, 1845 ("...Surely you have been happy in the tone and spirit of these lyrics .. broken as you have left them. Where is the wrong in this?") do not prove B thought of the poem as broken, nor does her allusion, in the same letter, to "sixty lines thrown away!" (Kintner, RB-EBB, i, 173). On October 29, after several queries about further progress on the poem she urges him to "print it in the meanwhile as a fragment confessed . . . sowing asterisks at the end" (Kintner, RB-EBB, 252). In place of asterisks, however, B ended the 1845 and 1849 versions with a more definite promise: "End of Part the First."

Her critical comments on the poem in the letters discovered in 1913 were digested by Kenyon in his Preface to *New Poems*. Most interesting of these criticisms is her objection to the short lines: "The ear expects to read every long and short line, in the sequence of this metre, as one long line,—and where it cannot do so, a loss . . . an abruption . . is felt—and there should be nothing abrupt in the movement of these pastoral, starry images—do you think so?" (*MacMillan Edition,* p. 1325). B shifted mainly to long lines in 1855.

1] *Abner* "And the name of the captain of his (Saul's) host was Abner, the son of Ner, Saul's uncle." I *Samuel* 14:50.

9] *the Spirit* "Now the Spirit of Jehovah departed from Saul, and an evil spirit from Jehovah troubled him." I *Samuel* 16:14.

12] *lilies still living and blue* When EBB inquired about his authority for "blue lilies" B wrote (March 16, 1846): "Lilies are of all colours in Palestine—one sort is particularized as *white* with a dark blue spot and streak—the water lily, lotos, which I think I meant, is *blue* altogether" (Kintner, RB-EBB, I, 508, 536, 539).

27] *Then a sunbeam, . . . showed Saul* EBB singled out this image for special praise but objected to the original wording of the line: "Then a sunbeam burst thro' the *blind* tent-roof/Showed Saul." She wrote: "Now, will you think whether to enforce the admirable effect of your sudden sunbeam, this first line shall not be rendered more rapid by the removal of the clogging epithet 'blind'—which you repeat, too, I believe, farther on in the next page?" She then suggests the present wording (*New Poems,* 158). James McPeek, "The Shaping of *Saul,*" has pointed to a similar image in Wyatt: *Seven Penitential Psalms*, ll. 509–516.

36] *And I first played the tune* While A. S. Cook (P-C, IV, 376) has suggested that B may have found the general inspiration for these songs in Longus's romance of *Daphnis and Chloe,* Part 1, no specific source for these seven songs has been found.

60] *Levites* The service required of the sons of Levi is described in I *Chronicles*, 23:24–32.

65] *male-sapphires* A superior sapphire showing a bright star.

203] *Hebron upheaves* A city of Palestine SSW of Jerusalem in modern Jordan. The city, southernmost of three biblical cities of refuge, is situated on a hill.

204] *Kidron* A brook near Jerusalem.

213–14] *ere error had bent/The broad brow* Before Saul disobeyed Jehovah's command to destroy the Amalekites and their goods utterly and spared Agag together with certain valuables. See I *Samuel* 15.

291] *Sabaoth* Hosts, armies.

TIME'S REVENGES

Title and source] The title appears to be from Shakespeare's *Twelfth Night*, V, i, p. 384: "And thus the whirligig of time brings in his revenges."

DeVane, p. 180, takes the poem to be largely autobiographical, "a highly precedence in his affections from Alfred Domett to EBB, though he is convinced she is not the lady of the poem (See DeVane, p. 180). B submitted the MS. to her for criticism several months before its publication. She evidently did not care for the poem; at least, after several sharp criticisms of its wording, she concludes, "It seems to me, while I appreciate the conception of the poem fully, and much admire some things in it, that it requires more finishing than the other poems—I mean particularly the first part, but may be as wrong as possible notwithstanding" (*New Poems*, p. 156).
46] *the Florentine* Dante.

THE GLOVE

Sources and Composition] As with *The Flight of the Duchess*, it has been customary to point to both literary and personal sources for this poem. DeVane believes that Leigh Hunt's ballad, *The Glove and the Lions,* published in 1836, spurred B to write his own version of the old French story. Hunt apparently derived his poem from Schiller's *Der Handschuh* (1797). Schiller's source, in turn, was the brief story told by Poullain de Saint-Foix in his *Essais Historiques sur Paris* (1754–1757); "One day while Francis I amused himself with looking at a combat between his lions, a lady, having let her glove drop, said to DeLorge, 'If you would have me believe you love me as much as you swear you do, go and bring back my glove!' DeLorge went down, picked up the glove from amidst the ferocious beasts, returned, and threw it in the lady's face; and in spite of all her advances and cajoleries would never look at her again." Schiller and Hunt add a few details to the incident, but the deeper motives given to the lady, the silent youthful lover, the mortification of DeLorge, Ronsard as narrator—all are B's inventions. DeVane (*Browning's Parleyings*, pp. 81–89) suggests a source for the Lady's character in the life of Marianne Pajot as recounted by the Marquis de Lassay in his *Memoirs* (1756), but it may be equally sensible to seek B's inspiration in his particular interest in the psychology of character and in his own situation at the time with respect to EBB. It is strange, at least, that *The Glove* was not submitted to her in MS. for criticism. She first saw the poem in printer's proofs on October 29, 1845. Her comment at that time shows that she perceived the special case B made of his subject: "And for your 'Glove,' all women should be grateful,—and Ronsard, honoured, in this fresh shower of music on his old grave . . though the chivalry of the interpretation, as well as much beside, is so plainly yours, . . could only be yours perhaps. And even *you* are forced to let in a third person . . close to the doorway . . before you can do any good. What a noble lion you give us too, with the 'flash on his forehead,' and 'leagues in the desert already' as we look on him. And then, with what a 'curious felicity' you turn the subject 'glove' to another use and strike DeLorge's blow back on him with it, in the last paragraph of your story! And the versification! And the lady's speech—(to return!) so calm, and proud—and yet a little bitter!" (Kintner, RB-EBB, i, 252).

Subtitle] *Peter Ronsard* (1524–1585), the narrator, began as a page and became "prince of poets and poet of princes" at the French court and most illustrious of the "Pléïade." According to Claude Binet (*Life of Ronsard*, 1586), "his life and his writings bore an indefinable stamp of nobility and in all his actions shone forth the characteristics of a true French gentleman." His erudition, mastery of classical forms, and noble conception of the poet's mission made him the leading poet of the French Renaissance.

1] *King Francis* Francis I (1494–1547), succeeded to the throne of France in 1515. He was known for his passion for sports and amusements.

12] *Naso* Publius Ovidius Naso, the Roman poet Ovid (43 B.C.-A.D. 18).

14] *Ixions* Ixion, the Greek mythological figure, murdered his father-in-law and repaid the pity of Zeus by attempting to seduce Hera. As punishment for his crimes he was condemned to be tied to a burning wheel which would turn forever. For B's attitude see his own *Ixion* (1883).

45] *Clement Marot* Marot (1496–1544), the author of sonnets, pastorals, and translations of the Psalms, was court poet under Francis I. Marot was twice imprisoned for heretical leanings. His translations of the Psalms were immensely influential, advancing the cause of the Reformation in France, but were condemned by the Sorbonne. He was a literary reformer of considerable significance, though his efforts were shortly eclipsed by those of the Pléïade. His best verse is noted for its unaffected vernacular style.

50] *Illum Juda Leonum de Tribu* "That lion of the tribe of Judah." See *Revelation* 5:5.

82] *Marignan* In 1515 Francis I defeated the Swiss troops of the Duke of Milan at Marignan (Melegnano).

96] *Kaffir* The Arab, his keeper, l. 33. Kaffir may mean here, simply, a non-Moslem (in the disparaging sense used by Arabic Moslems), or a member of the people of the Hindu Kush range in NE Afghanistan, or a native of Kaffraria, now the Transkeian territories of the Cape of Good Hope province, South Africa.

162] *Nemean* The first labor of Hercules was the destruction of the famous lion of Nemea.

171–88] For suggested interpretations of these lines see *Explicator* 1: (1943): Item 54; 2 (1943): Item 13 and Item 23.

189] *Venienti occurrite morbo*! "Go meet the coming ills." It has been suggested that this Latin proverb came from Persius Flaccus (see Louis Friedland, *Explicator* 2 [1943]: Item 30).

190] *theorbo* A seventeenth-century lute with an S-shaped neck and two sets of tuning pegs, the lower set holding the melody strings and the upper the base strings. Louis S. Boaz has suggested that these features of the instrument can be read as a clue to B's moral in the poem (*Explicator* 2 [1943]: Item 13).

EDITORIAL NOTES

LURIA

Emendations to The Text

The following emendations have been made in the 1889 text:
I, 193: The 1868 reading *up!* does not necessarily end a sentence but the 1888 reading *up.* does. It makes ll. 192–193 almost meaningless. The 1846–1863 reading has been restored.
II, 100: The 1863 reading *lands."*—syntactically isolates the rest of Luria's speech. The 1846–1849 reading has been restored.
II, 179: The 1888 reading *links* runs two separate sentences together. The 1846–1868 reading has been restored. This is confirmed by D. C.
II, 204: An obvious omission; the possessive Florence', 1846–1868, has been restored. This is confirmed by D. C.
II, 303: An obvious omission; the 1846–1868 reading *forget.* has been restored.
III, 135: *The after* is found in all editions, but the sense requires a word other than an article. The best candidate permits the reading *Then after,* making sense to the line. B probably overlooked it repeatedly because *The after* begins an independent clause.
IV, 257: The 1888 reading *wit* runs two syntactically independent elements together. B entered a colon in the D.C. copy, the reading adopted here.
V, 208: The 1889 reading *forgone* was an acceptable spelling change and B removed the *e* in the D.C. copy.
V, 242: There is no apparent reason to recapitalize *Him* since the other *hims* in the passage were not recapitalized. This is possibly a printer's error.
V, 293: The two point ellipsis is inconsistent with the regularization of ellipses in the 1888 and 1889a editions to three points. The length of the line probably accounts for the two point ellipsis. The 1846–1848 reading has been restored.

Composition

The history of the composition of *Luria* can be gleaned from the B–Elizabeth Barret Browning correspondence. Browning had *Luria* in his mind by Feb. 11, 1845. By May 24 he had begun writing it. Sometime later he put it aside but resumed work in October. By Jan. 22, 1846 it probably was all but finished in draft. The all but final version was done by Feb. 10. On March 18 he asked EBB for the return of the MS that printing might begin. By March 22 he was discouraged with it and decided to print it just to get rid of it. A week later he read the proofs and liked it better. He made a few cuts and changes, some suggested by EBB. It was published with *A Soul's Tragedy* as *Bells and Pomegranates. No VIII and last* on April 13, 1846.

Sources

B uses very little historical background in *Luria*, and ignores much of what was historical. Of works easily available to him, J. C. L. Simonde de Sismondi, *Histoire de Républicques Italiennes du Moyen Age*, 16 vols. (Paris, 1809–1818) has a clear and succinct account of the conquest of Pisa (8:133–52); the account of the rivalry of the two field commanders of the Florentine army might have either suggested or justified the rivalry between Luria and Puccio. Since from his work on *Sordello* B was familiar with L. A. Muratori, *Rerum Italicarum Scriptores*, 28 vols. (Milan, 1723–1751), he probably examined Mattheus Palmeri's *De captivate Pisarum Liber* (vol. 19) and the more interesting and detailed *Commentari di Gino di Neri Capponi dell' Acquisto ovvero Presa di Pisa seguita l'Arno 1406* (vol. 18). Several touches in *Luria* suggest that he was familiar with this chronicle, which was written by a member of the *Dieci di Balia*, the committee conducting the war in 1406; the author was also one of the Dieci's commissaries, and became the Podestà of Pisa after the conquest. Some justification for B's bringing troops from Lucca to the aid of Pisa is to be found here (see I, 11n). The name Lapo is found in several places, and a notary assisting Gino Capponi is named Ser Jacopo di Messer Bartolommeo di Castel San Giovanni. The military authority in the field of Gino Capponi is at least a justification for the authority of Bruccio and his activities, if not a source. Vol. 2 of the supplement to Muratori, *Cronica di Piero di Giovanni Minerbetti*. ed. G. M. Tartini, contains an account of the Florentine conquest of Pisa and suggests further justification for the idea of introducing troops from Lucca. Several unsuccessful efforts were made by Lucca to get food into the besieged city. Minerbetti also mentions that in the course of the war the Florentines appointed a new commander, Luca dal Fiesco, a member of a famous Genoese family. This appointment provides a justification for Luria's taking the place of Puccio. In the 1840s the best and then still standard history of Florence was Scipione Ammirato's *Istorie Fiorentine*, first published in 1600 and richly annotated in subsequent editions by the younger Ammirato. In 1889 Henry S. Pancoast published in *Poet-lore* what was said to be a translation from "Sapio Amminato's 'Istoria [*sic*] Fiorentine," (I:557).

> And when all was ready, the expedition marched to the gates of Pisa, under the command of Conte Bartoldo [Bertoldo] Orsini, a Ventusian captain, in the Florentine service, accompanied by Filippo di Megalotti, Rinaldo di Gian Figliazzi, and Maso degli Albizzi, in the character of commissaries of the commonwealth. For although we have every confidence in the honor and fidelity of our general, you see it is always well to be on the safe side. And in the matter of receiving possession of a city. . .these nobles with the old feudal names! We know the ways of them! An Orsini might be as bad in Pisa as a Visconti, so we might as well send some of our own people to be on the spot. The three commissaries therefore accompanied the Florentine general to Pisa. (Am. xvii., Lib. Goup. 675)

Not only is there no such historian as "Sapio Amminato," although the name is repeated in all references to Pancoast's essay up to and including DeVane's *Handbook*, but the passage cannot be found in Ammirato, for which "Amminato" is an obvious error, probably arising from misreading of a hand-written note. Further, the passage is not typical of Ammirato. Nor is the passage to be found in any of the other accounts of the taking of Pisa in Muratori. Pancoast's description of the historical background is brief and vague and does not argue a reading of Ammirato. The misspelling of name and title also suggests that this discovery was not Pancoast's. Whether his or an informant's, it was carelessly recorded.

Dedication

The quotation comes from "To the Reader" in *The White Devil* (1612) by John Webster:

> Detraction is the sworne friend to ignorance: For mine owne part I have ever truly cherisht my good opinion of other mens worthy Labours, especially of that full and haightned style of Maister Chapman: The labor'd and understanding workes of Maister Jonson: The no lesse worthy composures of the both worthily excellent Maister Beamont & Maister Fletcher: And lastly (without wrong last to be named) the right happy and copious industry of M. Shake-speare, M. Decker, & M. Heywood, wishing what I write may be read by their light: Protesting, that, in the strength of mine owne judgement, I know them so worthy, that though I rest silent in my owne work, yet to most of theirs I dare (without flattery) fix that of Martial.
>
> —*non norunt, Haec monumenta mori.* [These monuments know not how to die. 10.2.] (*Complete Works*, ed. F. L. Lucas, London, 1927, I, 107.)

Browning probably met Walter Savage Landor for the first time on May 26, 1836, the occasion being a supper to celebrate the successful first performance of *Ion* by T. N. Talfourd. Later that year Landor wrote his friend and

Browning's, John Forster, that *Paracelsus* placed Browning among the great poets. In *Sordello* (1840) Browning called him patron and friend (III, 950–966). In Nov. 1845 Landor received a copy of *Dramatic Romances and Lyrics* and wrote to Browning praising it and enclosing a poem dedicated to him. On Nov. 22 the *Morning Chronicle* published the poem:

TO ROBERT BROWNING

There is delight in singing, tho none hear
Beside the singer: and there is delight
In praising, tho the praiser sit alone
And see the prais'd far off him, far above.
Shakespeare is not *our* poet, but the World's,
Therefor on him no speech; and brief for thee,
Browning! Since Chaucer was alive and hale
No man hath walked along our roads with step
So active, so inquiring eye, or tongue
So varied in discourse. But warmer climes
Give brighter plumage, stronger wing: the breeze
Of Alpine highths thou playest with borne on
Beyond Sorrento and Amalfi, where
The Siren waits thee, singing song for song.

Persons

Luria A name of unknown origin, it might have been suggested to B by the Lurio River in Mozambique, conquered by the Portuguese early in the 16th century. There is a slight possibility that the name was suggested to him by the Luri or Alurs, a cattle-breeding people in the swamps of the Nile N of Lake Albert, an area being explored in the 1840s. Another possibility is that B developed the name from the Greek *lura*, lyre, suggesting that Luria is played upon by the Florentines and by his idealism. Luria is clearly black; the Moors are in fact a white race, though darkened by exposure to the desert sun. B continues the traditional confusion between Moors and Negroes, preserved in "blackamoor." This confusion is to be found in *Othello*, from which B seems to have taken the idea of a black Moorish *condottiere*, "mercenary military leader," in the service of an Italian state. For Othello's dependence on Desdemona, B substitutes Luria's dependence on the idea of Florence.

Puccio A name B could have found in volume 7 of the *Biographie Universelle* (1813). The entry refers to *Capanna*, a fourteenth-century follower of Giotto.

Braccio The name appears in volume 5 of the *Biographie Universelle* (1812) as that of an Italian condottiere b. 1368 in Perugia. In 1409 he fought for the Florentines and in 1416 became lord of Perugia. The statement that he had an extraordinary skill in gaining the hearts of his soldiers might have caught

B's eye, but since this is so frequently said about great military leaders, no source for such a character trait is needed.
Tiburzio Tiburzio di Maso was one of a fifteenth-century anti-Papal group in Rome. For *Commissary* see I, 27n.
Domizia Or Domitia was the name of the wife of the Roman Emperor Domitian. She joined in a successful plot to assassinate her husband. Since B's Domizia wishes to destroy Florence and attempts to inspire Luria to do so, there may be a connection. See also III, 291n.

Scene

Pisa By 1402 Gian Galeazzo Visconti, Duke of Milan, had conquered Pisa, as well as Siena and Perugia, and in that year captured Bologna. The independence of Florence was in extreme peril. Suddenly Gian Galeazzo died. Pisa, with which Florence had been fighting for centuries, was inherited by Gabriele Maria, Gian Galeazzo's third and illegitimate son. With the aid of his mother he governed Pisa stupidly and oppressively. The Pisans resisted, and in 1405 the Florentines secretly bought from Gabriele the title to Pisa. The Pisans rose against him and refused to honor the purchase. This was the excuse the Florentines had long been looking for, since if they controlled Pisa they controlled the main Tuscan access to the sea, the river Arno. Gabriele turned the citadel of Pisa over to the Florentines, but the Pisans drove them out, and offered peace. The Florentines refused and in 1406 the attack began in earnest. It consisted mostly of a siege, though there was some fighting in Pisan territory (*contado*). In a matter of months the Pisans were reduced to starvation, since the Florentines had cut off every avenue of help, including blocking the Arno below Pisa and destroying or capturing the Pisan grain ships from Sicily. Giovanni Gambacorti, the captain of the Pisans and virtual ruler of the city after the siege began, secretly visited the Florentines, and in return for a rich reward promised to open the gates. In any case, the Pisans could not have held out for even a few more days. On the night of Oct. 8, 1406, one of the gates was opened; the city fell and lost its independence Oct. 9, 1406. It was a victim of Florentine expansionist policy.

ACT I

6] *Signory* In Italian *signoria*, or lordship; principally the eight priors and under them the podesta, or chief magistrate. The chief of the priors was the Gonfalonier (standard-bearer) of Justice.
10] *Pisa* In the war of 1406, the Florentines saw to it that no aid came to the city by completely surrounding it, and by paying several city-state lords not to help. There is little historical basis for the land battle in *Luria*.
11] *Lucchese* The troops of Lucca. Pisa and Lucca had long been enemies; however, at the beginning of the siege of Pisa the Lucchese did help briefly in the destruction of a Pisan tower occupied by the Florentines. Lucca feared

that after Pisa, the next Florentine victim would be itself. Florentines in Lucca on business were forced to leave the city for fear of being badly handled by the people. The idea that Lucca sent troops toward the end of the siege may be based on these incidents, but it is equally possible that it is a reasonable invention of B's.

21] *Ser* Short for *Messer*, master, a title of respect for a commoner.

27] *Commissary* Commissioners were sent as representatives by the *Dieci di Balia*, the committee of ten in charge of conducting a Florentine war. The commissaries had the task of seeing that the orders of the Ten were carried out, and of reporting any treasonable moves on the part of the mercenary generals, who were easily tempted by a sufficiently large offer from the opposite side. One of the Ten usually served as one of the commissaries, and in the Pisan war, at least, other commissaries were drawn from the members of the Ten previously in office. The Balia was a device to carry through a reform manipulated by the oligarchy then governing Florence under the increasingly hollow forms of a constitutional republic.

68] *Piazza* The Piazza, or Place, of the Signoria before the Palace of the Signoria, now known as the Palazzo Vecchio (the Old Palace). It was then the residence and headquarters of the priors and the podestà while they were in office.

107–8] *saint . . . wheel* St. Catherine of Alexandria was martyred on a wheel, her iconographical attribute.

123] *Duomo* Originally S. Reparata, the cathedral of Florence was begun Sept. 8, 1296, by Arnolfo di Cambio. Construction proceeded slowly and fitfully. By 1406 the body of the church was done, except for the dome. In 1412 it was dedicated to S. Maria del Fiore. By 1420 a third of the facade had been completed. It was demolished in 1587; the present facade was not begun until 1871 and was finished in 1887.

124] *Moorish front* In Spain there had been for centuries a fusion of Gothic and Arabian architectural styles.

176] *House's fall* There were various ways in medieval and Renaissance Italy of getting rid of one's political enemies. A common way was to get a man declared, together with his male relatives, enemies of the state, exile them, and confiscate their property. Exile to and confinement to a remote country town is still a method of punishment in Italy.

299] *walls are peopled* Exterior walls were frescoed in medieval and Renaissance Italy, though it was not a Florentine custom, being more characteristic of northern Italy.

300] *statue to its niche* Possibly a reference to the church of Orsanmichele, recently built. The walls had niches for statues for which some of the greatest Florentine sculptures were created.

316] *East* If Luria is a Moor, he comes from Morocco, W of Italy. East here probably has the usual early nineteenth-century meaning, the desert lands of Arab territory, extending from the Atlantic to India.

364] *statist* Politician.
383] *Mage Negro king* In pictures of the Adoration of the Magi one of the magi is often presented as dark skinned or clearly Negro, particularly in the late Middle Ages and the Renaissance.

ACT II

18] *thou . . . sacrifice* Toward the end of the fourteenth century the oligarchy, the current rulers of Florence, exiled a number of their political enemies and business rivals. Among such families were the Albizzi and the Alberti.
26] *Porzio* Possibly derived from Shakespeare's Portia. The *Biographie Universelle*, 35 (1823) lists a Porzio, a Neapolitan physician, b. 1639.
41] *Florence . . . falseness* Justified by the fact that the republican constitution of Florence had already been virtually destroyed by the oligarchy. The way was being prepared for the take-over of total power by the Medici a few decades later.
75–76] *triumphal arch / Or storied pillar* Rome, where several triumphal arches still stood, as well as the columns of Trajan and Marcus Aurelius, sculptured in continual spiralling bands with the campaigns of those emperors.

ACT III

291] *Traversari* The name of a family of Ravenna. The most famous was a fifteenth-century humanist, Ambrogio Camoldenese, who died in Florence in 1439.

ACT IV

201–10] *him who first ordained*, etc. Legend, with some basis in fact, was that Florence was founded by Julius Caesar. The rest of the passage appears to refer to Caesar's terminating the Roman Civil Wars and using his power to protect and foster the life of the people to restore Italy after the devastations of the wars.

ACT V

27] *Pesa . . . Lupo . . . San Romano . . . Evola . . . San Miniato, Scala, Empoli* Fifteen mi. from Florence on the road to Pisa (about fifty mi. from Florence) the third stream crossed is the Pesa, which was forded just above its outlet into the Arno. Just to the E is Montelupo. San Romano is thirty mi. from Florence on the Pisan road, San Miniato twenty-five mi., Scala about twenty-three mi., and Empoli nine mi. By Evola B probably means the R. Égola, a stream between San Romano and San Miniato. A village where the road crosses the stream is Ponte a Égola. Forts or towers at these places would defend the road to Pisa and control the Arno valley.

35] *Staggia* is about thirty mi. S of the intersection of the road to Siena with the road from Florence to Pisa, and about thirteen mi. N of Siena, near what was then the Florentine-Sienese frontier. There is no historical basis for the notion that Siena attempted to help the Pisans. In 1429, however, when Florence attempted to conquer Lucca, the Sienese came to Lucca's aid. Had Siena attempted to send help to Pisa, Staggia would have been a good place to stop it. In 1405 the Pisans attempted to hire a condottiere, Agnello della Pergola, who tried to reach Pisa through Sienese territory. The Florentines met him, defeated him, and dispersed his troops.

Cumulative Index of Titles

(Titles of long poems or of collections of short poems are capitalized.)

Cumulative Index of First Lines of Shorter Poems